Prime Ministers and Whitehall
1960–74

Jon Davis

hambledon
continuum

Hambledon Continuum is an imprint of Continuum Books
Continuum UK, The Tower Building, 11 York Road, London SE1 7NX
Continuum US, 80 Maiden Lane, Suite 704, New York, NY 10038

www.continuumbooks.com

Copyright © Jon Davis 2007

All rights reserved. No part of this publication may be reproduced or transmitted in any form or by any means, electronic or mechanical, including photocopying, recording or any information storage or retrieval system, without prior permission from the publishers.

First published 2007

British Library Cataloguing-in-Publication Data
A catalogue record for this book is available from the British Library.

ISBN 978 1 84725 169 5

Typeset by Egan Reid, Auckland, New Zealand
Printed and bound by Biddles Ltd, King's Lynn, Norfolk

Contents

Foreword by Peter Hennessy		vii
Introduction		ix
1	Cracks	1
2	Hardware	23
3	Software	51
4	Strategy	83
5	Pressure	113
	Conclusion	159
	Appendix	173
	Chronology	177
	Notes	183
	Bibliography	233
	Index	243

Foreword

What do new prime ministers inherit? A large pot of public expenditure; the bulk of the legislative time in Parliament; and the Whitehall machine. To be true artists in the use of power, they have to use all three assets with intelligence, coherence and care. Yet, in recent times, very few new incumbents in No 10 have given the Whitehall leg of the governing tripod more than fleeting attention.

Jon Davis's study, however, embraces three premiers (Macmillan, Wilson and Heath) who had, in their differing ways, a real feel for the Whitehall machine. Ted Heath saw it as a first-order problem of government. And taken as a whole, the period 1960–74 is bursting with lessons for today's premiers or aspirant prime ministers in terms of both 'dos' and 'don'ts'.

Tony Blair has said more than once that he wished he had read history rather than law at Oxford. Gordon Brown did read history – masses of it – at Edinburgh. Dr Davis's *Prime Ministers and Whitehall* is history with a high and enduring utility, practical scholarship at its best. He has mined the archives for every grain of ore and milked his interviewees for every last drop of insight.

Would-be prime ministers, read on …

Peter Hennessy, FBA
Attlee Professor of Contemporary British History
Queen Mary, University of London

Introduction

The study of prime ministers and the reform of British central government in any era is fascinating. The interaction between the temporary, often inexperienced but largely elected ministers – especially those in the top job, and the always highly educated and usually experienced yet theoretically subservient senior civil servants who comprise the permanent side of government – would provide great interest on its own. The analysis of personalities is intrinsically attractive. But if you add in rivalry between and inside the 'governing tribes',[1] and the rise of a class of 'special advisers' somewhere in between, you have the makings of an absorbing analysis. Set this against a backdrop of a powerfully felt relative economic decline which lasted several decades, years which also saw an absolute reduction in the UK's global clout alongside a fast-changing social scene, and the story becomes compelling for anyone interested in the workings of British governance. During the years 1960–74, all these elements mingled and engendered numerous myths and legends – as well as real lessons – which are remembered in British government to this day.

Several treatments of the period 1960–74 have appeared before. There is the cumulative, daily 'first rough draft of history' in the press.[2] Then there are countless articles and books which concentrate on one or more of the specific elements. Finally, we have the books which attempt to gather all the issues and synthesize them. Perhaps the best-known of these is Peter Hennessy's *Whitehall*.[3] Another which dealt with the themes in a much more concise way was Kevin Theakston's *The Civil Service Since 1945*.[4] Gavin Drewry and Tony Butcher's text book, *The Civil Service Today* (published in 1988 and updated in 1991), offered a highly valuable introduction to the world of Whitehall and 'how things came to be' by the late 1980s.[5] *Manipulating the Machine*, Christopher Pollitt's excellent inquiry into the reform of the government's central machinery, published in 1984, offered an admirable analysis of the changes which took place through many interviews with many of the most relevant figures in the years 1960–83.[6] Pollitt's study was completed without access to the official documents of the time. Geoffrey Fry's highly detailed work on the Fulton Report, *Reforming the Civil Service*, published in 1993, did, however, have the distinction of being based on the relevant documents some time before the 30-year rule released them to the general public.[7] The declassification of Fulton-related records for the period *after* 1968, which is covered in Chapter 3 of this book, adds intriguingly to Fry's work.

The overall narrative in all these books is mostly similar. For the history of British administration is largely, at the highest level, uncontentious. It is not a story of competing policies – that would be political history, or even the history of ideas. Administrative history is concerned with a political party's plans and, more specifically, how those plans are put into practice, or at least attempted.

This book retraces ground previously trodden, but for the first time with virtually all of the central government archive open. What emerges diverges little from Hennessy and Theakston's work at the top end. There are, however, many new leads, angles and fragments of documentary evidence which throw fresh light on familiar events. Declassified documents often loosen the tongues of heretofore notoriously discreet retired senior officials. The archive plus the oral testimonies of these aged 'desk warriors' gives what Churchill might have described as the 'beginning of the end' of the story. For though this study attempts to be as comprehensive as possible, it covers many years of activity, and so some areas might well benefit from much closer scrutiny in the future. It is in a sense a hybrid of specialization and generalism, something of which officialdom itself (especially after the Fulton Report) should heartily approve. It has proved challenging to keep exactly to the topic in question – the why, how and evaluation of administrative reform – when so many other aspects affect it; for example, economic performance and the ebb and flow of political support. The context is important but has been kept brief.

The hybrid nature is most keenly seen in the manner in which the study has been conducted. The methodology began with a comprehensive trawl through all of the secondary material available alongside biographies, autobiographies, memoirs and diaries. The period studied here has been particularly well covered, the Wilson governments of 1964–70 especially so. Just about every significant figure has given his or her account, sometimes in different formats, including the Cabinet diarists Richard Crossman, Barbara Castle and Tony Benn. A good knowledge of all of these occasionally misleading accounts (for example, the conflict of opinion between Harold Wilson and George Brown over the early days of the Department of Economic Affairs) is essential if one is attempting to find the gaps in the history and seeking to bring new value to existing knowledge before developing a fresh synthesis. Once this was completed, immersion in the primary material followed.

For any study of prime ministers and the reform of British central government there is only one place that can bring the necessary illumination to a story that requires an understanding of the political and bureaucratic interface, and that is the Public Record Office now under the umbrella of the National Archives. For this study, the Prime Minister's Office, or PREM, files are crucial as they hold virtually all of the papers and letters which the Prime Minister sees, writes and comments upon (though documents relating to intelligence matters are usually not included here). It is these files, created for Harold Macmillan, Sir Alec Douglas-Home, Harold Wilson and Edward Heath, which form the backbone of this work. But, being a hybrid, if a particular lead encourages investigation into departmental records, this has been pursued leading to a thesis which has a strong central trunk with many offshoots. If work has sometimes been suggested in archives other than those at Kew, these too have been investigated.

The final element is oral testimony – vital because so much of the history of government is not written down. This can be for several reasons, not all sinister. There is, understandably, a reluctance on occasion to write down very sensitive matters which might then be leaked or used in future as evidence. But the modern problem of leaking, while undoubtedly a difficulty for Wilson in his governments of the 1960s (but scarcely one at all in the Heath Government that followed), was not on the scale of the 1980s, the 1990s and in the aftermath of the invasion of Iraq in 2003. Another reason is that while a great many meetings in Whitehall are minuted, the sheer weight of consultation that occurs between colleagues, within and between departments, with Parliament, companies, overseas governments, international institutions and other outside interest groups means that much is necessarily lost. A further point is that personal observation, not written down at the time, can be compelling. This is naturally a danger given the passing of time and the blurring and selectivity of memory. One way of keeping interviewees 'on the rails' of what actually happened, sometimes over 30 years ago (and in some cases, such as the interviews conducted with Sir Frank Cooper, former Permanent Under Secretary at the Ministry of Defence, about events over half a century ago), is to present them with documents unearthed at the Public Record Office and to conduct the interview around the papers. This brings great benefit in maintaining relevance but, more importantly, it jogs the memory as nothing else can.

The investigation, though inevitably tracing some threads back before 1960, starts at that date because it essentially marks what Sir Samuel Brittan, economics commentator on the *Financial Times* since 1966, described as 'the re-appraisal of the 1960s'.[8] Just as the Thatcherite reforms of the 1980s can reasonably be said to have begun (however slowly) with the Callaghan Government in the aftermath of the 1976 sterling crisis, an account of the reforms which Harold Wilson enthusiastically pursued after his election victory in 1964 would be incomplete without an explanation of Harold Macmillan's change of direction. This occurred after the Conservatives' landslide majority in the 1959 election. The reasons for Macmillan's shift towards what he described as 'a little dirigisme'[9] and which resulted in the reorganization of the Treasury and the creation of the tripartite National Economic Development Council ('Neddy'), both in 1962 as part of his drive for economic growth, will be examined along with their effectiveness.

The Labour years of 1964–70, which entrenched and deepened Macmillan's interventionist shift, form Chapters 2 and 3. These were hectic years of enthusiasm, movement and disaster, all against a background of repeated and worsening exchange rate crises, deteriorating industrial relations and an economy seemingly falling ever faster behind its major competitors. The creation of the Department of Economic Affairs (DEA) was meant to take on the work of 'Neddy' and to ally this limited 'dirigisme' to a much more statist and interventionist view of how to turn the country's economic fortunes around. The DEA was born of high hopes but was laid to rest just five years later after a battle royal with the Treasury over who controlled the direction of economic policy. An investigation into its creation and its perhaps inevitable demise forms much of Chapter 2.

The other big department created in 1964 was the Ministry of Technology or Mintech. (There were three other newcomers: the Ministry of Overseas Development, the Ministry of Land and Natural Resources and the Welsh Office.) Mintech's establishment was in response to a growing unease over Britain's perceived failure to convert its scientific prowess into economic advantage. The new department was supposed to be in the frontline of Wilson's battle to forge a new scientific socialism which would bring sustained and high levels of economic growth. Yet Mintech started off slowly and only by the late 1960s – when it assumed some of the dying DEA's functions – was it beginning to look as if it might achieve the size and power that would enable it to be a major player in Whitehall.

The importation of several high-level politically appointed special advisers in 1964 will also be covered. With Whitehall slow to recruit economists after 1945 and the belief on the left that the Civil Service was irredeemably centre-right, Labour decided to bring in such figures as Thomas Balogh to the Cabinet Office and Nicholas Kaldor and Robert Neild to the Treasury. Wilson's appointment of Marcia Williams as his Personal and Political Secretary in No 10 was perhaps the most significant of all. How they fitted into the Whitehall ecosystem and the long-term significance of these developments will be considered throughout the book but mostly in Chapter 2.

Eighteen months after coming to power, Wilson set up the Fulton Committee to look at the recruitment, training and management of civil servants, though steering it away from key areas such as Minister–official relations and the machinery of government. The Fulton Report, which emerged in 1968, became legendary for its difficult gestation, its immediate reception and the mini civil war which developed within Whitehall over its partial implementation, as will be seen in Chapter 3. The aftermath of the report, though effectively over by the early 1970s in terms of immediate impact and implementation, reverberated throughout that decade (and beyond, as many of its recommendations were enacted in a piecemeal fashion over three decades), with question-marks over the power of elected politicians to exert their will vis-à-vis their permanent officials. The Fulton Report remains an undoubted landmark in the administrative history of Britain.

With Heath's unexpected election victory (unexpected to all but him, that is),[10] the era of faith in the state's ability to effect a step-change in economic performance reached its zenith. Although elected on a platform with a vague commitment to reduce the role of government in the economy and society,[11] the reverse in fact took place. Two significant new additions to the institutions of Whitehall, the Central Policy Review Staff (CPRS or 'think tank') and Programme Analysis and Review (PAR), were established, with the hope not of reducing government machinery but of making what was already there work much better. Both had several parents, often a political and an official one, who wanted very different outcomes for their offspring. For example, PAR was originally planned by the Conservatives in opposition as a ruthless apparatus to concentrate minds on deciding whether a particular government activity was being done well, could be done better or should not be done by government at all. But by the time of its creation it had mutated into a highly bureaucratic scrutiny machine for long-term policy. Subtly different as this may at first appear, it was in practice a world apart as it had no real cutting edge with which to axe failing or unnecessary projects as was first envisioned.

An even greater gap existed between the original planning of the 'think tank' for the Prime Minister and what transpired. This began in the minds of Heath's advisers as a way of coldly analysing competing spending paths. Within Whitehall, meanwhile, there was a growing sense of a need for an analytical unit at the very heart of British government which could bring wisdom and clarity to intricate and frequently thorny problems, ones which often involved several departments. Again, the bureaucracy won the battle of ideas (perhaps more specifically the battle of practicality) and the CPRS was established in 1971 under the highly entertaining but idiosyncratic leadership of the third Lord Rothschild. The CPRS became an analytical unit effectively under the control of the Prime Minister as the political planners wanted, but without the purely financial focus they had deemed necessary in their pre-election analysis. The CPRS became the flagship for the Heath reforms, enjoying a first two years of great influence before it gradually became just another analytical component at the Prime Minister's disposal.

Heath's 'quiet revolution',[12] as he described his administrative changes, were heralded in *The Reorganisation of Central Government* of October 1970.[13] The White Paper included other elements beyond PAR and the CPRS, the most significant of which was the move toward merging several departments into fewer larger ones. The creation of super-departments such as the Foreign and Commonwealth Office, the Department of Health and Social Security (both in 1968), along with the gradually enlarging Mintech (throughout the later 1960s) which became the Department of Trade and Industry, and the Ministry of Housing and Local Government which turned into the Department of the Environment (the latter two developments in 1970), was often for different specific reasons, but all fitted in with the prevailing management theory of 'big is beautiful', due to the internal economies of scale that could be offered. This was taken to a new level in the early Heath years as it also coincided with his wish to have a smaller Cabinet. But events conspired to undo the attempt. The Heath Cabinet got bigger as the DTI was broken up under immense political pressure. The gestation of *The Reorganisation of Central Government* White Paper, its implementation and how the developments handled the growing political, industrial and economic malaise of the 1970s is analysed in Chapters 4 and 5.

The book ends with the resignation of Heath in March 1974. Wilson's return did not provide for a re-run of his earlier administrations' lust for institutional reform, save for the creation of the Downing Street Policy Unit, a formalization of advice from the special advisers whom Wilson had incorporated into government in 1964. The fact that the PREM archive for 1976 will only become available at the National Archives in January 2007 also means that the end of the Heath Government in 1974 provides a neat cut-off point.

Several themes will be examined in this book. Firstly, the aforementioned relative economic decline. This proved to be a touchstone of those working in and writing about central government from the late 1950s to the 1990s. But by the early years of the twenty-first century, and with the UK having enjoyed unbroken and substantial economic growth between 1992 and 2006, the general view has consequently altered.[14] But though the post-war period of the UK's severe and rapid relative decline undeniably came to an end, it does not lessen the palpable feelings which living through the decline engendered in the minds of those who worked in Whitehall or wrote about government. It formed a backdrop which coloured analysis and stimulated many of the reforms of central government which will be covered.

A theme which proved much more contentious among analysts was that of the post-war consensus. This notion saw a country essentially at ease with itself in the post-war era where a mixed economy (albeit with fierce arguments about the public/private proportions of the mix)[15] and a comprehensive welfare state were accepted across the mainstream political spectrum and where opponents of these found their voices heard only with difficulty. An acceptance of a broad consensus did not mean, of course, that everything was agreed as there were always many specific items which were beyond consensus, aspects of public ownership especially. The dates of this consensus are generally thought to be the mid-1940s (the publication of the Beveridge Report of 1942[16] and the Employment White Paper of 1944[17] are the cornerstones) through to the late 1970s. But as this book shows, among those in the Conservative Party who conducted detailed planning in the run-up to the Heath Government were some keen to destroy the mixed economy aspect of the consensus equation. Many of the changes the Heath Administration enacted had at their heart an attempt to roll back the state. As we shall see, the bulk of these, if not all, were thwarted. This brings us to further themes which will be woven in.

Firstly, the whole question of Civil Service power. Sir Warren Fisher, Head of the Civil Service 1919–39, tried hard in the inter-war period to make his Civil Service respected as one of the 'four Crown Services', alongside the army, navy and air force.[18] The power of the Civil Service was strongly underpinned by its sterling work in organizing the country during the Second World War, alongside gifted outsiders recruited for the duration.[19] It was further enhanced by the post-war move to draw much of the economy into the state and the creation of a comprehensive welfare system, largely administered by the central state, as 2,304,200 people moved from the private to the public sector between 1945 and 1951.[20] As its responsibilities and reach grew, so did the size and the might of the Civil Service in relation to the wider public sector (in 1938 there existed a total of 581,000 civil servants; in 1960 there were 996,000).[21] In the period dealt with here, there were many questions, from both left and right, over whether the senior Civil Service wielded too much power – and if the right kind of individuals were being recruited and promoted in the first place.

Another related theme was that of the widespread belief in the considerable use of state power as an instrument of modernization during the first 30 years of the post-war era. This book in effect looks at the why and the how of the attempts by both Conservative and Labour governments to use the state to bring about economic renaissance and social advance in Britain. Its main protagonists were Macmillan, Wilson and Heath. The failures of some aspects of this ambitious approach, with the major economic indicators of inflation, unemployment, growth and the balance of payments all performing poorly and industrial strife destroying hopes of a tripartite solution, led quite clearly to the late-1970s rise of the New Right and the dawn of Thatcherism. Such ideas had been around for some time (even the word 'privatization' was coined before Heath entered Downing Street in June 1970)[22] but it took the undeniable failure of the state and its civil servant operators from the late 1960s to allow these relatively extreme ideas (certainly compared to those dominant during the heyday of the post-war consensus) to come to the fore.

Other, more specific, themes that will be addressed include an analysis of how the individual prime ministers viewed the Civil Service – as a whole and more particularly the centre – and what they planned for it, both in government and when in opposition. There will also be an ongoing look at the relative importance of Civil Service, party-political and other pressures upon the prime ministers and how all these varying influences, combined with their personal views, affected their ability to effect change. A link will also be made to other analyses of the dynamics of administrative reform. Finally, an assessment of the impact the prime ministers had on Whitehall will be provided.

How British prime ministers attempted reform of British central government during the years 1960–74 is, therefore, a substantial story. It deals with both long- and short-term institutional, social, economic and political issues. It encompasses all areas of central government, from the 'hardware' of state (its structures and institutions) to the 'software' (the people who formulate policy, take decisions and shape it every day).[23] It looks at the many changes which took place in 14 years which in retrospect appear as the high-watermark of faith in government-framed and administrative solutions to economic problems. The present work analyses why this was so, what was done as a result of this belief, evaluates each reform and examines why so much activity was followed by so little as the appetite for administrative reform waned for 20 years after the fall of the Heath Government.

1

Cracks

PRESSURE FOR REFORM OF THE BRITISH CIVIL SERVICE 1853–1964

THE HIGH WATERMARK

The Civil Service was under great pressure in 1964. It was accused in the years running up to Harold Wilson's first electoral victory of everything from under-skilled impotency to wielding too much undemocratic, elitist power. A seemingly failing economy, a speedy retreat from empire and a country adrift of the integrating nations of Western Europe meant that British confidence was at a low ebb. Disaffection was given form by a rash of publications which attempted to demonstrate how a once proud country was in swift decline. Books such as Andrew Shonfield's *British Economic Policy Since the War* (1958),[1] Michael Shanks' *The Stagnant Society: A Warning* (1961)[2] and Anthony Sampson's *Anatomy of Britain* (1962)[3] differed in their analysis of decline but all included the British State among their reasons for the UK's failure.[4] Though not as initially famous, an article from a left-wing Hungarian-born economist in 1959 was to prove more significant for the Civil Service of the 1960s. 'The Apotheosis of the Dilettante' by Thomas Balogh (who was to become Economic Adviser to the Cabinet in 1964) had as its sole target the senior civil servants themselves, castigating them for their amateurism, self-righteousness and self-protection.[5] Just before the election in 1964, Balogh was part of a Fabian group which developed the themes he had previously expounded, in a more measured way, in *The Administrators*.[6] This pamphlet sought to avoid simply pointing out shortcomings and offered practical roads to reform. All of these writings, amid an atmosphere of general dissatisfaction, led Professor W. J. M. Mackenzie to note in 1963: 'Administrative reform is a phrase that has hardly been heard since the eighteen-fifties until recently.'[7] This was a great contrast to the mood just a decade-and-a-half before. For, in the afterglow of victory in the Second World War, the British Civil Service was widely held to have been the most effective bureaucracy of the warring nations.[8] In order to chart this extraordinary turnaround, we must begin in that 'adventure playground for all the talents'[9] – wartime Whitehall.

When Britain declared war on Germany in September 1939, a complex planning operation that had been gearing up for several years sprang into action. Learning the lessons of the opening months of the First World War when many of the young and best-educated men of the British Isles had been killed on the Western Front[10] and when it took several years to get the structure and people right, a substantial list had been compiled of those whom the State felt it could profitably use in the wartime bureaucracy and how they would be used.[11] Individuals from all walks of professional life, academics and industrialists, young and old alike, were to be absorbed as the State mushroomed. As existing ministries expanded and new ones grew exponentially, the 'irregulars'[12] merged into the machine and some truly excelled. Oliver Franks, philosophy don on the outbreak of war, was the best example. He unprecedentedly rose from Principal to Permanent Secretary in just six years.[13] Although the star performer, he was not alone in his success, with 'Many of the established civil servants who were originally most opposed to the new recruits [coming] to regard them as a stimulating influence.'[14]

Civil servants had their moments, too, as the suffocating inter-war grade cementation was temporarily swept aside.[15] The role of experts was also crucial as Winston Churchill, Prime Minister from May 1940, came to depend on analysis from newly created groupings such as the Statistical Section (created in 1939 when Churchill returned to the Admiralty and which followed him across Horse Guards Parade when he became Prime Minister). The wartime Civil Service, with its blend of established and temporary, expert and generalist officials, raised its game impressively during the war to make Britain probably the most fully mobilized society on either side.[16] The Whitehall fort had been overrun and was unquestionably the better for it.

The State also set in motion during the war the study of future responsibilities which were to change the political landscape of the United Kingdom out of all recognition. The Beveridge Report of 1942[17] drew up plans for a comprehensive welfare state while the wartime coalition's 1944 *Employment Policy* White Paper[18] looked at ways in which government could sustain high and stable employment (but significantly not total employment).[19] Moreover, there were also the substantial nationalizations which Whitehall had not planned during 1940–5 (the National Health Service apart) but which Labour enacted after its 1945 victory. The acceptance of these new responsibilities was to bring difficulties to a Civil Service keen on largely unbending continuity with pre-war practices, as would gradually become apparent.

The Civil Service, therefore, entered the post-war world rejuvenated and supremely confident. Yet, in its moment of triumph, the seeds of future underperformance were sown. For, as soon as hostilities ended, the very high quality irregulars left virtually en masse,[20] not attracted by the pay or the atmosphere of Whitehall once the wartime emergency was over.[21] Those irregulars with previously established careers went back to their universities and firms, while many of the younger ones sought pastures new. This severely depleted the Civil Service of exactly the kind of enthusiasm and skill that the bureaucracy needed as, over the space of only six years, it substituted administering total war for making real the ambitious wartime plans for welfare and economic management. This was to be explicitly recognized by the Head of the Civil Service, Sir Edward Bridges.[22] Bridges did not, however, allow his regret to get in the way of the newly emboldened Civil Service's 'institutional conservatism'.[23] He simply felt that the irregulars had proved wonderfully effective and now that most of them had gone, the service must go back to doing things as they had done prior to the war and with the same people.

In fact, by the early 1950s there were very few of the wartime temporaries left. Some, like Richard 'Otto' (a pseudonym from his pre-war financial journalism days[24] which apparently referred to his trademark spectacles)[25] Clarke, became permanent but those who did not were gradually removed. Sir Frank Cooper, who joined the Air Ministry in 1948 after wartime service in the Royal Air Force, explained that 'people well up the ladder wanted to get back out into the private sector and earn some money again' and that those not in senior positions 'could be held to have got in through the back door by some kind of favouritism'. 'The Civil Service in those days', Sir Frank explained, 'was very prudish and rules were not meant to be broken.'[26] The staleness which many began to note in the 1950s was partly due to the return to 'normality' as the war years receded.[27] Reviews of the Civil Service did take place during this period, but they were invariably internalized affairs (in practice if not in theory) and ultimately unambitious.[28]

This generally blasé attitude contrasted sharply with the approach of a Labour backbencher and businessman, Geoffrey Cooper, who wrote to Clement Attlee on 12 February 1946 urging the Prime Minister to conduct a reform of the Civil Service. Cooper pointed directly to the massive new responsibilities the State had taken on which negated any possibility of business as usual.[29] But his points were effectively ignored. For Attlee and his senior ministers had served in the wartime coalition and had found it highly effective.[30] Furthermore, the left's fears in the 1930s that the Civil Service was anti-socialist were assuaged as one nationalization bill after another rolled off the production line.[31]

Attlee, as well as many others (including Professor Harold Laski of the London School of Economics),[32] observed that the Civil Service had proved itself democratic and effective. Pressure for reform was for Attlee, according to Richard Crossman, 'left-wing clap-trap',[33] though he had had some interesting, and quite radical, thoughts of his own on the machinery of government reform after his early governmental experience in the second Labour government of Ramsay MacDonald and his senior role in the War Cabinet during the Second World War, thoughts which he did not implement once in Downing Street. These included a forerunner of Churchill's 1951–3 peacetime coordinating 'overlords' experiment and significantly strengthening the Prime Minister's Office.[34]

That the Civil Service survived the return of Sir Winston Churchill as Conservative Prime Minister in 1951 unscathed, especially after the example of 1945, demonstrated its political neutrality. This was despite Churchill's private remark soon after re-entering Downing Street that the Civil Service had been politicized and was 'drenched with socialism'.[35] This throwaway aside fitted well with the traditional Tory suspicion of bureaucracy (bar defence – the Armed Forces were always seen as something different from civil servants in the service ministries). But it was to be short-lived as Churchill settled into the other traditional Conservative approach to the Civil Service – a high level of intellectual dependence.[36]

The Civil Service was, therefore, highly self-confident during the immediate post-war period, something graphically illustrated by Bridges' amazingly self-congratulatory 1950 lecture 'Portrait of a Profession', which was rightly described by Samuel Brittan as 'an inexhaustible quarry of quotations for radical critics'.[37] Bridges did understand, though, that the Civil Service had a poor public reputation when he observed that 'I confidently expect that we shall continue to be grouped with mothers-in-law and Wigan Pier as one of the recognized objects of ridicule'.[38] How the Civil Service went in such a small space of time from supreme self-confidence, able to brush aside all criticism, to a position of questioning its own abilities is truly intriguing. The cause, primarily, was economic.

ECONOMICS CASTS A SHADOW

With the successful conclusion to the war, Britain was generally on something of an understandable high. The exemplary sacrifice of so much to prosecuting the war meant that many Britons looked forward to a relaxation of effort once it was won. Before this could happen, however, the British had to undergo one final push. Britain had to be made to pay for itself again, since it had been since 1941 financially reliant on America[39] (in the form of Lend-Lease initially, and when that was abruptly halted the American Loan and then Marshall Aid).[40] A tremendous export drive was launched as it was widely felt that the United Kingdom was in a favourable position to take advantage of mainland Europe's devastation to make large strides in post-war world markets.[41] The feeling was that the British could now look forward to a rosy economic future.

As the 1950s opened, the Korean War erupted. Widely feared to be the opening skirmish in World War Three,[42] the British re-armed substantially, directing resources away from the consumer to the military industries through a quadrupling of the defence estimates thereby halting the great upswing in exports.[43]

Mercifully, a third world war failed to materialize but so, unfortunately, did a successfully renewed export drive even though the Korean emergency's pressure on resources proved short-lived. Lord Croham, generally agreed to be 'one of the most economically literate civil service permanent secretaries' as Permanent Secretary to the Treasury (1968–74),[44] felt that the Labour Chancellor, Hugh Gaitskell, was politicking and panicking when he diverted the country's resources in such an extreme way and that 'we could have had a German-style recovery here' but for him.[45] Persistent balance of payments crises and the drag of administering the world's second reserve currency alongside a business cycle politically, though not very effectively, manipulated from 1955 to produce economic booms to coincide with general elections, meant that the decade was instead one of fitful growth.[46]

Although growth in the early-to-mid 1950s was not given the primacy it later attracted (unemployment was still the main preoccupation)[47] the feeling began to develop that the British economy was underperforming. The Treasury's 1954 *Economic Survey* was perhaps the first publication to draw attention to the UK's dwindling share of world trade,[48] though there had been private unease in Whitehall since before the end of the war.[49] This was increasingly underlined by the comparative statistics that institutions such as the Organisation for Economic Co-operation and Development were beginning to publish, which continuously pointed to lagging British performance.[50]

The decline debate which fascinated a generation of historians demonstrates a powerful warning about the use of statistics. Depending on the start and end points, almost anything can be 'proved'. As Hamish McRae of the *Independent* has indicated, Britain began the twentieth century enjoying the world's largest economy and finished it in fourth spot behind the United States, Japan and Germany – hardly a crash.[51] (An even starker statistic is that Britain also had the fourth largest economy way back in 1820, behind China, India and France respectively.)[52] With this in mind, the post-war acceptance of significant and sustained British decline was clearly misplaced. This is not to suggest that Britain did not lose ground economically during the 1950s, 1960s and also the 1970s, as it most certainly did. But, while one duty of the historian is to dissect the past, another is to try to understand why individual protagonists thought and acted as they did. It is entirely understandable why decline felt so palpable to contemporary observers, as we shall see.

Some historians, most notably Correlli Barnett, have unequivocally blamed British decline in the 1950s, 1960s and 1970s on the creation of a comprehensive welfare state during the final months of the Coalition Government and Attlee Administrations;[53] he has also argued that the creation of a generalist career Civil Service in the nineteenth century was another great failing.[54] The considerable burden which the welfare provision imposed, so the theory went, meant scarce resources were directed to unproductive consumption as a way of the UK patting itself on the back for a (war) job well done. This superficially persuasive theory is not borne out by closer scrutiny. As José Harris has demonstrated, by 1950 the UK's spending on social services as a percentage of gross domestic product was less than West Germany, Austria and Belgium; in 1952 it was passed by France and Denmark; in 1954 by Italy; in 1955 by Sweden; in 1957 by the Netherlands; in 1970 by Norway and Finland. For health care the position is even clearer. Studies during the 1950s and early 1960s show that 'the aggregate volume of per capita health expenditure through central, local and private agencies was lower in Britain than anywhere else in Europe except Italy and Ireland'.[55]

Higher European spending on social programmes did not mean poorly performing economies either. Poor growth in Britain contrasted eye-catchingly with that of continental Western Europe. Despite the same world financial crises that faced Britain in this period (but always remembering that no other country had the combined burdens of a reserve currency, an empire and a big defence budget), Germany's growth averaged 7.8 per cent per annum over the period 1950–8, Italy achieved 5.8 per cent, and France 4.6 per cent. Britain could only muster 2.6 per cent[56] – interestingly, not dissimilar to America's.[57] This was respectable by historical standards but clearly very poor by contemporary comparison.[58] (The trend continued: between 1950 and 1973, Germany averaged 6 per cent in GDP per hour worked, France and Italy 5.1 per cent and the UK 2.9 per cent.)[59]

Looked at in world economic terms, the quarter-century after the war is regarded as the 'Golden Age'[60] – 'Everywhere growth was faster than before.'[61] It subsequently dawned on many in the British circles of influence that the jump in continental growth that reconstruction from a low base inevitably brought was continuing for a suspiciously long time.[62] This recognition turned into something of a 'national neurosis'[63] (though this was not the first outbreak of declinist gloom – that began in the 1870s[64] and was followed by another in Edwardian times) fuelled by unsubstantiated scaremongering that the UK was heading for 'technical inferiority and spiritual weakness in the face of the Soviet challenge'.[65] Even Prince Philip joined in when he said in 1962 that 'we are suffering a national defeat comparable to any lost military campaign, and, what is more, self-inflicted'.[66] The burgeoning declinism reached a crescendo with publications such as the best-selling *The Anatomy of Britain* which pictured the UK as 'becoming to the twenty-first century what Spain was to the eighteenth'.[67]

CRITICISM BECOMES FOCUSED

Powerfully underpinning the burgeoning economic self-doubt was the foreign policy debacle of the Suez Crisis, whereby a hostile USA flexed its financial muscle to such effect – in the face of sterling's fragility[68] – that it spelt the end for British pretensions to independent world-powerdom. As the Prime Minister, Sir Anthony Eden, privately put it in 'a kind of political last will and testament'[69] penned less than a fortnight before stepping down from the top job, 'we must review our world position and our domestic capacity more searchingly in the light of the Suez experience, which has not so much changed our fortunes as revealed realities'.[70] The combination of economic and foreign policy failure festered and led to palpable national self-recrimination, which in turn led the search for scapegoats.[71]

The re-evaluation was to encompass all aspects of British life in a far-reaching re-evaluation of where the country was, how it had got there and where it should go. Anthony Sampson, in the early 1960s, felt that the seemingly inexorable decline in the country's power and prestige – and the non-reaction from the Civil Service – was 'producing a crisis almost comparable to the war'.[72] That the government of the war years and those since had accepted state economic management as a primary responsibility largely by means of the 1944 Employment White Paper, yet things appeared to be going wrong economically, meaning that governments and therefore their civil servants were very much in the firing line.

Much of the detailed criticism came from left-leaning thinkers who discounted the Attlee line that there was nothing wrong with the Civil Service's democratic credentials or its ability. For example, Thomas Balogh felt that a future radical Labour administration would require root-and-branch reform of the system of public administration as an 'essential pre-condition'[73] to extensive social and economic change. Moreover, the Fabian team which produced *The Administrators* included not only noticeable left-wing political figures such as Balogh himself, Shirley Williams and Anthony Crosland, but also serving civil servants in a private capacity (the Fabian Society allows for non-party members), two of whom went on to be permanent secretaries[74] (although these dropped out, claiming the Fabian work was poor).[75]

There were two main elements of criticism which the senior Civil Service faced: that they possessed a distinct lack of expertise and a hopelessly elitist attitude, two mutually reinforcing drawbacks. Ever since 1853–4 and the founding of the modern Civil Service with the Northcote-Trevelyan Report and, much more specifically, during the inter-war tenure of Warren Fisher as Head of the Civil Service (1919–39), there had been a definite bias towards what was known as the 'generalist'.[76] The idea was that the expert should be the first one consulted yet the last to take the decisions – 'on tap but never on top' as the phrase went.[77] The expert, Fisher believed, had too narrow a viewpoint, wanting to solve a problem by the shortest route. This was a recipe for tunnel vision. Having been moved between disparate tasks and fields of expertise over many years (what Fisher described as 'musical chairs'),[78] the generalist had been schooled continuously in the on-the-job *art*[79] of official-political decision-making reality, the generalist believing that the expert was irredeemably impractical. This produced, to Anthony Sampson's mind, a 'cold war' between experts and generalists.[80] Balogh contemptuously dismissed 'the absence of training [which] does not make for an absence of "theory". It usually results in a bias towards a policy of "do-nothing" in the fond – and jejune – hope that a negative absolves them from any responsibility'.[81]

Although the amateur ethos was not completely reversed, the post-war Treasury recognized that Fisher's views were becoming outdated. It took the major step of establishing in 1963 the Centre for Administrative Studies,[82] 'which inaugurated formal courses for Assistant Principals in economics and related subjects' and which led to a growing professionalism throughout the 1960s.[83] The traditional lack of expertise in the Treasury – Sir Donald MacDougall was appalled at the general economic illiteracy when he became Economic Director of the National Economic Development Council in 1962[84] – had a further repercussion. It left the Treasury very dependent upon the Bank of England for advice in monetary matters.[85] (As BWE Alford has pointed out, 'the nationalisation of the Bank of England was regarded as a crucial first step in gaining [political] control of banking and finance ... the reverse would be nearer the truth'.)[86]

Leaving aside the anomalous wartime emergency experiences, the supreme merit of the generalist was underpinned by the iron commitment to sustaining a recruitment processes whereby high-fliers were admitted straight from university and expected to stay for life, a practice which had developed since Northcote-Trevelyan. Earlier in the twentieth century more mature appointments were sometimes made, occasionally all the way up to Permanent Secretary.[87] This was gradually phased out and the almost total reliance on recruitment straight, or very soon after, university became standard practice.[88] Not only was this fact criticized, but also that during the years 1957–63, 85 per cent of those recruited by the Civil Service Selection Board (CSSB) to the (top-ranking) Administrative Class were from the Oxbridge colleges.[89] As such a high proportion of Oxbridge students came from the public schools – between 1948 and 1956 30 per cent came from boarding schools alone[90] – the charge of elitism had much foundation.

Public schools came under attack at this time from many quarters. There were those who felt that they fostered the antiquated ethos of the Victorian gentleman, personified by the archaic figure of the imperial administrator, qualities unsuited to the new era of highly specialized, innovatory international capitalism, let alone running huge public businesses.[91] Apart from the honesty of the average civil servant, Thomas Balogh could see little virtue at all in this recruitment system.[92] Others claimed that it was a socially divisive practice[93] perpetuating snobbery and, just as powerfully held, inverse snobbery (in its wake fuelling the destructive industrial relations[94] which, for many historians, accounted for much of Britain's apparent economic anti-miracle).[95]

The Civil Service ignored these specific criticisms by pointing to the unbending merit inherent in their recruitment systems – 'the first great meritocracy'.[96] Michael Young, in his remarkable study of the past and future of British society, *The Rise of the Meritocracy*, written largely in the early 1950s and eventually published in 1958, explained how the perpetuation of privilege at this time was inevitable:

> The rest of society, and in particular education, was not yet run on the civil-service principle. Education was very far from proportioned to merit. Some children of an ability which should have qualified them as assistant secretaries were forced to leave school at fifteen and become postmen ... Other children with poor ability but rich connexions, pressed through Eton and Balliol, eventually found themselves in mature years as high officers in the Foreign Office ... The limits were the deficiencies of the general education system. Only when the school did its job were the Civil Service Commissioners able to do theirs.[97]

Meritocracy was, therefore, only applied from the age of 21. The elitism this practice created collided heavily with the accelerated social change which Britain experienced in the post-war period. The civil servants themselves were seen by many as antiquated symbols of a discredited past.

The creation essentially of 'night-watchmen'[98] civil servants, with a 'mentality of maintenance',[99] was the inevitable culmination of Civil Service recruitment and training. This produced a mismatch, as the Civil Service was in effect now running huge enterprises. 'Though the Keynesian state was to have highly sensitive new responsibilities', wrote Professor David Marquand in *The Unprincipled Society*,

> He [Keynes] had no theory of state and appears to have seen no need for one. He assumed that, demand management apart, the Keynesian state would behave as the pre-Keynesian state had behaved. The possibility that it could not discharge these new responsibilities successfully without a change in its character – that they would generate new expectations and demands, which could be accommodated and reconciled only by a new kind of state, engaging the public in a process of consultation, negotiation and mutual-education – does not seem to have occurred to him.[100]

The resultant lack of what Marquand called a 'developmental state' therefore meant that there was no accommodation between formal parliamentary sovereignty and ministerial accountability on the one hand and the 'great powers of the real economy' on the other.[101] Defence is a major area in which that thesis was not wholly true. David Edgerton has explained how the defence arm of Whitehall was consistently successfully interventionist, offering encouragement and co-operation, all with informed and high quality technocratic civil servants.[102] Agriculture was another example of Whitehall-influenced technical prowess, certainly up to the British accession to the European Economic Community in 1973, but these were very much exceptions to the rule.

REFORM BEGINS

The Treasury was at the forefront of criticism. That 'most political of all the Departments',[103] as Bridges called it, faced attack from all sides. What was most interesting, and most significant for its workings, was that much disquiet came from *inside* (especially after Keynes's death in 1946 left it without a respected external stimulus)[104] so beginning the Treasury's rolling internal reappraisal of the late 1950s and early 1960s.[105] Some officials were coming to see the Treasury's aims and methods as anachronistic. They thought the departments were too decentralized[106] and that the Treasury had too few people properly to scrutinize other departments' programmes, yet too much power when it came to imposing simplistic, wholesale economies which could prove counterproductive. They also felt, along with the rest of the Treasury, that the piecemeal scrutiny of programmes and the way the Chancellor was being ambushed in Cabinet by spending Ministers was undermining the Treasury's role in expenditure control (in the words of one Treasury official, 'trying to avoid this system of being nibbled to death').[107]

All-encompassing machinery needed to be constructed on the model of the fledgling defence and social security forward surveys,[108] begun in the mid-1950s, which were an attempt to add serious analysis to the politics of spending.[109] An opportunity for Treasury officials to enact big change arose in late 1957 with an investigation by the all-party House of Commons' Select Committee on Estimates. Reporting in July 1958, the committee was broadly favourable to the Treasury, but felt that a more expert investigation into the public expenditure machinery was required (after suitable briefing and encouragement by the Treasury reformers).[110] A year later, the Chancellor of the Exchequer, Derick Heathcoat Amory, announced an inquiry under the chairmanship of Lord (Edwin) Plowden, Chief Planning Officer in the late 1940s – early 1950s Central Economic Planning Staff and latterly Chairman of the Atomic Energy Authority.

The investigation took place privately under the auspices of the Chancellor. The membership of the Committee was interesting in that it included three businessmen, all with some experience of Whitehall.[111] Five anonymous senior civil servants also sat on it as 'assessors' (Burke Trend, Otto Clarke and Evelyn Sharp were among them).[112] The Plowden Report was to prove a landmark in the post-war history of the Treasury. For not only was it the first investigation to take Keynesianism as its point of departure,[113] but it also had the same effect in government circles as the legendary wartime Beveridge Report in that it signalled a true change of heart at the centre of government – 'It was in effect a statement of Government policy.'[114] According to Otto Clarke, the senior internal Treasury critic and wartime temporary who stayed on, this was because of three elements: it asked practical questions; it had a chairman of great standing and government experience; and the Civil Service was bound in from the start.[115]

Sir Samuel Goldman, a successor of Clarke's in Treasury public expenditure control, was later to write that 'It is an open secret that the principal ideas and analysis which made the Plowden Report so seminal a document came from the mind of Sir Richard Clarke'.[116] The outcome of the Report was, therefore, totally in accordance with the wishes of many in the Treasury and was, according to Sir Leo Pliatzky, another successor of Clarke's, 'a great conceptual achievement. To secure its acceptance by Whitehall was a feat of will and organisation. I say this as someone who – to understate the point somewhat – owed nothing to patronage from that quarter [i.e. Clarke's].'[117]

There were several elements to Plowden. It led to the then world-beating sophistication[118] (later much criticized for being a motor of inflation) of the Public Expenditure Survey Committee (PESC) – but not to a permanent Cabinet committee solely devoted to public expenditure which Plowden also recommended privately.[119] Only ad hoc ones were created[120] until some three decades later when the Major Administration created a system, long after PESC had been abolished, in which projected government revenues were matched against all public spending over the forthcoming five years, all within the standing EDX Cabinet committee.[121] 'With PESC', said one Treasury official, 'power is shifted to the centre, that is, to the Treasury', all in an attempt to make sure the Treasury would not be defeated in future.[122] PESC also reflected the growing realization that emergency across-the-board cutbacks in public spending were irrational and often counter productive.[123]

The Report led to the most extensive Treasury peacetime reform since 1919.[124] In October 1962 the Treasury was internally divided into two, the 'Pay and Management Side' and the 'Finance and Economic Side',[125] according to an Otto Clarke–William Armstrong blueprint (Armstrong had been made Permanent Secretary to the Treasury earlier in 1962).[126] The split happened because (setting aside the institutional reform represented by PESC) the true crux of the Plowden Report was to change the nature of the Treasury or, in Otto Clarke's words: 'Instead of being a back-seat driver, the Treasury's job is to ensure that every Department has the best possible cars and drivers and is properly equipped with maps.'[127] In effect, there was to be a new ethos for a new era of intervention in the economy.[128] (In Henry Roseveare's view, the split was also due to the Treasury having to raise its game in rivalry to the creation of the National Economic Development Council, of which, more later.)[129]

The 1962 reorganization made *management* the modern successor of negative *control*[130] (the age-old criticism being that the Treasury was more interested in counting 'candle-ends'[131] which counterproductively produced irresponsibility on the part of the departments).[132] Thus 'management' firmly entered the Civil Service lexicon, in this instance as a way of delivering more sophisticated public expenditure oversight. The drive for better management was to prove a recurrent theme[133] as complexity and cost of programmes increased.[134]

At the same time as the visible failure in domestic economic matters and humiliation along an overseas canal, a more intangible shift was happening with the increasing breakdown of social deference. This was powered by such factors as the spread of affluence, the rise in the number of students attending a form of higher education (from 69,000 in 1938–9 to 216,000 in 1962–3, an increase of over 300 per cent),[135] the steady decline in church-going[136] and the ending of national service, each of which would separately bring change but combined to produce a social revolution. The rise of satire, exemplified by the stage show *Beyond The Fringe* (1960), the television programme *That Was The Week That Was* (1962) and the magazine *Private Eye* (1962), ushered in a new era of nearly no-holds-barred public discourse. Britain was changing fast and the results included continuing attacks on the allegedly old-fashioned, class-ridden totem poles of British public life and the 'the whole matrix of official and social relations within which power is exercised', as Henry Fairlie put it in 1955. Fairlie went on to revive the catch-all phrase 'The Establishment' succinctly to describe Britain's governing tribe.[137] The Civil Service was clearly a prime candidate for assault as it could be described – even parodied – as holding to procedures and traditions a century old, with a middle-class, male-dominated, old school- (and university-) tie-ruled upper echelon which had presided over undeniable failure.[138] That its political masters in Harold Macmillan's Cabinets were at this time increasingly from an identifiably privileged social stratum intensified criticism.[139]

Macmillan's intellectual life prior to becoming Prime Minister proved him to be quite the progressive, calling in his 1938 book for 'The Middle Way' to be found between total state planning and unbridled *laissez-faire*.[140] 'By far the most radical man I've known in politics ... He was a real left-wing radical in his social, human and economic thinking', Clement Attlee recalled privately in 1951.[141] In fact, Macmillan had even gone as far as having a pre-war conversation with Aneurin Bevan about his potential defection, who advised caution.[142] In any event, this was highly significant for the Civil Service as there was now a Conservative Prime Minister who did not find state power *per se* distasteful (as many, if not most, Conservatives did),[143] but one who had actively called for its thoughtful and extensive application.

Macmillan formed his government with his party at a low ebb after Suez. But he managed to turn around the Conservative Party's fortunes to produce a landslide victory in the October 1959 general election.[144] The post-election honeymoon was not to last long, however, and the Tories found it increasingly difficult to prolong the good times.[145] Macmillan had to lean heavily on his own economic thinking and writing in trying to escape this tight spot.

Palpable relative economic decline in the 1960s really began with the sterling crisis of 1961. 'July Measures' from the Chancellor, Selwyn Lloyd, imposed 'rather savage deflationary measures'[146] on the British economy, which included a curb on government spending and bank advances and a rise in the Bank Rate to 7 per cent.[147] One of the most controversial factors in British economic decline in the 1950s and early 1960s was the policy derided as 'stop-go', largely by economists such as Christopher Dow who ridiculed attempts at fine-tuning,[148] scapegoated as a prime accelerator of relative economic decline (though Geoffrey Owen has argued persuasively that 'stop-go' was the *result* of poor growth).[149]

Fundamental to Keynes's philosophy of demand-management (published by Macmillan in 1936 as *The General Theory of Employment, Interest and Money*)[150] was the idea that it was for the government to encourage economic activity in times of slump and to discourage it when overheating threatened. Overheating happened rapidly in Britain at this time. Because of the commitment to as full employment as the government could create, demand for labour was constantly high. This obviously led to consistent upward pressure on wages, and hence to inflation. More money in the economy therefore ate into the quantity of goods and services which ideally should have been exported. It also led to increasing imports as demand remained high.[151] There were several problems with this as a paucity of supply and little by way of productivity gains meant, for a fixed exchange rate economy like Britain's, great pressure on the balance of payments during times of growth.

With growth widely accepted as the new goal, and becoming a driver of British political competition, Macmillan's old thinking came into its own. Macmillan was consumed by the commitment to higher growth. His experiences as a young Conservative hopeful in depression-ravaged Stockton-upon-Tees during the 1930s had seared into his psyche the perils of the free market when it went wrong (officials kept a secret tally of the number of times Macmillan's old stomping ground cropped up in conversation).[152] He subsequently urged expansionary measures at all points during his tenure, something consistently urged on him by the economist Roy Harrod,[153] thinking that 'writing cheques', as Peter Thorneycroft sardonically put it, was the best way to solve the problems of places such as Stockton.[154]

Thorneycroft was made Macmillan's first Chancellor in 1957 but resigned a year later when the Cabinet only offered £100 million of cuts to planned spending when he had somewhat precipitately demanded £150 million. His belief that inflation was stoked by excessive government borrowing led to him becoming a totemic figure in the monetarist movement of 1970s and 1980s.[155] But there was no room for this kind of thinking during the Macmillan years. Thorneycroft's successor Derick Heathcoat Amory, Chancellor from 1958 to 1960, proved more flexible in allowing Macmillan, 'almost a wild inflationist at that time'[156] (in Amory's words), to pressurize him into producing the boom for the 1959 general election. But even Amory let it be known that if he had not been granted his request to retire in 1960, there would have been a parting of the ways in any case over the need for a 'stop' to the booming, but fragile, economy.[157]

A powerful reason for Macmillan's pressure for expansion on his Chancellors was because of his hatred of the Treasury's traditional methods of dealing with the economy, which went back to the desperate days of the 1930s and even into the 1920s, August 1931 in particular, when the National Government was formed and deflationary measures imposed on an already depressed economy, all in the perennial effort to save the pound. This was to instil in Labour politicians and, as we have seen, Macmillan too (due to his somewhat ambiguous philosophical sympathies) a deep distrust of 'Treasury orthodoxy'.[158] He subsequently felt that deflation was 'more dangerous, really, than inflation',[159] though his celebrated 'never had it so good' July 1957 Bedford speech,[160] and his lecture to the Conservative Political Centre (which formed the introduction to the 1958 reissue of *The Middle Way*), each clearly demonstrated an understanding of the dangers of excessive inflation.[161]

The 1961 'stop' was delivered by the new Chancellor, Selwyn Lloyd. The Treasury had calculated that if the outflow of reserves continued at a constant pace there would be none left by Christmas.[162] Macmillan felt powerless to avoid the deflationary measures.[163] But the expansion-minded Prime Minister was determined not to be trapped again and so began the search for a solution to the problem of 'stop-go'. The 'July Measures' were botched in the eyes of the business community who lost confidence in the Treasury after it singled out consumer goods and car production, two of the biggest growth markets.[164] This produced a gulf in outlook between business and the government exacerbated by the Treasury's assertion that deflation was not boosting exports as it should, and that this was down to the poor way industry was run by employers on the one hand and the behaviour of trade unions on the other.[165]

CONTINENTAL TILT

Sir Frank Lee, the Permanent Secretary to the Treasury, was convinced that Britain needed a strong dose of competition (an analysis that was by no means unanimous in the Treasury) alongside continuous deflationary pressure, in order to counter the rigidity of the labour market.[166] The application in 1961 to join the six-nation European Economic Community (EEC) was clearly a way of intensifying competition and therefore efficiency, but Lee was convinced that the British economy needed a cold shower, whether or not the application was successful.[167] The EEC was increasingly seen by Macmillan as a major threat to British economic success due to the tariff wall erected around what were fast becoming the UK's most important high-value trading partners,[168] in direct contrast to earlier analysis that too much European involvement would damage what eventually became seen as low-value Commonwealth trade.[169] This was largely ignored in the Foreign Office but the economic need to turn to Europe was understood in the Treasury, ever the hard-headed part of government.[170] Lee was supported by a growing band of younger Foreign Office officials who fervently believed that Britain's future was European.[171] Thus began a technocratic takeover of UK–EEC policy which in effect lasted until the accession in 1973 and involved a somewhat unconstitutional push for eventual UK entry by many senior officials even when government policy was against it (during Harold Wilson's first years as Premier).[172]

The 1961 application to join the EEC, with a negotiating team comprising the cream of Whitehall and headed by Edward Heath (Lord Privy Seal, 1960–3),[173] was knocked back unilaterally by the French President, Charles de Gaulle, in January 1963. To Macmillan, de Gaulle's precipitate action meant that 'all our policies at home and abroad are in ruins'.[174] The subsequent British exclusion from the rapid, stable growth in intra-European trade from the EEC's inception in January 1958 through to the early 1970s[175] was, for Geoffrey Owen, along with the aforementioned lack of competitiveness, the true determinant of Britain's relative economic decline.[176]

A different path to the cold-shower effect of greater competition was taken when the divergence of view between the Treasury and the organized employers' groups provided the springboard for one of the elements which formed part of Macmillan's 'post-Suez rethinks'[177] for across-the-board modernization and expansion. In 1961 the Federation of British Industry (FBI) conference called for planning to be adopted in Britain.[178] This was because the French system was seen as dynamically capitalist but underpinned by a government which fostered a benign environment for business.[179] The FBI move was, therefore, an attempt to wrestle some aspects of economic management away from the Treasury[180] (which was already happening separately with independent investigations such as the Beeching Report on the railways, the Buchanan Report on traffic in towns and the Robbins Report on higher education,[181] and with Lord Hailsham's appointment as Minister for the regeneration of North-East England).[182]

The concept of 'planning' was an enigma in itself. While few people regarded a step backwards to the wartime days of physical controls to be practical or indeed desirable outside the hard-left of the Labour Party and left-wing extremists, the tide of intellectual opinion was at this time moving towards the advocacy of some form of state-involved planning, and that pointed to just across the English Channel.[183] The French wanted the UK to adopt their own 'indicative planning'

– or 'planning by influence' as Edmund Dell called it[184] – so that it would tip the balance towards the Germans adopting greater dirigisme if ever Britain joined the EEC.[185] To that end, they entertained several unpublicized group visits to France in 1960[186] and attended a conference in London on 20–2 April 1961.[187] Sir Donald MacDougall was one of those present and described the British thinking:

> We noticed that French growth had been rapid, that they had had a succession of four year 'plans', and thought there might be some connection between the two. I had been to France, on a visit ... in a team of civil servants, businessmen, trade unionists, politicians and academics, and we were told by the chief planner, Monsieur Massé, that French planning – on a tripartite basis – had indeed increased their rate of growth.[188]

It is highly debatable whether Massé's claim was true.[189] For Alec Cairncross (Professor of Applied Economics at Glasgow in 1960, and subsequently Head of the Government Economic Service, 1964–9) the whole idea of politicians claiming credit for rapid economic growth was fanciful.[190] But it was certainly attractive for those who visited France who were, it seems to modern eyes, clutching at straws, trying to discover just what the Continentals were doing which Britain was not.[191] The Cabinet, however, was wary of being too closely linked to the French model. During the Cabinet meeting of 21 September 1961, Macmillan told colleagues that 'It would be wrong to suppose that any form of organisation would resolve the fundamental difficulties of economic planning in a free society, but progress might be made in practical respects, if the co-operation of industrialists and trade unions could be secured in the studies and investigations which the council would promote.'[192] The government eventually decided on the planning route, albeit a British version.[193]

As it was supported by so many people right across the political spectrum, it is clear that there was no one definition at the time of 'planning', but broadly it seemed to be a synonym for forward thinking.[194] (Eastern European planners, used to almost total control of the economy, who visited Sir Donald MacDougall were very confused as to how planning UK-style could work: '"You've got your plan, now how do you make people invest and do what you want them to do?" ... They weren't at all convinced and they were probably right.')[195] Specifically, the British form entailed the attempt to rationalize spending, avoid unnecessary waste and forge a mutually understanding, socially cohesive bond between government, employers and the unions[196] in order to agree on a growth target and minimize the industrial conflict which was beginning to blight the British economy. (Those favouring an injection of competition were suspicious of this move towards what they regarded as cartelization,[197] but, crucially, Sir Frank Lee backed NEDC as an independent institution.)[198]

The creation of the National Economic Development Council, funded by the taxpayer and thus as an instrument of public policy, was announced by Selwyn

Lloyd during his statement on the July 1961 measures to counter the negativity of their content.[199] Although the idea of NEDC was widely credited to the Chancellor, as Macmillan did himself in his memoirs,[200] there is more than a hint of NEDC in *The Middle Way*. In it, Macmillan called for a 'National Economic Council' which 'with all the facts before it, would survey the whole field of economic activity, and, in consultation with the responsible representatives of the Government, formulate a comprehensive plan for general guidance' – a very similar brief to Neddy.[201] Furthermore, Neddy demonstrated a determination by the Macmillan Government to absorb and act on the pro-planning criticism, thereby redirecting the anti-establishment impulse in a technocratic fashion.

The NEDC's birth was opposed by several in a Cabinet bounced into acceptance. The Cabinet complained that its creation would cause confusion and duplication, and that its strong association with government would give it too much credence.[202] The most notable dissenter was Reginald Maudling, President of the Board of Trade, who also disliked the idea of a powerful agency beyond democratic control.[203] (Maudling replaced Lloyd as Chancellor in July 1962 and, therefore, took the chair of the NEDC. His initial opposition was reversed, especially after the EEC veto left the government's economic policy in ruins).[204] Macmillan saw the Cabinet opposition as 'corresponding to whether they had old Whig, Liberal, *laissez-faire* traditions, or Tory opinions, paternalists and not afraid of a little *dirigisme*'.[205]

Neddy was established as a non-statutory, purely advisory, tripartite economic forum with a few independent members.[206] Tripartism had a long history in Britain and reached its height in the wartime emergency. Deemed a great wartime success, it was to be dusted down once again when new difficulties challenged.[207] The Trades Union Congress (TUC) eventually agreed to join Neddy on 24 January 1962[208] (overcoming their distaste of 1961–2's public sector 'Pay Pause').[209] The NEDC was buttressed by a series of Economic Development Committees (EDCs or 'Little Neddies'), a micro-economic attempt to help the economy, which scrutinized individual industries and pointed out improvements (a supply-side measure which signified a departure from the solely demand-minded philosophy of Keynesianism proper). It was backed by a staff, the National Economic Development Office (NEDO).

The first head of the NEDC was Sir Robert Shone, a former Chairman of the Iron and Steel Board (chosen because of his familiarity with the French plan).[210] The inaugural Economic Director of the NEDC, Sir Donald MacDougall, somewhat touchingly described the hope of its first meeting: 'The lift was not working, so members had quite a climb to the room where we met. This was regarded as symbolic of the run down state of the economy. Neddy would change all that. By 1966 all the lifts would be working all the time everywhere.'[211] The feeling that Neddy represented the future of British economic management, and therefore the place to be, was reinforced by *That Was the Week That Was* which contrasted the dull, orthodox, antiquated Treasury with the thrusting, iconoclastic, new NEDC.[212]

Staffing Neddy also proved to be significant. The Civil Service as a whole had worryingly few professional economists at this time, in actual fact only 25 in 1964.[213] The Civil Service acknowledged the astonishment this provoked[214] but claimed it was very difficult to attract them.[215] MacDougall pointed out that this did not stop this period becoming known as the 'Golden Years'.[216] But the lack of economic professionalism was worrying to all during a time of massive investment in publicly funded infrastructure projects – the roads programme, the rail modernization plan and civil nuclear power – many of which were planned without the help of an economist.[217]

Shone and MacDougall went about making NEDO as expert as they could. They proved so effective – recruiting nearly as many economists as there were in the Treasury[218] – that Neddy came to be regarded as an intellectual rival to the Treasury and therefore a threat to the economic hegemony carefully built and jealously guarded over many years.[219] As it was so expert, Samuel Brittan surmised that it may also have exerted valuable behind-the-scenes pressure on the Treasury.[220]

There were two major studies which the NEDC completed in its first years. The 'Green Book' predicted an annual rate of growth of four per cent for the years 1961–6 and the 'Orange Book' dealt with obstacles and efficiency.[221] The Treasury vetoed a section of the Orange Book written by a former student of Sir Donald MacDougall's, Maurice Scott, which looked at the possibility of a floating rate for sterling; 'most people refused to talk about it, it was quite extraordinary'.[222] This matter alone demonstrated a determination by the Treasury to avoid being usurped by the NEDC as the central shaper of economic policy and showed its fear 'that NEDC should embark on such a question in semi-public circumstances [which] seemed to confirm fears that it would turn out to be a Frankenstein Monster'.[223] The Treasury was otherwise very impressed by the analysis of the Orange Book.[224]

The four per cent 'target' for growth essentially became an estimate for growth. This was because the government could hardly refute the predictions of a panel *it* had set up and which had the Chancellor as chairman.[225] Nevertheless, the Treasury remained very sceptical about four per cent growth.[226] Yet it was factored into the public expenditure estimates, against the Treasury's own forecast, which proved more accurate at just over three per cent. The overriding principle which Otto Clarke and the other Treasury reformers had tried to instil into future public expenditure plans, that government spending growth (as detailed in the PESC machinery) must not outpace that of growth in the economy, was fundamentally undermined.[227] This period was described by Otto Clarke as 'anti-PESC'.[228]

CIVIL SERVICE SELF-CONFIDENCE SHAKEN

The Treasury's 1961 miscalculation regarding the immediate future for the balance of payments was so significant that it not only damaged the Chancellor but also undermined the Treasury's confidence in itself.[229] Unsurprisingly, the Cabinet became highly wary of the Treasury's forecasting skill.[230] Macmillan was chief among the ministerial critics but his scepticism went deeper – and had lasted longer – than most. In fact, giving the Budget speech as Chancellor himself in 1956, he had warned against economic forecasting and statistics:

> Some people feel that what passes for such is more like astrology than astronomy ... I do not share this extreme view. Nevertheless, I think that we should all agree that if there is such a science, it is not an exact one. There are too many unknowns and to[o] many variables. Then I am told that some of our statistics are too late to be as useful as they ought to be. We are always, as it were, looking up a train in last year's Bradshaw.[231]

Macmillan was a bitter opponent of 'stop-go' (it being 'like those young ladies who oscillate daily between the stimulant and the tranquillizers'),[232] wanting just 'go', and he cast around desperately searching for a remedy. His major decision was to ditch what he came to see as his ineffective Chancellor, Lloyd. His replacement was Reginald Maudling, the most economically literate and experienced Conservative Chancellor for many years (having been Economic Secretary to the Treasury 1952–5, Paymaster-General 1957–9 and President of the Board of Trade 1959–61).[233] July 1962 also saw a new Permanent Secretary for the Treasury. Sir William Armstrong, probably the first Permanent Head to have a contemporary approach to economic management, was promoted from Third Secretary over the heads of his superiors in a clear sign that Macmillan was displeased with the official side of the Treasury.[234]

The Treasury appeared at this time to be in a somewhat chastened mood. The critical assault it suffered over the forecasting mistake of 1961, as we have seen, lost it the confidence of Ministers and many captains of industry. According to Samuel Brittan, this made 'very senior Treasury administrators' anxious 'to persuade sceptical industrialists that stop-go had at last been abandoned in favour of steady growth'.[235] The Treasury was therefore committed to the Prime Minister and Chancellor's expansionist plans which lasted until Labour's narrow victory in 1964. What became known as the 'dash for growth' was ended when the incoming Labour ministers took fright amid fears for the fixed exchange rate. As Brittan later lamented:

> A period of steadily rising demand, at slightly above trend levels, might in the early and middle 1960s, before the inflationary explosion of the end of the decade, have speeded up the underlying growth rate via its effects on expectations and business investment.

Because of the devotion to an arbitrary exchange rate the experiment never had a chance, and we shall never know whether it could have worked.[236]

Apart from the economic apparatus, there were several other machinery-of-government reforms in the last years of Macmillan's reign, before his sudden retirement forced by ill health in the autumn of 1963.[237] Macmillan's successor, Sir Alec Douglas-Home, had little time to refashion the State himself during his short-lived Premiership from October 1963 through to the Labour election victory in October 1964. He was certainly interested in technocratic questions, though, as he explained in his memoirs:

> I confess that I would like to have been given a bit longer at No. 10 so as to get more grip on the machinery of government.
> The keys to this are: short and precise paper-work; a chain of government committees each charged to take decisions, resulting in a Cabinet agenda which is cleared of all but the absolute essentials; Ministers who can be relied upon to insist on these rules ... and lastly a programme of legislation for Parliament which is not overloaded.[238]

Douglas-Home was privately working on plans for a radical reform to reduce the workload on the Cabinet and Civil Service if the electorate returned him to Downing Street, to be overseen by Enoch Powell (who knew nothing of this at the time[239] and who held very minimalist views regarding bureaucratic arrangements as he made clear in his evidence to the Fulton Committee).[240]

There was a minor innovation with another experiment in 'overlordship' from December 1963. The wartime practice that had been discredited with its peacetime resurrection in Churchill's 1951 Government was again tried, this time with Edward Heath becoming Secretary of State for Industry, Trade and Regional Development. As a coordinating Minister, Heath was supposed to hold the Prime Minister's authority in deciding issues from the Board of Trade or from the Ministry of Housing and Local Government, Transport, Power or Public Buildings and Works. There was little extra support given to Heath, however, and he had no statutory power to direct other Ministers. The Head of the Civil Service, Sir Laurence Helsby, felt that this experiment had again failed but Douglas-Home did not believe that it had had long enough to prove itself by the time the Conservatives lost the October 1964 election.[241] Home's rational mind also led to the creation of the Douglas-Home Rules which to this day ensure authorized access for the opposition to discuss the machinery-of-government changes to be enacted in the event of election victory, as we shall see in Chapter 2.[242]

In 1945, the Civil Service could feel rightly proud of itself. But it undoubtedly made a strategic error in thinking that things would quickly reassume the pattern of the pre-war years. For the 1942 Beveridge Report and the 1944 Employment

White Paper had signalled a fundamental shift in the ambition and reach of the public sphere. To quote Oliver Franks, the State 'had changed from being purely regulative ... and had become more and more [that] of management'.[243] This 'missed opportunity' coupled with the despondency created by accelerated relative economic decline in the 1950s and 1960s, which proved such a millstone around the neck of the Civil Service due to the responsibilities imposed by the 1944 Employment White Paper, meant the service understandably came in for tremendous criticism once problems became apparent.

How did the Civil Service face this barrage of cynicism? Some buccaneering souls such as Otto Clarke tried to shift the culture of an increasingly demoralized Treasury almost single-handedly. But much remained the same, and this is unsurprising. For in a culture as hidebound as the Civil Service then was, conditioned by generations of cautious practice, 'men of push and go' (as Lloyd George liked to say)[244] rarely prospered. It was therefore left for the politicians to step into the breach, Macmillan being the first, and much changed during his Premierships, with his stab at tripartism and clear disapproval of Treasury orthodoxy. Macmillan fell before he could really begin to see the results of his policy shifts and within a year of his retirement it was left to Harold Wilson's reinvigorated Labour Party to run with the torch of modernization.

2

Hardware

HAROLD WILSON AND THE REFORGING OF WHITEHALL 1964–68

BIRTH OF THE DEA

The Labour Party's electoral victory in 1964 after 13 years in the wilderness provided an injection of enthusiasm to the 'little *dirigisme*' that Harold Macmillan had embarked upon (though with no credit given to Macmillan's ideas or actions). The Conservative Party had been slightly uneasy about its unorthodox and Whiggish leader. The Labour Party, by contrast, was fully behind the manifesto's declaration that 'the machinery of government must be modernised'[1] – and intended to embrace economic planning at a gallop. This is not to suggest that all Labour members were in accord over what or how to plan. But, at least in the autumn of 1964, hopes were high within Labour that intensifying the planning already begun would lead to improved and more equitable economic growth – and a shift in the country's political balance leftwards.

Aneurin Bevan, the godfather of Britain's post-war left-wing tradition, in his last speech to the House of Commons, a response to the Queen's Speech, on 3 November 1959 said:

> There is one important problem facing representative Parliamentary Government in the whole of the world where it exists. It is being asked to solve a problem which it has so far failed to solve: that is, how to reconcile Parliamentary popularity with sound economic planning. So far, nobody on either side of this House has succeeded, and it is a problem which has to be solved if we are to meet the challenge that comes to us from other parts of the world and if we are to grout and to buttress the institutions of Parliamentary Government in the affections of the population.[2]

Interestingly, Bevan's words formed the epigraph of Harold Wilson's *The Labour Government 1964–1970* (and was repeated in his *Final Term: The Labour Government, 1974–1976*).[3] In this chapter, we shall look at Labour's attempts during the 1960s to enhance the British State's ability to manage its ever more complex economy. As we saw in Chapter 1, much of the criticism of the British

Civil Service in the run-up to Labour's 1964 victory was aimed at the Treasury and its handling of economic policy. It is therefore unsurprising that the bulk of Labour's initial reforms to the Civil Service centred on the splitting of the Treasury and the subsequent creation of several rival outposts of economic power. This, along with many other reforms, represented the 'hardware', as opposed to the 'software',[4] changes on which Harold Wilson set great store by in his re-jigging of Whitehall.

Economic planning – in short, the attempt to mitigate the vagaries and waste of an unadulterated price-mechanism as a distributor of resources – had been the Labour Party's touchstone since the interwar years[5] (partly because the Great War had shown just what a government could do when it put its mind to it).[6] Attlee's 1945–51 governments had delivered mightily on nationalization. But the government was deemed by most commentators to have been unsuccessful when it somewhat half-heartedly attempted to 'plan' the resulting semi-controlled economy with units such as the Central Economic Planning Staff, the Economic Planning Board and a myriad Cabinet committees.[7] This sense of relative failure resonated throughout the 1950s in Labour circles.

The shrinkage in support for the Conservatives during the years 1960–2 (Gallup calculated Macmillan's personal rating to fall from 79 per cent satisfaction in May 1960 down to 52 per cent dissatisfied in July 1962)[8] meant the Labour Party was increasingly buoyant and began confidently to plan for the day it would return to government. These preparations, due to the Macmillan Government's increasing embrace of planning, were, however, comparable to shooting at a moving target.[9]

When the Labour leader, Hugh Gaitskell, died suddenly in 1963, the winner of the subsequent bloody leadership election was Harold Wilson.[10] Wilson was, remains and probably always will be an enigma, both personally and politically. Beginning working life as an Oxford don (from a lower middle class, North of England background), he was appointed to the War Cabinet Secretariat as a temporary civil servant during the Second World War, joined the Cabinet in 1947 as its youngest member since Pitt and resigned from it in 1951 with Bevan over defence estimates and cuts in social spending, apparently on principle.[11] During the long years of opposition from 1951–64 he was initially a leading Bevanite (albeit a mistrusted one, both by ultra- and anti-Bevanites),[12] Shadow Chancellor and Chairman of the powerful House of Commons Public Accounts Committee. All in all, a man of great ability and even greater experience, yet one dogged by accusations of shiftiness which led to a poor subsequent reputation.[13]

The battle to succeed Gaitskell scarred Labour for several years.[14] The leading right-winger, George Brown, felt that the crown rightfully belonged to him, but his unpredictable nature split the vote and allowed Jim Callaghan to steal valuable support. Harold Wilson won comfortably.[15] But, unlike 1992 when Bryan Gould completely left British politics soon after losing the contest to John Smith, Callaghan and Brown (especially) were still hugely ambitious. This left Wilson with a problem. For Callaghan was highly placed in the Shadow Chancellorship (though he found his brief difficult to master and personal seminars in economics at Nuffield College, Oxford, were provided to help),[16] while another leading right-winger, Patrick Gordon Walker, was firmly positioned as Shadow Foreign Secretary. Where to place George Brown?

With Macmillan ailing and soon gone, the economy overheating and Macmillan's successor, Douglas-Home, largely unimpressive, Wilson was right to see No 10's door beckoning. He began to plan for the day when he would move into the famous terraced house he had been photographed outside as a child. Right from the beginning of Wilson's leadership, it was clear that Neddy and the Treasury's reforms in 1962 had been dismissed as inadequate by the Labour high command and that major reforms were being considered. Intelligence began to filter through in July 1963 to the Head of the Home Civil Service, Sir Lawrence Helsby, from Macmillan's Principal Private Secretary, Tim Bligh, that 'It has come to my ears that if he becomes Prime Minister Mr Wilson has one or two ideas floating about in the machinery of government field.'[17] Bligh was referring to widely conducted consultations that some high-ranking Labour politicians were undertaking on a variety of economic planning mechanisms and approaches.[18] Here was a chance to square the Brown circle.

Lord Roll of Ipsden, who, as Sir Eric Roll, was to be Brown's right-hand man as Permanent Secretary of the Department of Economic Affairs (DEA), was clear how limited was Brown's initial interest in the economic sphere: 'George's principal desire was the Foreign Office, he really wanted to be Foreign Secretary basically [shades of Ernest Bevin, the formidable father-figure of Brown's union, the Transport and General Workers, and Foreign Secretary 1945–51]. But it was quite clear at this stage that he couldn't be as it was already spoken for in a way, so that's why he turned himself more to economics.'[19] With this switch, Brown attacked his new target with gusto.

Brown began to carve out for himself a role that he believed befitted his true position in the Party. What he wanted to be was economic overlord, a kind of supreme coordinator of everything with an economic and industrial aspect – and one buttressed by a dynamic new department. This overlordship was not to be of the vague, discredited 1951–3 Churchillian breed,[20] but one with statutory powers underlining who was boss.[21] This would have turned the Treasury, the Board of Trade and the Ministry of Labour, in effect, into specialized executive agencies, all carrying out the will of the overlord.[22] As Brown later wrote, the new department '(as I always saw it) would be superior to the Treasury in determining the country's economic priorities. Looking back, it seems that my own thinking may have gone further ahead than that of the Prime Minister and some of my other colleagues, and it is possible that I made assumptions in my mind which the others did not, in fact, share.'[23] It seems clear that Brown picked up the ball and ran with it, for Wilson himself was later to write that 'George Brown had interpreted the DEA mandate liberally ... DEA had developed more than I had originally intended'.[24] Samuel Brittan, the unrivalled Whitehall-watcher and very temporary DEA temporary from 1964–5, thought that Wilson's wish was to have 'rival views on economic strategy, instead of being argued out in the depths of the official machine ... represented by different ministers, which would bring the Prime Minister into the picture in a way that had not happened under the Conservatives'.[25]

Tim Bligh's intelligence feed, this time directly to the Prime Minister, Sir Alec Douglas-Home, continued into 1964 when he reported on Brown's 'private conversation away from Whitehall with Sir William Armstrong', Permanent Secretary to the Treasury:

> Apparently, Mr Brown claimed to be speaking on behalf of Mr Wilson but this seems unlikely on two counts. Mr Wilson plays his cards very close to his chest and leaves no room for the space of a fly, let alone George Brown; secondly, Mr Brown claimed that Labour Party policy was to have a Minister for Production who would be an overlord in the economic field (and this would be him), helped by a whipper-snapper Chancellor of the Exchequer (who would be Mr Callaghan).[26]

How had it happened that Brown had strayed so far from Wilson's thinking? Lord Roll of Ipsden believed he knew why: 'It was to some extent stimulated by people like Tommy [Balogh] ... Tommy was the inspirer, Tommy used to say "I'm a visperer." [sic]'.[27] Balogh was central to the pre-election planning. The man who had vented his spleen at the 'Establishment' and the Civil Service in particular with his celebrated late-1950s essay 'The Apotheosis of the Dilettante'[28] was now given what *he* saw as a free hand (Wilson was very self-confident in economic matters) to help shape the future Labour administration as a true intimate of Wilson, having known him at Oxford in the early days of the war.[29] Balogh began to draw up plans for a 'Ministry of Expansion or Production'.[30]

Sir Donald MacDougall, Economic Director of the NEDC 1962–4 and Director-General of the DEA 1964–8, observed that 'Balogh didn't trust the Treasury or the Bank of England one little bit and wanted a department to keep an eye on the wicked things the Treasury wanted to do.'[31] This was a deeply held belief across a wide swathe of the Labour Party, not just its left wing. 'Take economic planning away from the Treasury ... they know nothing about it' said Bevan in his already quoted 1959 Commons response to the Queen's Speech.[32] It was also widely shared throughout intellectual circles sympathetic to Labour[33] and Wilson himself disliked the Treasury all his life, although he had been offered a job there after his stint in the wartime Civil Service; working round it became his leitmotif.³⁴ Balogh was convinced that sustained British economic success could never be achieved without the humbling of the myopic Treasury and the installation of a more pro-growth bias at the heart of government. Through losing the leadership battle and having no big shadow seat to slip into, George Brown was ripe for Balogh's 'vispering'.

Some of the unofficial consultations between Brown and senior civil servants began to reach the ears of Bligh. These conversations were quite different from the 'Douglas-Home Rules' meetings which facilitated official contact between Her Majesty's Opposition and senior members of the mandarinate, but were recorded for posterity by Lord Roll. Roll was involved in many of the discussions in the early summer of 1963 and had been invited to

> a large and very agreeable luncheon party by Roy Jenkins at which I was placed (deliberately, as I later discovered) next to George Brown ... I admitted the theoretical case against having the whole of economic policy run by a department with the 'candle-ends-saving' tradition of the Treasury ... But I remember very clearly ... stressing three things: first, that it was far from easy for government in practice to take account of all the economic factors that were significant and that finance in the broadest sense could often be the most useful focus of diagnosis and therapy; that the Treasury was so powerful by statute and tradition that any new department would have an almost impossible task in trying to assert itself, and, above all, traditionally in British government departmental machinery was rarely as important as the relative power of Ministers. A Minister who was powerful by status and personality would soon make his department powerful, too.³⁵

A year later, Roll was privately sent the most up-to-date thinking on Labour's desired reform of economic administration. While thinking the planning was 'workable', he again warned, extremely presciently and specifically, that

> There is a danger, I think, which it is well to recognise at the beginning, that if there is a tug-of-war between relatively short-term considerations that must influence immediate decisions on fiscal or monetary policy, on balance of payments etc. the longer-term considerations that are to be the special concern of the new department will take a back seat. If this is so, then the danger is that the new department will become essentially a 'backroom boy' outfit with relatively little impact on current affairs.³⁶

Fascinatingly, Roll was offered the job of Permanent Secretary in the new department despite – or, more likely, because of – his words on just how difficult it would be to supplant the Treasury (and also his considerable reputation as a planner during the War and the late 1940s, not least the end of Marshall Aid for the UK).³⁷ Brown was later to lament his choice of Roll, surmising that the resultant battle with the Treasury would have gone better had Sir William Armstrong been at the DEA helm.³⁸ As we will see, the quality of the staff in the DEA was never in question, though the rationale of its creation most certainly was.

The opposition to a 'Ministry of Expansion or Production'[39] was as fervent as its supporters' advocacy. The legendary Lord Bridges, erstwhile Cabinet Secretary and Permanent Secretary to the Treasury and, therefore, a former gamekeeper of machinery-of-government issues, was a vocal critic, believing that management and finance should never be divorced from one another.[40] Another most vociferous opponent was Douglas Jay who had been Attlee's economics adviser in No 10 from 1945 to 1946, Economic Secretary to the Treasury 1947–51 and was to be Wilson's first President of the Board of Trade. Jay tried hard to persuade Wilson that splitting Treasury control was madness, basing his criticism on the experience of 1945–7. These two years saw the Lord President of the Council, Herbert Morrison, attempt to coordinate economic policy, with Hugh Dalton in the Treasury handling domestic and international finance and public spending. Sir Stafford Cripps was appointed Minister for Economic Affairs in 1947 in charge of planning, while Dalton remained Chancellor in charge of fiscal policy.[41] Dalton resigned just six weeks later, ostensibly over his Budget indiscretion but physical and mental exhaustion played their part,[42] with Cripps assuming both tasks. The 'discredited muddle'[43] which could only have intensified if the arrangement had continued[44] was, therefore, brought to an end, but Wilson appeared to be determined to recreate it in another form. (Paradoxically, George Brown's biographer, Peter Paterson, hands the credit for inspiring the DEA to Jay, citing a May 1963 paper he wrote for the Labour Party's Finance and Economic Committee which suggested that a Minister of Economic Affairs be appointed, but, crucially, one that should report to the Chancellor in an enlarged Treasury.) [45]

Jay was sufficiently worried by developments in Wilson's mind to arrange for Lord Normanbrook (who as Sir Norman Brook was Cabinet Secretary between 1947 and 1962) and Lord Plowden (the public/private sector amphibian who had directed the Central Economic Planning Staff during 1947–53), who, between them, 'knew more about the higher government machinery for managing the economy under several governments than anybody else',[46] to give their unsupportive views to Wilson in the months running up to the 1964 election. Jay invited Wilson and Lord Normanbrook to lunch in the Commons:

> Brook was forthright as ever; Wilson listened politely. But it became pretty clear to me that he had promised George Brown to put him at the head of the DEA. This was a prime example of creating bad organization in order to appease personalities – a classic recipe for trouble. Wilson, I am sure, knew the scheme was ill-judged, but for some reason put personal appeasement first.[47]

Wilson did not 'know' the scheme to be ill-judged,[48] as his support of it through its gradual deterioration to its eventual death in October 1969 was to prove. He was truly wedded to his 'specifically socialist measures'[49] of technological and scientific progress coupled with a firm agreement on prices and incomes policy to bolster the balance of payments.[50] As Wilson outlined in his 'white heat' Party Conference speech at Scarborough in the autumn of 1963, 'unless we can harness science to our economic planning, we are not going to get the expansion that we need'.[51]

Wilson did, however, place 'personal appeasement' higher. Creating a new, high-level department partly solved the Brown-conundrum (Brown's temperament would make him a problem for the Prime Minister wherever he was located in Whitehall). Brown himself was very pleased to be given such a role. With all of the warnings that Wilson had been given, he knew that the DEA was not going to have a smooth ride, so placing Brown there helped ease another problem. This was succinctly described by Marcia Williams, Wilson's Personal and Political Secretary, who later thought that 'George Brown seemed to feel that he was not so much a Deputy Prime Minister as the alternative Prime Minister'.[52] Giving Brown just such a role meant he would have more on his mind than the leadership question. This was a key Wilson tactic, to avert potential threats by creating balances of power. One of the justified criticisms of Harold Wilson was that he had a great belief that improving the higher State machinery was an essential preliminary to better governance generally and healthier economic performance specifically, yet a 'political penchant for playing things by ear'.[53] This contradiction was to be replayed again and again.

1964 marked the inauguration of the so-called 'Douglas-Home Rules' which were needed due to the many years that had elapsed since Labour was last in office and the burgeoning aspirations of Wilson and his entourage. Bligh wrote to Douglas-Home conveying his concern:

> I wonder if I might add a personal thought on all this. The Civil Service are servants of the Queen and serve the government of the day. They cannot also serve the Opposition. But there is a real problem here ... because a newly-elected Prime Minister has, in practice, very little time to form an administration. Certainly there is not enough time for an in-coming Prime Minister to have long discussions with officials about machinery of government problems ... There is every possibility of a hasty ill-thought out decision being taken which might ... do real harm to the country. If, however, discussions between the Opposition and the Civil Service were to be regarded as tolerable I would have thought that the particular case of machinery of government on economic affairs was such a case.[54]

While neither a man lacking ambition nor oblivious to securing party advantage, Douglas-Home *was* rightly concerned with the welfare of his country and saw the benefits of this development, with the proviso, as Douglas-Home intriguingly told Helsby, that the Prime Minister 'must know nothing whatsoever about this' (i.e. what transpired at the sessions).[55]

PLANNING (IN)ACTION

The consultations resulted in Labour's Civil-Service-prepared brief being considerably larger than that written for the Conservatives,[56] which is unsurprising as a re-elected government is, to a considerable degree, a matter of continuity. Contained within the brief was a Treasury-designed provisional blueprint for the creation of the DEA.[57] The Civil Service was unenthusiastic about the DEA. Sir Lawrence Helsby had responded to Bligh's 1963 information that Labour was considering altering the economic machinery by deeming it 'troublesome, but I think there may be ways in which we can contain it'.[58] Whereas Lord Croham was convinced that Sir William Armstrong 'would not have approved the Treasury split – he had, after all, just taken over the Treasury'.[59]

The Treasury's plan was to give the fledgling Department of Economic Affairs enough responsibilities to make it important rather than dominant, but no more. To this end, the Treasury blueprint for the DEA envisaged the new department having a unit for creating an all-embracing economic plan, a section devoted to prices and incomes policy, and capability to take responsibility for industrial policy and regional economic development[60] (in effect taking on board most, but not all, of the NEDC's work and secretariat).[61]

In view of George Brown's pre-election discussions, Sir Donald MacDougall's observation that Brown 'didn't understand it [the battle over the DEA's functions]. He hadn't done any preparatory work at all, really'[62] appears to be erroneous, but evidence at the Public Record Office supports Sir Donald. For the 'Concordat' ('the Treasury presumably cast in the role of the Pope and the DEA in that of a secular power, although George Brown on occasion liked to refer to himself as "the Pope"')[63] was agreed on 27 October 1964.[64] Tom Caulcott, Brown's long-to-suffer Private Secretary who had been sacked and reinstated three times within the first month,[65] wrote to William McIndoe, Sir Burke Trend's Private Secretary in the Cabinet Office, that the Concordat 'is agreed between the First Secretary and the Chancellor of the Exchequer', less than a fortnight after polling day, Thursday 15 October.[66] Wilson himself was later to claim of the Concordat that it 'did not take more than a few minutes to dictate its terms'.[67]

Yet two days later, Peter Jay, Private Secretary to Sir William Armstrong, wrote to Ian Bancroft (Principal Private Secretary to the Chancellor) and Otto Clarke (Second Secretary in charge of public expenditure): 'Apparently the Concordat is now back in the melting pot.'[68] This followed Balogh, now Economic Adviser to the Cabinet, and Anthony Crosland, the Labour MP and author of *The Future of Socialism*, given the no 2 job to Brown in the DEA (though ostensibly employed by the Treasury as Economic Secretary due to too many Ministers being appointed), reacting with horror to the Treasury's view of the Concordat – and also to Brown's ready acceptance of it.

Only a relatively small number of 'irregulars' were brought in by Labour in 1964, among them several economists. The most important among them were Balogh (stationed in the Cabinet Office), Nicholas Kaldor and Robert Neild (both to advise Jim Callaghan at the Treasury) along with John Allen and Michael Stewart. While this small number could not cause great alarm to the mandarins, the fact that Balogh, Kaldor and Neild were 'at a high level, at the centre of the administration' certainly did.[69] As Peter Hennessy described it:

> For some Whitehall regulars, this appeared, still does, to be the thin end of a wedge of politicisation which has advanced ever since. One seasoned Treasury man, for example, traces to October 1964 a growing tendency among some career officials to trim their advice to ministerial preferences. Certainly there was a degree of mutual wariness in Whitehall between the old and the new blood ...[70]

This was one innovation of Wilson's which was going to last, and indeed deepen and grow – so much so that by 2000 there were 77 special advisers in government, 26 of them answering directly to the Prime Minister.[71]

Balogh and Crosland were upset that, as a note from the Treasury's Organisation Committee put it, the DEA 'will not have executive functions in the ordinary sense of the form. Its organisation therefore will be more like that of a strong secretariat, with a comparatively small supporting staff.'[72] This was not what the two economists believed the DEA was created for, since they wanted the DEA to be superior to the Treasury: the Treasury plan was clearly to maintain the status quo *vis-à-vis* ultimate policy-making power.

When Brown, bolstered by Crosland and Balogh, attempted to renegotiate the formerly agreed Concordat by demanding the transfer of some or all of the Treasury's public expenditure responsibilities, the Treasury knights began to man the ramparts. Otto Clarke, undisputed general of public expenditure and 'a very clever man at arguing, very clever',[73] led the defence. Clarke wrote to Ian Bancroft, pointing out that,

> It is impossible for us to carry out our work of control of current expenditure unless we control the whole of public expenditure (this is literally the case); and it would be utterly impracticable to have the departments negotiating one part of their Vote and other expenditure authorisations with the Treasury and another with the DEA. I emphasise that we are here in the field of *literal administrative impossibility* [emphasis added].[74]

Clarke went on in the same letter to express his wish to see the DEA thrive – a comment which provokes deep scepticism. The next day Clarke reported to his boss, William Armstrong, that MacDougall had had a long chat with him at Roll's suggestion. According to MacDougall, Roll was very concerned to foster good relations with the Treasury, in direct contrast to Brown who often viewed it as the 'enemy'[75] – another sign of the difference in outlook between the permanent and the temporary government. MacDougall 'explained the First Secretary's preoccupations on familiar lines, including the consideration that Labour Party opinion had expected that public investment would be controlled by the new department'.[76] This was a real battle over the very heart of Whitehall and one that was remembered for many years.[77]

With the Chancellor keeping quiet and Brown digging in his heels, it was left to the officials to look for a solution – or a fudge. At a meeting on 2 November, Helsby, Armstrong, Clarke and Jay of the Treasury met the DEA's Roll and MacDougall to thrash it out. MacDougall produced a theory and supporting wording that all could agree to. Sir Donald

> suggested that, while it might not be practical to divide the subject matter of public expenditure between the two departments, it might be possible to distinguish the points of view from which each department approached it. The Treasury's prime interest was in the 'vertical' division of the public sector outlay between the various public services etc. (i.e. the functional blocks). By contrast, the D.E.A.'s predominant interest was in the 'horizontal' division of this expenditure between the various categories of resources and particular industries.[78]

The notion of 'horizontal' integration is intriguing as Lord Croham thought that much of the Wilsonian machinery of central government reforms had the aim of providing greater cohesion of government.[79] This was a fascinating pre-echo of the early Blair Government's obsession with 'joined-up government', to provide more efficient delivery of policies and to counter the 'wicked issues' which slipped between departmental silos.[80]

MacDougall's diplomacy did not put an end to the conflict. For on 11 November, Roll wrote to Helsby stating that Brown and Crosland were still unhappy and that Crosland, in particular, was uncompromisingly confident that the DEA would assume responsibility for public investment and that he was personally redrafting the Concordat.[81] Moreover, Clarke had not let his defences down. He now attacked MacDougall's accommodation, writing to Armstrong on 17 November that 'The distinction between short-term and long-term, useful in considering economic policy, is not meaningful in public sector expenditure.'[82]

But suddenly on 4 December, Brown wrote to Helsby and appeared completely to capitulate. He told Helsby that due to the good working relationship between himself and the Chancellor, the direction of higher economic policy needed no further reform.[83] In light of the battle royal which had raged for over a month, at a time when the Labour Government suffered its first exchange rate crisis and subsequently introduced an emergency Budget, it seems incredible that the First Secretary would quietly back off on the key issue of public investment. (Though the big initial problems the new Labour Ministers encountered may have meant that there was little appetite for a protracted fight.) The answer, according to Lord Roll, was maybe that the Prime Minister finally intervened:

> I suspect that what happened was that Wilson must have had a chat with George ... and more or less warned him off by saying 'Don't fight the Treasury on this sort of ground' but in addition he must also have said 'As you are Secretary of State for Economic Affairs and First Secretary of State you will in fact have as much power to counter Jim as you can reasonably expect to have in our system of things.'[84]

This was understood by Brown, especially as the First Secretaryship led Wilson to give him the chairmanship of both the Cabinet's main economic committee, Economic Development Committee, ED,[85] and that of the NEDC, so that Callaghan did have to consider the DEA in Treasury decision-making[86] – in the final analysis, a powerful position.[87] The DEA was also allowed a small team to shadow the Treasury's public expenditure work and to offer suggestions when they impacted on growth.[88]

Wilson's probable intervention is illuminating for he accorded the DEA a less than dominating role, something that clearly ran contrary to Crosland and Balogh's beliefs and wishes. This was powerfully underlined on 28 October, soon after the conflict began, when Wilson scribbled on a letter from Balogh regarding the need for public investment to be assigned to the DEA. In a note to the Cabinet Secretary, Sir Burke Trend, Wilson wrote 'We discussed this. NFA [no further action] on this.'[89] It is easy to understand why the Chancellor kept quiet and allowed Brown, Crosland and Balogh 'to swing slowly in the wind' (to borrow a phrase Callaghan himself used ten years later over Edward Heath's desperate attempts to retain the Premiership).[90] Wilson, therefore, allowed the battle to play itself out for over a month – during an economic storm – until he finally weighed in to demand Brown's acquiescence. It was a foretaste of his Cabinet management style to come.[91]

The Concordat eventually approved by Wilson on 14 December 1964[92] was based on the short-term/long-term division, with the Treasury retaining power over the Budget, public expenditure, the balance of payments, exchange rate policy and overseas financial relations, and the DEA taking responsibility for physical resources, incomes policy, economic growth, regional and industrial policy.[93] This division frustrated the Treasury because it could not look at the long-term, and the DEA due to the ban on the short-term.[94] The Chancellor was later to write that

> The Concordat represented a verbal truce rather than a true meeting of minds with a genuine and rational division of responsibility. The principal officials in the Treasury and DEA tried to make the agreement work, but there were what the Americans call frequent 'turf fights'. It was sometimes said that No. 10 believed in something called 'creative

tension' and that the friction between the Departments would produce the desired pearls. This was not my experience.[95]

Officials from both sides of the divide were unconvinced by the Concordat as well, and it was never used to sort out any difficulty.[96] Clarke backed Callaghan's appraisal, believing that 'It was never possible to establish a meaningful division of functions between the two departments' while Croham felt that much 'was not politically or organisationally viable'.[97] He did, however, think that it 'had worked better than he had thought possible at the outset'.[98]

Wilson's actions also demonstrated a private U-turn on economic policy-making. For one of the key ways the enforced schism in economic policy was originally to be managed was through a coordinating committee chaired by the Prime Minister (something 'strongly' supported by Sir William Armstrong),[99] overseeing the Treasury, the DEA and the newly bolstered Cabinet Office containing Balogh, all of them vying for influence.[100] But the Prime Minister shied away from this, apparently under pressure from Callaghan,[101] leading to Wilson being in charge of economic policy only at critical moments[102] – a fact, naturally, pleasing to the Chancellor. In any case, Wilson was always keen to avoid internal disputes,[103] especially if they concerned the 'brilliant but uncontrolled personality'[104] of Brown.

The way in which Brown approached the creation of the DEA was grandiose and totally unrealistic. He blamed the subsequent difficulties the DEA encountered on the lack of a detailed, Labour-Party-prepared blueprint for the Concordat[105] (missing largely because of the difficulty in drafting it)[106] but also felt that the economic crisis Labour inherited 'meant that we simply couldn't give as much attention as we should have given to establishing the relationship between the department and the Treasury in formal minutes'.[107] He also claimed that the Concordat 'never got itself formally accepted between Jim Callaghan, the Prime Minister and myself'.[108] Yet, he had readily agreed the Treasury-designed split within a fortnight of the election, and the subsequent Balogh-Crosland-inspired row lasted for over a month due to the impossibility of reconciling[109] 'diametrically opposed policies', with the Treasury wishing to retain the exchange rate parity at all costs and the DEA determined to raise Britain's growth rate.[110] Brown himself wrote to Helsby, 'I do not think it necessary to spell out all the details, especially in a document which we intend to circulate to other departments.'[111]

It is a pity that Wilson and Brown did not live to see the lifting of the 30-year rule from their 1964 files and so escaped the cross-questioning demanded by the contradiction between their accounts (both published in 1971) and the declassified documents. Politicians in struggles with officials, intra-Civil-Service strife and a turf war over the most important department in government provided one of the most strange and fascinating stories in the reform of post-war central government. But the conflict was not the only thing to linger over the years as the actual reason for splitting the Treasury was in Jim Callaghan's thoughts when he considered creating a Ministry of Finance and an Office of Management and Budget if he won the 1979 general election (a different and admittedly more rational split).[112] Newspaper reports suggesting a modern cleavage in the Treasury appeared again in January 2005.[113]

How different the Treasury might have been if the major reorganization two years before Labour returned had been given time to settle is impossible to know. Callaghan, who claimed he had originally 'supported fully' the concept of the DEA,[114] later explained how

> William Armstrong had convinced me that as a result of a reorganisation at the Treasury department in 1962 there was a change in atmosphere – that the Treasury would no longer operate perhaps as it had done in the 1950s, to a large extent. Putting a dampening hand on something was always going to be realistic, but the Treasury did ... fall for the fallacy of trying to get a higher growth rate, being able to achieve these things, and saying 'Yes, we are going to do our part in order to do this'. And this is one reason why I think if the department [the DEA] had not been set up we might have had perhaps a slightly different result.[115]

It is difficult to envisage the reforms of 1962 delivering the grandiose aims of the Labour, and Labour-supporting, planners who dreamt of sustained economic expansion. Planning through the DEA represented the 'big idea' of the incoming Wilson Government. It demonstrated dynamism and modernization, in direct contrast to the seemingly ineffective Conservative approach. 'Critics of the civil service', wrote Sir Leo Pliatzky,

> as unreceptive to new ideas cannot have witnessed the missionary spirit, sometimes spiralling over into an uncritical enthusiasm for practically any fresh initiative, which the new Department generated among its recruits. There was also a certain amount of promotion going there, which is generally good for morale.[116]

The DEA was created with hope and not a little expediency. But it was not thought through and was dominated from the beginning by the wishes of Wilson, Callaghan and, initially, Brown to maintain the parity of $2.80 to the pound[117] – and, therefore, by the Treasury. A lot of effort went into creating the DEA and to bedding it down into the Whitehall matrix, all for so little return.

THE CIVIL SERVICE AND LABOUR

If the DEA was created to provide growth through economic planning, then another department created in 1964, the Ministry of Technology, was to provide growth through the planning and application of high technology.[118] 'The other major new department', as Wilson described it, had been foreshadowed at Labour's 1963 Scarborough Conference,[119] when Wilson claimed that 'In all our plans for the future, we are re-defining and we are re-stating our Socialism in terms of the scientific revolution'.[120] The 1964 manifesto also heralded its arrival 'to guide and stimulate a major national effort to bring advanced technology and new processes into industry'.[121] Wilson later described exactly why he created it:

> I had long felt that we needed a ministry to discharge two functions which existing departments were inadequate to perform. It was to be a 'Ministry of Industry', starting with a relatively small number of industries, but taking on a wider and wider sponsorship, with a very direct responsibility for increasing productivity and efficiency, particularly within those industries in urgent need of restructuring or modernisation ...
>
> The second task of the Ministry of Technology would be to speed the application of new scientific methods to industrial production ... Britain had always been good in the scientific laboratory, but all too often the results of fundamental research done here had been clothed with the necessary know-how only by foreign industrialists ... The process had continued apace after the war and I decided something must be done about it.[122]

But although the concept of Mintech had long been in gestation, Wilson had not settled on a clear scheme prior to assuming office and the new Ministry, designed very much 'off-the-cuff' according to its Economic Adviser,[123] suffered a rough first year.[124] This was also due to the Prime Minister's choice of Frank Cousins as its first ministerial head. Cousins had been General Secretary of the Transport and General Workers' Union and there are suggestions that one reason for Mintech's creation was that Wilson wanted a major trade unionist in his Cabinet.[125] If true, the totally inexperienced new Minister would fit the new Ministry nicely.[126] Although Cousins was liked – Barbara Castle thought it an inspired choice from an industrial point of view[127] and Callaghan thought him 'dynamic, forceful and self-confident'[128] – the Minister was initially very uncomfortable in the House of Commons,[129] naïve about the workings of Whitehall[130] and administratively weak.[131] An inauspicious beginning for the other new institutional pillars upon which Wilson was to base his growth strategy.

The Prime Minister did not leave his immediate machinery-of-government reforms there. The Department of Technical Co-operation was transformed into the Ministry of Overseas Development, with a seat in the Cabinet for Barbara Castle. Its duties were enlarged so that it could now foster real development, particularly in the Commonwealth.[132] The year 1964 also saw the creation of the Welsh Office, a manifesto promise. This was given responsibility for functions such as local government, housing, roads and forestry.[133]

The final newcomer was the Ministry of Land and Natural Resources which was set up in order, Marcia Williams wrote, to combat 'the more vicious sides of the housing'.[134] The MLNR was quickly abolished, lasting just 18 months, before its functions were reabsorbed back into the Ministry for Housing and Local Government.[135] It was not in the manifesto and was simply invented at the last minute, causing difficulties with the MHLG.[136]

Wilson wrote to Helsby on 21 October 1964 to offer his thanks for the Civil Service's reforming efforts: 'I am not unaware that the changes that have been announced involved fundamental changes in the government machinery such as we have not seen in peacetime in the last generation ... much as I love you all, I do not want to see you on Sunday and I hope that Saturday will, as far as is possible, be a free day for all those who have borne the heat and burden of the past few days'.[137] Wilson genuinely liked the company of civil servants and respected their abilities hugely, to the dismay of some of his more politically motivated intimates. Marcia Williams, his Political Secretary, felt this was a major problem:

> Some of us who were very close to him were worried it would be the civil servant who would dominate him, and I think it is fair to say that our fears were in fact justified to some great extent through the years of the two Labour Governments.
>
> It is the fact that he does have such an admiration for and such a working knowledge of 'the System' that he tends to lean over backwards in his relationship towards it. He gives it the benefit of the doubt. He doesn't really want to argue with it. He admires the way it is organized and its methods of working. He admires its efficiency and he is often myopic about its failings and its short-comings and its inefficiencies, and this is a great drawback.[138]

Williams is a true boon to the historian. Her memoir of the 1964–70 governments is embittered, vitriolic and Thatcheresque in its sense of struggle. It is also lengthy and an unadulterated case for the prosecution.

Williams was Wilson's Private and Political Secretary throughout his Premierships (paid for by the Labour Party) and by his side from 1956 to 1983, a confidante of the utmost centrality. How she achieved this longevity has been the cause of intense speculation since the very early days of their relationship. Some, such as Peter Hennessy, believe Williams 'suffered as strong-minded women in politics often do from being deemed shrewish and shrill in a way that does not afflict comparably insistent men'.[139] Further claims were provided by Joe Haines, Wilson's Press Secretary from 1969 to 1976, who wrote in 2003 that documentary evidence held by Williams of a pre-1964 affair between herself and Wilson is probably the best explanation of how she could act in such a bizarre way for so long.[140] Haines details so many examples of Wilson, and almost everyone else around him, being humiliated by Williams, events 'so unreal the average fiction writer would have rejected' them[141] – even in an era used to the embarrassment George Brown could cause – that it is interesting, to say the very least, how she retained her role. Perhaps only if rumours prove correct of a manuscript written by Williams, lodged with a London publisher and embargoed until Mary Wilson's (Harold's widow) death, will the full story of her and Wilson's unprecedented relationship be known.[142]

Whatever the truth behind the Wilson–Williams relationship, there was undeniably a close meeting of minds which, according to Ben Pimlott, rendered rumours 'a technicality'.[143] When Labour returned to office, there was never any doubt that Williams would follow Wilson into Downing Street. There were questions, however, over the role she would play. 'Some considerable time before the 1964 election,' Williams explained,

> I had been taken to dinner and lunch several times by the late Sir Timothy Bligh, who was Principal Private Secretary to Sir Alec Douglas-Home ... Tim Bligh made it clear during these meetings that there was no place for me, or my office colleagues, at No. 10. I reported these views back faithfully to Harold, and there was a joint decision to disagree with Sir Timothy ... They knew I had been running Harold's Private Office in opposition, and if he succeeded in capturing power in 1964, they wanted to make certain that they captured him.[144]

Williams' pre-election difficulties with the Civil Service were imported exorbitantly into Downing Street. The chief battle was between her and Derek Mitchell, Bligh's successor as the Prime Minister's Principal Private Secretary. The problem was that Williams' Political Office, which she situated in the waiting room next to the Cabinet Room, handled many of the functions which had previously fallen to the Principal Private Secretary and his staff. When asked if there was any administrative point to Williams' role beyond personal and spiritual support to the Prime Minister, Sir Derek replied:

> I think if you put it like that, the answer's 'no'. She had the skills of a good constituency secretary ... she could see the politics of any situation and understand it. If a situation required statesmanship instead of simple political nous, she was lost, it was beyond her ... But not a great brain, not a[n Alistair] Campbell or a [Peter] Mandelson, nowhere near it, but it was coupled with the deep suspicion [detailed in her book]. She felt more strongly than anyone else who worked near him that there was this great conspiracy, that all of Whitehall was against him, the press were against him and it was up to the likes of her, all too few of them, to save him and somehow bring him through this. Dreadful situation. A bit weird.[145]

She even called for a complete purge of what she considered to be the Tory-supporting No 10 staff, something which was utterly impracticable.[146] Her 'volcanic and neurotic' nature (Williams' reported description of herself)[147] alongside her bond with Wilson meant that 'Civil servants, almost without exception, hated her', wrote Joe Haines.[148] The resulting turf war between Williams and Mitchell became Whitehall legend.[149]

To be taken more seriously were Williams' claims that the Civil Service obstructed her and the entire Labour Government and its programme. Williams' distrust of the Civil Service machine was great: 'I hold the view very strongly that Ministers, and particularly Prime Ministers, should automatically suspect many of the activities of the Civil Service.'[150] Why was this? First, 13 years of opposition had made Labour very suspicious of the Civil Service.[151] In reality, the Civil Service was keen for the changeover and the new ideas that went with it.[152] Next, Williams personally equated the senior civil servants with the 'Establishment', ergo all civil servants simply must be closet Tories (the Conservatives 'controlled the Civil Service, more or less').[153] This was paranoia on a high level, if she felt the Civil Service as a whole was trying hard to scupper the Labour manifesto due to Tory sympathies. It was true that many of the senior civil servants did belong to the clubland of St James's as did many Conservative politicians. But the two different breeds rarely mixed there, as civil servants were typically members of the Reform or the Travellers, not the Carlton or White's. Moreover, many senior civil servants found soul mates among high-ranking Labour figures like Jenkins, Crosland and Healey who shared their schooling (grammar as well as public schools), university formation, outlook and interests. Furthermore, as Douglas Hurd has written, the Civil Service 'works in practice to the advantage of Labour Governments because allied to it is a firm belief in the merits of action by the state' (especially if a Conservative wish is to reduce the reach of the state).[154] What Williams really meant was that the senior Civil Service did not conform to her tastes and her view of what Wilson's tastes should be.

But did the Civil Service obstruct? There was clearly no love lost between Williams and Mitchell. The latter adhered scrupulously to the dividing line between Civil Service lifers and temporary political appointees; due to the inevitability of another election in the near future, thought Williams, 'We were treated as ships passing in the night'.[155] The impartiality of the Civil Service was unquestionably observed during these years.

Bearing this in mind, was the Civil Service's heart in the Labour programme? This is much more vexatious. When asked to judge how he, Armstrong and Trend rated, on a scale between blind enthusiasm for the government and *Yes, Minister*-style cynicism, Lord Roll admitted

> More the latter. Not entirely. But there was never real reforming drive, it was modest. It was 'Well there it is, these ideas are here, and these things come and go' ... To some extent William [Armstrong] was a bit of an old-style civil servant, shrugging his shoulders and saying 'There we are, here we go again; something will stick but not an awful lot.' Anyway, there's always the feeling: how long is this minister going to be here – he could be gone tomorrow so let's not take it too seriously.[156]

Perhaps Williams had a point after all. But perhaps not. For, upon closer inspection, Roll's honesty betrays a keenness to provide a fine service, just based upon experience and a lack of faith in what Peter Hennessy christened the 'Tommy Cooper Trap' whereby everything changes just because somebody says it will – 'just like that'. Government had become too big to change overnight, or even in a few years. As Mitchell commented, 'It must be extremely frustrating to see the sheer inertia of government activity'[157] – especially for someone of Williams' temperament. There is also the fact that just as Williams herself bemoaned the fact that No 10 was never transformed from the monastery into the powerhouse of Wilson's pre-election rhetoric,[158] the monks were likely to be nervous of outsiders (a problem that afflicts much of the service, then as now). 'It is possible that she misrepresented people because she didn't understand them', lamented Sir Derek.[159]

Marcia Williams and her office did prove difficult to bolt onto Downing Street's machine, something that was eventually put to rest when Michael Halls somewhat inappropriately succeeded Mitchell as Principal Private Secretary in 1966 against the wishes of the Civil Service hierarchy, when Sir Derek moved on (see Chapter 3). Wilson knew that he – and doubtless Williams – would find Halls a more accommodating colleague, as the Prime Minister and he had worked together at the Board of Trade in the late 1940s.[160] This proved true, but Halls was deemed to have failed on several professional fronts and worked himself into an early death just before Labour left office in 1970.[161]

What became known as the 'kitchen cabinet' was another Wilsonian development which provided succour directly to the Prime Minister, especially during the period 1964–6. In essence it was a group of left-leaning Wilson acolytes, though ones often prepared to confront him, like Barbara Castle, Richard Crossman and Thomas Balogh. These political obsessives met in Downing Street and chewed the political fat and drank the prime ministerial brandy into the early hours, though they were often frustrated afterwards at the lack of influence they could bring to bear on the chameleon-like Wilson.[162]

PLANNING RUNS AGROUND

As we have seen, a majority of the first significant peacetime wave of what we now call special advisers were economists. The unelected yet often centrally positioned temporary civil servants appointed by a Prime Minister or Minister to offer specialist skills that the Civil Service could not provide, or political activity it would not, found themselves in the thick of the action from the very first days. For the attempts of Reginald Maudling to break out of the 'stop-go' cycle had led to Armstrong presenting the new Chancellor with a dire prediction of a balance of payments deficit for 1964 of 'about £750 million', quite beyond the realms of credibility at that time.[163]

The Labour ministers, all 'expansionists at heart',[164] were crestfallen. The ruling triumvirate, Wilson, Brown and Callaghan, agreed to meet in secret (the cover story was that the future of Crosland and Robert Neild were to be discussed) on Saturday 17 October without any advisers or civil servants.[165] The troika decided that the new government's 'specifically socialist measures'[166] of planning and technology would swiftly right the imbalance,[167] and so they plumped for reductions in the increase of public expenditure instead of devaluing the pound. Crosland was infuriated by the decision and the manner of its taking. All the special advisers on the economic side were aghast, barring Balogh who backed the ruling threesome only to renege three weeks later.[168] Yet all the civil servants – again, barring one, Sir Donald MacDougall, not a career civil servant[169] – supported the decision not to devalue. This was because, as Sir Samuel Brittan, an economic adviser in the DEA from 1964 to 1965 saw it, the decision was not whether to devalue or deflate but to devalue *and* deflate or to deflate much deeper.[170] The civil servants were unconvinced (rightly) as to whether a devaluation would have been coupled with the necessary deflationary measures.[171] This was also the view of the Governor of the Bank of England, Lord Cromer.[172]

The decision not to devalue in October 1964 cast a shadow over the first three years of the government[173] as the currency remained overvalued.[174] It certainly meant that the Labour Government's pride and joy, the centrepiece of the 1964 manifesto and of their economic policy, the National Plan, was put under pressure before it had even begun to be written. The spectre of an overvalued pound had caused the government great concern in the last months of 1964 as the currency markets turned against the new Labour Administration. This abated but the markets returned to the attack in July and August 1965.[175]

Sir Alec Cairncross was the first head of the newly established Government Economic Service, created in order to maintain an apolitical head of economic advice upon the appointment of the special adviser Robert Neild (in actual fact Cairncross and Neild sometimes shared direction of the GES).[176] Cairncross was very concerned that 'Ministers seemed oblivious to the situation that was building up and were busy discussing the National Plan',[177] once again favouring theory over reality. But the pressure intensified and the government was forced into a hasty series of public investment cuts,[178] virtually indistinguishable from the hated 'stop-go' policies of the Tories.[179] By this time, Brown had come to understand that inevitable balance of payments crises, coupled with an overriding commitment to the existing parity of $2.80, meant deflation – and less, if any, emphasis on expansion, the *raison d'être* of his DEA. From this point on, Brown became an increasingly vocal internal advocate of devaluation (but not deflation).[180]

The Chancellor's and, more importantly, the Prime Minister's staunch support of the existing parity was due to the fear of being forever condemned as the party of devaluation after the two previous Labour Prime Ministers had devalued in 1931 and 1949 (Ramsay MacDonald, the Prime Minister, was not actually leader of the Labour Party at the time of devaluation, but the point holds). Added to this was the belief that devaluation would damage the standard of living[181] (of the working classes mostly),[182] that sterling balances held by many of the world's poorest countries would have their reserves devalued, too, and that it was simply immoral; the 1964 manifesto criticized the Conservatives for allowing the pound to shrink in value.[183] Wilson had also promised the New York Federal Reserve Bank while still in opposition that there would be no devaluation (provided financial help was forthcoming, naturally).[184]

However, promising no devaluation and delivering it were two very different things. Super-secret contingency planning in case the parity could not be maintained went on in an official committee humorously entitled the 'FU [Forever Unmentionable] Committee'. Set up by Armstrong, probably early in 1965, possibly due to Neild's warning that 'devaluation is going to happen one day and I trust the Treasury has a contingency plan for it', its membership was interesting.[185] Senior Treasury officials were, of course, represented along with the Bank of England and the Chancellor but, at least initially, the Prime Minister was not notified of its existence.[186] Meanwhile, as the contingency planning proceeded, Ministers continued publicly and privately to stress the impossibility of devaluation – Samuel Brittan encountered George Brown in the DEA corridor one day in 1965, asking 'What shall we do about the Unmentionable?' 'Don't mention it' was Brown's reply.[187] Whatever the reasons – though these soon became secondary to not losing face – the decision to place the balance of payments above all else meant that the National Plan was under a cloud from the beginning.

What George Brown described as 'our main object' was 'the first attempt at economic planning on such a scale that has ever been made in Britain'.[188] In essence, the National Plan was a development of early-1960s NEDC work. It tried to form a big plan from all the little plans of individual industries and to foster a meaningful prices and incomes policy (which George Brown, through his own idiosyncratic skills, did achieve, to universal praise)[189] all with the intention of achieving an annual rate of 4 per cent growth and thus avoiding the necessity of a devaluation.[190] According to Pliatzky, 'Much of this document struck me at the time of its preparation as a sort of What's On In Whitehall. That is to say, various Departments tabled statements of what they were doing and would in any case have been doing in their respective fields, which became the National Plan.'[191]

The National Plan would succeed where the Tories' version had failed, thought Brown, because this time all of government would be behind it.[192] By August 1965 the Plan was almost complete. On 4 August, Brown got wind of preparations, the night before the crucial NEDC meeting to agree the Plan, for the industrialists' corner of the tripartite triangle to pull out of the agreement. Using his staff's detective capabilities to their limit, the industrialists' meeting was tracked down to Sunningdale in Berkshire. Although Brown was told the meeting was over, he raced down there with MacDougall (in effect the author of the Plan) bearing the only copy. By two o'clock in the morning, Brown had persuaded the group to back the Plan, a superhuman effort. This was not the end of the story, however, as Brown then left the document in the Mini of a motorist who had deigned to pick him up – after the Civil-Service-provided car had broken down – and drop him at the DEA's headquarters at the back of the Treasury. The man duly returned it the next day – the blueprint for future British economic success being rescued by a startling symbol of contemporary British design.[193]

The Plan was confidently introduced to the House of Commons by Brown on 3 November 1965, an attempt to map out the economy for the next six years.[194] It was interesting to hear, in contrast to Roll's admission of collective scepticism, MacDougall had truly *believed* in it at the time.[195] He soon appreciated his misplaced faith. The National Plan was born of a moment when the belief of the middle ground in Britain was firmly placed in the benefits of 'indicative planning' – and this represented the high point.

The Plan was comprehensive, stretching to nearly 500 pages, and covered macro-economics (efficiency, productivity, the balance of payments, etc.) and micro-economics (the state of individual industries) with copious appendices and annexes in a kind of mid-1960s economic Domesday Book. Nobody could say that its production was half-baked. What critics could say was that it was based upon an over-ambitious and weak understanding as to how an economy grows, especially when there were few or no physical controls at the government's disposal. Even this could have been ignored for years if the general economic climate had been propitious.

The Plan had some life between September 1965 and July 1966 but slipped into desuetude and was not replaced.[196] The dynamic history of the DEA died with it[197] (although a more detailed Concordat was considered around the time of the March 1966 General Election,[198] but was swiftly abandoned).[199] For, although the Plan formed the centrepiece of Labour's highly successful appeal to the country in the 1966,[200] a third currency crisis – this time a much deeper one – hit the country again in July. This time Brown fought hard for devaluation, the timing of which subsequent commentators supported,[201] with more than an eye on toppling Wilson. But once Callaghan had fallen into line beside Wilson, after initial sympathy for Brown's economic analysis[202] and further deflationary measures were announced, Brown's move was thwarted. In a Cabinet meeting recorded only in a 'Confidential Annex', Wilson managed to hold his anti-devaluation line but only by agreeing that 'All measures, including devaluation, would be open to examination'.[203]

Wilson wasted little time in moving Brown, this time to fulfil his heart's desire, to the Foreign Office.[204] Roll left soon afterwards to become chairman of Warburgs, as 'the fun had gone out of it in a way ... seeing George fighting all the time was great fun',[205] illustrating the paradox of Brown – a sexual harasser by modern standards, a poor drinker by any measure and a man of irrational exuberance, yet one of power and passion. But Brown's assertion that 'The story of the D.E.A. ... is the record of a social revolution that failed'[206] is almost ludicrous. For, as Roy Jenkins was later to write in a slightly different economic context, but one that bears direct comparison to the DEA and its National Plan: 'This was nonsense, and rather dangerous nonsense. It implied that you could control the allocation of resources in an economy with the precision of air-traffic controllers allowing planes on to a glide path.'[207] With few or no physical controls, certainly nothing like those which existed in wartime Britain or early post-war France, upon which so much of the economic planning thinking was based, the only ways to influence an economy were by exhortation (which would be 'an exercise in make-believe')[208] or managing the fiscal and monetary elements. The latter was problematic due to the overriding commitment by the Prime Minister, the Chancellor, the vast majority of the senior Civil Service and the Bank of England to maintain the parity of the pound at virtually all costs.

A positive balance of payments despite all the various travails since 1964, declared Wilson in his 1971 memoir, demonstrated economic success under a Labour Government and thereby made a good export record synonymous with successful socialism according to Edmund Dell.[209] Interest rates and exchange rate policy were completely geared to that end. The belated realization of this spelt the end for the dream of 'purposive' (a favourite Wilson word in those days) expansive economic planning.[210] The destruction of the left's 1964 and 1966 election economic *raison d'être*, which killed Labour's short-lived reputation for efficiency and modernity,[211] foreshadowed a decades-long decline in Labour fortunes. This was one factor which would eventually lead to the neo-liberal Conservative dominance of the 1980s.

The DEA might have succeeded. Most saw a positive role for the NEDC (indeed, it survived until 1992), and if the DEA had been a bolstered Neddy then good results might have flowed.[212] This was in essence the view of Douglas Jay in 1963–4, which failed to prevail with Harold Wilson. Perhaps, as Callaghan later lamented, the Treasury's 1962 reorganization, aimed at encouraging sustainable growth, should have been allowed to settle.

Few, however, have supported with the benefit of hindsight the decision to make the DEA a major department of State in direct competition with the Treasury. This truly was folly, as retired Civil Service luminaries such as Lord Bridges and experienced economic ministers such as Jay had foreseen. 'Creative tension' inevitably took shape as energetic conflict. Moreover, the reputed Wilson ploy of balancing (and therefore thwarting) pretenders to his crown did little to enhance his reputation for statesmanship.[213]

The DEA was reduced, in Harold Lever's words, to 'a very agreeable form of adult education' (Lever was Joint Parliamentary Under-Secretary of State at the DEA in 1967).[214] With the instruments of fiscal and monetary power staying firmly in the hands of the Treasury throughout, the DEA was doomed from the beginning, as Roll had tried to make Brown understand in 1963. Not only was the DEA less volatile after Brown's transfer but it was also palpably less important. Brown swapped jobs with the Foreign Secretary, Michael Stewart, the proverbial safe pair of hands, donnish and quiet,[215] and under him the DEA inevitably withered. It was, however, more under Wilson's control than it had ever been.[216] The Department toyed with the idea of producing an updated National Plan in March 1967,[217] as had originally been envisaged. But what with recurrent economic crises and a totally understandable lack of enthusiasm, bearing in mind what had happened to the first National Plan, the atmosphere was never going to be as conducive again. However, a Green Paper, *The New Version of the Former National Plan*,[218] was published as an 'Economic Assessment' on 26 February 1969.[219] (In September 1969, when the DEA's days were finally numbered, there was official talk of a second National Plan, this time it was to be authored by the Treasury.[220] It never materialized.)

Wilson moved a frustrated Stewart (he had been sold the DEA as the dynamic department of Wilson's imagination)[221] in August 1967, complaining that getting anything out of Stewart was akin to 'throwing darts at cotton wool'.[222] He replaced him with Peter Shore, a Wilson protégé. Shore was given the title of Secretary of State for Economic Affairs (but not the First Secretaryship, which Brown and Stewart held, and which later went to Barbara Castle at the Department of Employment and Productivity). Shore was given responsibility for the day-to-day running of the Department. But the big news of this change was the fact that Wilson himself assumed overarching control of the DEA, now *his* DEA. Wilson ambitiously explained to Shore that 'Defence in wartime was the best precedent for a Prime Minister assuming strategic control of a department, assisted by a Secretary of State'.[223] He told Dick Crossman that 'If I can't run the economy well through the DEA, I'm no good. I was trained for this job'.[224] The Prime Minister believed planning could save the day right up to devaluation in the autumn of 1967.[225] This, in the view of a very senior economic official, was Wilson demonstrating his all-too-frequent – and highly damaging – penchant for dreaming.[226]

The Chancellors, whether Callaghan or his successor Roy Jenkins, would never have allowed their power to be usurped in such a way. But we have also seen how the DEA had been effectively emasculated by the absolute adherence to the sterling–dollar parity, and this point is key. For the economy, which had been looking 'deceptively favourable' in the spring of 1967 with some rebuilding of the reserves and better news on the balance of payments front, took a turn for the worse in the summer and autumn and this time the effects were decisive.[227] In November 1967 the Prime Minister and the Chancellor finally conceded that the pound was overvalued compared to the dollar, that the parity was unsustainable, and an ignominious devaluation from $2.80 to $2.40 followed after so much defiant rhetoric, dubbed 'Operation Patriarch'.[228] The Chancellor, Jim Callaghan, resigned but was persuaded to move to the Home Office, swapping jobs with Jenkins. The Prime Minister was a man who, according to Edmund Dell, 'had been devalued along with sterling'.[229] The last vestiges of the 'specifically socialist measures'[230] were swept away as all attention turned to deflation and getting the balance of payments to balance (though the Industrial Reorganisation Corporation, an institution announced in the Queen's Speech of 1966 to merge smaller concerns into larger companies and to invest in already burgeoning ones, lived on until the Heath Government abolished it).[231]

Peter Shore's tenure at the DEA was not a successful one. Being the new boy in the Cabinet and one widely regarded as there purely on the Prime Minister's patronage, Shore found it difficult to effect coordination.[232] Lord Croham, Permanent Secretary at the DEA during this period, observed that his Minister was roundly ignored by the big beasts in the Cabinet.[233] Shore's position was not helped by a poor performance when steering the 1968 Prices and Incomes Bill through the Commons.[234] This failure led Wilson to ponder moving the up-and-coming Barbara Castle to the DEA, something she began to agitate for,[235] with a brief to prepare a major reform of industrial relations (what was to become the infamous *In Place of Strife* White Paper and proposed legislation in 1969). But the new Chancellor, Roy Jenkins, had no intention of allowing a rival to the Treasury to spring up once again and he left the Prime Minister in little doubt that he would not tolerate Castle's appointment (Jenkins was, in many respects, an ally of Castle's and personally explained his veto to her as a compliment to her strength).[236] Wilson decided not to provoke Jenkins head-on. Instead, he promoted Castle into something approximating the role he had originally envisaged by moving her to the Ministry of Labour and re-jigging it to form the new Department of Employment and Productivity and giving her the title of First Secretary, in the process taking away the prices and incomes function of the DEA.[237] Wilson also relinquished control of the DEA at this time when, in a parliamentary statement just eight months after his do-or-die conversation with Crossman, he explained to the House of Commons that

> I took over that responsibility last August because I was not satisfied with the co-ordination among the industrial departments ... With the new changes ... of course I retain my present and previous responsibility for the co-ordination, not only of industrial

matters, but of economic matters in general ... But I am all the time trying to take steps to ensure that the industrial departments are able to do even more than they have done so far for industrial productivity and efficiency.[238]

The DEA was left to study the long-term.[239] The end was nigh.

October 1969 saw the Department's final demise, something that Jenkins had long lobbied for [240] (as had Callaghan, unsuccessfully, in 1966).[241] Although Wilson had earlier in the year written to its Permanent Secretary, William Neild, talking of future plans,[242] the DEA was now an irrelevance. Defeated over its original founding brief, shorn of senior ministerial authority[243] and having functions carved off, there was little left to abolish at its end.[244] Some of its responsibilities went to the Board of Trade and the Treasury. But the major gainer was the Ministry of Technology and Tony Benn as its Secretary of State.[245]

Mintech had been steadily accumulating functions since its inception – with aircraft manufacture and shipbuilding. Now it was turned into the 'counter-balance' it had originally been created to be.[246] Marcia Williams stepped into the debate when she wrote that 'It would only have been possible to challenge the Treasury if a department had behind it a vast backing like the Board of Trade and the DEA amalgamated together.'[247] Although Mintech did have some statutory powers, especially for industrial sponsorship, this was Wilson and Williams the dreamers once more.[248] For, as we have seen on several occasions, no Chancellor would have allowed a rerun of the 1964–6 DEA–Treasury conflict. Due to devaluation (and his own deft handling of the aftermath), Jenkins was just too powerful throughout his Chancellorship for Wilson seriously to cross. Anthony Crosland landed another new super-ministry, the Department of Local Government and Regional Planning, which subsumed the DEA's regional functions at the same time (and which was to evolve into the Department of the Environment after the Conservative triumph in 1970).[249]

Wilson tinkered with the machinery of government throughout his first two administrations, mostly in the pursuit of 'joined-up government' (the DEA excepted). Not only were there the big changes we have been examining but also myriad minor ones. Such changes can be a permanent temptation for some premiers as, being a prime ministerial prerogative, unless offices exist on a statutory basis (as does the Ministry of Defence), changes can be made using orders in council – a clear symbol of authority.[250] Some changes were beneficial in the late 1960s, as when the continuing logical rationalization in the UK's overseas representation culminated first with the merger of the Commonwealth Relations Office and the Colonial Office in 1966 to form the Commonwealth Office, and with the Foreign Office to form the Foreign and Commonwealth Office in 1968.

Another major creation was the Department of Health and Social Security in 1968 (Social Security itself had been formed in 1966 with the merger of the Ministries of Pensions and National Insurance). This was roundly denounced subsequently as a poor decision for the two departments and was described by Peter Hennessy as 'organisational nonsense'.[251] The two departments had little or no common functions. It was another example of Wilson displaying the curious tendency to create baronies to suit particular personalities, in this case Richard Crossman's, regardless of the administrative mess this caused (a pattern repeated around the person of John Prescott in the Labour Governments, 1997–2005). Wilson later viewed the DHSS amalgamation as a mistake, telling the House of Commons' Expenditure Committee in 1977 that 'I think that that was probably the wrong step. In fact, soon afterwards – I take full responsibility for it – they were saying to me that they were not sure they ought not to have advised me to merge social services with the Home Office'.[252]

The Cabinet system itself was also partly reformed. Perhaps the greatest bout of Cabinet committee-making ever saw a wealth of MISC committees created in what Robert Armstrong called 'proMISCuity'.[253] There were also two half-hearted attempts to foster a formal strategic inner cabinet, the Parliamentary Committee set up at the same time as Castle's Department of Employment and Productivity in 1968 and which evolved into the Management Committee in 1969 until the afternoon of June 1970's election defeat.[254] Both of these attempted to bring some cohesion to the government's strategy but ultimately foundered on Wilson's fundamental disdain for forward-thinking, the *raison d'etre* of an inner cabinet.[255] They both degenerated into short-term political tools, similar to the 'kitchen cabinet'. The most important committees were the belated attempt to bring cohesion to economic matters with the Steering Committee on Economic Policy (SEP), which announced its creation to the Cabinet on 10 August 1966,[256] and MISC 205 the 'most secret and powerful of the Cabinet groups'[257] which was created to deal with the 'gold-dollar-sterling crisis of March 1968'.[258] The Joint Intelligence Committee (JIC), located in the Cabinet Office, was also reformed, which saw a 'sharpened, bespoke, all-source analytical capacity in the form of the Cabinet Office Assessments Staff' which proved highly successful and endures to this day.[259]

The 'hardware' reforms of the 1964–70 Wilson Governments were plentiful. These varied from short-term political fixes, such as the repeated creation of departments to suit personalities, to far-reaching and effective reforms, such as the re-jigging of the JIC and the first large-scale peacetime importation of political appointees to government. They demonstrated Wilson's inexhaustible belief in the power of administrative reform to effect change not only in the running of Whitehall but also in that of the wider society and especially of the economy. But the story of the Department of Economic Affairs became a mighty weight upon the shoulders of future advocates of administrative reform. Though there was a case for an agency tasked with the pursuit of sustainable growth, its birth, infancy and subsequent reincarnations were mired in fantasy and political expediency. While the commitment to detailed economic planning by government was effectively ended here, the belief in the efficacy of dramatically reforming Whitehall's ecology and, through this, its performance, also began to be undermined.

Intriguingly, the Leader of the Opposition, Edward Heath, was privately and enthusiastically engaged at exactly the same time in preparing his own transformation of the hardware of state. For all their undoubted mutual personal antagonism, Wilson and Heath demonstrated a very similar commitment to the State and its potential to improve the country and thus the lives of the people. That they both saw reform of central government as a first-order question essential to a wider picture of national renewal was partly due to their both having worked in its higher echelons both as officials and ministers prior to attaining the highest political office. Though, as we shall see in subsequent chapters, this shared view did not entail an identical approach.

3

Software

THE FULTON REPORT AND ITS PARTIAL IMPLEMENTATION 1966–70

GENESIS OF THE COMMITTEE

The 'software' of the state, 'the people involved', in Lord (Ian) Bancroft's vivid metaphor, came under substantial, at that stage unprecedented, scrutiny during Wilson's 1964–70 Governments.[1] The result was the Fulton Report of 1968. The last of the great investigations into the workings of the Civil Service achieved legendary status within the Service for the simple reason it happened at all, the reforms which were enacted, those that were not, and the way in which it attracted controversy at the time and subsequently.

As we saw in Chapter 1, the years leading up to 1964 witnessed growing criticism levelled at the Civil Service and at the calibre and attitude of the senior civil servants themselves. The beginning of the post-war 'decline' debate, and the linked idea that the UK had swapped the positive, 'can-do' spirit of its industrial and imperial apogee for a bureaucratic caution, was the subtext for an argument which centred on the Civil Service's supposed lack of professionalism (more specifically, its traditional peacetime disdain for specialists). This was especially apparent when compared with the allegedly dazzling and technocratic French. The 'what's wrong with Britain' debate[2] was, moreover, incomplete without a sizeable dash of class-based criticism which contrasted the elitist British bureaucracy with that of probably imaginary meritocratic societies which were thought to exist in competitor countries.

With part of the Labour Party's electoral success in 1964 based upon the promise of across-the-board modernization, and doubts over the efficiency of nearly all State or State-related institutions, the stage was set for far-reaching changes to the machinery of government. The Labour manifesto stated 'we shall need to make government itself more efficient'.[3] Yet the impetus for change did not manifest itself immediately. Indeed, compared to the highly visible (and audible in George Brown's case) reforms to the departments of Whitehall undertaken within the new government's first few weeks, the initial steps towards an investigation of the role of civil servants in the machine took over a year, with the Fulton Committee only being announced some 16 months after the 1964 general election on 8 February (just before the March 1966 election campaign began).[4]

Throughout the history of British administrative reform it is noticeable just how much the Prime Minister of the day alone is required to get things moving and for sustaining the momentum. The machinery of government, both hardware and software, is his or her traditional bailiwick. Yet the establishment of the Fulton Committee owed much to Jim Callaghan, the Chancellor of the Exchequer, certainly more than to Harold Wilson (although Callaghan in 1988 described Wilson as the 'moving spirit in getting the Fulton Committee established').[5] Callaghan wrote to Wilson on 1 November 1965, pointing out that

> I think that the case for a wide ranging inquiry has been made out. There has been a good deal of criticism of the Service, and it is many years since the last comprehensive inquiry. There are also specific problems that are becoming urgent, for example those of recruitment ... The Committee should be given wide terms of reference to review the structure, recruitment and management of the Service. It is important that their field of work should not seem to be restricted ...[6]

Callaghan's letter is important in many ways. As Chancellor, Callaghan was the Minister responsible for the Civil Service as establishments had traditionally been part of the Treasury, and, since the 1962 reorganization, it had become one of the two sections into which the Treasury had been split (the other being finance and economics). Given that the issues were not of the highest political controversy, and that it was typed, the letter was most likely prepared by officials as they nearly always are, at least in the first draft. Trying to unearth who exactly was behind the letter is more difficult. Professor Robert Neild, special adviser to Callaghan and co-author of the Fabians' *The Administrators*, replied when asked:

> The short answer is that I cannot remember this message from Jim Callaghan to Harold Wilson, but I may have been somewhere behind it ... I certainly talked to William Armstrong [Permanent Secretary to the Treasury] about it at many stages and found him sympathetic to my views ... I think it is most likely that it was put forward by Armstrong-Helsby [Head of the Civil Service], while I stayed in the background. It should not be read to mean that the initiative for Fulton came altogether spontaneously from the Treasury. Tommy Balogh at No 10 was a passionate critic of the Civil Service and told me, I remember, that he was pressing Harold Wilson to establish an inquiry. The Treasury will have known this; and they also knew that there was a tide of public criticism of the Civil Service; there was some recognition of the need for an inquiry and modernisation. Hence I guess Jim was responding to a suggestion from Harold Wilson, spoken or written, that there should be an inquiry, and doing so guided by the machine.[7]

Although a civil servant must theoretically do whatever the Minister bids him or her do, from the language it appears that officialdom was broadly supportive of the letter's content, for it pointed out three reasons why an inquiry was required. First, the outside criticism. Second, the argument that it had been 'many years since the last comprehensive inquiry' was powerfully supported by the retired, but still hugely influential, Lord Bridges, ex-Cabinet Secretary and Permanent Secretary to the Treasury. In *The Times*, ten days after the announcement of the Fulton Committee by Wilson in the House of Commons on 18 February 1966, Bridges wrote that the investigation 'follows the long standing practice whereby, at intervals of about twenty years, there has been a major inquiry into Civil Service organisations.'[8] (Peter Kellner, writing 14 years later, was unimpressed – 'an inquiry every three-and-a-half decades scarcely suggests the watchfulness of a hawk'.)[9]

The third reason Callaghan stated was that of recruitment. Pressure from the Treasury was pivotal in the creation of the investigation into the Civil Service, due to a continuing recruitment shortfall, a nagging doubt that this was due to the Service becoming less attractive to the burgeoning graduate population (the numbers of university students had gone up 44 per cent in the years 1955–63, from 82,000 to 118,000)[10] and a growing belief that the traditional method of recruiting a small number of high-quality entrants alongside many school-leavers with A levels 'no longer represented the output of the educational system'.[11] In June 1965, Sir Laurence Helsby wrote to the Prime Minister expressing concern that 'The present shortage of Principals is about 100, or some 10% of the total cadre. Such a shortage at this level is a serious impediment to good administration, and it is in my view beginning to have harmful effects on morale and on the organisation of departmental work.'[12]

This practical reason for the investigation was underlined at a 'Fulton: 20 Years On' symposium when Richard Wilding, secretary of the Fulton Committee, later the coordinator and planner of the Report's implementation and secretary to all the committees set up during 1968–70 to carry out Fulton,[13] said that the Committee's establishment was due to 'the considerable increase in the number of graduates produced by the educational system, and the feeling that the civil service arrangements for recruiting them were not actually up to date and well devised ... A person who attended the early meetings of the committee could have been forgiven for supposing that it had actually been set up to settle that problem alone!'[14] In another letter to Wilson, in September 1965, Helsby underlined the concern when he informed the Prime Minister that 'In recent years competition to enter the Service has not been strong enough to exclude any acceptable candidate simply because a better was available.'[15]

Once again, internal Treasury nervousness over an issue proved to be the key reason why a major inquiry was set up, as with the Plowden Committee. It is also the case that, in Lord Allen of Abbeydale's words (as Sir Philip Allen he was Second Secretary in the Treasury when the Committee was announced and was appointed Permanent Under-Secretary of State at the Home Office soon afterwards), although the Committee was set up with deeper, declinist, anti-elitist, anti-generalist feelings 'floating about in the atmosphere, I don't think they were quite as specific in motivating Callaghan himself, at any rate, towards taking action'.[16]

The main reason why the Chancellor pushed for the inquiry at this time came from within the Civil Service itself and it was due to practicality, a source of Treasury pride throughout its history (compared to the rest of Whitehall, including No 10). Even the Committee's terms of reference as announced were almost identical to Callaghan's original memo: for 'review the structure, recruitment and management of the Service' substitute 'examine the structure, recruitment and management, including training, of the Home Civil Service'.[17] While the Fulton exercise may have owed much to outside pressure, its direct creation was essentially a Treasury affair.

There was another direct factor, however. That came early in 1964 when the House of Commons' Estimates Committee, chaired by the former ICI industrialist, Dr Jeremy Bray, recommended the establishment of a hybrid committee of insiders and outsiders, on the model of the successful Plowden Committee into public expenditure control appointed in 1959.[18] During the debate in which he announced the Fulton Committee, Wilson, addressing Bray, gave fulsome praise to 'an extremely valuable contribution to the study of this subject. The factual examination was done in greater depth than almost any other inquiry for a very long time.'[19] The Plowden Committee's creation was due to Treasury pressure – most notably from Otto Clarke – channelled discreetly through the Estimates Committee.[20] Thus two of the most significant scrutinies of the Civil Service were heavily influenced by the Commons. Parliament can be a very useful ally for a Whitehall reformer.

Fulton's terms of reference caused controversy over the subsequent years due to what was *not* in it. Machinery-of-government issues, and potential tinkering with the Minister–Permanent Secretary partnership, were ruled out from the very beginning: 'the Government's willingness to consider changes in the Civil Service does not imply any intention on their part to alter the basic relationship between Ministers and civil servants [who] remain the confidential advisers of Ministers, who alone are answerable to Parliament for policy; and we do not envisage any change in this fundamental feature of our parliamentary system of democracy ... [though] within the terms of reference and competence to inquire into all aspects of the functioning of and recruitment for the Civil Service'.[21] This later caused Lord Crowther-Hunt angrily to denounce this move as 'a nice illustration of the way the Civil Service helped to narrow the Committee's terms of reference – and later was able to argue that this restriction invalidated much of what the Committee said!'[22] Norman Hunt, as he was when a member of the Fulton Committee's inquiry, was a tutor in politics (but no authority on the contemporary British Civil Service)[23] at Oxford, who had struck up a friendship with Wilson during the run-up to the 1964 election when Hunt interviewed him for the BBC Radio series *Whitehall and Beyond*.[24] He proved to be the leading radical on the Committee, and became the *bête noire* of many in the senior Civil Service.

Peter Hennessy was very clear that the terms of reference represented a huge missed opportunity. Fulton, he thought,

> was steered away from the start from fundamental, fascinating and important questions which, to my mind, needed to be settled before the second-order questions such as recruitment, training and management were addressed. The specifications of the machine and the ground-rules for its operation surely should have been considered before the choice and man-management of its minders were pondered ... Its enforced removal from machinery-of-government questions *and* minister/civil servant relationships made Fulton a one-dimensional inquiry rather than the three-dimensional investigation that was needed.[25]

These are strong words, indicative of the frustration the Fulton Report caused. At the time of its publication, Sir William Armstrong himself thought that the lack of machinery-of-government questions may well lead to 'pressure for a "new Haldane"'[26] (the 1918 report which looked at British central government as a system in the round from a theoretical, yet practical, viewpoint).[27]

So much was excluded from the start of what was billed as a comprehensive exercise. Lord Allen provided an answer for this: 'Machinery of government was not included because it was too big a subject, like criminal justice.'[28] There simply was not the scope to deliver tangible recommendations for reform *and* practical changes to the machinery of government, all within a timeframe of two years. Moreover, a Prime Minister very rarely allows machinery-of-government responsibility to slip from his or her grasp. It is far too powerful a tool. Allen went further:

> It is difficult to see any modern Government allowing an outside body to review machinery and what Ministers do. Even if such a review body was thought to be suitable, it would have to have been a different and much weightier body than the Fulton Committee could ever hope to have been. The Haldane Committee had been such a body but it didn't achieve very much.[29]

LORD FULTON AND NORMAN HUNT

A complex investigation requires deft chairmanship, the selection of which was by no means easy. Lord (John) Fulton was not the first choice. On 3 November

1965, Wilson suggested to Callaghan that Lord Simey, the Charles Booth Professor of Social Science at Liverpool University (his wife, Margaret, a veteran Labour activist,[30] was based in the city[31] – near to which Wilson had his constituency) should be shown 'serious consideration'.[32] Richard Wilding was blunt about this suggestion: 'That wouldn't have done. Simey was a very nice man and had a lot of common sense but he was really on the downhill with health and age and so on. He wouldn't have been able to manage.'[33] If Simey had been appointed, the 'Simey Report' would have had a very different flavour to that of Fulton, as Simey attached to it a minority report defending the conduct and achievements of the existing Civil Service, as we shall see. The Chancellor on 25 November 1965 recommended the Cambridge scientist Sir Eric Ashby for the chair. This was accepted by the Prime Minister on 29 November. No evidence has been uncovered to suggest if Ashby was ever approached and, if so, why he was not appointed.

The reason why Fulton was finally chosen is unclear from the archival evidence. His name was first mentioned by Wilson's Principal Private Secretary, Derek Mitchell, in a letter to Callaghan's Principal Private Secretary, Ian Bancroft, on 28 January 1966. Fulton had been a friend of Wilson at Oxford from before the war,[34] and later when they were temporary wartime civil servants in the Mines Department of the Board of Trade sharing fire-watching duties.[35] After teaching philosophy and politics as a fellow of Balliol College, Oxford, Fulton became Vice-Chancellor of Sussex University.[36] Crowther-Hunt and Kellner observed in hindsight that 'he was doing so many jobs when he was made Chairman ... that it must have seemed to anyone who took the trouble to think about it that he simply would not have the time to spearhead any serious probe into the operations of the Whitehall machine'.[37] These preliminary fears were underlined when Lord Allen much later observed that 'Fulton was not first choice, nor the happiest choice.'[38] Allen was alluding to the, by all accounts, appalling chairmanship demonstrated by Lord Fulton.

Robert Neild, economic adviser to the Chancellor and a member of the Fulton Committee, thought Fulton among the worst chairmen he had ever encountered,[39] while Richard Wilding saw Fulton as 'A very incompetent chap. A nice man of excellent qualities, liberal thoughts and that sort of thing. But he could not manage a committee.'[40] As the Committee drew to a close in the spring of 1968, Wilson's Principal Private Secretary, Michael Halls, had dinner with Fulton and afterwards sent the Prime Minister an account of the meeting along with a general appraisal of the inquiry. Halls wrote that 'there is a certain amount of unease in his Committee about the way in which he is handling the Report ... It is said he jumps about like a grasshopper and re-opens issues which the Committee have already decided, not necessarily with new views but often with irrelevant comments.'[41]

Lord Shackleton, the first political head of the future Civil Service Department, recalled that, in the years after the Report, 'it became very apparent when you talked to Fulton himself that he didn't really know what he was proposing'.[42] This was the view of most members of the Committee, yet Geoffrey Fry, author of the authoritative history of the Fulton inquiry, felt that, on paper at least, Lord Fulton was a good choice for chairman owing to his record as a university administrator and wartime temporary civil servant, and his background knowledge of the Civil Service as a whole.[43]

At the 'Fulton: 20 Years On' seminar, the chair, Peter Hennessy, described it provocatively as 'a classic "good and the great enterprise"'.[44] He suggested this by looking down the list of people on the Committee. This was roundly rejected by Allen who pointed out 'There had never been a committee like this; Callaghan said it was an experiment of mixed insiders and outsiders. On reflection, he thought there ought to be more outsiders than insiders but I'm not conscious of any precedent for it – I don't think anyone was at the time.'[45]

The nearest example (at least for Whitehall aficionados) was the Plowden Committee on public expenditure which blended insider Civil Service lifers with outsider amphibians like Edwin Plowden himself, who had experience of both Whitehall and industry. But that was a private committee, conducted under the aegis of the Treasury, and it delivered initially only a series of reports to the Chancellor of the day personally and confidentially[46] (though an edited summary was subsequently published).[47] Why was something as important as this not conducted as a Royal Commission but as a Committee of Inquiry? After all, Wilson was not averse to this form of inquiry, having established seven such investigations between 1964 and 1970.[48] Again, the answer lies with Callaghan, who thought that 'A body of this kind ... should work more quickly and flexibly than a Royal Commission'.[49] 'To some this seemed to be a downgrading of the inquiry even before it got underway; and the suspicious at once smelled a Civil Service plot', wrote the leading critics of the Fulton exercise:

> This is partly indicated by the fact that its chairman does not receive the traditional silver ink-stand which marks the conclusion of the work of a Royal Commission. More important, though, a Committee of Inquiry is not given the power that a Royal Commission has 'to send for persons and papers'. But if this was a Civil Service plot, it made no difference. The Committee never had any difficulty in getting anything it wanted.[50]

The first meeting of the Committee was held on 10 March 1966 with the last taking place on 19 June 1968. The Committee only slightly exceeded its estimated life – the government urged Fulton to deliver in eighteen months to two years.[51] Normally convening on Tuesdays, there were 32 meetings in 1966, 35 in 1967 and 18 in 1968. The task undertaken was huge, and herein lay one of the key dilemmas for the inquirers. What kind of investigation and report were required? Opinions differed, with some wanting a no-nonsense document as pithy, judgemental and high-minded as the Northcote-Trevelyan Report of 1854. 'I was a strong advocate of a brief, forceful Report,' explained Neild, 'I circulated copies of the Trevelyan-Northcote Report and the Macaulay Report [the precursor to Northcote-Trevelyan which dealt with the Indian Civil Service]. It seemed to me that our Victorian ancestors had set us a fine example of being outspoken, brief and robust.'[52]

The Northcote-Trevelyan Report offered little in the way of specific reform but was still being cited nearly a century-and-a-half later as the core ethic of public service which informs the *spirit* of reform.[53] As Allen observed in a letter to Halls,

> The Chairman is aiming at providing a new 'Northcote-Trevelyan' Report – a broad and philosophic state paper rather than a minute analysis of every problem of grading and structure. This is probably inevitable if the Committee is to report in reasonable time, since the field is so vast ... This broad approach however has some dangers:–
> Exceeding the terms of reference: some members (including the chairman) and some witnesses are inclined to go pretty wide.[54]

The machinery of government *was* looked at by the Fulton Committee but only in areas such as the 'hiving-off' of executive functions from the day-to-day control of Ministers, and the creation of the Civil Service Department,[55] of which more later.

John Rosselli, an historian at Sussex University, employed more clarity and eloquence than heretofore when he wrote to Fulton saying: 'You cannot really have a latter-day Macaulay or Trevelyan-Northcote statement; the issues and the organization your Committee has to deal with are much more complex than anything the investigations of the 1850s looked into; nor are people today as sure of having found the key as those men were'.[56] The result was a report which was neither succinct nor sufficiently sophisticated.

The Fulton Committee certainly mixed insiders and outsiders. There were the three serving civil servants: Sir Philip Allen of the Home Office; Sir James 'Ned' Dunnett, Permanent Secretary to the Ministry of Labour upon appointment to the Committee and later Permanent Secretary at the Ministry of Defence; and Sir William Cook, 'a superb organizer, and a decisive project manager, with a powerful grasp of detail',[57] who was Deputy Chief Scientific Officer in the Ministry of Defence (though he 'didn't say very much' according to Richard Wilding).[58]

The outsiders were numerous: along with the aforementioned Norman Hunt sat Sir Norman Kipping, Vice-Chairman to Fulton and former Director General of the Federation of British Industries; Walter Anderson, a solicitor and General Secretary of the National Association of Local Government Officers; Sir Edward

Boyle, Conservative MP for Birmingham Handsworth;[59] Robert Neild ('thus ensuring that the Committee's agenda would take full account of his Fabian pamphlet [*The Administrators*]';[60] John Wall, Deputy Chairman of the Post Office (and former member of the Plowden Committee); and Robert Sheldon, Labour MP, replaced Shirley Williams after its first meeting as she had been made a junior minister. The initial Secretary of the Committee was Mary Loughnane, a Principal in the Treasury. She stepped down on grounds of ill health in May 1966 and was replaced by Richard Wilding, also a Treasury Principal (Loughnane's 'headaches rapidly turned into a continuous migraine ... I very soon came to feel a lively sympathy with her distress' the sardonic Wilding later commented).[61] An assistant secretary, Michael Simons, an Assistant Principal from the Ministry of Labour, was appointed in April 1966.

Fulton's was 'an unhappy committee' according to Allen.[62] Wilding recalled (laughing to himself, it has to be said) that

> They were a nasty lot of people and they didn't like each other. There was lots of ill temper. Being secretary of that body was not a pleasant experience ... We used occasionally to have some dinners on Monday nights before the Tuesday meetings. Norman Kipping used to lay rather excellent little dinners for an inner group to which I used to go. Robert Neild and Norman Hunt and Ned Dunnett and Fulton. Philip Allen used to go but because he lived [outside London] he used to leave early which was a pity because as people had more and more to drink, the atmosphere used to get nastier and Philip Allen wasn't there with his mollifying influence.[63]

However, Allen's sentiment was not shared by all. Robert Sheldon, for one, was very satisfied by the way the Committee operated.[64] But there was an undercurrent of dissatisfaction at best, distrust at worst. There was no outright warfare – Neild was clear that politeness prevailed, 'it wasn't a rumbustious committee'[65] – that is not to say that cold, very 'English' antipathy did not take place. But the haphazard manner of Fulton's chairmanship, alongside Committee members either preoccupied with very heavy workloads (for example, Allen, who returned to the Home Office on promotion as Permanent Secretary after a stint in the Treasury, was not replaced because Wilson did not want another change after Williams' departure)[66] or lacking in confidence, background, energy or plain interest, meant there was a power and energy vacuum at the heart of the Committee. The stage was set for Norman Hunt.

Hunt became fascinated by the role of the Civil Service and obsessed with the eventual implementation of Fulton. He became the leading champion of the pre-1964 Civil Service critics, advocating dramatic reform to rid the bureaucracy of the inefficiencies which elitism and generalism allegedly wrought. Hunt threw himself into the investigation. Once it was complete, he wrote to the Prime Minister to express his thanks for being appointed in the first place – maybe to toady a little – but also to inform Wilson that 'The last 2½ years have been the most stimulating I've ever had.'[67]

Hunt took full advantage of the generous, year-long sabbatical leave from Exeter College, Oxford (it was said that his college was only too pleased to give him leave)[68] to drive the Committee forward and to lead one of the spin-off investigations the Committee sanctioned to run in parallel and to inform the members along the way. The one Hunt oversaw was the Management Consultancy Group (MCG), with John Garrett, future Labour MP and Whitehall-watcher, as deputy. The other three were the sociological survey, undertaken by Professor A. H. ('Chelly') Halsey of Nuffield College, Oxford; Richard Wilding's study of those entering the Administrative Class in 1956; and the comparison by John Pickering of Durham University of how those who had joined the Service in 1951, those that had been accepted through the recruitment process but turned down the offer, and those who had been rejected, did in the subsequent years of their careers.[69] None were thought to have much influenced the Committee[70] and Neild later spoke of the irrelevance of it all – 'There was a core of us and we were just anxious about the main stuff, which didn't rest on that kind of research material'.[71]

The MCG was set up, according to Hunt, 'to carry out its own investigation of what civil servants were actually doing'.[72] More specifically, it was to look at the newly expanding field of management theory and its application in the private sector (though 49 per cent State-owned at this time, BP was the model)[73] and whether there were lessons the Civil Service could learn from this. It was also the fount of new thinking whereas too much of Fulton was concerned with entrenched, clearly distinctive 'us and them' positions.[74] Hunt and Garrett drove the MCG with the idea that it must produce the finest analysis, regardless of the cost or time taken. It was finally delivered to the Fulton Committee on 29 December 1967, and so was in plenty of time to inform the Report, unlike Halsey's findings.[75]

The first draft of Halsey's Social Survey was delivered in July 1967 but was only cleared for publication after myriad objections by those on the Committee and departments in September 1969.[76] It painted a highly socially exclusive picture of the senior Civil Service which many, not least in the Civil Service Commission and the Treasury which had given Halsey most of his statistics, felt presented an incomplete picture.[77] A supporter of the Halsey survey, Sheldon offered perhaps the best epitaph when he claimed that it was 'interesting' but 'we had already made up our minds' by the time it became available.[78] The fact that Hunt led the MCG and was perhaps *the* leading member of the Fulton Committee proper meant that cross-fertilization had to take place.[79] Members of the Committee were divided over just how powerful the MCG's report was, but it is clear that it did influence the drive towards recommending single unified grading and accountable management.[80]

Hunt produced the first draft of the Fulton Report late in 1967.[81] If any chairman, especially a Prime Minister, controls a meeting by dictating the agenda, then he who writes the drafts often steers a committee. Hunt's drive and, most importantly, his free time meant that he became by far the most significant member on the Committee, indispensable almost. This was resented by several other members, Simey the most keenly, who felt they were being railroaded by Hunt's determination. As indeed they were. Simey wrote to the chairman in October 1967 stating that 'I don't propose to come to London for the next meeting, as I cannot think that anything useful will be served by ploughing through drafts produced by Norman Hunt'[82] (Hunt repeatedly accused Wilding of 'circulating minutes designed to sabotage the Committee's conclusions').[83] After a dinner with Fulton on 8 March 1968, Halls told Wilson that 'While he [Fulton] paid tribute to the enormous work which Norman Hunt had done and his enthusiasm he gave the impression that Hunt's enthusiasm was beginning to irk some members of the Committee (probably including himself) and he told me quite bluntly that Simey just could not stand Hunt.'[84]

Another member of the Committee, more sympathetic to Hunt's ideas, thought that his enthusiasm and determination were inappropriate, concerning what were, after all, relatively dry questions of administration over which there was little dispute about the main recommendations (tone was a different matter): 'He was a rabbit. Eager rabbit ... One didn't waste time on him.'[85]

The civil servants on the Committee had other causes for concern. In the first place, how could they independently advise their respective Ministers when the Report came to Cabinet?[86] Furthermore, if they appeared to obstruct any recommendation for reform, however innocently and on the basis of experience, and this leaked to the press, 'Mandarins obstruct equal opportunity!' would have been the inevitable headline. Allen felt that 'we were in a terribly embarrassing position, Ned [Dunnett] and I.'[87] Sir William Armstrong, at this time still Permanent Secretary to the Treasury but now about to succeed Helsby on the establishments side and therefore take the lead on the Civil Service's appraisal of Fulton, told Sir Laurence that there

> is the possibility of a highly embarrassing disclosure that there was a rear-guard action on the Committee on the part of the permanent secretaries to modify any of the conclusions other members of the Committee might want to see; or even a suggestion that they tried to tone down the wording in the analytical part of the Report which sets out the reasons for any recommended changes.[88]

They therefore felt in some ways gagged.[89] More troubling for them was that word began to filter into the Whitehall grapevine that Fulton and Hunt were suspiciously close to Wilson. It was felt, as Allen enunciated during the 'Fulton: 20 Years On' seminar, that the Chairman and leading protagonist 'used to go and see Harold Wilson and together they would get their instructions ... Not usually No. 10, but somewhere else to get the line. We weren't party to these instructions.'[90] These are unambiguous words from a usually cautious retired senior civil servant and point to a resentment of outside interference, especially from the man who would, in effect, accept or reject the Report's findings.

HAROLD WILSON AND MICHAEL HALLS

For Fulton and Hunt to be seen to have prime ministerial backing for their involvement meant that it was doubly hard for others – especially serving civil servants – to object to their wishes. But Allen, while correct in saying there was contact, does not give the full picture. There was no lobbying with a coherent end-game in mind. For example, Hunt requested a private meeting with Wilson 'without Fulton' towards the end of February 1968.[91] We can only speculate what Hunt wanted, but it seems likely that he wished to cut the – for Hunt, at least – inadequately focused Fulton out of the prime ministerial loop as the Report came to be published and thoughts turned to implementation. As for getting 'the line', Neild, firmly on the more radical side of the Committee, believed that 'Harold Wilson was a great lover of busy-body meetings, at which nothing whatever would happen ... it was busy-bodying, seeking reassurance, keeping the PM in the picture, getting his blessings, whatever you care to call it. I cannot remember anything emerging from those meetings that in any degree influenced me.'[92] But the real unfolding story during the Fulton Committee and after was of the relationship between Hunt and Halls, something which only truly became apparent with the declassification of the PREM files for 1968–70.

Halls was solidly behind the Fulton Report. He and Hunt became firm allies, they and their wives going out for dinner together,[93] but there was also a true meeting of minds between the two. Halls had been promoted to Principal Private Secretary to the Prime Minister after special intervention by Wilson who had worked with him when President of the Board of Trade in 1947–51.[94] The usual Civil Service procedures did not deem him worthy of the position (a negative appraisal powerfully underlined by Roy Jenkins).[95] Helsby recommended that Wilson see five other candidates, which Wilson did, but stuck to Halls. Helsby suggested that this could be construed as patronage. In an uncharacteristic display of opposition to Civil Service procedures, Wilson stood up to Helsby, writing:

> If I am told that this is a question of patronage and challenged to choose between Prime Ministerial patronage and patronage exercised by a small, self-perpetuating oligarchy of Permanent Secretaries, I have no alternative but to say that patronage, if patronage it be, must be exercised by me.
>
> I certainly cannot accept the implied suggestion that such an appointment would imply a deterioration of standards since the arrival of the present administration ... My

suggested appointment has no political implications, I have not the slightest idea of the political views, if any, of the five I saw.

But I do not regard the appointment as patronage, reward for past services, or as a promise for the future ... I regard it as the means of ensuring that my office will work ... as efficiently, smoothly and agreeably as possible. What I want is a Private Secretary, actual or in embryo. No. 10 is an office, not a Government Department; it is also a small and necessarily intimate community – it is also a home.[96]

Given the force of that letter, it was unsurprising that Wilson got his man. But the episode must have fostered in Halls some animosity against his seniors. Coupled with the fact that the Prime Minister could not pay anywhere near as much attention to the Fulton Committee as he would undoubtedly have wished (with the needs of the post-devaluation economy, trade union reform and rebellion in Rhodesia taking up much of his time), and the Chairman's lackadaisical approach, this meant that the Halls-Hunt axis provided the strongest support for the Fulton Report's findings.

Evidence-gathering was long and laborious. The Secretaries, Wilding and Simons, were very critical of this, especially of evidence taken orally by the Committee, Wilding describing it as 'fairly chaotic' and something which 'wasted a lot of time'.[97] This was only remedied once Hunt had produced his first draft during the summer of 1967.[98] The bureaucracies in France, the United States, Holland, Sweden, West Germany and Canada were examined[99] (but, according to Michael Simons, 'did not result in serious studies of other Civil Services)[100] and consultation was invited from all interested parties. One of the most eye-catching testimonies was that of Richard Crossman, then Lord President of the Council and Leader of the House of Commons, who told the Committee that his time in government had not diminished his sympathy for Tommy Balogh's 'Apotheosis of the Dilettante' but had rather strengthened it.[101] Another was that of a serving Treasury official, William Ryrie, who produced what Peter Hennessy described as a 'mini-Haldane' in which he juxtaposed what he saw as the reducing responsibility officials exercised with the staggering and often banal workload expected of civil servants.[102] This stepped over the boundary imposed by terms of reference which specifically warned the Committee off machinery-of-government issues. Throughout the inquiry, Wilding later suggested, 'certain opinions were held so widely that they were almost taken for granted'. They were that

(a) The Treasury had failed, both in its task of giving economic advice to Ministers and in its management of the civil service ...
(b) The civil service was failing in its duty to do long-term policy planning and to provide ministers with a coherent basis for long-term decisions.
(c) It was also intolerably amateurish in its approach to complex technical and investment matters ...

(d) The administrators sat on the specialists and allowed them neither their full-share in decision-making and management nor proper career opportunities to become administrators.
(e) Administrators moved around far too often, thus developing a kind of butterfly mentality which reinforced their amateur status.
(f) Too few civil servants saw themselves as managers and developed the appropriate skills.
(g) The service was too much a closed world, drawn from too narrow a social and educational base.[103]

In late February 1968, the fundamentals of the Report began to take shape – and the lobbying began. This was when Halls began to operate very significantly behind the scenes. To a considerable extent, the history of the Fulton Report can now be seen as a story of two civil servants, Halls and William Armstrong – certainly in terms of the fight for Wilson's ear. Fulton sent the Prime Minister a copy of the penultimate draft; Halls wrote a lengthy memorandum to accompany the draft, giving his assessment of it. Urging the Prime Minister to bear in mind 'what Hunt calls "the ethos of professionalism"', Halls observed:

> Of course, there are many practical problems in implementation, but the Fulton Report is not looking to the Service in the next five years, it is seeking to establish a Service with opportunities for all (eliminating the defects of what is in fact, at present, 'class snobbery') and a new found professionalism which would determine its role over the next generation or so. As you will see, my own personal view [Wilson scribbled next to this 'And mine'] is that it is just the kind of radical reform that is essential, indeed without it, the Fulton Report would finish up by producing merely one step forward.[104]

Wilson, Hunt and Halls therefore shared a common vision.

Halls went on to 'remind' Wilson of the five main elements of the Report as it took shape. They were:

(i) The Classless Uniformly Graded Service.
(ii) The structure of the Civil Service in three broad groups, (a) Economic and Financial, (b) Social in its widest sense, (c) Scientific and Technical.
(iii) The establishment of a Civil Service Training College.
(iv) A new department for the Civil Service.
(v) Recruitment.[105]

We will take these points in reverse order, beginning with recruitment. This was a tough and inherently controversial issue for the Committee to consider. Pre-Fulton recruitment to the Civil Service had come into question from both socio-theoretical and practical stances – from Balogh (among others) over elitism and non-specialism, and the Treasury which simply wanted to get educated brains in.

Statistics demonstrating that between 1957 and 1963 85 per cent of those recruited to the Administrative Class came from Oxbridge were hard to defend.[106] Wilson was a critic, even though he had been a high-flying Oxford don himself. In September 1965, Helsby wrote to the Prime Minister, stating 'My own view is that the Civil Service dilemma reflects a basic unbalance in our educational system which arises from the capacity of Oxford and Cambridge to attract a disproportionate share of the ablest undergraduates.' Wilson responded sharply: 'Membership [of the Administrative Class] seems to me to be heavily weighted against L.E.A. [Local Education Authority] types – and even if these things are not taken into account like tends to perpetuate like'[107] (it is worth pointing out that most grammar school students at Oxbridge *were* 'L.E.A. types'). Both men were merely reprising the long-standing wish for a Civil Service that reflected the society it served along with the need to preserve merit in its appointments. The late Michael Young, writing in the mid-1950s, observed that whatever the case for recruitment to a Civil Service on the basis that appointees should represent the community they serve, the need for efficiency always emerged victorious.[108]

The Fulton Committee's consideration of the recruitment problem did not get very far. It resulted in a largely semantic argument between those who favoured a written examination (Method I) and those who advocated a blend of that plus tests, exercises and an interview (Method II) as the chief means of recruitment to the higher grades. The organization with most clout in this area, the Civil Service Commission, had made clear its wish to discontinue recruitment based on Method I and this took place in 1969.[109] The (Jack) Davies Committee into Whitehall recruitment (Davies was a personnel expert in the Bank of England), reporting in 1969 after being set up by Wilson on 24 October 1968, backed this move alongside strong support for Method II.[110] (Thomas Balogh was a very keen supporter of Method I as a way of measuring merit without heeding the accent of the candidate.)[111]

A new department for the Civil Service seemed a big change (although it had been first mooted by Harold Laski many years earlier).[112] Responsibility for the Civil Service, as previously noted, was part of the Treasury's remit. Splitting the Treasury once again (after the DEA experiment), in effect making explicit the implicit division of 1962, became important for more reform-minded members of the Committee, such as Hunt, Neild and Sheldon (an interesting omission from this list was Sir Edward Boyle whose 'heart was not in the Fulton business').[113] It was felt that greater concentration could be given to personnel matters if the service was taken out of the Treasury's grasp. It was also believed that the Treasury's domination in Whitehall would be fundamentally undermined by this action. This was not just a practical move for, as Helsby reported to the Prime Minister in May 1967, 'Some members appear to think that the image of the Treasury is a serious disadvantage ... some members of his [Fulton's] Committee seem to think that a move away from the Treasury would help to create a brave new world'.[114] The Treasury's bad PR, which had led to distrust in the wider Civil Service, was counting against it once again.

The creation of a Civil-Service-specific college was a largely uncontroversial recommendation. Clement Attlee had urged Sir John Anderson's wartime machinery-of-government committee to support one in 1942,[115] as did the Committee on the Training of Civil Servants chaired by the Financial Secretary to the Treasury, Ralph Assheton, in 1943.[116] Both came to naught despite the need for training appearing obvious. The establishment of the Centre for Administrative Studies in 1963, an attempt to bring greater economic expertise to the Treasury and Whitehall generally, provided a successful blueprint.[117] A 'Staff College for the Civil Service'[118] became something of a pet subject for Wilson in the Summer of 1965, but the Prime Minister was far from being the first to advocate it. Since the First World War there had been thoughts regarding how to improve the skills-set of higher officials,[119] and the Civil Service was itself becoming uncomfortable. As Balogh wrote to Wilson in July 1965:

> Sir Philip Allen's Management Committee has been considering how to ... train up people and I am sure your idea of enlarging the Staff College into a fully-fledged university-level institute ... is by far the most likely to yield results. As you said yourself, the Mendes-France reforms have made all the difference to the knowledge and morale of the French Civil Service and enabled them to dominate the scene in the Common Market and beyond.[120]

Pierre Mendès France was French Premier, 1954–5, and 'represented just the kind of left-of-centre technocratic attitudes which Balogh was trying to inculcate into the Wilson Government ... All the enthusiasm for planning and the Ecole Nationale d'Administration' which was created in October 1945.[121] Wilson and his intimates were, therefore, concerned about not only the British but also more importantly, the French bureaucracies. This is not to say that Wilson was consumed by the need for Civil Service reform, or encouraged it in members of his 'kitchen cabinet'. For, as another letter shows, from Derek Mitchell to Helsby, the Prime Minister was keen to escape being the focus of attention in this area (perhaps with good reason):

> The Prime Minister suggested that it would be appropriate for a Treasury minister – presumably the Financial Secretary – to take a closer interest in all this with a view to reporting his impressions to the Prime Minister in due course. One point he has in mind is that the nomination of a minister for this purpose would enable him to provide Mr. Balogh with an audience other than the Prime Minister himself for his many ideas on Civil Service training.[122]

Wilson much appreciated Balogh's input, thinking of him as a one-man think tank able to counter conventional machine advice. But he could clearly prove too much at times.[123]

The first two points on Halls' list are essentially one. The 'single, unified grading structure' was, according to Halls, 'the major issue'.[124] Robert Sheldon agreed completely.[125] The myriad classes – there were literally thousands of them[126] – within the service were essentially seen by critics as a barrier to the efficient use of personnel *and* a tool of the classics-educated Oxbridge elite within the Administrative Class to aid its self-perpetuation. The wish of reformers was to abolish the barriers which would allow bright young things from the Executive Class a free run through to the very top.[127] This troubled many, especially those with responsibility for recruitment like the Civil Service Commission, as they feared that the traditional high-calibre applicants for the Administrative Class would be discouraged if they were not given special treatment.[128]

There was also a secondary aspect, and this concerned the lamentable lot of specialists in the Civil Service. The dominance of the generalist in the Civil Service came under critical pressure during the 1960s. The wish of reformers – and Wilson himself was of course a trained statistician who had been a wartime temporary civil servant – was to take the shackles off gifted specialists and allow them to progress to the very top. That meant access to the administrative tree, a diminution of job-classification obstacles and possibly a 'preference for relevance' regarding the subject that a civil servant had studied at university.

The widely accepted incompetence of the generalist compared to the specialist argument must not be allowed to pass without question, however. Lord Allen, like many others in the senior ranks (including Dunnett at the relatively technocratic MoD)[129] recognized the need for greater specialization, especially in accountancy. Allen was somewhat rueful when later explaining that 'the problem was when you brought them [specialists] into the limelight, ministers couldn't understand what they were saying!' This translation explanation was 'a very difficult point for me and Ned [Dunnett] to argue in the presence of Kipping and Cook'.[130] Not wanting to embarrass themselves or others meant that they did not curb the hyperbole surrounding the merits of specialists and the failure of all-rounders.

Moreover, generalists, according to the critics (see Chapter 1), were vastly more generalist than rational argument could sustain, a practice which prevented an official from becoming an expert in his or her field. Thus the recommendation for Whitehall work to be split into three strands – economic, social and scientific. This was a compromise which provided for an official to be able to gain gradually greater relevant expertise yet still be able to switch roles. The single, unified grading structure was, therefore, both a vertical and a horizontal attack on the fortress of the Administrative Class.

Further to this, recently released documents at the National Archives offer a fascinating insight into the wishes of those demanding urgent reform along more professional lines. This was the simple question of the *kind* of civil servant who should occupy the service's higher echelons in the future. In a letter to Wilson, Halls recalled from his conversation with Hunt how the reforms envisaged

> the creation of a powerful Civil Service. Hunt recognises this ... But it will not merely have the potential of power which he describes, it will <u>be</u> powerful. Will it be adaptable to ministerial change, or flexible enough to implement quickly fundamental changes of policy? Will it need the counter-balance of 'kitchen Cabinets' [most likely Halls had in mind French-style ministerial *cabinets*] of a kind and scope with which you disagree?
> Hunt recognises that this new Civil Service will need strong democratic control ...[131]

Hunt, as the chief reformer on the Committee, was not interested in diminishing the service at all. He wanted to make it marvellous. He wanted to give senior civil servants much sharper teeth. But he did not think the current cohort could ever deliver his wishes. Root-and-branch reform was needed to achieve success.

Once this improvement had been carried out, serious thought would have to be given to controlling the newly emboldened civil servants who might have even more power over politicians, the true amateurs of government. Hunt thought that this could be achieved in five ways (as Halls related it to Wilson). First, public scrutiny must be improved by lifting Whitehall's 'veil of secrecy'. Next, the legislature must be brought into greater balance with the executive by expanding the powers of the select committee system. The third proposal was for Permanent Secretaries to extend their new-found public voice – hardly very loud at this time but apparent with more lectures, briefings and even television appearances, most notably by Sir William Armstrong[132] (this proposal was rejected immediately by Halls and Wilson). Fourth, the idea for greater mixed ministerial-official committees was mooted as a way of controlling purely Civil Service might. The last point (though there was a vague plea for a streamlined machinery of government which was not elaborated upon)[133] was for a special committee, with a similarly eclectic membership, to review the progress of reform. Halls was disdainful of this but Wilson commented that it 'might be useful'[134] (Armstrong was very antagonistic to this proposal, seeing it as 'another example of the Committee's suspicion of bureaucratic inertia').[135] All in all, the Hunt-Halls line involved a detailed attempt to *limit* the power of a deliberately *empowered* mandarinate – a fascinating paradox.

As with some of the hardware reforms detailed in Chapter 2, these ideas had more than a touch of fantasy surrounding them. Although several of the recommended checks were indeed acted upon – there was a half-hearted attempt at a reform of the Official Secrets Acts in 1969 (of which, more later) and Crossman oversaw changes to the select committee system (which involved seven new ones set up between 1966 and 1969)[136] – there is little or no reason to believe they were due to Hunt's fears of over-mighty officialdom. The overall 'ethos of professionalism' and the accompanying checks and balances, therefore, turned out to be simply irrelevant, even if they help historians to understand the impetus behind such aspirations.

In May 1968 Sir William Armstrong moved from the economics and finance side of the Treasury, replacing Helsby as Head of the Home Civil Service, and was replaced in turn by Sir Douglas Allen. ('It astonished Whitehall that he gave up the Treasury', said Allen much later.)[137] An important characteristic of Sir William's management style was his determination to create thinking time to mull over big issues. Prior to becoming Head of the Home Civil Service, he spent a fortnight at Nuffield College, Oxford, looking at the evidence presented to the Fulton Committee.[138] After receiving a copy of the final draft of Fulton, Armstrong took it upon himself to represent what he felt to be the Civil Service angle.

In a huge memorandum to the Prime Minister in early May of 1968, Armstrong began by assuring Wilson (and Halls) that he had kept his own counsel on the draft, showing it to neither his fellow permanent secretaries nor his Minister, the Chancellor of the Exchequer Roy Jenkins: 'It was [agreed] that I would not bring the Chancellor in until we have an official text of the Report, when it is signed in a week or two's time.'[139] Even though the Prime Minister is technically First Lord of the Treasury (a fact of which Margaret Thatcher occasionally reminded Treasury officials),[140] for the Joint-Permanent Secretary to the Treasury to keep the findings of the Fulton Report from his Chancellor, the Minister responsible for the Civil Service at this time, is eyebrow-raising. Allen readily agreed when interviewed, believing that 'The only time you can withhold something from your minister is over security.'[141] (Yet Samuel Brittan saw nothing untoward in this.)[142] More likely, Armstrong and Wilson were acting as if a separate Civil Service Department under the control of the Prime Minister had already been created.

The level of outside interference in the Committee has long been an interesting issue. Earlier we saw how Allen was unhappy with Fulton's and especially Hunt's easy access to No 10. With the opening of the National Archives' files relating to the Fulton Committee, we now have documentary evidence of Armstrong's influence over the Committee, if only in a minor way ('I've always been puzzled as to how far William was operating behind the scenes', mused Allen[143] while Lord Croham observed that Armstrong 'apparently had a lot of contact "round the back" as it were').[144] For in reference to an earlier conversation regarding Wilson's wish to see a limit of two special advisers for each Minister (a limit which survives to this day),[145] Armstrong responded, 'I aim to try to get the Committee's Report modified accordingly'.[146] It must be noted, however, that Neild rejected the idea that the Committee was led from outside. While conscious of Wilson's, Halls' and Armstrong's interest in the Committee, he feels that the interference theory had been overdone. 'Look at the Fabian and Fulton reports. Do you find much deviation?'[147] Neild is correct. In fact, Richard Wilding describes the Report as 'a kind of sandwich with a piece of Fabian rye bread on top and a piece of managerial white bread underneath'.[148] If the concept of meritocracy, according to its creator Michael Young, is computed by adding IQ and effort, then Fulton is *The Administrators* plus the Management Consultancy Group.[149]

Armstrong tried hard to appear upbeat in the memorandum. Arguably the most contentious issue was one of wording and especially that of paragraph one. Many felt that it was an own goal by the Committee. The Chairman had tried hard to foster agreement but, as Wilding observed, '[s]ome members made it clear that they would accept nothing less than a public execution with all drums rolling, and that they were not open to discussion on the point.'[150] Halls, however, told his boss that Fulton felt the need to placate the civil servants on the Committee by avoiding 'too much of a condemnation of the existing Civil Service'.[151] Yet the final Report opened by boldly stating that

> The Home Civil Service today is still fundamentally the product of the nineteenth-century philosophy of the Northcote-Trevelyan Report. The problems it faces are those of the second half of the twentieth century ... It is still too much based on the philosophy of the amateur (or 'generalist' or 'all-rounder'). This is most evident in the Administrative Class, which holds the dominant position in the Service.

Richard Wilding, writing nearly three decades later, declared that '[t]o this day, I still do not know whether the civil service members were right or wrong to go along with Chapter 1. I was glad as secretary not to have to make my own decision.'[152] Several years after this assessment, he was to describe it as 'a misconceived hand grenade.'[153] Wilding was also highly critical of the 'amateur' accusation, finding it 'unjust' and 'vindictive':

> although a sustained push from the Prime Minister is a necessary condition of keeping things moving along in this field, it is not a sufficient condition. You also have to persuade the people who are in the key jobs with responsibility for translating broad proposals into detailed plans, promulgating them and bringing them into effect that the changes are right, should be adopted and will in effect become their own property and their own achievement ... The result was that Fulton got a bad press in precisely those places where he needed a good one. Damage resulted.[154]

Even Hunt and Kellner were to deem the inclusion of the word 'amateur' as '[t]he decisive tactical mistake'.[155] Sir William responded to this in a letter to Halls which contained wonderful mandarinese, a blend of understanding and contempt:

> In my own personal view much of the criticism is justified, though it would have been better from the point of view of getting across the positive recommendations accepted if

the Committee had recognised more fully both the improvements that have been made in recent years, and the difficulties under which the Service has been labouring ...

Armstrong went on to list the omissions, from his point of view, in the Fulton Report. He highlighted discipline, security, the political activities of civil servants, departmental welfare activities, financial control, the honours system ('The Committee appears to find nothing strange in the notion that a group of civil servants should in effect decide, subject to the approval of the Prime Minister, which of their number should be admitted to the various orders of knighthood'), and virtually nothing regarding the 'psychology of office workers or the sociology of bureaucratic communities'.[156] In a letter to the Prime Minister, Halls countered Armstrong's reservations:

> In my view the Committee could have been much stronger in their criticism and indeed the chapter has been somewhat modified against the more critical views of Norman Hunt, Neild and Sheldon ... we are really turning our backs on Northcote-Trevellyn [sic – Wilson in his memoir referred to the 1854 Report as being authored by Harcourt-Trevelyan,[157] both hardly inspiring confidence that either had intimate knowledge of it] – let us turn our backs on the "Ministers without Portfolio and without Ministerial responsibility" – the Warren Fishers of the Civil Service.

Halls went on to further criticize Armstrong because he had not confined himself purely to the acceptance of the Fulton Report and the challenges involved in its implementation.[158]

Armstrong was also critical of the overall nature of the Report, which gave little in the way of definite recommendations and settled more for 'rather general and even woolly'[159] wishes, something which was to plague the Report's implementation (or lack of). This was to result in the process, described by Sir Donald MacDougall, who had become Head of the Government Economic Service in 1969, after which he was

> obliged to read, and sit through discussions of long papers by the CSD which I thought were sometimes like sermons. First there was the text – a paragraph from Fulton; then ten pages discussing what it might mean; then another ten considering what might be done about it; and a final section quite often saying why nothing was possible or, worse still, with no conclusion at all.[160]

Armstrong's negative tone spurred Halls into action.

The 1960s and 1970s (especially after the first of Richard Crossman's diaries were published in 1975)[161] were decades of great mistrust of Civil Service attitudes. Conspiracy theories grew as to the obstructionist tendencies of the machine when confronted by radical policies and politicians. Yet there were serving civil servants who perhaps went too far the other way in trying to facilitate politicians' wishes. Halls sits in this category. He was very comfortable in the Prime Minister's 'kitchen cabinet'. In a word, he had gone 'native'. In response to Armstrong's long memorandum, Halls wrote to the Prime Minister and his letter is here quoted at length due to its lucidity and its criticism of the man who was the ostensible head of his profession:

> It is not only the young civil servants who will welcome the criticisms [contained in the Fulton Report]; there is a wide range of middle rank civil servants, of whom I am one, who have been making many of the criticisms which Fulton brings out ... Another point which is relevant to this and which William himself cannot, of course, make is the dominance of the Civil Service by Treasury personnel; Armstrong, Trend,[162] Johnson,[163] Morton,[164] France,[165] Padmore,[166] Philip Allen,[167] Pitblado[168] and Otto Clarke,[169] all permanent secretaries who have served in a senior position in the Treasury and most of whom secure the breakout appointments under the influence of Bridges. Of course, many of these will feel that the criticism is unjustified because they in fact have been pillars of the system.

(Sir Warren Fisher would have been mightily proud of this trend.) Wilson minuted simply: 'Agree with your comments.'[170] But for all Halls's agitation and access to the Prime Minister, his influence was limited, as Wilding has observed:

> As far as I'm aware, Halls didn't have any very great impact inwards into the Service. He didn't seek allies there ... He didn't himself carry the kind of weight with the rest of the Civil Service that people who had been Principal Private Secretary before him and after him carried. You could as I did occupy yourself with, as it were, what to do about Fulton without having any very strong impression that Halls was having an influence on the course of events. I was aware he was writing things and he was briefing Hunt ... It was curiously detached.[171]

As the Fulton Committee neared its reporting stage, the time for Wilson to decide what he wanted to see enacted drew close. It appears that there was never a possibility that the Report would be accepted in its entirety as the Cabinet was unconvinced. Indeed, there was a distinct chance of two reports, one majority and one minority, provoked by the aggressive tone of the final draft. In the event, only Lord Simey provided a 'note of reservation'[172] because he felt that the Report's belligerence was 'unfair to the Civil Service'[173] and because, so Wilding felt, 'the two Permanent Secretaries were in a very difficult position. I think they went along with quite a lot.'[174] According to Whitehall folklore this minority report was written by Sir William Armstrong himself – Simey told Allen and Dunnett (the latter no friend of the Treasury or of Helsby)[175] that Armstrong and the Treasury were 'helping him out'.[176] (The civil servants on the Committee, so gossip in Whitehall said, stayed only to act as a restraining influence – if they had not and the Report had taken a more radical turn *and* Labour had won in 1970, the consequences for the Civil Service could have been much more far-reaching.)[177]

The Prime Minister needed to decide exactly which of the many recommendations he was to endorse personally. But this was not a decision he could make in a political vacuum for the dispute between the future Head of the Home Civil Service and his own Principal Private Secretary was mirrored in the Cabinet. The spring of 1968 saw Wilson at one of the lowest points of his political life. Devaluation, and the mishandling of the aftermath,[178] left him in a very weak position. The economy was not coming right and industrial relations were beginning to be a major headache. The strategy upon which Wilson and Halls based their approach was to immediately accept three points – a Civil Service College,[179] a Civil Service Department[180] and single unified grading[181] – and to leave the rest for later (there were 22 main recommendations[182] and 158 in total).

Armstrong had previously feared that the civil servants on the Fulton Committee could be accused of fighting a rearguard action, but now he launched his own attempt to halt what he regarded as a truly problematic and counter-productive recommendation – that of single unified grading. The first evidence of Armstrong's attempted obstructionism came when he wrote a full appreciation of the Report which he hoped would form the basis of the paper to be circulated to the Cabinet. He suggested that Wilson accept only the Civil Service College and the Civil Service Department immediately, with the rest to be considered later. He then went on to highlight the cost of the reforms.[183]

Halls and Wilson were not impressed. Halls wrote to Armstrong stating that the Prime Minister 'thought that the cost of the implementation of the Committee's Report in full might, as it was presented in your paper, cause some concern among Ministers who were at present preoccupied with the PESC [Public Expenditure Survey Committee] exercise.'[184] Halls was consistently suspicious of Armstrong's costings and by 1969 was, quietly, obtaining a second opinion from Colin Gilbraith, Armstrong's Private Secretary, such was the level of mistrust.[185]

On 13 June 1968 Armstrong accepted the principle of single unified grading.[186] But a day later he provided an updated brief for Wilson's Cabinet discussion in which he again contested the Report and its recommendations when he gave the options as 'to implement this report now and to accept in principle a substantial outlay of manpower and money *or* to shelve the report until better times ... (I naturally hope that the decision will be in favour of implementation)', he added somewhat unconvincingly.[187] This was followed up four days later with even greater backtracking when he wrote to Halls, telling him about the conference of leading scientific and professional civil servants that he had attended: 'I must tell you that what was said makes me more concerned about the dangers of becoming committed to the unified structure before examining it'.[188] Armstrong's repeated underlining of the problems, as he saw them, made a mockery of his professed support for the Report.

The Chancellor of the Exchequer, earlier kept out of the Fulton loop by Armstrong, now made noises that 'though he liked the report' there was a 'need for delay while we [the Cabinet] considered it'.[189] Either Roy Jenkins was disingenuous at the time or changed his mind later for in his autobiography he described Fulton as 'the midwife of a not very good 1968 report on the civil service'.[190] Jenkins' real feeling was quite understandable, though, as Wilson did not consult him over the plan to create a new Civil Service Department from a slice of his Treasury, and in the sometimes juvenile world of politics this mattered greatly. A deal was struck between Jenkins and Crossman, Lord President of the Council (who wrote at the time in his diary that Fulton was 'a second rate Report written in a very poor style by Norman Hunt').[191] Crossman recorded Jenkins as saying, "'If I agree with you about postponing the decision on Social Service cuts for a week will you give me your full support on Fulton?" "Yes", I said, "if you will support me on Lords' reform as well"' (that perennial quagmire of an issue).[192]

The Cabinet initially considered the Report on 20 June 1968. Wilson announced his intention of immediately accepting the Civil Service Department, the Civil Service College and single unified grading, while considering the rest of the proposals at a later date. But Cabinet Ministers were not to be bounced. They questioned the cost of Wilson's wishes at a time of economic crisis, especially as the Cabinet had previously agreed a freezing on Civil Service recruitment only to be informed that the Service would grow by 1,000 by April 1969.[193] The Cabinet also expressed the feeling that 'The criticisms in Chapter I of the report, which though not without foundation were over-simplified and lacking in balance, were likely to receive undue publicity'. A chastened Wilson agreed that 'the Cabinet needed more time to consider the handling of the Fulton report'.[194] At Cabinet a week later, the Cabinet gave Wilson a much easier time, with 'wide support for the view that when the report was published the Government should make a positive statement announcing their acceptance in principle of the three main recommendations'.[195] In the Commons debate that followed, Edward Heath, the leader of the Opposition, welcomed the Report but saw it as only 'one part of the changes which have to be brought about in the structure of government as a whole' (reforms he was already planning, as we shall see in Chapter 4).[196] The Prime Minister 'readily agree[d]'.[197]

THE BATTLE FOR FULTON

Now came the issue of implementation. Two of the agreed three recommendations were easy to deliver. The Civil Service College took two years to open with several sites canvassed, including the Royal Naval College at Greenwich. The former Civil Defence College in Sunningdale was the eventual location for the main premises and its opening in June 1970 became Edward Heath's first official engagement as Prime Minister.[198] Lord Croham added a fascinating aside when he explained that Norman Hunt's determined behaviour throughout the period 1966–70 was because he had his eyes fixed on becoming the CSC's first head, a post which went instead to Eugene Grebenik (Professor of Social Studies, University of Leeds, 1954–69).[199]

The Civil Service Department began life on 1 November 1968, the same day as the Foreign Office and Commonwealth Office and the Department of Health and Social Security. The Prime Minister decide that the CSD should follow the ministerial model of the Department of Economic Affairs during 1967–8, whereby Wilson was in overall control but Shore in day-to-day charge – hardly a successful precedent.[200] Wilson did assume control of the Civil Service as First Lord of the Treasury with Lord Shackleton donning the Shore role. Lord Croham, head of the Treasury in 1968 and successor to Armstrong in the CSD, thinks that the CSD was another Wilsonian attempt at creative tension aimed at his Treasury, also observing that 'the Treasury often won when there was a fight'.[201]

The third item was where the bad blood had been created and where further bloodshed was to come: single unified grading. This was also to become the leitmotif of whether one was pro- or anti-Fulton. In the two years after its acceptance in Cabinet, little in effect happened. The key moment in the story came when Armstrong, Head of the Home Civil Service and also, essentially, of the Civil Service Department (his political 'boss', Lord Shackleton described their relationship as 'he was the head and I was his political adviser'),[202] began the abolition of all grades above Principal in the Administrative Class. The process was negotiated in the Whitley Council[203] (Halls was convinced that 'Whitleyism in the Service has probably been one of the main features contributing to our present rigidity').[204] This led to Armstrong having a running battle with No 10 – Halls at the forefront with, rather surprisingly, Norman Hunt, who was given a room in Downing Street at regular intervals so that he could review the current state of play and fire off sharp letters to Armstrong, all with the support of the Prime Minister.[205]

The Hunt–Halls–Armstrong trialogue became known as the 'inner circle' – 'a good description this', thought Hunt, '[w]e certainly went round in circles. And Michael Halls and myself were mostly taken for a ride!'[206] Even Peter Shore, who upon the DEA's abolition in October 1969 was made Minister without Portfolio, but with special responsibility for the presentation of government policy, was also asked to review Armstrong's activities.[207] Among the choice comments that Hunt fired off to Armstrong, with the Prime Minister's blessing, was his observation that: 'It is quite clear ... that the remit to the Civil Service Department is to devise a practicable scheme for the implementation of a unified grading system to replace all of the different Civil Service classes. The remit is NOT to see whether such a practicable scheme can be devised.'[208]

Halls manned the defences of Fulton's single unified grading recommendation as he had fought all the feet-dragging by Armstrong (Wilding described the 'chief villains' as Armstrong and said he was 'in the minor role of Third Murderer, myself').[209] He thought Armstrong's proposal fell 'well short of the unified grading structure',[210] and reminded Wilson that Armstrong 'as you know, tried at literally the twelfth hour ... to prevent you from accepting the unified grading structure as an objective of government policy'.[211] 'Working down', Halls had earlier written, 'which put rather crudely was the original Treasury evidence which Fulton did not accept ... put another way, has not the time come to start at the bottom as well as at the top'.[212] (The Treasury had submitted evidence to the Committee which spoke about the managerial need to increase the efficient use of manpower, to abolish all grades above Principal but, crucially, nothing more).[213] Halls continued: 'the proposal which will attract most interest, namely the merger of the Administrative, Executive, and Clerical classes, will not even be negotiated until next year [1970] and not come into effect until 1971'.[214]

These were the last months before Halls' fatal heart attack on 3 April 1970. Marjorie Halls was adamant about who was responsible for her husband's death. After some deliberation, she finally issued a writ in February 1973[215] for £50,000 over Halls' non-transfer to an agreed position away from the very heavy workload of No 10 and Marcia Williams's bizarre behaviour. In fact, the job that Mrs Halls cited in her writ was that of 'implementing the Fulton Report', something she said was agreed by both Wilson and Armstrong.[216] 'That's completely news to me and, I would have said, deeply unlikely', says Wilding: 'I would be surprised to hear that Armstrong would want to have Halls [in that role as] Armstrong actually thought he was implementing the best of Fulton'.[217] The Civil Service Department settled out of court.[218] Halls' replacement, Sandy Isserlis, took over his place in the 'inner circle', but the 1970 election swiftly put paid to that. Hunt tried to interest David Howell in the battle after the Conservatives won but Howell, who was made Parliamentary Secretary to the Civil Service Department after his opposition work for Edward Heath on Civil Service reform, was understandably more concerned with his own ideas.[219] As Hunt and Kellner somewhat melodramatically put it: 'Armstrong and the CSD had seen off the one man capable of challenging their actions.'[220] Certainly, the change of government in 1970 meant that even the modest support for single unified grading largely dried up, to the extent that Armstrong was able to 'draw a line under Fulton' in 1972.[221] ('It was not until the 1980s', according to Wilding, 'that the reform was carried through at those levels where it would make most difference: the middle management grades of assistant secretary and principal'.)[222]

But Halls was getting agitated over what was, at the end of the day, an issue of bureaucratic management, something most people would find relatively insignificant. He clearly saw it differently, and wrote to Roger Dawes (a Private Secretary to the Prime Minister 1966–70) in July 1969, asking: 'Are we being taken for a ride? Is this really a step towards a unified grading structure of the type envisaged by Fulton or is it a presentational step which achieves only a very limited contribution – if at all – to a unified grading structure?'[223] In one of his final submissions to Wilson regarding Fulton, Halls lamented that 'Throughout the last year we have seen a slow but fairly determined withdrawal from a commitment to single unified grading. This is a great shame, particularly since it will delay the advantages for the junior staff. But I doubt whether you have the time at present to press further on this'. 'I've every wish to return to it when I have more time'[224] was the Prime Minister's response. Wilson elaborated on this in 1976, when he told the House of Commons' Expenditure Committee hearings on 'The Civil Service' that by 1969 implementation of the Fulton Report 'was tailing off a bit ... with so many urgent problems at that time, I was not able to give my mind to it sufficiently ... the sheer rush and pace of Government at the present time ... has prevented as much being done on this as I think should be'.[225] An interesting sub-point was made by Wilding:

> When Armstrong backed the creation of the CSD, and agreed to become its first head as Head of the Home Civil Service, I think he believed that it would be a major job, closer to the Prime Minister than it turned out to be. Part of the trouble in 1968–70 was that it began to become clear what later heads of the CSD certainly found ... it didn't make necessary the kind of daily or weekly meetings and dealings with the Prime Minister that would really shore up the importance of that position. I think that happened at the same time as I dare say Wilson felt that though he didn't have the time to do anything about it, things were falling behind on the Fulton front, that Armstrong was not doing all he hoped there.[226]

Wilding developed his point regarding the Head of the Home Civil Service's position, juxtaposing it with previous holders, beginning with Armstrong's immediate predecessor Helsby, who rarely saw the Prime Minister *or* the Chancellor:

> This was of course part of the reason why it was decided to have a CSD because the critics of the Treasury's management of the Civil Service felt that the management of the Civil Service always trailed home behind the rest of the field when it came to the Chancellor's attention. He had to cope with the balance of payments, the running of the economy, taxation and everything else, and there, way back in the distance, was the management of the Civil Service. That certainly was true that Helsby didn't see the Prime Minister and this was a slightly new problem because when Norman Brook had had the job he was Secretary to the Cabinet, and that, of course, meant that he was central and that

when he wanted to bring to the attention of whoever was Prime Minister at the time some essential Civil Service matter, which would often usually be the appointment of a permanent secretary or some trouble that was going on between some permanent secretary and some Minister, that kind of thing, he had only to knock on the door and go in and talk because he was there talking about Cabinet Office business. I think Armstrong didn't foresee this. I'm sure that Fulton and his Committee and Hunt didn't foresee this and it dawned on people during 1968–70.[227]

With Wilson settling on forcing through just three of the Fulton Report's recommendations, the majority were therefore ignored at the time. The Committee called for a continuous review of Civil Service functions and recruitment;[228] a greater emphasis on career management;[229] an expanded late entry into the service;[230] the creation of accountable management units;[231] the establishment of departmental planning units, to be headed by a new Senior Policy Adviser;[232] and the right for all Ministers to recruit temporary special advisers.[233]

Perhaps the most eye-catching recommendation that was immediately rejected (and, in 2007, still unimplemented), the so-called 'preference for relevance',[234] an idea first recommended by Dr Benjamin Jowett of Balliol, the keen university reformer, at the time of Northcote-Trevelyan.[235] The Report stated that 'a majority of us consider that the relevance to their future work of the subject-matter of their university or other pre-Service studies should be an important qualification for appointment'.[236] None of the Civil Service members of the Committee were among the majority.[237] It was another, this time lightly-veiled, attack on the classics graduates in the Administrative Class.[238] Douglas Allen (along with Helsby)[239] was a firm believer in this recommendation, observing that just as graduates with an eye on a private sector job tailored their studies accordingly, the same approach could benefit the Civil Service.[240] Armstrong and Shackleton took the proposal seriously[241] but it was dismissed 'out of hand' by Wilson because it 'would close to the Civil Service a very wide field of candidates who have started ... on their chosen university courses long before they had decided that they wanted to become civil servants'.[242]

The Fulton Report recommended that four further studies should be undertaken. The recommendation to reform the Whitley machinery was shelved.[243] The aforementioned Davies Committee on Civil Service recruitment was, in effect, one of the investigations. The third was the inquiry into official information, examining if the British bureaucratic obsession with secrecy actually needed to be relaxed at all as it could be hampering efficiency. This particular inquiry was a farce. Wilson had initially 'doubted whether there would in fact be much of a demand for a review of the [Official Secrets] acts'.[244] Indeed, the Prime Minister was apparently happy to see the issue 'in limbo' (Halls' words).[245] The only reason he opened it was in response to Edward Heath who, while presenting the prizes at Granada's awards for journalism in January 1969, argued forcefully in favour of an inquiry when he said 'politicians should make it possible for the media to improve the level of political discussion by reducing and eliminating the obstacles that stand in their way'.[246] In response,

> The Prime Minister said that when he had considered this matter both at the time of the debate and shortly afterwards, he had doubted whether there would in fact be much of a demand for a review of the Acts but he had been thinking further about this. In particular, he had noted that Mr. Heath ... had called for a review of the Official Secrets Acts. The Prime Minister said that this might lead others to call for this ...[247]

The government's review did produce a 'truly feeble' White Paper, favouring ever-so-slightly more open government but nowhere near true freedom of information.[248] In fact, it only really pointed out that 'departments are adopting a more liberal attitude towards the release of information than in the past'.[249] Wilson was powerfully supported in his lack of desire for greater openness by both Trend and Armstrong.[250] In such circumstances, there was no chance of anything of substance ensuing, which lent no credibility to Wilson's fast-disappearing reputation as a modernizer.[251]

The final investigation recommended by Fulton dealt with the possibility of 'hiving-off' current central government responsibilities. This, like almost all of the Fulton proposals, was not a new idea. The late-1960s version was concerned with managerial efficiency.[252] As the Confederation of British Industry succinctly put it to the Fulton Committee,

> Accountable management is most effectively introduced when an activity is separately established outside any government department ... These boards or corporations would be wholly responsible in their own fields within the powers delegated to them. Although they would be outside the day-to-day control of Ministers and the scrutiny of Parliament, Ministers would retain powers to give them direction where necessary.[253]

But there is no evidence (apart from the interest that Heath was taking in it and his question to this effect during the Fulton Report debate in the Commons in November 1968)[254] as to why suddenly, in 1969, Wilson became fascinated by this, going as far as pointing out to his Principal Private Secretary that 'I should like to feel that a very high priority is being given to the review'.[255]

The investigation was handled by the Civil Service Department and resulted in two large reports prior to Labour's election defeat in June 1970. While it was felt that some bodies could be hived-off and others could not, yet all were ripe for reform, the actual results were thin on the ground.[256] (The most frivolous candidates for removal from the public sector were the state-owned breweries and pubs in Carlisle, Gretna and Cromarty, hangovers, literally, from the First World War. This was scotched as these were Labour-voting districts which would not take kindly to this form of efficiency drive.)[257] Armstrong was nervous about even this turn of events. In a letter to his fellow Permanent Secretaries he alerted them to 'a factor that should, I believe, weigh heavily with us is the possibility of implying a judgement that the Civil Service in the post-Fulton era, is disqualified from managing large executive operations of a commercial kind'.[258] Robert Neild recalls that this was almost precisely why he was so interested in hiving-off, as civil servants were taking responsibility for more and more roles.[259] While nothing resulted from this inquiry, it is significant as the first time that a government had looked at some of its activities, however small, and considered them for what was in effect privatization – and under the auspices of a Labour government. It is also interesting that the idea of devolving power by creating executive agencies came to be muddled with privatization.[260]

CONCLUSION

The Fulton Report has gone down as one of *the* key moments in British administrative history. It is still talked about in Whitehall to this day. Does it deserve its legendary status? Though it is undeniable that the Fulton Report is important in the history of the Civil Service and that it provides an intriguing story, its significance in explaining the development of British central government cannot be seen as pre-eminent. In no way was it as significant as Northcote-Trevelyan. The recommendations it contained were not radical. Nothing in the Report's recommendations was new at the time. Richard Wilding was right to observe a quarter of a century later that 'an odd feature of the Fulton story was the disproportion between what the critics said about the civil service and the proposals that were put forward for improving it, between an apocalyptic diagnosis and a rather modest, even pedestrian, prescription for cure'.[261]

Moreover, from the vantage point of the twenty-first century, compared to decades of continuous radical reform, from Margaret Thatcher's financial cuts and sustained disdain through John Major's entrenchment of the *Next Steps* agency culture and first moves towards a codification of constitutional conventions all the way to the Blair Governments' surrendering of interest rate setting, devolution to Scotland, Wales and (some of the time) Northern Ireland, the rising power and numbers of special advisers and the near-fusion of the Prime Minister's Office and the Cabinet Office, the Fulton Report is not nearly so significant as it once seemed.

But legendary it remains. There was the head of steam which built up through theoretical criticism of the Balogh kind which the Civil Service appeared both bemused and troubled by, and the more practical critique by the Treasury in its concern over the quality of future recruitment. Then there was the inquiry itself which proved tortuous for the Committee's members and controversial due to the alleged influence of the Prime Minister and the Head of the Home Civil

Service. Perhaps only Norman Hunt was subsequently proud of his involvement in the Committee's deliberations – certainly Lord Allen, Robert Neild and Richard Wilding all demonstrate varying degrees of dismissiveness.

The unnecessary and controversial introductory assertion that mandarins were hopelessly amateur in an unprofessional sense rankled and demoralized the very people who were supposed to engineer Fulton's multiple recommendations and ensured that stories regarding dissatisfaction were abundant from one of the most private institutions in the realm. The Report's longevity was assured due to the Olympian stature of Sir William Armstrong locking horns with the energy and radicalism (in the sense of wishing to shift the status quo) of Norman Hunt, displaying all the zeal of somebody new to a topic and only having read the case for the prosecution. (The Civil Service has always undergone constant change, yet being accountable to Parliament and needing to care for Ministers' reputations has also led to immense but understandable risk-averseness.) Add to this the Prime Minister's Principal Private Secretary becoming ever more partisan in his opposition to the head of his own profession, before his sudden death, and there is conflict, always helpful in deepening and perpetuating the memory of an event. From an administrative history point of view, few, if any, episodes have been more controversial.

The Fulton Report proved to be the last of the big Civil Service investigations to date. Inquiries which followed were often internal and directed at a specific function of government. Though the machinery of government and its practitioners are central to understanding the state we live in, it is a curiously under-examined and often ignored subject. The daily press are progressively less interested as the years pass and few comprehensive publications appear; highly specific studies are written but often by experts for experts. One of the few books to capture the public imagination was Peter Hennessy's *Whitehall*. In this as in other works, the Fulton Report is treated as a hugely significant inquiry. Hennessy's views have, rightly, become the received wisdom.

That most of the Report's recommendations were eventually implemented is another reason to see it as a major event. From the Civil Service College and the Civil Service Department in 1968–70 to single unified grading and the late 1980s–90s creation of 'hived-off' autonomous executive agencies as part of the *Next Steps* initiative, and even the eventual reform of the Official Secrets Acts, the implementation may have taken up to two decades but it happened. Though none of the reforms were individually radical, taken together the package most certainly was compared to what had gone before. Fulton was never going to be the twentieth century's rival to Northcote-Trevelyan, but it was a landmark – and remains so.

4

Strategy

HEATH'S PRE-ELECTION PLANNING AND *THE REORGANISATION OF CENTRAL GOVERNMENT*, 1964–70

CONSERVATIVE PLANNING IN OPPOSITION

We have seen how the two Harolds, Macmillan and Wilson, made significant changes to the machinery of central government during each of their six-year stints as Prime Minister in the years 1957–63 and 1964–70 respectively. Yet the Government of Edward Heath which lasted just over three and a half years, from June 1970 to February 1974, introduced reforms which were more ambitious and strategically coherent than anything that had been attempted before or, indeed, since. The attempt to ally extensive forethought about the purposes and practices of government with robust determination in facing the country's challenges remains a highly commendable lesson to all who aspire to shape the fortunes of their country. This chapter will centre on the extensive research conducted by several groups which reported to Edward Heath in the run-up to the 1970 election and how the Civil Service reacted prior to the publication in October 1970 of *The Reorganisation of Central Government* White Paper, which detailed the practical results of the plans.

The Labour Party's narrow electoral victory in 1964 consigned the Conservative Party to its first taste of opposition for thirteen years. The former Prime Minister, Sir Alec Douglas-Home, intended to remain as leader for the general election expected to be in the near future, given Wilson's slender majority of five. Douglas-Home ordered soon after the defeat 'the most extensive and businesslike policy review that the party [had] ever mounted'.[1] It was headed by Edward Heath, the Party's new Shadow Chancellor.[2] Heath had ended the 1964 government as *de facto* 'overlord' for industry, trade and regional development. He had also been the power behind the politically controversial but economically necessary abolition of resale price maintenance (Douglas-Home believed it cost them support on polling day[3] though David Butler and Anthony King thought it 'figured hardly at all').[4] His promotion to Shadow Chancellor seemed a natural progression.

Douglas-Home was not in a strong position. The nature of his 'emergence' as leader had split the Party (some of the ablest younger Tories such as Iain Macleod and Enoch Powell refused to join his Cabinet in protest)[5] while the narrowness of the defeat was largely irrelevant to Conservative MPs used to repeated victory and the trappings of power. Discontent with his low-key leadership style began to grow and Douglas-Home, a truly honourable man and a hereditary landowner in the borders of England and Scotland to boot (and hence a man with much else in his life besides politics), announced his resignation on 22 July 1965 amid internal Conservative Party criticism. The subsequent leadership election, the first for the Tories, was essentially a two-horse affair between Heath and Reginald Maudling, the former Chancellor of the Exchequer.

Maudling's record as partner to Macmillan and then Douglas-Home in the failed 'dash for growth' during the years 1962–4, along with his languid style, did not endear him to the Party and it turned to Heath.[6] The contrast between the two could not have been greater. Heath had ended the Second World War as lieutenant-colonel in the artillery and was Chief Whip at the time of Suez, retaining his air of discipline and solidity throughout. Douglas Hurd, who ran Heath's office in opposition, later becoming his Political Secretary 1970–3, thought that Heath had been chosen 'because of his reputation as a tough negotiator and his thoroughly professional approach to politics'.[7] The Conservatives were desperate for a self-made man of direction and strength, as much to underline a break with the past as for a champion to take on Harold Wilson. Heath embodied great hope.

Heath continued the wide-ranging policy review, but the chairmanship passed to Sir Edward Boyle.[8] While Wilson governed as if 'he had a hundred-seat majority', the reality was that a fast-disappearing majority meant that another election was imminent.[9] Heath, therefore, oversaw a hasty conclusion to the policy review and all was complete by the time of the 1966 election. It included some highly detailed analysis[10] and a final report overseen by Boyle on the machinery of government; machinery issues were under consideration almost immediately under the initial chairmanship of Rab Butler until Boyle succeeded him in February 1965.[11] The report advocated, among other things, only one central economics and finance department[12] – in direct contrast to Labour's Department of Economic Affairs – and was delivered to Heath in March 1966.[13] The landslide Labour majority of 97 seats was not unexpected. As Heath had only been in the top job for eight months, his robust performance during the campaign meant that there was never any question of his being dumped as Douglas-Home had been.[14] He entered the 1966 Parliament determined to make sure he was not beaten again.

Heath was remarkably consistent in his belief that he would be the winner second time around. Through double-digit opinion poll leads (in May 1968 the Conservatives were 28 per cent ahead of Labour)[15] and Labour Party recoveries,

Heath was convinced that he would get his chance due, as Douglas Hurd put it, to 'the logical result of the long years of preparation, and of the fact that the people of Britain ... were at bottom a sensible lot'.[16] This inner confidence meant that Heath spent less time worrying about *if* he was going to lead his country and more time planning for what he would do *when* he did so.

The policy review which ended with the 1966 manifesto *Action Not Words*[17] was followed up by one after the election which did not question the fundamentals of the first but added flesh to them,[18] all in the spirit of a government-in-waiting and with the next election in mind. Most aspects of government were considered alongside machinery of government though, interestingly, the changes brought about by the Labour Governments after 1964 were ignored.[19]

Heath had seen the way Whitehall worked from the inside, in a way akin to Wilson. For all their undoubted personal animosity and difference of style, Heath and Wilson offered similar histories and analyses of those experiences. Heath had been a Cabinet Minister for five years in 1959–64 (Wilson for four during 1947–51) and also saw government from the inside when he came joint-top in the post-war reconstruction Civil Service exams in 1946, spending a brief time in the Ministry of Civil Aviation as an assistant principal[20] (Wilson spent the war inside the Cabinet Secretariat and the Board of Trade and thus both men tasted an invaluable flavour of how the Civil Service operated, though Wilson had naturally had a much more central experience). Heath later half-joked that if he had been given a Treasury posting he might well have stayed inside Whitehall[21] – and would have been a Permanent Secretary during the years 1970–4.[22] In fact, he left after two years upon being adopted as prospective parliamentary candidate for Bexley, disillusioned by the pace and atmosphere of his department.[23]

Heath came of age in the 1930s and 1940s. The mass unemployment (which did not leave his family untouched),[24] travelling through Germany just as it turned out the lights over much of Europe for the second time in a quarter of a century and his aforementioned successful army career in Germany at the end of the war gave him deeply held principles. They also provided him with twin pillars for his future Premiership – finally to anchor the UK to an integrating Europe and to put Britain on a much firmer and coherent economic path[25] (the two were mutually reinforcing). This outlook was further cemented by his extensive exposure, at a relatively young age, to the two Conservative greats of the century (as Heath saw them), Winston Churchill and Harold Macmillan. Due to Heath's life-long bachelorhood and Kentish base he was always available for late nights and weekend socializing at Chartwell and Birch Grove, Churchill and Macmillan's respective country seats. Churchill's patronage of the young Heath meant that he witnessed the gravitas of the great man's leadership qualities (though very much on the wane compared to his war years).[26] But the real impression was made by Macmillan.

In many late night whisky sessions, the Macmillan view of politics and the world, with its air of perspective and detachment, almost Whiggish in its robust centrism, was expounded to his Chief Whip and later Labour Minister. Heath found he shared Macmillan's 'One Nation' beliefs,[27] especially once he had moved away from the whips' office to the Ministry of Labour as Macmillan's interest in planning developed and grew.[28] But he believed that an injection of efficiency and dynamism into the country was necessary in order to sustain these values.[29]

What Heath wanted was a mixed economy with government doing all it could to provide economic success alongside social fairness – which he passionately believed to be absolutely right – vigorously pursued to a successful end. Heath's critique of the years 1951–64 was that insufficient energy and strength had been shown. 'Harold Macmillan had taken things far too easily so he was wanting to be up and at them', as Douglas Hurd described Heath's view, 'he was out for the slaying of dragons'.[30] Heath was, in Martin Burch's words, 'a classic exponent of the alternative governmental approach to opposition leadership'.[31]

To this end, and with his experience of the permanent and temporary sides of British government, he became deeply interested in the machinery of government. 'This was a subject', Heath wrote in his memoirs, 'that engrossed me to some people's surprise, because I was concerned that Ministers spent too much time on day-to-day matters, instead of on strategic thinking.'[32] Heath's thinking ahead coincided with the Fulton Committee, an investigation the Conservative leader was careful not to endorse (although several ex-Ministers gave evidence and Heath himself had an informal meeting with Fulton in which he praised highly the overall calibre of civil servants, in particular his Brussels team during the first application to join the Common Market in 1961–3, but criticized some of the structures of government, most especially the Cabinet system).[33]

Immediately following defeat in the 1966 election, Heath wrote to Ernest Marples, Conservative MP for Wallasey 1945–February 1974, a successful example of the businessman-in-politics,[34] who was also crucial to Macmillan's early-1950s housing drive.[35] Heath wanted to know if Marples was interested in heading research into the machinery of government, specifically regarding enhanced efficiency through the reduction in the size and scope of the state.[36] Marples readily replied agreeing to the task and set about recruiting a small number of high-quality young Conservative would-be technocrats.[37] David Howell, MP for Guildford, who had worked in the Economic Section of the Treasury during 1959–60, Mark Schreiber, who was the Conservative Research Department Desk Officer for Science and Technology, and David Alexander,[38] along with a part-timer, Laurence Reed,[39] were brought on board.[40] The unit was announced on 22 April 1967.[41]

Marples's political career had waned – he had been dropped from the Shadow Cabinet in 1966 – because of his profound contempt for the political world.[42]

He was sceptical of Whitehall practices, too. He believed that figures such as Enoch Powell were right to lambast the extravagance and inherent inefficiency of the State but, as Howell put it, 'their ideas and speeches were like paper arrows, crumpled and useless when fired against the great bureaucratic brick wall which lay across every path'.[43] (Powell's strictures over bureaucratic profligacy and misjudgement did undoubtedly help push the Conservative leadership into a war on waste. He wrote in 1969 of 'a hatred of bureaucracy, above all, lawless bureaucracy', and his rejection of 'the modern assumption, which this country has been brainwashed into accepting, that the solution to every problem must be a government solution and that nothing can be well done, or perhaps done at all, unless the State has a finger in it'.) [44] Heath knew that Marples had brains but that his contempt, including that which he felt for his leader (Heath himself), was making him a liability.[45] Howell said that 'this was generalised contempt but focused on the current leader, he just felt that all the new generation of Conservatives were wafflers entrapped in the same web as Labour, and that he, Marples, was the only dynamic character who could break out of the box'. Though Marples remained an MP until February 1974, there was no chance of him taking office again as '[h]e was a pretty impossible team-player!'[46] Corralling Marples and focusing his undoubted talents was wise man-management.

THE PSRU'S BLUEPRINT

Marples believed there was an answer to the seemingly intractable problem of inefficiency and waste and that it lay in American business methods.[47] With this in mind, he, Schreiber and Howell scoured the think tanks of North America (as well as Japan[48] and Italy),[49] imbibing the newly developing management theories, and forged links with the Johnson Administration in Washington which was putting many of these new ideas to the test.[50] Arguably, the most significant, certainly in terms of what was actually going on at this time within Whitehall under Labour, was the decision to split the US Treasury in two, creating a Bureau of the Budget and separating finance from management.[51] This, of course, was a similar, but far from identical, approach to that pursued haphazardly with the creation of the Department of Economic Affairs, the key difference being that public spending allocation and control remained with the UK Treasury between 1964 and the DEA's demise in 1969.

Splitting the Treasury, under a Conservative Government and along different lines, interested the Tory planners. They keenly believed that the machine over which ministers in successive governments presided had proved incapable of delivering the spending reductions which politicians kept promising.[52] According to the analysis of the Marples team, the Treasury was the only department with the capability of taking a strategic look at the whole of government, and as government grew ever bigger, against the professed wishes of Conservative and Labour governments alike, the Treasury was clearly not delivering. Heath claimed that public spending rocketed from 44 per cent of GDP in 1960 to 50 per cent in 1969.[53] Planning for another cleavage was not the only way in which the Marples Unit,[54] or Public Sector Research Unit (PSRU) as it became known, demonstrated their dissatisfaction with the Treasury.[55] A British-style bureau of the budget would mean that one department would draw up the plans for public expenditure, while another would find the means to fund it. But it would not solve the way in which the centre of British government was constantly defeated by the great departmental interests. The PSRU decided that the only way to stop this once and for all was to create a much stronger centre, something influenced by the support provided for the German Chancellor at the time[56] and also found in Canada, France and Italy.[57]

The British way of government traditionally relied upon a small centre, part of the theory that the Prime Minister is nothing more than *primus inter pares*. There was a growing belief among Marples' team that this was no longer realistic. Once a major project had got under way in government, especially if responsibility was shared between departments, it became almost impossible to halt or amend its progress and there was an air of good money following bad into a bottomless pit. Many technological projects fell into this category, most notably those of a defence nature and those such as Concorde where the UK had overseas partners.[58] The PSRU came up with a plan for a new 'analytical capability' which would look at such issues and offer clear guidance whether funding should be continued as before, amended or stopped altogether. In effect, it was an attempt to bring the American idea (or 'fad' according to *The Economist*) of Planning, Programming and Budgeting (PPB) to Britain.[59]

Perhaps most significant, though far from new, was the idea to create a 'central capability', too. (It must be understood that the 'analytical capability' and the 'central capability' went through many gestations, had several authors and were never clearly contained in one single blueprint. They therefore meant different things at different times.) This had gone through several mutations among Heath's planners: a Public Sector Efficiency Unit, a Crown Consultancy Unit, a Cost-Effectiveness Department, and an Office of Government Reorganisation and Efficiency.[60] They felt this was needed in order to bolster the Prime Minister's control over government, and its strategy, through an injection of high-level information and guidance, traditionally lacking in the small centre.

Twice in the twentieth century there had been forms of 'think tanks' answering directly to the Prime Minister. David Lloyd George's five-strong[61] 'Garden Suburb' led by the Oxford Professor W. G. S. Adams (so called because it was housed in makeshift huts in the Downing Street garden) was the first, followed by Winston Churchill's 'Statistical Section' of six academic economists under

Professor Lindemann, both in wartime.[62] The PSRU made extensive studies of these.[63] In its entirety, the plan to build a powerful Prime Minister's department was a bold statement of intent. There was not, however, a completely clear and unanimous decision even within the PSRU on what the 'central capability' should do and engender, and this was to prove confusing after its creation. David Howell wanted a war on waste and inefficiency, while for Mark Schreiber the whole point was to sharpen the analytical side of government.[64]

The planning did not end there. Alongside this reform of the centre were many ideas to refashion the wider machine. A smaller Cabinet was desired, able to take a much more strategic view of proceedings ('strategic' was the word of the moment, as 'purposive' had been in 1964). This would be made possible by the creation of super-departments. This, essentially, was a far more rational and practical attempt to develop a more efficient and smaller Cabinet than Churchill's 1951–3 'overlords' experiment.[65] The move towards larger departments, it will be recalled, was already happening under Labour with the establishment of the Foreign and Commonwealth Office, the Department of Health and Social Security, the continuing growth of Mintech and Crosland's late-1969 near-overlordship of what was to become the Department of the Environment (the planning being well advanced by the time Labour fell).[66]

Central to the PSRU's planning was the employment of a tough but simple managerial logic to the business of government. In a three-step approach, they asked what government was trying to achieve in all its myriad forms, could this be better done by the private sector, but if not, how could it be improved?[67] The idea of 'hiving-off' state agencies was a key aspect in the PSRU's blueprint – as it had been in Whitehall during 1969–70 after being mentioned as a subject requiring a follow-up enquiry in the Fulton Report. Indeed, Heath later wrote that he was keen on hived-off executive agencies 'following the advice of the Fulton Report'.[68] (Though it is interesting to note that in 1967 Heath had told Fulton at his informal discussion during the Fulton investigation that '[t]he Conservative Party had come to the conclusion that hiving-off could work where the organisation was commercial in character, but was doubtful elsewhere.')[69] As Howell wrote in 1970, Fulton 'failed to take the next logical step and discuss the idea of taking functions right out of the public sector. But since they were already outside their terms of reference in dealing with machinery questions at all, this is perhaps understandable.'[70]

If much government activity could be farmed out to the private sector (or at the very least placed in autonomous agencies), the overarching aim of less – but better – government could be achieved. To attain this, the PSRU wanted a team of top businessmen to be seconded for two years or more to launch a war on waste and inject business ideas and energy throughout Whitehall[71] – not a new idea, of course – alongside a much greater use of management consultants, something relatively rare at the time.[72] (Heath had always been keen on consultants since he employed a group to audit the accounts of the Oxford Union when he had been its President in 1938–9.)[73] All this would, the PSRU felt, also demand a fundamental reform of Parliament to improve its scrutiny function,[74] something very similar to Norman Hunt's views of the parliamentary implications of developing super civil servants during the Fulton Committee's deliberations. All in all, the PSRU enterprise was human and structural planning on a grand scale – planning for a 'quiet revolution'.[75]

The Conservative Party and its institutions were uneasy with the degree of Heath's interest in the technocratic side of government, especially as not everyone shared his belief in inevitable victory. It was widely felt that as the onus was on thinking like a 'government-in-waiting' some of the tactical opportunities of opposition were being ignored – for example, not being able to find a House of Commons bruiser like John Boyd-Carpenter a front bench job.[76] It was also felt that concentration on the 'how' was ignoring the necessity of the 'why' as regards the detailed policies being produced. As the Director of the Conservative Research Department, Brendon Sewill, privately wrote to a predecessor, David Clarke, 'the public want to know where he [Heath] wants to go just as much as how he means to get there'.[77] Enoch Powell thought it also due to Heath's inability to talk grand theory.[78] As Powell told Phillip Whitehead, Heath 'believes there is an answer to all problems which can be worked out by proper bureaucratic means – I'm not using that word abusively for once – by the proper approach. If all the relevant facts are assembled and put together by competent people, and logical analysis is made, then that will provide the answer.'[79] Heath's critics were concerned that all this, as they saw it, technocratic nonsense was getting in the way of telling people what a Conservative government would be *for*. That, as Angus Maude, Shadow spokesman for the colonies, wrote in his controversial 'Winter of Tory Discontent' in *The Spectator* in January 1966, 'for the Tories simply to talk like technocrats will get them nowhere'.[80] Heath sacked Maude for this. The apprehension in the Conservative Party that this engendered – especially inside the Conservative Research Department – meant that Heath created and kept the PSRU outside the usual Conservative Party structure. (Howell was also dissatisfied by Conservative Central Office as he explained in another *Spectator* article.)[81]

The Conservative Research Department's consistent resistance to radicalism partly explained this: 'So pervasive was this negative attitude that those who wanted to break out from it had to conduct a kind of covert operation'.[82] This subterfuge was necessary, thought David Howell, as 'The reality was that we were digging very deep indeed into philosophical issues. We were questioning the very nature of the state apparatus and we were proposing to carry forward that question in a more systematic, ordered and analytical way than ever attempted.'[83] He believed that the opposition to the PSRU was rooted in the belief that 'the idea that the collectivist state could be unravelled was seen as just as unrealistic as the idea that the Soviet Empire could be dissolved. Neither was ever going to happen'.[84] The PSRU's true aims were shrouded under the cloak of a dry-as-dust machinery of government re-jig.[85]

Discontent with the apparent failure of the economy and inefficiency within the State, something felt palpably across the political spectrum,[86] was fostering the beginnings of an organized backlash against the previously – at least for the previous quarter-century – mostly unquestioned tenets of heavy statism. Howell claims the first published use of the word 'privatization' was in the *A New Style of Government* pamphlet in 1970.[87] This was why the road these Conservative planners were beginning to travel was hidden from the more politically and electorally conscious in the Conservative Party, although some Tories were beginning to reject the small-scale corporatism (especially compared to that on the Continent) and interventionism.[88] Enoch Powell and, to a lesser extent, Keith Joseph (shadow Trade spokesman), among others especially in the constituencies, felt that these issues would cost the Party votes, both through antagonism and indifference.[89] The whole edifice of the 'post-war consensus', discussed in Chapter 1, was beginning to be questioned.

A conference was arranged at Sundridge Park in Kent incorporating the PSRU, most of the future businessmen's team, industrialists and academics along with the Shadow Cabinet and selected backbenchers.[90] Sessions took place between 15 and 26 September 1969 and were a blend of presentations by the planners and guests on the theory of the proposed changes and talks by the future Ministers on how it was to be done in practice.[91] Charles Schultz, former Director of the Bureau of the Budget and later at the Brookings Institute, gave two lectures on 'Planning and Programming the Budget in a Political Setting'.[92] The participants' reactions were mixed, with some Shadow Ministers very sceptical.[93] (It also has to be said that for all of the talk and writing about Planning, Programming and Budgeting and a possible Bureau of the Budget, there is no actual evidence of a blueprint for this in the PSRU papers at the Conservative Research Department's archive, nor in The National Archive, unlike the impressive detail of the 'future legislation exercise' undertaken during the winter of 1969–70 and delivered to Heath on 10 March 1970.)[94]

The conference was followed by a dinner for the Shadow Cabinet in November 1969 in which 'the whole approach [to machinery of government changes] was thrashed out'.[95] Lord Carrington, the chairman of the Shadow Cabinet sub-committee concerned, which included Robert Carr (spokesman on industrial relations) and Keith Joseph as members, regarded machinery issues as 'very important'.[96] Carrington supervised action groups set up after the Sundridge conference to go into specific aspects of 'the new style' and reported just before the 1970 election.[97]

No one could say the plans were half-baked. One could say, however, that the planning was only half-supported, if that. Reginald Maudling, Conservative spokesman for home affairs and deputy leader, was somewhat bemused by it all when attending a meeting on 2 December 1969 dealing with the same machinery issues: 'What's all this balls we're having dinner about at the Carlton tonight ... I can't say I understand what it's all about'.[98] David Howell's contemporary note of the meeting demonstrated that Maudling was not alone in his cynicism: 'the wretched Sewill piped up saying he didn't see what the point of it all was while in opposition – that the C.S. [Civil Service] was doing it all anyway etc.' Howell was positively glowing in his praise for Heath's response to Sewill, 'I can only say I don't agree', noting that Heath's address to the dinner was 'Flat as usual but authoritative – obviously well ahead of most of his audience – an evidence of leadership over his dissident colleagues, I thought – very refreshing.'[99] All of these ideas were contained in various pamphlets and letters, which Howell wrote in order to 'send out some smoke signals' to the Civil Service, and culminated in the 'Black Book' which was published just prior to the 1970 general election.[100] The 'Black Book' was made up of 'a relatively unimpressive "impressionistic" "Urgent Action Dossier"'[101] and what also formed a draft PSRU submission to Heath. The latter boldly stated that 'the next Conservative government must have a much better decision-making capability, which must include the means of implementing decisions, than any government of Britain has had before'.[102]

There were other teams, comprised of retired senior civil servants, working on machinery-of-government issues, which reported directly to Heath and, though aware of each other's existence, were kept separate from each other.[103] Heath received advice from Lord Plowden (former head of the Central Economic Planning Staff and Chairman of the committee which recommended the five-year plans of the public expenditure survey) and Lord Roberthall (the former Chief Economic Adviser to the Treasury)[104] who told him that businessmen floating around Whitehall unattached to a specific department could only be a bad thing.[105] A team was chaired by the former Cabinet Secretary, Lord Normanbrook (who had initially turned down membership of Rab Butler's 1965 machinery-of-government committee and who died in 1967),[106] and another chaired by Dame Evelyn Sharp, formerly Permanent Secretary at the Ministry of Housing and Local Government, which covered ground similar to Boyle's 1965 review.[107] (Sharp was not the first choice, with many others considered earlier including Anthony Barber, Conservative Party Chairman 1967–70, and Lord Eccles, one of Macmillan's victims during the 'Night of the Long Knives' in July 1962.)[108]

Sharp told William Plowden, who had been Heath's Private Secretary at the Board of Trade in 1963–4 and was secretary to the Sharp Committee, that the 'whole project originated with some remarks of hers to H. [Heath] about the need for any future government to handle questions of government structure better than had the current Labour administration'.[109] (Sharp's first contact with Heath's advisers was actually Mark Schreiber.)[110] Sharp's group contained Sir Henry Hardman, Permanent Secretary, Ministry of Defence, 1964–6; Sir Freddie Bishop, Permanent Secretary, Ministry of Land and Natural Resources, 1964–5; Sir Eric Roll, Permanent Secretary, Department of Economic Affairs, 1964–6; and James Robertson, a former senior official in the MoD who had also been Private Secretary to the Cabinet Secretary.[111]

This powerful group eventually recommended an ambitious blueprint. The Prime Minister was to have his own department which would subsume the Prime Minister's Office, the Cabinet Office and the recently created Civil Service Department in a 'Prime Minister's Department'.[112] There was also to be a central planning staff to help maintain priorities[113] and a more rational demarcation of departments.[114] Sharp's views were influenced by Harold Macmillan's analysis of his years as Premier (she had got to know him well when Macmillan was at Housing in 1951–4).[115] These groups often presented their findings, and were asked their opinion of other groups' work, at Heath's flat in Albany.[116] It added up to the most significant attempt to refashion the central machinery of Whitehall since Lloyd George's administrative revolution of 1916–17.[117] The detail of the plans would also make it more difficult for the Civil Service to obstruct or reject.[118] The idea of a think tank or some form of central capability was also under consideration *within* Whitehall. Lord Trend later talked of 'a quite remarkable coincidence of diagnosis'[119] (although one must always be aware that Civil Service words often hide myriad meanings, as we shall see later).

The concept of a central capability unit was agreed on all sides. This was made apparent during the 'Douglas-Home Rules' discussions between the Civil Service and the Opposition in the last days before the General Election of June 1970.[120] No previous record of these discussions, nor indeed of those in 1964 and 1966, have ever been unearthed at The National Archives. Documents relating to the 1970 discussions have, however, been found. These show that Schreiber had three meetings with Sir William Armstrong; one session with Messrs Douglas Henley (Third Secretary, Treasury), Peter Baldwin (Treasury Under Secretary 1968–72) and Tom Caulcott (Under Secretary, Machinery of Government Group, CSD, 1970–3); a meeting with Otto Clarke; and a meeting with Sir Burke Trend and Armstrong.[121] David Howell remembers attending one of the meetings,[122] while Derek Rayner of Marks and Spencer and Richard Meyjes of Shell, both from Heath's team of businessmen, also went to see Armstrong.[123] The reason Schreiber conducted these most important conversations was that all the other major figures were politicians nursing constituencies in what was a snap election.[124]

For it appears that while the two redoubtable knights, Armstrong and Trend, were in favour of reforms to the centre of government, they had their own idea of what they should be and what they thought possible. At a conference of officials which took place at Sunningdale concerned with machinery-of-government matters, it was understood that 'Sir W Armstrong will want to follow up [the Conservative] proposals with Mr Schreiber and seek to guide him gently along the lines of thinking which emerged at Sunningdale. Briefly, this envisaged building up a series of staffs inside the Cabinet Office designed to service official and Ministerial interdepartmental groups ... These staffs would assist Ministers to reach decisions on priorities as between Departments, acting on material collected during the PESC process and in close consultation with Departments ... In effect, these staffs would be providing Ministers with a central analytical capability to enable them to discharge the constructive task of planning priorities in the medium term – year 4 and after.'[125]

It would also be fascinating to find out exactly what the future Conservative ministers had in mind. For, as we have seen, the plans of the PSRU were not universally embraced. Iain Macleod for one, as Shadow Chancellor, was naturally irresolute on the need to split his potential future fiefdom, as James Callaghan had been in 1964, though Macleod did ask Howell to brief him on his ideas for government just before his untimely death on 20 July 1970, a month after the election.[126]

Breaking up the Treasury was not explicitly broached by anyone during the 'Douglas-Home Rules' conversations, nor during the run-up to the publication of *The Reorganisation of Central Government* White Paper. Lord Howell has explained that as regards splitting the Treasury, 'Our ideas, which were very fully developed in some areas, were not fully developed here,'[127] due to the earlier-than-expected election. However, Richard East of Guest, Keen and Nettlefolds, one of the businessmen expected to be recruited should the Conservatives form the next government, did circulate, among the Conservative reformers, less than a month before the June 1970 election, a quite detailed plan for a Programmes Department and a new Minister of Programmes, based heavily on the USA's Bureau of the Budget experience.[128] Howell himself, in his 1970 *A New Style of Government* pamphlet, did not advocate an immediate cleavage but something far more organic by way of bolstering the 'expenditure "half"' of the Treasury with 'a better capability than exists today for effective budgetary analysis'. This could possibly develop into a 'full-blown department of the Budget'.[129] When Schreiber went to see Henley, Baldwin and Caulcott on 1 June 1970, the Conservative planner hinted at the idea of splitting the Treasury.[130]

Lord Croham, then Sir Douglas Allen and Permanent Secretary to the Treasury, had no knowledge at this time of the Tory planners' keenness to separate the spending and finance functions of his department.[131] Armstrong and Trend still sported bruises from trying to make the Department of Economic Affairs experiment work and had no interest in seeing history repeat itself. Already the plans of the PSRU were beginning to founder on the rock of Civil Service pessimistic scepticism. (Joe Haines, Wilson's Press Secretary 1969–70 and 1974–6, thought that 'Their impatience and frustration is understandable ... They labour to create a policy and then they labour to dismantle it, only to be told to start building again.')[132]

THE CIVIL SERVICE IS HANDED THE PLANS

After some of the worst years a peacetime administration had suffered in recent times, the Labour Government's morale and poll-ratings quickly recovered by the early months of 1970. After being 28 per cent adrift in May 1968, Labour posted its first lead at the end of April 1970 and five polls then gave it an average 3 per cent advantage on 14 May.[133] This was largely due to Roy Jenkins' determined stewardship of the balance of payments after the devaluation, and Wilson called a general election for 18 June (he could have held on until the Spring of 1971). This caught Howell and the PSRU on the hop and meant that the detailed blueprint for change was rushed,[134] another reason why the Tory reformers did not experience a smooth implementation of their plans. Howell, however, under Heath's patronage, was able to add his own technocratic phrases to the foreword of the Party's manifesto, *A Better Tomorrow*,[135] which included the sentence 'There has been too much government: there will be less.'[136]

The surprise Conservative victory gave Heath a majority of 30 seats, leaving him in a solid position to plan for a full term, and for the Civil Service to be able to do the same. The Prime Minister followed Wilson's example with Marcia Williams in 1964 and appointed a party member and the former head of his private office in opposition,[137] Douglas Hurd, as his Political Secretary. Heath was very adroit in keeping the worlds of politics and officialdom apart in No 10.[138] We saw in Chapter 2 just how disruptive an influence Williams had been. Hurd was under no illusions that the tone he must set needed to be almost entirely the reverse of his predecessor, relatively easy for someone who knew the ways of Whitehall as a former civil servant, and an ex-diplomat at that, between 1952 and 1966.[139] (It is noteworthy how many reformers of Whitehall have experienced Whitehall from the inside.) 'I understood only', wrote Hurd, 'that I was expected to make peace where Mrs Williams had made war.'[140] And where Williams was almost Wilson's political wife,[141] Hurd's relationship with Heath was more like that of a civil servant with a Minister.[142]

Hurd was also, as opposed to Williams' ongoing struggle, happy to work with and through Heath's official Private Secretaries.[143] This was helped immeasurably as Hurd and Robert Armstrong, Heath's second Principal Private Secretary, were old school friends.[144] Hurd was later to claim that Williams' demands had established the job of Political Secretary as one to be taken seriously, especially as she had successfully commandeered an office adjacent to the Cabinet Room which Hurd inherited – a nice allusion to the geography of power.[145]

Heath decided to abandon Wilson's practice of having a politically appointed Press Secretary in No 10. He had thought about this deeply.[146] The job was given to Sir Donald Maitland who became his first Chief Press Secretary.[147] Maitland had been Head of the Foreign Office's News Department, Principal Private Secretary to two Labour Foreign Secretaries and, at the time of his appointment to Downing Street, Ambassador to Libya. Heath and Maitland had worked together during the EEC application negotiations in 1961–3[148] and his Foreign Office background 'reflected in part the priority Heath intended his Government to give to Europe'.[149] He served from 1970 until 1973 when his 'fixed-term three-year civil service posting' came to an end.[150] Maitland was highly respected by officialdom and by much of the media as 'meticulous' and 'civilised'.[151] He even tried unsuccessfully to have lobby briefings 'on the record'.[152] Douglas Hurd later wrote that Heath

> Felt that Mr Harold Wilson had made a great mistake in turning the Press Office into a political fief. A Prime Minister needs to be sure that his Chief Press Officer is loyally expounding his views, but the press also needs to feel that it is getting a fair statement of the Government's problems and intentions. It is very difficult to reconcile these two requirements. I doubt if it can be done by a political partisan. But there is a strong case for appointing someone from outside the narrow caste of Government information officers … It is an exposed position, and there will always be grumbles. But he came as near as anyone could to reconciling the different demands of an almost impossible job.[153]

All ran smoothly until Maitland's departure. He was succeeded by Robin Haydon, another former Head of the News Department at the Foreign Office, who was forced to leave a job he loved, as High Commissioner in Malawi (1971–3), for a role in which 'he had little natural aptitude. He was not cynical, or wily, enough to face the press corps successfully.'[154] Peter Hennessy thought this judgement harsh. His real misfortune was to have to explain the crises which engulfed the Heath Administration in its final phase.[155]

Somewhat surprisingly, Heath did not refashion No 10 as a whole. All continued as before, even to the extent that he allowed Barbara Hosking, who had joined Harold Wilson's Press Office from the Labour Party's headquarters, to remain in Downing Street; they got on very well.[156] Being a bachelor meant that No 10 and Chequers were run very differently from the way they had functioned under almost all Prime Ministers before and since. Heath expected his top officials to work with him and keep him company through long hours and weekends.[157] A flat at Chequers for his Private Secretaries, to make weekend work less onerous, was being considered when he left office.[158] It was as if Churchill's wartime practices had returned (though Heath did not work through the small hours or conduct business from his bed in the morning).

The newly returned Conservatives found the Civil Service in thoughtful mood in June 1970. After 13 years of Conservative rule, the service was very happy to welcome a new set of Ministers and new ideas in 1964. But the never-ending economic difficulties that Labour faced, self-induced in some instances, and the short-term measures which were frequently the result (piecemeal cuts alongside the abandonment of once heralded innovations such as the DEA and the National Plan), led to a degree of cynicism within official circles. Some senior civil servants were also disenchanted with Wilson's tactical style of government. Almost all found Heath admirable with, as Hurd saw it, his 'Substance first, then tactics and communication' approach.[159]

Even the Fulton Report, which senior civil servants had called for, as we have seen, turned into a near administrative civil war of attrition during the late Labour years over its partial implementation. The Fulton personnel reforms were not deemed to conflict with what the Conservatives had in mind. John Chilcot, in 1970 Assistant Secretary in the Civil Service Department, thought 'that while the Fulton Report was concerned with the Civil Service itself, that is the resources of skilled manpower available to government, improvements in the structure and machinery of government organisation were equally necessary. The changes [Heath required] are directed to the structure and are complementary to the Fulton reforms'.[160] David Howell, in *A New Style of Government*, agreed: 'The Fulton Report, so excellent in parts, gave the dominant weight of its attention to personnel. Most of the energies being applied by the Civil Service in implementing Fulton are directed to problems of staff reorganisation. This pamphlet in no way contradicts that approach. It merely argues that neither excellent men nor efficient machinery are much good without each other.'[161] The Conservative Party reformers and the Civil Service were in complete agreement on this.

The ongoing Fulton reforms have already been mentioned. But the key contentious issue arising from the Fulton Report, whether or not to implement single unified grading (SUG), continued to prove problematic. On 18 November 1971, Robert Armstrong wrote to Brian Gilmore, Private Secretary to the Lord Privy Seal Lord Jellicoe (Cabinet Minister for the CSD), informing him of the doubts that the National Whitley Council were expressing over extending SUG beyond under-secretary: 'The Official Side took the view that the objectives which had led the Fulton Committee to recommend unified grading could be met and were being met by other means, including a conscious attempt to reduce the number of classes and grades in the Civil Service and to promote mobility between them.'[162] The bitter dispute over SUG was coming to a quiet end. The attention of the Civil Service turned to quelling any possible embarrassment Hunt and possibly Fulton could cause over the abandonment of their cherished reform.[163] 26 November 1971 saw the final 'shelving' of SUG.[164]

Heath's commitment to long-term administrative planning and his pledge to put the country before political considerations ('a cheap and trivial style of government')[165] caught the Civil Service's imagination. 'Mr Heath's reformers were', as Peter Hennessy has rightly pointed out, 'preaching to the converted'.[166] Contrary to Lord Croham's belief that the reason why machinery-of-government issues were not included in the Fulton Committee's remit was because no Prime Minister would ever give away authority over such an important power,[167] Heath immediately handed the responsibility over to William Armstrong. Heath wanted his reform of Whitehall to be apolitical. There was also the fact that incoming Conservative Ministers were, on the whole, trustful of the Civil Service (though Keith Joseph had his doubts),[168] a rare occurrence in British post-war administrative history.

William Waldegrave, a member of the think tank in 1971–3 and then Political Secretary in No 10 in 1973–4, thought that Heath 'was perhaps the last Prime Minister ... who truly respected the British administrative and academic establishment'.[169] The Head of the Home Civil Service was asked to plan for the fundamental change that Heath required. The Civil Service Department used the summer recess – and the lengthy absence of Conservative Ministers – to go back to basics regarding the fundamental organization of government for the first and last time since the Haldane Committee in 1918.[170] ('One of the best presents which Labour left behind at No. 10 for Mr Heath', wrote a slightly caustic Marcia Williams, 'was the best present any Prime Minister can be given – time. The new Prime Minister inherited a situation in which he could plan his tactics, consult with his friends and sail his yacht in the weeks immediately following the Election.')[171]

In 1986, Lord Trend (as Sir Burke had become on retirement) opined that 'A comprehensive job on the Haldane model badly needs to be done'.[172] He had become a fan of Haldane in 1970 when he began to think closely about Heath's machinery-of-government reforms.[173] (Geoffrey Rippon, Chancellor of the Duchy of Lancaster 1970–2, had called for a Haldane-style inquiry in 1968.)[174] Indeed, 1970 has proved to be the closest Britain has come to a 'new Haldane'. There was one crucial difference between 1918 and 1970, however. The investigation that took place at the end of the First World War was peopled by a broad swathe of some of the finest thinkers from many of the professions central to the conduct of the Great War (including politicians and trade unionists).[175] In 1970, only senior members of the Civil Service took part. After the disjointed changes to the central machinery during the Wilson years – something Heath thought gimmicky[176] – the Civil Service was raring to have a chance to produce a much more coherent series of improvements, reforms which this time would take hold and last a generation as opposed to a few years.[177]

On 19 June, just days after the new government had taken office, Colin

Gilbraith, Sir William Armstrong's Private Secretary, sent the Prime Minister's Principal Private Secretary, Alexander 'Sandy' Isserlis,[178] a minute on the 'background philosophy on the organisation of the Executive'.[179] Isserlis did not last long at No 10 being identified, like Halls before him, as personally close to Harold Wilson. This alone would not have endeared him to Heath, but his fate was sealed when, on the first night of the Conservative Administration, Isserlis only reluctantly produced beer and pork pies[180] for Heath and William Whitelaw, shouting 'Grub's up!' to his new Prime Minister.[181] Whitelaw, especially, was 'shocked': 'Much, he felt, had gone amiss with the standards of public life since Sir Alec Douglas-Home had left office six years earlier.'[182]

Upon Isserlis's departure, Harold Wilson launched a short-lived press campaign on Heath's victimization of Wilson-appointed officials and thus his politicization of the Civil Service.[183] Like all British Civil Service postings, none traditionally change with a new government and Isserlis, according to *The Times*, was apparently 'given no reason to believe that he would not have the customary three-year term'.[184] The next day *The Times* carried a full-blooded rebuttal of the story:

> At the level of private secretary it is said to be fully accepted that when there is a change of Government, Ministers – because of the personal relationship involved – are free either to keep or change the men whom they 'inherit' from the previous Administration ... in Government quarters yesterday it was stated categorically that when Sir William Armstrong ... saw Mr. Isserlis before the appointment it was made clear that it was not certain that his appointment would outlast the Parliament if there was a change of Government ...[185]

The article came complete with a statement from Isserlis, fully supporting his removal and expressing 'satisfaction at the choice of an excellent successor'.[186] Robert Armstrong was Isserlis's replacement, much to the satisfaction of Heath, who described him as 'an unfailing source of good advice'.[187] Armstrong had been selected by Burke Trend and William Armstrong due to his being the conductor of the Treasury singers, something they rightly believed would help the new Principal Private Secretary to forge a close relationship with the introverted yet music-loving Heath.[188] Indeed, Robert Armstrong's father, Sir Thomas Armstrong, had been Heath's musical mentor at Oxford.[189]

In the lengthy memorandum given to Isserlis, which demonstrated that it had been underway before Heath's victory at the polls, Gilbraith[190] pointed out that there would be another clear distinction between the two reviews, in what amounted to a formal response to the PSRU:

> It does not start de novo, as Haldane did, by laying down broad principles from which particular conclusions could be drawn: useful though this approach might be if there

were a thorough-going enquiry into the machinery of government. Instead it seeks to offer a pragmatic basis from which to assess particular proposals for changes in the machinery of government.

To this end, and in the same vein as the Fulton Committee, 'Ministerial accountability should be preserved; policy must remain the prerogative of Ministers.'[191] Haldane would have been very disappointed with this as the starting block.

There was, however, a keenness to go as deep as the project allowed. For example, Gilbraith went on to explain that 'the central truth about the basis of the machinery of government [is] that it expresses the distribution of political authority in the state, both within the central government, and between central government and other public authorities'[192] and that 'politics is people, and so is the machinery of government.'[193]

The CSD's administrative theorizing went further. Taking on board the ideas put forward by the Tory planners for 'hiving-off', along with the CSD's somewhat half-hearted reviews into this possibility under Labour during 1969–70 (as detailed in Chapter 3), Gilbraith explained how the CSD was taking it rather more seriously this time, treating it as a potential step-change in contrast to the thinking during the last phase of the Wilson Government. He described hiving-off, or how 'the over-concentration of power within the Executive might be remedied', as a process towards 'non-Ministerial boards and agencies. The practice is an old one and is one that has undergone marked fluctuations over the period since 1832.'[194]

The concept of hiving-off across the board clearly exercised the CSD. Gilbraith expounded its thinking by telling No. 10 'There is no easy solution to the problems of government through hiving-off. If it can help, it is likely to be in limited fields of commercial activity and often here with a retention of some ministerial responsibility and therefore control.'[195] He then went on to explain the difficulties the CSD saw in widespread hiving-off. There are 'dangers', he wrote, 'in terms of manageability, of finding the men to manage such departments, and of giving the staff a sense of identity and recognition. They can reduce the degree of central collective Ministerial discussion of issues, because more policy work and conflicts are internalised.'[196] Ian Bancroft, by now Director General of Organisation and Establishments in the newly created Department of the Environment, saw other difficulties including ministerial status, nomenclature and pay.[197] It is not surprising, therefore, that the first candidate for hiving-off, the supplies function of the Ministry of Public Building and Works, was deemed inappropriate.[198]

The creation of hived-off agencies was inseparably linked with the establishment of super-departments – less work done better, with scope for a considerable reduction in Civil Service numbers.[199] This was not new, for the process had largely begun under the previous government and was anyway very much in tune with the prevailing management theory which preached that big was best with corresponding benefits of economies of scale and internal cohesion.[200] But it was now being contemplated with far greater forethought and as part of a larger reform framework. Problems were seen here too, especially, as the CSD believed, in the context of collective Cabinet government:

> The need for an efficient committee system cannot be reduced by the creation of super-Ministers or very large departments save to the extent that one is prepared to recognise that the indispensable processes of reconciling conflicting aims and co-ordinating divergent policies will merely be transferred to within the large departments themselves at the risk of eroding the collective responsibility between Ministers who are equal members of a government and accept equal responsibility for the sum of its policies.[201]

There were several targets for possible combination into super-ministries. First, the Board of Trade and the Ministry of Technology, which were, naturally, at the forefront of the drive to rejuvenate the British economy and arrest its perceived relative decline. Under Wilson, Mintech became a monster, eventually subsuming much of industry-sponsorship, too. All this was brought under one umbrella organization, the Department of Trade and Industry, with 'a real captain of industry', John Davies, the former Managing Director of Shell-Mex and BP and Director-General of the Confederation of British Industry, brought in from outside Parliament as its first Secretary of State.[202] It was clear where the new Department's heart was to lie when Sir Antony Part, from the traditionally *laissez-faire* Board of Trade,[203] was made Permanent Secretary over Otto Clarke (who, admittedly, was much nearer retirement age than Part) from the interventionist Mintech.[204] (Clarke's subsequent move to the Civil Service Department on a 'special duties' basis for only a few pre-retirement months[205] allowed the great 'Ottoman Empire-builder'[206] to dream up unilateral plans, akin to Baroness Sharp's prior to the election, to split the Treasury, to merge the public expenditure side with the CSD and, surmised Sir Samuel Goldman, to install Otto as its head.)[207]

The ongoing planning from the previous government ensured that the fusion of the Ministry of Housing and Local Government and the Ministry of Public Buildings and Works was made concrete with the creation of the Department of the Environment. The detail of the merger was, of course, handled in-house by the Civil Service. The man in charge of it was the head of machinery of government issues in the Civil Service Department, Ian Bancroft. Mark Schreiber (later Lord Marlesford) thought Bancroft very helpful and keen to make this part of the reform agenda a success. He also thought him 'a wonderful, typical, typical civil servant'. Marlesford has recounted a meeting in which many of the issues thrown up by the merger were thrashed out. 'Somebody said, more or less at the end, "Well, what are we going to call this new department?" and Ian Bancroft said,

"Ah! Now there's something the Ministers can decide!"[208]

Lastly, the Conservatives' down-playing of the role of overseas aid compared to the emphasis Labour had placed upon it meant that the Minister of Overseas Development was no longer given a Cabinet seat. The department was merged into the Foreign and Commonwealth Office,[209] not without some difficulty over whether the Foreign Secretary would answer relevant questions – or would they go directly to the Minister for Overseas Development Administration.[210] Other changes mooted by Armstrong and the Civil Service Department but not acted upon included establishing a Ministry of Construction, Social Services being given to the Home Office, or the Children's Department of the Home Office being given to the Department of Health and Social Security[211] and a merger between the Lord Chancellor's Department and the Home Office (something favoured by the ubiquitous Haldane).[212]

As we saw, the Tory planners and Heath were persuaded that a smaller, more strategically minded Cabinet would be essential.[213] The practical pursuit of a smaller Cabinet foundered on the experience of Sir Burke Trend. He informed Heath that the evolution of the Cabinet committee system necessitated a small number of senior Ministers in sinecure offices – such as Chancellor of the Duchy of Lancaster and Lord President of the Council – to chair committees as honest brokers with, as Sir Burke put it, 'no particular axe to grind'.[214] The Cabinet was reduced to 18 (from Wilson's 21) but was back up to 21 by 1973. The Government's total number of Ministers was cut from 88 to 71[215] (the First Parliamentary Counsel told the new Prime Minister that, under existing legislation, there could have been a total of 110 paid ministerial offices).[216] Trend was not entirely comfortable with the theory of super-departments either. In a letter to Heath, he thought that 'it would be a pity if the result were to disinterest other Ministers in the work of some of their colleagues; and it could be damaging if questions which are either important on merits or politically sensitive did not emerge for collective inspection until it was almost too late to affect the outcome'.[217] (One of the key reasons for splitting the Treasury in 1964 was that it was effectively handling very political dilemmas in-house, as it were, and not bringing the controversies to Cabinet.)

Another possibility for reform was the pursuit of federal departments, which was what the PSRU had in mind with fewer departments encompassing wider spheres of activity. This would be made possible by mass hiving-off,[218] super-departments squeezing the number of Secretaries of State and correspondingly increasing the significance of junior Ministers by delegating to them specific areas of responsibility.[219] It would also make 'departmental empires ... less clearly delineated' and so help to join up Whitehall.[220] The actuality diverged from the PSRU's ideas when the widespread hiving-off did not take place, yet what was left was the same mass of functions simply merged into bigger blocks, as witnessed by the Department of Trade and Industry and the Department of the Environment.

This was followed by a brief explanation on how the 'functional' approach to government, that is big departmental silos devoted to health, education, defence, etc., was more practical than one which was customer-driven or based on small territories, as evidenced by the overwhelming reliance upon this approach in the UK and abroad.[221] Moreover, a return to Churchill's discredited overlord system was discussed and dismissed.[222] The weighty document culminated with Gilbraith quoting J. S. Mill's *Representative Government*:

> As a general rule, any executive function, whether superior or subordinate, should be the appointed duty of some given individual. It should be apparent to the world who did everything, and through whose fault anything was left undone. Responsibility is null when nobody knows who is responsible. Nor, even when real, can it be divided without being weakened.[223]

This proved to be the last time the Civil Service was to have anywhere near the self-confidence to attempt such an exercise.

THE SIDELINING OF THE CONSERVATIVE PLANNERS

It may have been thought that after the immense legwork that organizations such as the PSRU and the former Permanent Secretaries' groups had undertaken, their efforts would be considered, and maybe that they would be consulted. This would be a reasonable presumption as the two main figures in the PSRU, David Howell and Mark Schreiber, were given posts in the new administration as Parliamentary Secretary in the Civil Service Department and as 'Special Adviser to the Government' ('a sort of gadfly' as William Armstrong described Schreiber's role), first based in the Treasury then the Old Admiralty Building.[224] (The PSRU ceased to function after the election.)[225] Not a bit of it. Trend and Armstrong believed and behaved as if the machinery of government was their charge, and theirs alone. As Lord Rothschild, who was to become the 'central capability's' first Director remarked after meeting the two knights for the first time, 'Until this week I never realised the country was run by two men whom I'd never heard of!'[226] Howell saw this as almost sinister:

> William Armstrong and Burke Trend moved in round the Prime Minister early on ... Armstrong and Trend moved in on me – lunch at the Athenaeum on the second day of the government. They said these were interesting ideas and they had also prepared a number of papers on how Whitehall could be run more effectively. And, hey presto, it was all in their hands, not mine. And Ted ceased to have any time to keep the momentum moving ... Momentum was lost as early as the first few weeks. I was a disappointed young man.[227]

The Tory reformers' work was essentially sidelined. The first Permanent Secretary of the new Department of Trade and Industry, Sir Antony Part, explained his ignorance of their work: 'I believe that a certain amount of study had been carried out by the Tories in opposition, and I know that they were advised by at least one former Permanent Secretary. But none of the detail of that came to our knowledge at the time when it was announced that the DTI was to be created.'[228] It is unclear to what extent Heath was an accomplice to giving William Armstrong almost complete control over the 'new style of government'.[229] But from the files deposited at Kew, it is quite plain that all roads led to Armstrong during the summer of 1970. They certainly did not lead to the Prime Minister, who spent August sailing for a week at Cowes and the rest at Chequers.[230] Joe Haines pointedly remarked that 'Edward Heath had decided not to do anything in his first hundred days'.[231] Heath, in an early attempt to avoid prime ministerial overload, thought August 'the proper time for politicians to cut down on their work in preparation for the coming parliamentary year'.[232] One of Heath's ministerial colleagues went as far as to describe Armstrong as one of Plato's fabled 'philosopher kings'.[233] It was certainly true that one of the most powerful civil servants of the twentieth century was approaching the zenith of his influence.

It seems likely that Heath asked Armstrong, after being impressed by the work of Howell and Schreiber *et al.*, to plan for the practical deployment of the new style. John Campbell was right to note that 'policies determined inflexibly in opposition ... may lack realism when they come to be implemented in office'.[234] Taking the power away from the pre-election planners frustrated them enormously. Just as was joyously depicted in the near-documentary first episode of *Yes, Minister*, the special adviser (Schreiber) was separated from his Prime Minister almost immediately and the Minister (Howell) was loaded with files which made his in-tray into a skyscraper[235] (I can still remember the late Sir Frank Cooper chuckling to himself when he admitted he was one of those officials overloading the naive Howell).[236]

Howell was also given the monumental task of collating the responses to the Prime Minister's call in August 1970, prompted by the Lord Privy Seal, for 'a review from first principles of all [government] functions and activities'.[237] As Lord Jellicoe wrote

> It was a major plank of our election platform that in our return to government we would reduce public expenditure and eliminate unnecessary activities ... It is therefore essential and urgent that we examine the whole range of government policies and the activities that flow from them which underlie the pattern of public expenditure which we inherited.[238]

Asking departments to analyse themselves and then to suggest and deliver savings was, in light of Sir Humphrey Appleby's later shenanigans, naivety on a colossal scale. But David Howell had to continue to push it along and produce periodic reviews of a government activity which, it became increasingly clear, had no chance of fruition. He was still greatly frustrated by this some 33 years later.[239]

Another ambitious attempt permanently to change the structure of the central machinery was the study in September 1970 to disperse government activity around the country (looked at again in the mid-1970s and also in 2003–4 by the Blair Government).[240] This project was ordered stepped up by the Prime Minister in December 1971.[241] By the autumn of 1973 there had been much research done but little actual dispersal partly, as Robert Armstrong wrote, 'because they themselves [civil servants] were very reluctant to be dispersed'.[242] A 'comprehensive statement', due for December 1973, was postponed as 'quite a lot of work [was] still to be done'.[243]

Immediately upon winning the June 1970 election, the businessmen's team was formed and injected into the government machine. They were to 'report directly to Ministers' but 'should retain their identity as a group under the leading businessmen and the Civil Service Department Ministers under the Prime Minister'.[244] The businessmen's team was expressly steered away from the Treasury by the Lord Privy Seal ('though the Treasury will have an important contribution to make').[245] It was headed by Richard Meyjes of Shell and comprised five others seconded for terms of around two years on salaries pegged at two-thirds of their current private sector pay – their companies generously paid the rest (some may think that this was not especially philanthropic but wise and relatively inexpensive investment).

The businessmen were thought by the PSRU to be a necessary addition to Whitehall, needed to bring fresh and vigorous business eyes to the lumbering and risk-averse bureaucracy. (Howell had to defend the concept, at a meeting of the forum of the National Staff Side of the Whitley Council, from charges of the businessmen being 'hatchet-men'.)[246] The men recruited, along with Meyjes, were A. Fogg of PA Management Consultants, R. East of Guest, Keen and Nettlefolds, K. F. Lane of Rio-Tinto Zinc Corp, H. R. Hutton of Hambros Bank and Derek Rayner of Marks and Spencer.[247] The team was in place by 1 August 1970.[248] The Management Projects Committee (MPC) with Heath in the Chair, Whitelaw (Lord President of the Council), Maurice Macmillan (Chief Secretary to the Treasury), Lord Jellicoe (Lord Privy Seal), Howell and Richard Meyjes met for the first time on 15 September 1970 to oversee the work of the businessmen.[249]

Jellicoe told the Prime Minister that 'Initially the businessmen would be concerned with analysing current procedures and making recommendations for improvements; later they may well be involved in implementation.'[250] Howell was more specific and thought that computer utilization, the nationalized industries, manpower, training, government-owned land and buildings and government construction were all worthy of the MPC's attention.[251]

The Civil Service was understandably suspicious of the businessmen. After all, was not the bringing in of these men on temporary contracts, to shed light on tasks and problems which officials had been struggling with all their working lives, a slur on their ability? (The same would be said of the Central Policy Review Staff, of which more later.) William Armstrong, however, understood the limited impact these men could in fact make. In a letter to Robert Armstrong he stated that 'There is no suggestion of the business team usurping the role of either Ministers or Departments. The main objective is to improve the performance of Departments by bringing extra expert resources to bear on certain problems which require analysis with the object of improving management.'[252]

The creation of 'central capability' and 'analytical capability', so crucial to the PSRU prior to the election, came to the fore around the end of September. The timing was due to Heath's wish to get the machinery in place as soon as possible; an October finish was wanted. It was thought that the central capability would direct the work of the analytical capability. Thus the priority was the central capability. Whereas the creation of the super-departments was largely down to William Armstrong and his team, the question of central capability fell to Trend, who, along with Armstrong, had come to believe that some form of bolstering was needed for the centre to handle its role more effectively. But, while he did indeed want it to work effectively, he had in mind a different kind of central capability. As Robin Butler, early member of the think tank and subsequent Cabinet Secretary to three Prime Ministers, puts it, 'I should think he did want it to work, within the limits of how he wanted it to work.'[253] ('I think Burke Trend, if he was the author of this, must have regretted it afterwards', observed Lord Hurd of Westwell.)[254]

We have seen how the PSRU envisaged a unit answering directly to the Prime Minister, but this was anathema to Trend, being one of the last of a powerful breed, the praetorian guards of the British Constitution. With so much of the Constitution based on convention, the man at the apex of officialdom is the highest form of authority as to what may and may not be done. Trend took this responsibility very seriously. It meant that Howell and Schreiber's wish for the Prime Minister to have sole control of the central capability[255] was simply never going to happen. It would mean that Trend had agreed to the Prime Minister becoming very definitely more than *primus inter pares*. This he could not countenance. Thus the new unit would be a resource for the whole Cabinet. This, though, did not stop it from acting on secretive prime ministerial missions on areas such as Northern Ireland[256] and Lord Jellicoe was later to describe its collective brief as 'a gloss' – for him it was 'primarily a device for strengthening the Prime Minister'.[257]

Trend fidgeted with what the PSRU and the Prime Minister wanted to call the central capability. Heath wanted it to be known simply and provocatively as the 'Think Tank'.[258] This made Trend nervous. Something so clearly different, with so eye-catching a title, could have given the unit too much independence – independence from Trend and, therefore, from what he judged to be legitimate Civil Service control. Trend later explained that

> It became known as the Think Tank, but they weren't quite the words you could see on the front of a White Paper ... And then it seemed to me that if you took the words which we finally did adopt, they came as near as I could come to being accurate about it. It *was* central, it *was* concerned with policy; and it *was* concerned with reviewing policy centrally and it consisted of a staff, not a political unit.[259]

Trend got his way and it was christened the Central Policy Review Staff, safely anchored in the Cabinet Office.

The Tory planners were losing the fight at every turn, but perhaps the biggest issue was who was going to head the think tank. Mark Schreiber had long planned for a think tank at the centre and was also very clear as to the type of person who was required to head it. 'The leader of the Central Capability will have to be', Schreiber wrote to Lord Jellicoe,

> 1. Intensely political in his motivation – that is to say passionately keen that the new Government succeeds, i.e. that the party is re-elected after five years ... Although he will of course have to have his own views of the national good he must be prepared to accept the ultimate bias of the Cabinet as his arbiter.
> 2. Able to think speculatively and intuitively.
> 3. Able to recognise when a piece of analysis which is presented is complete and technically sound.
> 4. Competent to decide which particular skills need to be applied for an interdisciplinary approach to any issue.
> 5. Able to organise and enthuse staff from varying professional backgrounds particularly getting the best from both career civil servants and from academics without infringing on the political impartiality and intellectual integrity of either.
> 6. Able to talk directly with Ministers and senior departmental officers without being patronised, feared or distrusted.
>
> It is clear that to fulfil these conditions, the Director of the Central Capability will have to be a committed Conservative.

Schreiber went on to recommend Peter Goldman, the Conservative candidate in the 1962 by-election at Orpington and former leading member of the Conservative Research Department, but also thought that either Charles Schultz or Thomas Paine, about to finish being Administrator of NASA and return to GEC – both US citizens – 'would, I believe, be a short cut to much of the experimentation'.[260] When asked about his wish for an overtly political appointee, Schreiber (now Lord Marlesford) confessed that it was really a *cri de coeur* for the head of the think tank to be anything but a civil servant.[261] In any event, a political Director was ruled out on 4 September 1970.[262]

A day earlier, the Lord Privy Seal informed the Prime Minister of the shortlist for the head of the Central Capability. The favoured top three were: Professor CR 'Dick' Ross (working for the OECD in Paris, lecturer in economics at the University of East Anglia and former Treasury man);[263] Ralph Turvey, Joint Deputy Chairman of the National Board of Prices and Incomes; and Robert Marshall, Deputy Secretary of the Central Economic Group within Mintech (soon to be the Department of Trade and Industry). The next four on the list were: Professor Hugh Ford, lecturer in engineering, Imperial College; Professor Alan Peacock, a free-market economist from York University; Christopher 'Kit' McMahon of the Bank of England; and Ian Fraser, working with the City Takeover Panel.[264] McMahon was the first to be offered the Directorship. He turned it down peremptorily – 'it had not proved possible to persuade' him, Lord Jellicoe reported to Heath. In the same meeting on 18 September, the Prime Minister, the Lord Privy Seal, Trend, William Armstrong and Robert Armstrong tried to thrash it out: 'The Prime Minister said that there would be an advantage in not moving Mr Marshall if it could be avoided ... the choice, therefore, lay between Professor Ford, who might not have quite enough breadth of experience, and Professor Ross, who might not have enough cutting edge.'[265] They plumped for energy over experience when, on 29 September, Professor Ford was chosen to head the new unit with Professor Ross to be offered the post of deputy.[266] David Howell made a late attempt to persuade the Prime Minister that the head of the businessmen's team, Richard Meyjes, would be the perfect candidate, owing to his sterling work since the election. Heath said that this was precisely why he did not wish to move him at this time.[267]

Ford was invited to Downing Street on 5 October and accepted the invitation to become the first Director of the Central Capability Unit, in the process asking the Prime Minister to write a couple of personal letters getting him out of commercial commitments. This Heath agreed to do.[268] And then, suddenly, a week later, Ford sent a handwritten letter to Heath explaining that due to these commitments he would not now, upon reflection, be able to take up the post.[269] This left precious little time for another candidate to be considered, agreed upon, consulted and accepted. As William Plowden, one of the first appointees to the CPRS, has explained, 'They were in a rush because Ford had turned it down very late in the day and the thing needed to get off the ground. They were probably in a panic.'[270]

Just then, one of those happy coincidences of life occurred. Victor Rothschild was visiting Downing Street as part of a review he was conducting into government research and development. R and D was part of the think tank's remit and Trend seized upon this overlap.[271] Rothschild had become known to the Cabinet

Secretary when he had been a part of the Kings Norton Committee looking at the future of the Atomic Weapons Research Establishment at Aldermaston in 1967–8.[272] This was a bold move by Trend. For Rothschild was larger than life. A third Baron of the English branch of the great banking dynasty, he had eschewed a life in the boardroom for one in the laboratory which eventually led him to the ranks of the Royal Society and the top of Royal-Dutch Shell's research team (taking in wartime service with MI5 and friendship with Anthony Blunt and Guy Burgess, two of the major British traitors of the twentieth century).[273] He had also joined the Labour Party some 20 years earlier, though his affiliation was never strong and, 'by the 1960s he had shed almost all his Labour beliefs'.[274] It was his enforced retirement from Shell at the age of 60 which left Rothschild with little to do and gave Trend his opening. The Prime Minister jumped at the chance and Rothschild's appointment was announced on 29 October 1970.[275]

The rush for appointments, appraisals and creations was driven by the Prime Minister's keenness to present a White Paper to the House of Commons as soon as possible. This fitted in with Heath's conviction that the machinery of government was, as Peter Hennessy describes, a 'first-order' question.[276] Heath wanted the tools to be correct and in place before the real work of policy could begin. The *Reorganisation of Central Government*, 'a monument to reason in Whitehall',[277] was unveiled on 15 October 1970. Heath was keen for the White Paper and the reforms contained within to be 'presented primarily as a considered reorganisation to meet the requirements of good management and thus something that can be regarded as lasting, not merely as a political move'.[278] It can therefore be seen as a thoroughly Fabian document – perhaps the last.[279] This made Douglas Hurd very nervous.

As the Prime Minister's Political Secretary, Hurd was in a difficult position, forever trying to balance Heath's wish to govern in a statesmanlike way with the basic political need for re-election. In a letter to Michael Wolff, special adviser and speech writer,[280] Hurd pleaded that it was 'important that the ancestry of tomorrow's White Paper should be traced back to the work which the Party and in particular the Prime Minister, did on this subject in Opposition.' Hurd was troubled by the news that Harold Wilson, still leader of the Labour Party, was going to claim 'that this is all stuff which he himself had prepared in his last months of Office and that there is no originality about it. There is a tendency in the Civil Service to take a similar view.'[281] Hurd pointed to Boyle's 1965 review, the PSRU, Lady Sharp's group, the Sundridge conference and the subsequent planning by the Shadow Cabinet.[282]

Even this document caused friction between the Civil Service and Howell. For Howell had been writing Heath's speeches on machinery of government for over five years and he had even provided the first drafts of the 1966 Conservative manifesto.[283] He had been led to believe it was to be he who would write the

White Paper.²⁸⁴ But now, in government, this access to power had been disrupted. Howell's writing was to form the first draft with Trend handling 'revision and editing'.²⁸⁵ In fact, the task of blending all the manifold changes was given to John Mayne, a member of the Cabinet Office on secondment from the Ministry of Defence (who joined the CPRS on its creation).²⁸⁶

To such deeply committed advocates as Howell, *The Reorganisation of Central Government* White Paper was a disappointment.²⁸⁷ What in retrospect now looks like a last-minute addition of philosophy on top of a technocratic blueprint (akin to the genesis of the *Modernising Government* White Paper of 1999 which literally had a last-minute politically written foreword foisted on it by a disappointed No 10),²⁸⁸ it opens with a sentiment the PSRU would have been proud of: 'This Administration has pledged itself to introduce a new style of government. More is involved than bringing forward new policies and programmes: it means resolving the issue of the proper sphere of government in a free society; and improving the efficiency of the machinery intended to achieve the aims it sets itself within that sphere.' The introduction was completed by similar thoughts:

> It [the months-long review] has been concerned not merely with departmental boundaries but with the central mechanism by which public policy is made and carried out. The results will therefore be longer lasting and will remove the need for continual changes for a considerable period in the future. The product of this review will be less government, and better government, carried out by fewer people. Less government, because its activities will be related to a long-term strategy aimed at liberating private initiative and placing more responsibility on the individual and less on the State. It will be better government, because the tasks to be done will be better defined and fewer in number, requiring fewer Ministers and fewer civil servants to carry them out.

This statement of intent was undermined a few pages later. In a classic manoeuvre, the White Paper began to blend political wishes with customary Civil Service caution:

> There will be a sustained effort to ensure that among those functions which remain a necessary part of central government, executive blocks of work will be delegated to accountable units of management, thus lessening the load on the departmental top management. These are, however, major changes *and will take some time to bring about* [emphasis added].

The White Paper degenerated into a dry list of machinery-of-government changes bereft of the philosophy which had given birth to them. There was even space for a lament about the lot of the contemporary public servant: 'The Civil Service itself, as it is given clearer objectives and more sharply defined responsibilities, will find that the work of public administration will again become more satisfying and that relations with the public it serves will improve.' The sentence was not penned by Howell.

Two sentences did, however, hint at what really informed the Civil-Service-authored White Paper: 'The fulfilment of these aims will improve the efficiency of government. This does not mean an increase in State power, nor any sacrifice of humanity and compassion in public administration.' This, in effect, is where Howell lost Heath to the ever consensus-seeking Civil Service. For Howell's ideas were unconcerned with 'compassion' but radically focused on making Britain an efficient nation once again. Howell's time was still to come; his beliefs were to be at the very centre of the neo-liberalism of the 1980s. Heath had supported, encouraged and listened to his young tyro. In his head, he knew he was right, but his heart contained too much of the 'compassion' for an iron adherence to market forces.[289]

The period from June to November 1970 witnessed one of *the* great showdowns between a still powerful 'permanent government' and the temporary occupiers of the UK's governing echelon. Two opposing views of how the State should operate, and in what fields, vied for the beliefs of a torn Prime Minister. In the event, he essentially opted for preserving the status quo. *The Reorganisation of Central Government* changes, alongside those that came as a consequence of the Fulton Report, meant that some new systems had been constructed and a few new people had been recruited to work alongside a tough old system run by tough old professionals. The Civil Service did not look very different in November 1970 following the decade-long rush of reforms. But Heath had spent six precious months putting it all in place. Now it was time to face the questions of policy that Heath thought demanded new and reformed machinery. The question was, had the changes equipped the Civil Service for the challenges of the 1970s?

5

Pressure

THE HEATH GOVERNMENT AND ITS NEW MACHINERY 1971–4

THE CENTRAL POLICY REVIEW STAFF

For Edward Heath the publication of *The Reorganisation of Central Government*, according to his Principal Private Secretary Robert Armstrong, meant that his interest effectively turned away from administrative matters towards policy.[1] How the new and reformed machinery fared will provide the bulk of this chapter. Yet, though the White Paper brought an end to the somewhat frenetic machinery-work of the summer and autumn of 1970, it did not signal a complete end to Heath's interest in Whitehall. The dark cloud of suspicion which had hung over the Treasury increasingly since the early 1960s became significant once again. And again, it was a Prime Minister who led the way, much as Macmillan and Wilson had done.

'Heath was known to be hostile to the Treasury', thought his second Chancellor of the Exchequer, Anthony Barber,[2] a man who did not want the Treasury.[3] This was another belief he owed in some part to Macmillan. Heath felt it had been lukewarm about the EEC negotiations in the early 1960s[4] and that its officials were habitually gloomy about the prospects for the British economy.[5] 'It is always the Prime Ministers who have not served in the Treasury who are the most suspicious of it', thought Robin Butler.[6] While Samuel Brittan (the country's leading Treasury-watcher of the day) thought Heath disliked the Treasury 'in a silly, mindless way. You must realize that I'm not very enamoured of Heath. It's like wanting to whip the messenger that brings bad news.'[7] The Treasury had begun a rearguard action in order to defend itself against any potential reduction in its power within days of Heath's victory at the polls, similar to that which saw it retain control of public expenditure when under pressure from the DEA.[8] The issue of curtailing the Treasury's reach had been brought up during the extensive planning for government by the Public Sector Research Unit, and by David Howell in particular. He did not drop his ideas once in government. On the contrary, for the first year in office, he kept the issue alive. His departmental boss, Lord Jellicoe, seemed to be captured by his Permanent Secretary, Sir William Armstrong, when in December 1970 he told the Prime Minister that

> One suggestion in the 'Black Book' was that there should be a Ministry of Programmes responsible for expenditure programmes. The Ministry would be produced by splitting the Treasury into two Departments either from the start or within two years. Our view is that such a split is neither desirable nor practicable now. Some strong arguments have been put forward against it at any time.[9]

Brian Reading, the Government's politically appointed economic adviser based in the Cabinet Office and an 'intellectually unconventional' figure,[10] was also very much against Lord Jellicoe's thinking. He believed that the Treasury's monopoly on advice simply had to be broken in a manner that went beyond the 1960s attempts.

Reading was fearful that even these modest attempts to break the Treasury's stranglehold were being reversed. 'From the Treasury's standpoint, Neddy [at this time the subject of a possible review][11] is a rival which has been satisfactorily disarmed and which they now intend should be stripped of any last pretence of influence over economic policy formulation ... I strongly challenge the Treasury's monopoly of policy formulation in the economic field because of – A. its disastrous record; B. its necessarily narrow and departmental approach.'[12] Robert Armstrong, formerly a Treasury man, tried to head Reading off:

> I am very much a believer in having properly thought out strategies, and for in-depth study of alternative strategies ... But I would myself stop short of your 'second force' solution, which assumes a separate source of authoritative advice to the Government advising in public, because I think that conflicting streams of public official advice would make it more difficult rather than easier for the Government to arrive at a sensible and coherent strategy.[13]

One might think that there are three 'I's too many for an impartial civil servant in that statement, and this leads us onto another key aspect of the Heath years. Though the William Armstrong–Trend axis was key to understanding who was giving the final advice that reached Heath's ears in the administration's first months, and Trend remained prominent until his retirement in 1973, the duet of Armstrong and Armstrong was increasingly influential. An early and powerful example of this was how Robert Armstrong finally put paid to pressure to split the Treasury in 1970–1.

David Howell proved to be the most consistent agitator for two central economics departments. He later regretted that the PSRU did not have a clear strategy for splitting the Treasury and also came to realize that it was wrong-headed to think that it could be done effectively at all.[14] What proved to be his final attempt was a letter sent to the Prime Minister in February 1971:

The Treasury for many years now has had two roles – on the one hand the control of expenditure, on the other responsibility for economic, financial and fiscal policies, etc. In the kind of structure envisaged in the Prime Minister's plans for the reform in government decision-making, these two functions are likely to become increasingly divergent and distinct from each other in character. Whether this points to the emergence of a separate Ministry of Programmes remains an open question. But the more that the expenditure side of the Treasury is developed under the influence of PAR [Programme Analysis and Review] into a capability for the analysis of departmental programmes, the more anomalous it will be to lump this part of the central government mechanism in with the rest of the Treasury's work.[15]

This prompted a response from Robert Armstrong to Heath which demonstrated the extent of Armstrong's personal involvement in policy advice:

Sir William Armstrong sees no future in splitting the Treasury and having a 'Ministry of Finance' and a 'Ministry of Programmes'. Mr. Macleod was against it; so is Mr. Barber. The split, or serious discussion of it, would be thought to undermine the Chancellor's position.[16]

I would add to those points that when the reform of government was announced last October you made a good deal of the point that, once it had been carried through, there should be a period of stability without future major changes. Dividing the Treasury would be inconsistent with that.

The suggestion here is that, if you agree, it should be made clear to Mr. Howell that this is not an idea with which you propose to proceed, at any rate during the present Parliament.

Heath simply scrawled 'Agreed' in the margin.[17]

It would be wrong to think that Macleod was totally against reform. In the few weeks of government before his death, he was drawing up a significant set of major public expenditure cuts.[18] He also called Howell in to listen to his ideas, suggesting that the PSRU's wish to see less but better government was also in Macleod's mind.[19] ('Tony Barber was not a strong Chancellor, Macleod would have been'[20] was Lord Hurd's appraisal, though Brittan thought 'There would have been little or no change if Macleod had not died – he once told Douglas Allen "you do the economics and I'll do the politics".')[21]

Armstrong wrote to Howell two days later and, with an inescapable tone of glee, told him that due to the stability issue 'and other reasons' a split had been ruled out during the present Parliament.[22] 'Now you know what we were up against' was Howell's response to being presented with this document 32 years later[23] (he was to 'give a wry grin' in early 2005 at the Conservative Party's plans to cut Whitehall bureaucracy by £35 billion).[24] Whether Heath agreed to rule out a Treasury split on principled or on pragmatic grounds is unclear, but in 1977 he would advocate a cleavage in ministerial economic responsibility. Speaking to the House of Commons' Expenditure Committee hearings on 'The Civil Service', Heath explained that regarding 'the question of what should be done about the Treasury, the CSD and public expenditure, my views have developed, I think, since that time [the publication of *The Reorganisation of Central Government*]. I think that today it is impossible for the Chancellor of the Exchequer to carry the burdens covering the whole of the field and to do so effectively ... it would be possible to have one Minister who was dealing with the question of expenditure ... [and another] with the question of taxation, overseas policy and so on.'[25]

Yet it would be wrong to think that Robert Armstrong was running away with his own ideas. He was simply embracing wholeheartedly his perceived role as gatekeeper and bureaucratic bodyguard to his Prime Minister, carrying out Heath's will as he understood it. His experiences here put him on the path to being one of the outstanding civil servants of the post-war period. Heath welcomed Armstrong's behaviour unreservedly, going so far as to describe Robert Armstrong as one of the most intelligent and companionable officials he had ever worked with.[26]

The question of Treasury influence in the Heath era is fascinating. While Wilson's 1964 creation of the DEA has caught the historical imagination, the decline of the Treasury's authority during 1970–4 has slipped by largely unnoticed. For the Treasury was at its lowest level of influence during these years than at any time since 1945. The combination of a relatively weak Chancellor, a suspicious Prime Minister persuaded of the damage that uncontrolled, unsophisticated Treasury power had wrought, and an empowered DTI (though headed by the ineffective John Davies until the more dynamic Peter Walker left Environment and replaced him as Secretary of State in November 1972) led to it being sidelined.[27] Its advice was increasingly marginalized.[28] Lord Croham, then Sir Douglas Allen, the Permanent Secretary to the Treasury in this unenviable position, went as far as to say that 'when the pound went soft [moving in May 1972 to the European exchange rate system and then eventually floating freely just six weeks later in June 1972],[29] Heath thought the Treasury was trying to pull the wool over his eyes'.[30]

The creation of the Central Policy Review Staff was part of the shift away from monopoly Treasury advice. Its establishment, as we have seen, was delayed over who was to head it. In the event, Victor Rothschild was appointed but added to the wait when he told a 'displeased' Prime Minister that he must have three months' holiday at his house in Barbados.[31] This was on the advice of Rothschild's friend, John Louden, Chief Executive of the Royal Dutch-Shell Group, who told him that he wouldn't know how exhausted his job with Shell had made him until he finished.[32] But it appears that Rothschild either did not want a total rest or interpreted his friend's advice very wisely. For he used the time between his appointment at the end of October 1970 and the official starting date of the CPRS on 1 February 1971 to do a milk-round of Ministers asking them the question 'You now have a new machine; is there anything it can do for you?'[33] Rothschild's initial appreciation of the CPRS's function was based on the Executive Office of the (US) President and so he also used his holiday to visit Henry Kissinger, National Security Adviser, and Charles Schultz, former Director of the Bureau of the Budget.[34] Rothschild quickly realized how different the competing visions of what the CPRS should be were.[35] John Mayne, effectively the draftsman of *The Reorganisation of Central Government* White Paper, flew out to Rothschild and spent five days arguing over the correct interpretation of his own words (though, it will be remembered, Trend's thoughts) as regards the CPRS's role and functions.[36]

As we saw in Chapter 4, there were many parents involved in the creation of a 'central capability' or think tank. Various elements in the Conservative Party and the Civil Service all saw a need to fill 'the hole in the centre' (as Lord Hunt of Tanworth, Cabinet Secretary 1973–9, described it in 1983).[37] But the detail involved in building the new unit proved controversial. These differing perspectives continued the debate of September–October 1970 over who should head the unit. Howell saw it as a force to bring greater economic coherence, especially with reference to the long-term, to the whole business of government.[38] For Mark Schreiber, the key was to consider government strategy in relation to reality – since previous governments' failure to do this 'explains many of the mistakes only revealed by time'. He also believed that facilitating the reduction of government activity, on which the PSRU had been so keen, should be a major factor.[39] The Prime Minister thought that the think tank should focus on the allocation of resources[40] and that his experience of Cabinet government showed there to be far too much short-term fire-fighting.[41]

For his part, the Cabinet Secretary was his usual 'congenital snag hunting' self (to borrow the glorious snipe of Hugh Dalton's at the mandarinate).[42] Trend had already in August 1970 assumed responsibility for the practical construction of the CPRS, as head of the Cabinet Office in which it was to be housed.[43] In December 1970, Trend asked for, and received, authorization 'to consider in more detail how the capability should be organised, staffed, related to the rest of the Cabinet Office, etc' as his concerns over how the think tank was to emerge, remained.[44] His unease continued past the CPRS's creation. For example, he sought from the Prime Minister in March 1971 'a very clear ruling [on] ... where the CPRS is definitely to take charge and to be able to require the departments concerned to provide full information and co-operation. Initially this may be a rather painful process, and a few tears may be shed in the course of it. Nevertheless, it is essential if the CPRS are to know where they are going, what their powers and duties are.'[45] The somewhat dry official terms of reference which were presented to Cabinet on 3 February 1971, just as the CPRS got underway, were as follows:

1. To examine and analyse selected major policy issues referred to the C.P.R.S. by the Ministerial Committee on the Central Capability.
2. To help Ministers develop a collective strategy to achieve their major objectives.
3. To assess the compatibility of government action, proposed action or non-action with this strategy.
4. To identify, and to brief the Cabinet and Ministerial Committees on, those selected policy issues about which decisions are necessary to achieve the Government's major objectives.
5. To help to select PAR programmes and to analyse the results.[46]

Added to this list was the issue of government-sponsored science. To give all science work at the heart of government to what was to become the CPRS was mooted by Trend in July 1970.[47] It would have meant that the Chief Scientific Adviser to the Government 1964–71, Sir Solly Zuckerman, an old friend and rival of Rothschild's, would have been subservient to him though potentially with right of direct access to the Prime Minister, as Heath suggested.[48] (Kenneth Rose describes the two as pursuing 'each other with malignant fidelity', though they proved they could work together during the deliberations of the Kings Norton Committee in 1968, a group of outsiders, of which Rothschild was a member but Zuckerman was not, being the Government's Chief Scientist.)[49] The issue returned to the fore in February 1971 when the Prime Minister suggested it might be better not to merge all central scientific advice within the CPRS.[50] But eventually this was done in March 1971, when Sir Alan Cottrell accepted the post of Chief Scientific Adviser, within the think tank.[51]

Rothschild immediately acquired a stature the magnitude of which was only previously enjoyed by the Secretary of the Cabinet or Head of the Home Civil Service. 'Lord Rothschild roamed like a condottiere through Whitehall,' Douglas Hurd wrote, 'laying an ambush here, there breaching some crumbling fortress which had outlived its usefulness. He wrote in short sharp sentences; he made jokes; he respected persons occasionally but rarely policies. He had the independence of position and personality which was needed to make the CPRS a success from the start'.[52]

Another way in which the CPRS differed from most of post-war Whitehall – certainly since the inter-war years which saw the entrenchment of university-to-retirement cloistering – was in its staffing. One of the key *raisons d'être* for the CPRS was in the perceived need to bring in fresh talent from outside the Civil Service and to establish links outside the bureaucracy. The criticism that the bureaucracy had become far too insular had been a particular refrain of critics for many years, certainly since Balogh's 'The Apotheosis of the Dilettante' and the Fabians' *The Administrators*. The CPRS was to have an exciting blend of high-flying young insiders and outsiders drawn from different walks of academia, commerce and industry.⁵³ The iconoclasm, however, did not extend to educational background – all of the first members of the CPRS were from Oxbridge.⁵⁴ Hugh Heclo and Aaron Wildavsky (visiting American scholars with excellent Whitehall access) noted that 'the Janus-like nature of CPRS personnel reflects the desire to plug into sources of information both inside the system, so as not to be surprised, and outside the governmental apparatus, so as to be better able to take the initiative. The mixture of insiders and outsiders epitomises the dual need to use the existing machine and to contribute something novel'.⁵⁵

Rothschild was instrumental in many of the appointments, more so for those outside Whitehall.⁵⁶ 'From the start,' Rothschild later wrote, 'it seemed to me that our job was to analyse problems and proposals and for that we needed excellent analytical brains: so that was what I tried to get.'⁵⁷

William Waldegrave, freshly back from Harvard, was one of the first to be given a post, after his father asked Lord Jellicoe, Lord Privy Seal, if he needed a 'messenger-cum-tea boy'.⁵⁸ Waldegrave was clearly identifiable as a Conservative after being politically active as a student, but he had to leave this aside as he became a 'proper civil servant, temporarily established' and was not even allowed to go to the Party Conference. The politically neutral tone of the CPRS was also set by Rothschild who was by now 'very apolitical'.⁵⁹ Lord Waldegrave was recruited by first meeting Rothschild and, once the Director was satisfied, seeing Trend (along with someone from the Cabinet Office's personnel office).⁶⁰ This was, according to Waldegrave, so that it could be said that the Secretary to the Cabinet had personal oversight of all personnel issues within his fiefdom.⁶¹ But the truth was that the CPRS was beyond Trend's jurisdiction – as it had to be. For it to function irreverently, it had to be free of the 'suffocating layer-cake of successive administrative generations filtering every initiative to purest innocuity', as Peter Jay described Civil Service grading and management.⁶² For Hurd, 'Because Ted believed in the efficacy of government, getting its organisation right, getting links with the private sector, getting people in who were not just civil servants by temperament but quite troublesome, ingenious, irritating people, getting them into government and getting the grit in the oyster was part of what he thought it was all about.'⁶³

The CPRS was in but not of the Cabinet Office.⁶⁴ Yet Trend was not a man to be beaten easily. He made sure that one of his chief lieutenants, John Mayne, was part of the CPRS from the start.⁶⁵ 'There were tensions right from the beginning,' observed Lord Butler, 'there were those who wanted to be iconoclastic and original and those who very much wanted to fit us into the machine, and the particular apostle of that was John Mayne.'⁶⁶ Rothschild was nothing if not subtle about the sinews of power and treated Mayne (and Professor Ross) with suspicion from the very beginning.⁶⁷ Mayne was widely thought to be 'Burke's Spy' in the enterprise.⁶⁸

The number employed in the Think Tank varied between 12 and 18 – never more than the physical limit that could be accommodated around Rothschild's table on a Monday morning for the CPRS's strategy meeting,[69] straight after Rothschild and Trend's regular weekly 'prayer meeting'.[70] This excluded secretarial and other support staff.[71] Above this, so Rothschild thought, benefits would only be achieved with an organization of around 200 to 300.[72] Rothschild recognized the limits to remaining miniature: 'so small an organisation made it essential to have outside consultants, so we built up a network of these, none of them paid'.[73] This kept the cost of the CPRS to a very modest £1 million a year (Rothschild's picking up much of the hospitality tab – the official expenses limit was just £100 – helped tremendously).[74] The Prime Minister told Rothschild to keep the £1m figure to himself.[75]

The Rothschild–Trend relationship, highly important, never really achieved great warmth. Mark Schreiber, joint-author of a CPRS Report into Concorde (Rothschild was forever co-opting non-CPRS members to work for him through his unparalleled network),[76] believed that Trend could not accept an outsider, even one as eminent and personally picked as Rothschild, as an equal. Rothschild perhaps anticipated this, for he negotiated a salary commensurate with the Prime Minister and only £1,000 less than Trend.[77] Such are the power-rankings of Whitehall explained – and Rothschild clearly understood it from the outset. Hurd remembered another minor friction:

> Once Victor got himself set up he spent a lot of time making fun of Burke Trend and teasing him and having quite a lot of quarrels with him. I don't say it was serious but Victor was a great tease, a very entertaining, witty man and Burke Trend was a rather solid fellow, very, very nice, very straight and not gifted with a huge sense of humour outside his particular area. Victor and his young men spent a lot of time teasing Burke.[78]

The CPRS had a 'very informal atmosphere'.[79] The average age of those in the early Think Tank was 35,[80] very young compared to other units of comparable seniority in the Whitehall hierarchy. It was heady stuff, thought Waldegrave, to be so young while addressing bureaucratic titans on equal terms, to their 'astonishment and alarm' – something largely unheard of.[81] For William Plowden, it was 'an extraordinary feeling to have in central Whitehall, this one of great flexibility and the possibility that with a sufficiently determined push one could get the machine to go in any of several possible directions. What worries me mainly is not having clear enough ideas about exactly where I'd like it to go …'[82]

Along with what Ted Heath retrospectively saw as its mission statement – 'if not think the unthinkable, then at least to express the uncomfortable'[83] – its young, dynamic membership and its fabulously wealthy Director, the CPRS was undoubtedly the place to be.[84] Plowden thought it 'The most enjoyable and exciting two years of my life.'[85] But apart from the glitzy appearance, in its first years it was certainly a unit with intellectual thrust. After the debate about how it would operate, the CPRS settled down to fulfilling three functions: early warning, keeper of government strategy and scrutineer of selective policy.

CPRS AND THE EARLY WARNING SYSTEM

The CPRS's early warning system (EWS) was not its most successful role. There were three EWS exercises, in August 1971, February 1972 and July 1972. The impetus for them came from two sources. Willie Whitelaw (Lord President of the Council 1970 and from March 1972 transferred to Northern Ireland) provided a political impetus by saying that 'he did not want to read about V & G[86] in the newspapers in his bath'.[87] Rothschild was more precise in his wish for an EWS:

> Worthwhile analysis of major issues could not be done in a short time. The CPRS therefore needed adequate early warning of impending major issues on which Ministers would be required to take collective decisions affecting the achievement of the Government's major objectives. Early warning of future problem areas could in certain cases be secured by analytical methods. But they [the CPRS] did not expect that such techniques could provide all the answers. It was more important that information about possible future problems should flow freely between departments and the CPRS ...[88]

In effect, Whitelaw wanted advance notice of political pitfalls and Rothschild practical help on what the CPRS was to focus upon. Rothschild suggested to Permanent Secretaries that the information he required would be '[e]vents or developments within a department's responsibility which, if they occurred, could either affect the collective strategy of the Government or be a source of major embarrassment to the Government and which would require urgent collective decisions at Cabinet level.'[89] A project like this could have ended up being huge. Rothschild avoided this by observing that '[t]he object must, I think, be to achieve the maximum effect with minimum labour'.[90] The first attempt at looking into the future, worked at over the summer of 1971, was disappointing. Responsibility fell to Robin Butler (with Plowden and Waldegrave also involved).[91] While most departments shared information well, some did not. The Department of Education and Science (with Margaret Thatcher at the helm) was unco-operative,[92] as was, much more significantly, the Treasury.

The Treasury was very concerned, with Douglas Allen informing Rothschild in May 1971 that 'Your proposed machinery is not suitable for certain kinds of highly sensitive problem which ... the Treasury may be concerned with from time to time.'[93] Allen was worried that a leaked warning over economic crisis – devaluation was again on the horizon – may become a self-fulfilling prophecy due to the financial markets' overriding fixation with confidence. Rothschild was convinced that to produce an early warning document without any economic or financial information at all was plain silly. In his diary, Plowden was musing over exactly this:

> Can we really stand back and let it possibly happen [devaluation] without any attempt to make considered decisions abt what shd be done if it does? Shd we not insist that this kind of failure to look realities in the face is what we're paid to prevent? But if we do insist, it may so incense the Tsy against our activities that they'll turn against us and thus threaten our existence, or certainly our effectiveness.[94]

The Prime Minister wrote to Rothschild on 26 July 1971 saying that he did not wish to see sensitive Treasury information in what was to be a paper circulated to the whole Cabinet.[95] Heath mused further over 'whether this memorandum should be restricted to use by himself and others at the centre, rather than be circulated to the Cabinet'.[96] This idea was not followed up and the document was distributed to his Cabinet colleagues, though with the Prime Minister's warning that 'handling of this requires very strict control'.[97]

The absence of economic information from the Treasury was not the only problem. How much material to include was another test. From the beginning, Plowden was uneasy over the EWS. In a letter to Butler, he wondered

> Whether you are right so much to emphasise in this procedure the need to give <u>Ministers</u> the chance to think about problems before they become problems ... In an imperfect world crises will happen weekly, and one should reluctantly be prepared for the fact that a Cabinet may not want to spend long discussing ... a list of issues some of which may never happen. In this situation what is important is ... the thought given to it by the CPRS against the day when despite our EWS it <u>has</u> become a crisis and the Cabinet have to deal with it at 48 hours notice.[98]

The first EWS report was divided into sections covering public expenditure; foreign affairs and defence; prices, industrial relations; pay claims; industrial policy; the machinery of government; home affairs and other items.[99] In a covering note for Ministers to the first EWS paper, the think tank noted that '[t]he problem has, of course, been to devise a net which will catch only fish of the right size. The CPRS does not expect, at this first attempt, to have got the size of the mesh exactly right. It will no doubt need altering in the light of experience.'[100]

The CPRS themselves were disappointed by their efforts: 'It was agreed that the first early warning schedule had, in retrospect, been the least successful of the CPRS papers to-date and that the exercise would only serve a useful purpose if it encouraged Ministers to think ahead and set in hand contingency planning against possible developments.'[101] That contingency planning for future events had not been a key, practical, initial aim of the EWS was a failure.[102] The lack of economic information, speculation on too many topics which may never cause a problem and little or no advice as to future action made the first exercise near to useless.

The Treasury, Allen in particular, were adamant that they would not share their sensitive information in any future exercise, 'unless there is an explicit instruction from the Prime Minister and the Chancellor that business is to be conducted in future in an entirely different way' than the usual Treasury–Chancellor–Prime Minister one-way bad-news system.[103] The unimpressive first stab at the EWS led to renewed efforts to make it more valuable. In November 1971 a deal between Butler and Peter Carey (prior to joining the CPRS, an Under Secretary in the Ministry of Technology and then the Department of Trade and Industry) with Allen of the Treasury allowed for *some* information to be provided by the Treasury on the proviso that future draft EWS memoranda would be given to the Treasury for vetting before distribution.[104] The second EWS memorandum was more focused than the first, with no 'purely speculative items'.[105] It was approved 'in principle' by the Cabinet in a discussion even shorter than that which greeted the first one.[106] But it still offered no solutions.

Rothschild demanded that for the third attempt 'the CPRS must be quite clear about the action which it wished to result from the exercise. There might be an advantage in linking it more coherently with the Strategy exercise [the CPRS exercise in plotting the Government's course for the future, which we will come to later]'.[107] Certainly, the CPRS knew that the EWS had to become far more practical. As Hurd has said, 'Early warning systems are no good if the doctrine is you don't take any action.'[108] Progress reports from the departments were uncomplimentary and inside the Treasury its very continuance was denigrated.[109]

The third EWS paper proved to be its last. Upon completion, it was sent to Trend in draft form. Trend was uncomfortable with its 'confidential' classification, thinking 'secret' more appropriate. The CPRS thought its circulation was too restricted already and that this would limit it further. At this time, Heath returned to his thought a year earlier, that perhaps the EWS should be just for him and selected other Ministers – Douglas-Home (Foreign Secretary), Barber, Whitelaw, Carrington (Defence) and Carr (Lord President). This was agreed on 19 July 1972.[110] A restricted readership meant that to collate the EWS would involve officials from departments whose Ministers could not see it – a constitutionally unsound practice. Rothschild and the CPRS were 'dismayed' by this turn of events.[111] They thought it undermined the whole point of the EWS which was originally constructed as a collective tool for the whole Cabinet. Rothschild thought that if the EWS was to be discontinued, 'the bi-annual strategic reviews would provide continuing opportunities for looking ahead at contingencies and identifying major strategic issues'.[112] Heath agreed and ordered that the July 1972 memorandum be the last.[113]

Fascinatingly, this was not the end of the story. One of the key critics in the unbelieving Treasury was John Hunt. By the autumn of 1973 he was Cabinet Secretary. On 26 October 1973 he wrote to Schreiber, who had suggested the reactivation of the EWS:

> I have heard nothing to suggest any change in the balance of argument which led to the Prime Minister's decision to allow the early warning system to lapse <u>in its original form</u>. I am however quite clear that we here (both Secretariat and CPRS together) need systematically to look further ahead at regular intervals and, after any necessary consultation with departments, to play a more dynamic role in bringing issues to Ministers at the right time taking account of both political and practical timescales and considerations. In other words we want a document which will be more a tool of management at the centre than something for the general edification (but non-use) of Ministers generally.[114]

The gamekeeper had turned poacher. It was agreed that 'a forward look exercise' should take place every parliamentary recess, but Heath felt that one was required before then, in January 1974.[115] On 7 November, Robert Armstrong suggested to the Prime Minister that it would be 'difficult to undertake a forward look at this moment, when the machine is under considerable pressure'.[116] A 'forward look exercise' was, however, begun in December 1973 and January 1974; 'The intervention of the Election', wrote Hunt, 'meant that this particular exercise never reached fruition, but it was generally agreed that what had been done had been useful and should be repeated.'[117] One exercise was duly completed for Wilson in May 1974.[118]

CPRS AND THE STRATEGY SESSIONS

The strategy aspect of the CPRS's remit was altogether more successful – at least until Macmillan's 'events, dear boy, events' hit Heath hard. The CPRS took the Conservative manifesto, looked at what departments were actually doing, assessed the political and economic climate in which the government was operating and prepared high-level presentations for the Prime Minister and the Cabinet, smaller ones for junior Ministers. According to Plowden's diary, this was

> Very interesting politically, as what we're doing is in fact to reinforce the <u>party-political</u> content of the govt's activities, as against the creeping paralysis imposed by the pressures of necessity and the permanent civil service. i.e. we reinforce the Cons. Central Office as against the departments, something which e.g. American commentators have always thought badly needed doing ...[119]

He returned to this question several times throughout the year:

A lot of talk about strategy, a lot of speculation about the attitudes towards ourselves of key ministers and officials. We are already in that way at least far more political than any normal department, as well as in the sense of their own priorities we're forced to develop quite strong values of our own. How far should we take account of the realities of existing departmental policy? of public or group opinion? of constitutional (?Political) theory, in not letting ourselves become the agents of the PM who is not to be thought of as more than the chairman of a collective cabinet.[120]

Just by doing their job, the CPRS was in danger of appearing 'more ideological than the ideologues'.[121]

When it came to the actual strategy sessions, Trend, ever the guardian of propriety, was very concerned that if Rothschild joined the sessions, along with some of his staff and various others including Schreiber, they must not therefore be called Cabinet meetings: 'Sir Burke Trend would like to preserve the principle that meetings of the Cabinet are attended only by members of the Cabinet and the Secretariat. He would therefore prefer to regard this as an *ad hoc* meeting of Ministers with official advisers, rather than as a meeting of the Cabinet'.[122]

This was Sir Burke succeeding in keeping Rothschild out of the highest forum in the land which just so happened to be Trend's personal domain. The actual fact of the strategy sessions provoked Robert Armstrong, a small-'c' conservative character to his fingertips, to ask 'Should we really waste the time of the CPRS on this primarily political task?'[123] As soon as a government wins an election, its manifesto transforms into the plan of government (perhaps uniquely among contemporary governments the Attlee Administrations' 1945 manifesto *Let Us Face the Future* does read like a legislative history of 1945–51 bar unforeseen events which heavily shaped the period – something rarely true). Armstrong's query was ignored.

These presentations, held at Chequers, charted the government's recent journey, where its current policies were taking it and where the CPRS thought the government actually wanted to be. They were divided into three parts: economic, social and employment policy – but did not include defence or foreign affairs.[124] (There is a fascinating file at the National Archives which details the very private discussion over what intelligence information should be shared with the CPRS. The result was that one of its members, Robert Wade-Gery,[125] was given clearance to see JIC reports, and Rothschild, who had been 'indoctrinated' in 1961 by the Ministry of Defence, was reindoctrinated so that he could see signals intelligence concerning oil matters.)[126]

Most commentators, from contemporaries until the present day, have seen these strategy sessions as an excellent way of infusing into a disparate governing team a continuing sense of common purpose and shared experience. Jock Bruce-Gardyne, Parliamentary Private Secretary to the Secretary of State for Scotland

1970–2, thought that the sessions were 'not there to prevent governments being blown off course ... [but] to make sure that Governments do not *steer* themselves off course – at least without realising that that is what they are doing'.[127] Heath thought the first one to be a great success and became interested in it being repeated every six months, for Cabinet and junior Ministers.[128] 'Rothschild,' Plowden wrote in his diary,

> Taking the independent and somewhat blundering line that is all too characteristic of him, effective though his non-Whitehall-establishment approach can often be, promptly told B.Trend that this was quite out of the question, as it wd mean grossly overloading the CPRS. He announced this to a general meeting of the CPRS ... and was greeted by universal dismay. The general feeling was that if we don't 'do' strategy, and that at fairly regular intervals, we don't really do anything, and that our other activities must flow from this exercise rather than being quite independent of it.[129]

The strategy sessions continued. But when economic and industrial strife, which had been ever-present since the electricity supply workers' action in the autumn of 1970, closed in on Heath's Administration from 1973 these sessions began to look luxurious. John Ramsden also concluded that Ministers felt somewhat unable, with their civil servants also in attendance, to abandon narrow departmentalism and embrace the collective spirit.[130] The CPRS's strategy presentations impressed a young Douglas Hurd immensely, with the

> High point, in my mind, [being] the sessions at Chequers. They were amazing. The Prime Minister made Ministers submit to lecturing by Victor, but also by Victor's young men, with blackboards and charts all showing that if they continued with their policies the results would be disastrous. You've got the Chancellor sitting there as if they were schoolboys. I remember thinking at the time that this was very odd. But this was Ted's authority, he wanted people, including himself, to be subject to this kind of thing ... It was a very remarkable thing. In my mind, it was the high point of the CPRS. They were actually asked to, and carried out, with great aplomb and elegance, that pedagogic role for Ministers.[131]

When asked how the Cabinet took it, Hurd said, 'I expect that they resented it a bit. I think there was occasional muttering. But they did it and they had to do it.' Hurd was right that some Ministers were unimpressed. Peter Walker and Jellicoe thought they added very little value.[132] Only three exercises were eventually held in the Heath era: in August 1971, May 1972 and June 1973. A fourth, pencilled-in for November 1973, was postponed till December, which was in turn put back to January 1974 because of negotiations on the Northern Irish crisis on 6 and 7 December 1973 (but not before all the preparatory work by the CPRS had been completed).[133] The gathering storm which led to the February general election then put paid to that, too.[134]

Such a bright start followed by a falling-by-the-wayside was, in effect, the fate of so many of Heath's machinery reforms, as we shall see. Howell was a lone voice in being highly critical of the strategy sessions, especially the last one. During this, the CPRS scared the Ministers present with spine-chilling tales of economic collapse coupled with unemployment only dropping gradually if policies continued on their present course along with unfavourable comparisons with Japan, Germany and France.[135] This 'emotionally upset'[136] Heath who considered the purpose of the June 1973 strategy session 'was to discuss economic expansion, counter-inflation and the concept of "One Nation"'.[137] Howell put this down to Rothschild having a none-too-developed grasp of economics and, more damningly, an insufficient sympathy for the burgeoning appeal of monetarism: 'He led everybody astray with his half-baked macro-economics, but he was only one of a tribe'.[138] Hurd contradicted Howell a little when he explained,

> What I was thinking of was when I got so angry with the 'coal war' and what it seemed to me was the mishandling the NUM [National Union of Mineworkers] and I was in favour of a tougher line. Whereas the young men, and I think Victor himself, were looking ahead really to what became much more orthodox in the Thatcher time of freeing the nationalised industries so that they could do more of their own thing prior to privatisation, to free them from the Treasury constraints and so on, and I was kind of horrified by that as they were opposite to my feelings at the time.[139]

Hurd wrote earlier that 'They were at once abolished by Mr Wilson'.[140] This is not true. There was a last CPRS Chequers strategy session under Harold Wilson in November 1974. Again, this scared the attending Ministers, unsurprisingly as the CPRS presentation began with the sentence 'The situation confronting Ministers is dangerously precarious.'[141] Wilson, a man who was reluctant to hear bad news unless absolutely necessary, was 'quite pleased with it', but did not arrange another.[142] It must be noted that, according to Bernard Donoughue, Wilson was persuaded to keep the CPRS after it was rumoured in the *Evening Standard*'s 'Londoner's Diary' column on 11 March 1974 that he might abolish such a Heathite creation.[143] Rothschild, however, claimed that Wilson had personally assured him in Autumn 1973 that 'I do not intend to make any institutional changes at the centre'.[144] In any event, the CPRS's first report to Wilson on public expenditure in June 1974 was heartily praised by the returning Prime Minister who thought it 'first-class stuff'.[145]

CPRS AND THE REVIEW OF POLICY

The other big CPRS function was the review of policy. This owed more to common sense and applied economics than to sophisticated policy analysis.[146] Rothschild understood very early on that there was a huge danger in all intractable problems being heaped on the CPRS's tiny membership, turning it into a repository for poisoned chalices.[147] He rightly had no intention of letting this happen, and largely picked the areas the think tank was to be involved in. The topics that the CPRS studied in Rothschild's era varied widely, from the future of Northern Ireland to Concorde; it had been previously written by Rothschild that Trend wished to steer the CPRS away from the supersonic sump[148] but, in fact, the Cabinet Secretary thought that 'the Central Capability will have to direct its attention to the major issues of policy (e.g. Concorde ...)'.[149] The complete list of 'CPRS specific in-house projects, 1972' was: 'Government Strategy; PAR; Early Warning; United Kingdom Population; Unemployment and inflation; Energy and Raw Materials; Resource allocation; Growth and declining industries; The Great and the Good; Foreign control of industries; Various carry-overs from 1971'.[150] Rothschild later wrote to Heath saying that he had omitted 'Wade-Gery's report on Northern Ireland and my report to the Lord President ... on the National Newspaper Industry'.[151] The list for 1973 was: six-monthly strategy reviews; ministerial strategy groups on the nationalized industries and social affairs; collective briefs; counter-inflation; technique of presenting information to ministers; public expenditure; energy; PARs; coordination and development of long-term planning (10–15 years); job satisfaction; 'Great and Good'; and race relations.[152] (The only published work of the CPRS during the Heath years was Rothschild's own *Framework for Government Research and Development* in 1971.)[153]

How the CPRS fared in its endeavours was not universally admired. Sir Frank Cooper, Permanent Secretary to the Northern Ireland Office 1973–6, felt that there was only a limited amount of fresh thinking an outside organization could give a question, especially those heavily bound up in secrecy and day-to-day experience.[154] This ignored a key CPRS skill in winkling-out ideas from civil servants below the top echelon of a department, ideas which had not permeated that department's official line.[155] (The CPRS review of Northern Ireland policy conducted by Wade-Gery was only possible after Heath by-passed the obstructions of Trend.)[156] Intelligence and foreign affairs were prohibited areas for the CPRS.[157] Rothschild strongly disagreed with Cooper's line. 'No particular class of investigation, such as those concerned with foreign affairs, defence, the Budget or the exchange rates, should be barred.'[158] One area he was definitely excluded from, and wished he was not, was William Armstrong's bailiwick – the machinery of government.[159]

Most Cabinet Ministers supported Margaret Thatcher's decision in 1983 to abolish the think tank as it was rightly seen to be a tool for strengthening the Prime Minister's power vis-à-vis them.[160] A few, however, did lament the CPRS's passing, among them Douglas Hurd who, in May 1993 when Foreign Secretary in John Major's Government, recommended the rebirth of the think tank.[161] A form of think tank did reappear in the New Labour Governments of 1997–2006, with groups such as the Social Exclusion Unit and the Centre for Management and Policy Studies, the Performance and Innovation Unit and the Forward Strategy Unit possessing some CPRS-like functions, before all were subsumed in 2002 into the Prime Minister's Strategy Unit. (Geoff Mulgan, head of the Strategy Unit 2002–4, explained that a detailed study had been made of the CPRS before the Strategy Unit had been set up.)[162]

The man tasked with the amalgamation of the CPRS's remnants with Margaret Thatcher's Downing Street Policy Unit was Robin Butler. As one of the first recruits into the think tank in 1971 (recommended by Trend and accepted by Rothschild, partly because of Butler and Rothschild's shared schooling, though many years apart, at Harrow)[163] and as one of its undertakers, his view of the CPRS is of special interest:

> I came to think that it couldn't operate advising the Cabinet as a whole. In a Whitehall sense it was too public and you were vulnerable to what happened which was that a minister or a department which didn't like the advice the CPRS was giving ... could leak it ... It was much better for such advice to be given privately to the Prime Minister rather than to the Cabinet as a whole.[164]

Trend's unshakeable conviction that the CPRS had to be an asset for the Cabinet as a whole, against the wishes of Howell and Schreiber who wanted it to be solely a prime ministerial resource, proved to be faulty. There was another perceived design flaw in the minds of the 1980s executioners. David Willetts, a member of Margaret Thatcher's Downing Street Policy Unit in 1984–6, thought that the grandiose strategies of the CPRS paid no attention whatever to the tactical nitty-gritty.[165] Willetts' point is strong in that the think tank can be seen as an institutionalization of Edward Heath's way of doing things.

The CPRS did, however, bring value to the Cabinet as a whole. Within its policy function was a commitment to making as clear as possible the various policy choices, both those contained within an issue and those between departments. The CPRS also strove to create a level playing field for anything to do with numbers: statistics, the costing of projects, and so on. Clarity of information – and brevity – underpinned an unsung side-effect of the CPRS. It bolstered the collectivity of the Cabinet (and thereby contributed to the coherence and 'joined-upness' of government). Rothschild's sense of constitutional propriety had been sadly dented when he noticed on a Cabinet Minister's notes that the official collating them had written 'This item is of no interest to you.'[166]

Sir Kevin Tebbit, Permanent Under-Secretary to the Ministry of Defence 1998–2005, explained how he had witnessed the collegiality first-hand:

> If you look at the numbers of Cabinet papers and meetings you'll find that there were almost twice as many as during the 1990s or the current Government. My personal

recollection of this was as an assistant private secretary and one of the jobs I performed then was in pulling together views for the Secretary of State on items that were nothing to do with the Ministry. In other words, the Cabinet agenda would come round on social policy, education or health and it would be my job to telephone the other departments, particularly the ones that were in the lead, and, with the use of the Cabinet paper that may have been provided for the discussion, tease out points and provide information for the Minister so that he could participate in a Cabinet debate even though it was not his subject. I think this illustrated the collegiate nature of the Heath Administration which, if you were to try to define the acme, as it were, the pinnacle of Cabinet Government, it would be during that period.

Now I'm not sure if this was Heath's nature, he was by nature a consensus individual who believed deeply in rational argument and in hammering out the pros and cons of issues before taking a decision. Indeed, he used to frustrate his colleagues by the length of time he spent agonizing over decisions, so there may be an element of the character of the Prime Minister there which was not necessarily always positive. But the fact is the process was always impeccably followed ... I remember briefing the Minister on educational policy. He said 'You understand these things, I don't, I went to Eton ... tell me about these issues,' and we had a long discussion. I mention this to illustrate the broad way in which Heath expected his Cabinet Ministers to behave and indeed the way in which he ran that system.[167]

Presenting difficult issues on one side of A4 (à la wartime Churchill) – or, in Rothschild's words, 'half a page of apparently innocent questions which one minister might put to his colleagues'[168] – could only help to interest members of the Cabinet in issues outside their narrow departmental silos. (In February 1971, Heath called for all submissions to the Cabinet to be on one page, but Trend thought complex issues such as Keith Joseph's social security reforms required two.)[169] Plowden, Private Secretary to Heath at the Board of Trade, was very clear on this point:

> I've always felt very strongly that there's a need to give countervailing advice. A body to withstand the powerful orthodoxies being expressed by all the spending departments and by the Treasury and pressing these views on Ministers without Ministers necessarily having any effective counter-briefing or any briefing which tries to set particular departmental points of view in its wider governmental context.[170]

Its greatest and best-known triumph was in predicting a significant and sustained hike in the price of oil. In fact it was one of the CPRS's – Rothschild's in particular – network of outsiders who foretold the oil crisis. Sir David Barran of Shell asked to see the Prime Minister in September 1971 to explain his fear of a severe risk to oil in the next decade.[171] Barran was granted an audience and sent him a detailed report which looked at global energy supplies and warned that 'The possibility also exists that Middle East countries would deliberately limit production to levels below actual world requirements. In this case take levels could rise above the high line ... and be sustained for perhaps 10 years while the developed consumer countries implement crash programmes.'[172] Rothschild wrote to Heath saying that if Barran's conclusions were right 'as I suspect they are ... the impact on the U.K. will be as serious and all-pervasive as our going into Europe or the Irish crisis'. Rothschild was dumbfounded by the Treasury, which forecast that it was 'probable that the relative price of oil would fall ... These remarks seem to me to have a certain dream-like quality in the light of the Shell appreciation.'[173] Hurd is very complimentary towards his former Prime Minister over this:

> I was very slow, even with my foreign affairs background I was very slow to realise what was happening and I think that was true in Whitehall, too. I think the Prime Minister was well ahead of us in understanding the importance for our economy and our politics of the price rise ... I don't think I was alone in it, I didn't mesh the two together to the extent that I think Ted did himself. They were in separate boxes as far as I was concerned ... It was the sort of thing he was good at.[174]

Rothschild envisaged a three-fold rise whereas it turned out to be 185 per cent in real terms during 1974,[175] but his prediction and encouragement of contingency planning was exactly what everyone thought that a think tank was for.[176]

The CPRS was not comprehensively loved in Whitehall – it trod on toes everywhere it walked. Sir Douglas Wass, Permanent Secretary to the Treasury 1974–83, contended that, 'As time went by, it concerned itself less and less with central issues and became a meddler in departmental business.'[177] One occasion illuminates much of the behind-closed-doors tensions which are always apparent in Whitehall but very rarely come to the boil. Rothschild wrote to the Prime Minister in May 1972, informing him that

> Sir Burke Trend called a meeting of the permanent secretaries this morning to review the activities of the CPRS, of whom four were present. I am too insensitive to appreciate nuances but the other three members of the CPRS who were present respectively thought that the permanent secretaries put the boot in; that they put the shoe in; that our shin pads were thick enough to cope with these eventualities. Sir Burke, needless to say, was neutral.

Heath minuted to Robert Armstrong at the top of Rothschild's memo 'Is there any reason why I shouldn't ask Sir Burke Trend for a report on [this]?' After a chat between the Prime Minister and his Principal Private Secretary, there was to be 'No further action'.[178]

Opinions on Rothschild's tenure as Director of the think tank vary. Everyone saw him as a larger-than-life figure, which indeed he was both physically and intellectually. Lord Waldegrave thought him 'formidable'.[179] For Lord Marlesford, Rothschild brought to mind what he thought 'an improbable quotation attributed to Lord Curzon: '"No man should be Viceroy of India to whom that job is an honour." Victor Rothschild totally fitted that. He had everything. He was a grandee, mega-rich, George Medal. They could give him nothing.'[180] (Rothschild once told Peter Hennessy that 'he was very misunderstood on this – having throughout his life a fear of failure'.) Robin Butler has described his former boss as a 'maverick' and 'a mixture between ingenuousness and sharpness', but that 'he had no idea how government worked'.[181] Not understanding how the bureaucracy operated could be one of the reasons he appears so successful in retrospect, testament to the importance of not knowing better (or caring). But Plowden felt that this in some ways 'created problems for himself and the CPRS, not being quite as oblique as he should have been',[182] while his interfering nature upset some of his subordinates.[183]

Howell went much further. While he thought working with Rothschild was 'thoroughly enjoyable'[184] and that Rothschild was 'the most stimulating and marvellous figure [who] produced an atmosphere of amusement, irreverence and excitement',[185] Howell expressed deep and continuing frustration at his appointment. After attempting a desperate rearguard action to get somebody much more business-minded when the Directorship was being decided in the autumn of 1970, he said that Rothschild 'knew absolutely nothing about programme budgeting and business planning and nothing about the Treasury and nothing about budget priorities, and when you think back to what we said before the election about the sort of person we needed, the sort of capability we needed, he obviously wasn't going to deliver the goods ... He was supremely uninterested in the minutiae of budgetary policy'.[186]

'It wasn't', concluded Howell, 'the mechanical, sort of almost steamroller effect that some of us were looking for.'[187] It is fascinating to see how the two powerful planners from the pre-election PSRU, Schreiber and Howell, differ in their retrospective appreciation. The reason for the divergence is contained in the think tank's multi-role functionality. For Howell the central capability was first and foremost about economic and financial policy. It was to be an instrument for fundamentally changing the nature of government, empowering a dramatic push to less but better government. What it actually became was a very small unit of high-powered intellectuals who could turn their attention to anything. 'The CPRS had more of the Civil Service in it than our ideas', lamented Howell.[188]

PROGRAMME ANALYSIS AND REVIEW

Rothschild had little interest in the Public Sector Research Unit's cherished 'analytical capability'. William Plowden thinks it may have been because 'it wasn't his baby';[189] Lord Butler because he may well have found it 'boring'.[190] The CPRS, as the embodiment of the PSRU's plan for a 'central capability', was supposed to be the main drive behind the analytical capability, though, as was shown in Chapter 4, there was no clear blueprint for what PAR was meant to be (leaving it open to manipulation by officialdom). As Jellicoe stated in a letter to Heath, 'PAR is indeed central to CPRS operations'.[191] The authoritative book on the CPRS by Tessa Blackstone and William Plowden described their involvement thus:

> Summarized, the formal procedure was that programmes to be reviewed were selected jointly by the Treasury, CPRS, and departments; choices agreed by officials were then ratified by Ministers. The main work on each review was done by departmental officials, but findings were again discussed jointly with the Treasury and the CPRS as they emerged. The final reports and recommendations were presented to Ministers for discussion. Ministers were also presented with a CPRS collective brief, commenting on the review and its conclusions and suggesting to Ministers decisions which they might want to make.[192]

The CPRS link with PAR 'was a way of getting us into departments' business', explained Plowden.[193] But the CPRS's even-handed approach to spending – sometimes the justification was to go higher, other times to cut it – largely served only to aggravate the Treasury which always wanted reduction.[194]

Rothschild's lack of interest in the analytical capability of course disappointed people such as Howell who had invested so much in the planning before and after the election. This contrasted noticeably with his continued interest in the Treasury's public expenditure function – he understood very well where power was located. Rothschild asked to be allowed to join a meeting of GEN 92, the Cabinet committee on prices and incomes policy. Robert Armstrong and Trend both advised the Prime Minister that it would be better if he was not included because it would make other officials, such as the Treasury's Douglas Allen, jealous.[195] Heath concurred but warned that he might change his mind in the future.[196] Rothschild's interest in economic policy made Howell uneasy, since Rothschild was very much still wedded to Keynesianism.[197]

With less of the CPRS's driving spirit than was originally envisaged, the analytical capability was born. Initially described to the Cabinet as 'Improved Expenditure Decisions by Government' before being christened Programme Analysis and Review (PAR), Richard Wilding thought 'a rather Fabian sort of idea ... [that] deep and thoughtful analysis in the hands of experts will produce the right answers'.[198]

PAR suffered from some teething problems from which it never really recovered. First of all, it suffered what amounted to a snub the first time it was brought before Cabinet, in early December 1970, Ministers being apathetic at best, dismissive at worst. Doubts over the burden and manpower requirements of PAR meant that, despite the Prime Minister's unambiguous support, it was not clearly backed by other Ministers.[199] It was presented twice further to Cabinet, on 5 January and 1 April 1971.[200] This time Ministers were persuaded to support PAR (and the Prime Minister).[201]

It soon became apparent that there was a distinct lack of manpower for these studies, just as Ministers had predicted in late 1970.[202] There was, after all, a major squeeze on Civil Service numbers throughout the Wilson and Heath years, a key part of which was Sir Robert Bellinger's 'Panel of Businessmen on Civil Service Manning', which finally reported in December 1970 after being set up by Wilson[203] (though total public sector numbers actually increased dramatically in the Heath years, up by 400,000[204] even with '[t]he statistical conjuring trick' of examples such as the Manpower Services Commission's 18,000 civil servants leaving the service and then rejoining two years later).[205] There was an even bigger shortage of relevant skills.

With Ministers' coldness clear, Heath attempted to answer their criticisms by making PAR more selective than originally envisaged, and contended that '[t]he extra manpower involved was small, and, once introduced, the system should more than pay for itself'.[206] The less ambitious topics which were presented to the Cabinet on 29 March for study in 1971 were:

> Ministry of Agriculture, Fisheries and Food: Lime and Fertiliser Subsidies (budget £45 million);
>
> Ministry of Defence: Service Manpower; Reinforcement Capability;
>
> Department of Education and Science: Higher Education (£500 million);
>
> Department of Employment: Employment Services (£50 million);
>
> Department of the Environment: Subsidies to Public Transport outside towns (£30 million); New Towns in Great Britain (£100 million);
>
> Foreign and Commonwealth Office Overseas Development Administration: Technical Assistance (£50 million);
>
> Department of Health and Social Security: Health and Personal Social Services for the Elderly (£350 million);
>
> Home Office: Treatment of Offenders (£80 million);
>
> Department of Trade and Industry: Promotion of Visible Exports (£40 million).[207]

Another problem was where PAR was to be located. There were three possible homes: the Civil Service Department, the CPRS or the Treasury. The CSD was initially chosen, largely because the only other real possibility would have to be the Treasury, the department which PAR was intended, in part, to rival. As William Armstrong stated, 'Although the Treasury would be closely involved, the implementation of P.A.R. should not be entrusted to the Treasury; and although it might in due course fall within the responsibility of the Central Capability, it might be desirable for the Civil Service Department to take the lead at least for the time being.'[208] Perhaps Sir William wanted to closely monitor it himself. But when PAR was launched in March 1971, it was located within the Treasury. The Treasury had made it known that it was in favour of such a function, but not of the CSD 'mucking about' with it.[209] Indeed, the CSD's PAR team was disbanded in June 1971.[210] At the end of March 1971, Trend and Armstrong suggested that its Treasury location might only be temporary, as it could still be given to the CPRS.[211] But it stayed within the Treasury until its abolition in 1979. If the think tank had been given PAR, the CPRS would have been far bigger and less fleet-footed than it was.

The PAR being given to the Treasury was nowhere near as fatal as it may seem. For the Treasury in the early 1970s had, along with its thinking on a central capability, diagnosed a gap in its financial planning. The Public Expenditure Survey system and accompanying Committee had proved successful (until it was modified in 1975–6 during the galloping inflation, of which PESC was a contributory cause, in favour of cash limits).[212]

From no planning, save somewhat ad hoc blueprints for defence and the social services, five-year plans had been created by the mid-1960s. This was a major improvement, and one with which the Treasury's public expenditure gurus were rightly pleased. But five years was the maximum. Long-term projects, of which Concorde was the most obvious and defence systems the most numerous, often had a life way beyond five years. The Treasury, therefore, saw that with PAR located within its fiefdom, it was now able to complete the PESC machinery. It also recognized shortcomings in big individual spending programmes.[213] Once it became part of the Treasury armoury, departments took PAR seriously.[214] (Otto Clarke wrote in 1971 that 'the idea of PAR was always implicit in the concepts of PESC'.)[215]

After a difficult start, PAR began to take shape. Indeed, Sir Samuel Goldman was almost glowing in his study of public expenditure published soon after his retirement in 1973.[216] Heath was certainly keen to see PAR become a central part of the public expenditure business when he wrote in November 1971 that he was 'anxious to develop the PAR system in 1972 significantly further than was possible in 1971'.[217] In December 1971, Mark Schreiber fretted that PAR needed an injection of energy and responsibility. According to Schreiber, the Prime Minister had recently said that

> 'Ministers should become more involved at an earlier stage in their PARs; and consideration should be given to devolving to second-tier Ministers special responsibilities for PARs.'
> ... I believe this to be terribly important and I don't think enough will happen if it is left there. I therefore suggest that the Prime Minister might wish the Cabinet to decide that a second-tier Minister should be nominated with personal responsibility for every stage of the preparation of each PAR.[218]

Robert Armstrong pointed out to Schreiber that his thoughts were unconstitutional: 'The Cabinet cannot decide for individual Ministers how they are to run their departments; but ... at Cabinet the Prime Minister will remind his colleagues of what has been said and point out the advantages of a general procedure on the lines you have indicated'.[219]

Howell found cause for pride when he informed Robert Armstrong in January 1972 of the Prime Minister's 'wish to see more informal meetings between Ministers, possibly in place of the traditional inter-departmental machinery': 'One of the most important outcomes of the developing system of Programme Analysis and Review is that it will encourage these meetings to take place frequently, regularly and within a well thought out framework ... I hope the Prime Minister will therefore feel that the proper policy planning system he seeks is now in fact emerging.'[220] Heath continued to press the Civil Service to adopt PAR wholeheartedly and to make it a success. In January 1973, he agreed a three-year rolling programme of PAR studies.[221] The studies themselves were placed within functional headings: resources deployed in facilitating industrial and technological change and for meeting the resultant human and social problems; and for enhancing the quality of urban and rural life; for preparation for employment and community life; in relief of poverty, illness and other forms of hardship; in support of law and order; in support of European and overseas commitments.[222] Slippage meant that 1974 was now to be the start date.[223]

Some Treasury insiders indicated their displeasure with 'a bloody excrescence', as one senior Treasury man privately called PAR.[224] Sir John Hunt, Trend's successor, thought that the 'system created a great deal of work but not much in the way of results'.[225] Trend discerned a wider dissatisfaction in late 1971 over an 'initial (and in some cases continuing) reluctance of departments to accept the new system'.[226] Yet PAR did have its supporters, with Wass calling in 1983 for a new, improved version.[227] PAR was, however, the object of perhaps *the* wittiest and certainly the most detailed satire on a public expenditure process. In a letter to Robert Armstrong from Robert Andrew, Private Secretary to Lord Carrington, the 'glossary' of PAR was gloriously explained (these are only the edited highlights):

> PARturient montes, nascetur ridiculus mus [the mountains are in labour, a ridiculous mouse will be born][228]
>
> | | |
> |---|---|
> | PARis | Lord R-T-S-H-L-D |
> | PARnassus | Office of the CPRS |
> | PARadigm | Example of Programme Analysis and Review |
> | PARamour | Person committed to PAR |
> | PARaphanalia | Programme review machinery |

PARdon	Academic member of review team
PARticipate	Take part in PAR
PARsnip	An in-depth study which satisfies all requirements
PARrot	An in-depth study which satisfies no requirements
PARalysis	Current state of PAR
PARoxysm	State brought on by PAR
PARsimony	Grudging attitude to PAR
PARtisan	Committed to PAR
PARtricide	Committed to getting rid of PAR
PARable	Skilled at telling the PAR tale
PARboil	Cook the books in preparation for PAR
PARanoia	A PAR bore
PARachute	PAR on the grouse moors
PARtridge	Victim of a PARachute
PARody	Form of *credo* sung on PARnassus
PARlez-vous?	Are you up to PAR for Europe yet?
PARfait knight	Watch the birthday honours[229]

PAR was to be the tool for cutting out waste in government activities which were necessary and for getting the government out of ones that were not. But it was completely undermined by the 1972 shift to turning on the taps of public expenditure (which is dealt with in more detail later).[230] As David Howell observed:

> The word came through from No. 10 and senior ministers and even from the Treasury, incredibly, that retrenchment was no longer the order of the day. On the contrary, 'expansion' was the word. So those very able civil servants, who'd risen to prominence in departments as analysts, saying 'Look boys, for years I've thought we were wasting money. We could cut this out or do it different', suddenly found they were in the pending tray, got a rather smaller office, pushed down the corridor, didn't get called into the permanent secretary so often. And the whole bit of Whitehall that had been geared to this terrific, thrusting reform rather got put on a back-burner.[231]

In the short term, PAR relied on the idea of rational continuity of government policy which was simply not in evidence after 1972. Looking at a longer time frame, PAR was too cumbersome and theoretical for the day-to-day, rough-and-tumble practicality of Whitehall. In its original form, it was doomed the minute it left the Public Sector Research Unit's drawing board. In its Treasury incarnation, it could only survive as the far end of PESC. PAR's abolition in 1979 went unlamented.[232]

THE BUSINESSMEN'S TEAM

Another aspect of the PSRU's work also delivered far less than the planners originally hoped. The businessmen's team had high hopes when it was established in the first days of the Heath Administration. They would bring business techniques and financial management to the job of government. But, six months later, Jellicoe was still trying to fix where they would be located.[233] Just as Lords Plowden and Roberthall had predicted before the election, not being anchored to a specific department or programme meant that they had little or no scope to influence the work of the bureaucracy. The businessmen themselves thought that, as Jellicoe reported to Heath, 'The initial period of adjustment to a strange environment was not easy for members of the team, though on balance the difficulties were less formidable than many had predicted, mainly because of the valuable preparatory work done before the Election.'[234] Lord Croham later described the businessmen's team as a 'failure' because they never became part of the machine, only wanting to talk to Ministers.[235]

There was one huge exception to this story. Derek Rayner would achieve legendary Whitehall status in the 1980s as Margaret Thatcher's Efficiency Adviser. Yet his career as a reformer of the Civil Service began a decade earlier when he headed a review into the procurement of defence materiel, much of it of a highly technical nature and correspondingly massive cost. So many programmes had suffered 'excessive duplication, cost overruns and long delays' that reform of this most important area was absolutely essential.[236] Rayner was tasked with creating a hived-off executive agency which would handle defence procurement. In this he was singularly successful. The report he wrote was clear and authoritative. In fact, it was so impressive that Rayner was asked to extend his two-year secondment from Marks and Spencer to four years, specifically until April 1974, which he agreed to do in March 1971[237] (although he made it clear that he still saw his future in Marks and Spencer[238] and actually left, with a knighthood, in 1973 to become joint managing director of the company).[239] He became the first Chief Executive of the Defence Procurement Agency, with the rank of Permanent Secretary and Head of Department.[240] Mark Schreiber was very satisfied with the Defence Procurement Agency and saw it as a model for a hived-off future:

> The essence of the work of the proposed Departmental Agency is that it would be of a dynamic and executive nature requiring entrepreneurial management rather than straightforward policy advice. The Defence Procurement Agency under Derek Rayner is a prototype on which to develop. I therefore believe that the 'executive heads' of the new departmental agency should in general be appointed from outside the Civil Service and possibly from business, where entrepreneurial talents are mainly to be found.[241]

But Rayner, and the Defence Procurement Agency, were largely exceptional. By 1972 Meyjes was downbeat: 'It has become clear that, in spite of a great deal of effort and much early euphoria, the areas in which the hiving-off solution can be applied are few in number and limited in significance ... In fact, in spite of strenuous efforts, so far only three activities have been found suitable for hiving-off, namely the nationalised pubs in Carlisle, the Civil Aviation Authority and the British Library'.[242]

The actual list of hivings-off in the Heath Government was: 1971, the Defence Procurement Agency and the Civil Aviation Authority; 1972, the Employment Services Agency, the Central Computer Agency, the Property Services Agency, the British Overseas Trade Board and the Industrial Development Executive, while Thomas Cook was sold to a consortium of the Automobile Association, Midland Bank and Trust Houses Forte; 1973, the Pay Board and Prices Commission and the establishment of the Director-General of Fair Trading; and lastly, in January 1974, the Manpower Services Commission. Though there are some sizeable ventures here, compared to the high hopes of the pre-1970 election planners and the businessmen's team, it adds up to little more than a damp squib.[243] (It is interesting to note Meyjes's description of the pubs which were sold to the private sector and the CAA and the British Library which were kept within the public sphere as being all hived-off. They would be explicitly recognized as two very different things by the 1980s with functions transferred to the private sector deemed, quite properly, 'privatized'. The *Next Steps* report of 1988 would lead a renewed effort to hive-off which saw functions ring-fenced and turned into executive agencies but rarely privatized.)

The businessmen's team recommended its own disbandment after its current projects were complete in March 1971.[244] In the final phase Meyjes was working on Ministry of Defence streamlining and the National Health Service; Herbert Cruickshank on a possible construction executive; Sainsbury on government real estate; Ronald East on PAR; and Hutton on the Public Trustee's Office.[245] Its leader, Meyjes, so lauded by Howell when he suggested to Heath that Meyjes should be the first head of the CPRS, became despondent with the lack of success, actual or even potential, and left.[246] But this did not prevent in early 1972 a rearguard attempt by Howell and Schreiber to continue with a businessmen's team of sorts at the very top of government. Howell urged a three-man group comprising Meyjes, Schreiber and one other businessman.[247] Douglas Hurd told the Prime Minister that 'in my view he would be a rash man who advised you that the present machine ran so well that outside talent of this kind could be dispensed with'.[248] William Armstrong advised that the group be abolished. He thought an industrial adviser located in the Treasury might bring better results.[249]

In April 1972, Jellicoe finally sealed the fate of the businessmen's team when he told Heath that there was no future for them – but a 'Central Business Adviser' may work.[250] Rothschild was not convinced. 'What is the probability of a firm releasing a really first-class man? I am not sure about the extent to which firms did this with the exception of M&S, in the first round.'[251] But Rothschild did see that the best businessmen injected into government, and with clearly defined roles, could really benefit the bureaucracy.[252] William Armstrong backed calls for a Central Business Adviser because he foresaw that the 'major task ahead of us is improving the performance of government at the interface with the individual citizen'.[253] (The public services in the 1990s and early 2000s were *very* focused on this precise issue.) Rothschild eventually accepted the idea of a Central Business Adviser, but encouraged a step-change in quality.[254] A week later he re-opened the debate by recommending government adopt a French-style *cabinet* system for Ministers, which would include a business adviser.[255] Mark Schreiber and a CSD official, Tony Hart, were dispatched to France to investigate the use of *cabinets* in Britain, but nothing came of it.[256]

REDRAWING THE WHITEHALL MAP

The super-departments which *The Reorganisation of Central Government* had thought so central, and were in fact already underway during the late 1960s, largely survived intact throughout the Heath Government. The re-creation of a Department of Energy in January 1974 (the Ministry of Fuel and Power had been incorporated into the Department of Trade and Industry in 1970) after a 'damaging delay' caused by the DTI's Secretary of State, Peter Walker, who was understandably reluctant to see his domain reduced,[257] was a step away, however, from the theory that big was beautiful. (A second Cabinet Minister, responsible for trade, prices and consumer affairs, was given to the DTI in 1972.)[258] As was the creation of the Northern Ireland Office (NIO) in 1972 due to the imposition of direct rule after four years of burgeoning violence and extensive civil unrest. The Northern Irish Parliament at Stormont was stripped of its devolved authority which returned to London, administered by the new NIO spun-off from the Home Office, with William Whitelaw appointed as its first Secretary of State.[259] All these moves put an end to the pre-election wish to see a smaller Cabinet.

Heath was reluctantly forced into several more machinery-of-government changes. The nature of industrial relations in Britain had seen a marked deterioration since the Second World War with increasing numbers of both official and unofficial strikes (certainly since Frank Cousins became head of the Transport and General Workers Union in 1958) and the early 1970s began its most destructive phase. The 1972 NUM strike involving substantial secondary picketing had demonstrated that the government was quite unprepared for a hardening of militancy in the union movement. Disputes of this magnitude had not been experienced since the Attlee Governments' difficulties with unofficial dock strikes, perhaps not since the General Strike.[260]

Though the Conservatives had done a great amount of work on industrial relations in the run-up to 1970, there were no plans for meeting serious industrial disruption. Hurd's political antennae sensed in December 1970 after an electricity industry go-slow that events were changing the landscape and he urged a review.[261] The Prime Minister took up Hurd's recommendation when he thought that 'in light of recent events, there are several aspects of our arrangements for dealing with industrial emergency situations which should be looked at as a matter of great urgency ... A team should be asked to start at once, and urgently, contingency planning for mitigating the effects of any future disputes affecting the basic services'.[262] On 30 December Heath went further: 'His [the Prime Minister's] reaction is, I am afraid, that the machine is just not good enough. He comments that every major emergency so far he has had to take over himself. He deduces from that that a central project team could operate effectively, and indeed logically.'[263]

Sir Philip Allen, Permanent Secretary to the Home Office, was 'not really persuaded' that the machinery needed radical change,[264] partly due to cost but also to potential information blockage.[265] Allen persuaded Trend, William Armstrong and the Prime Minister that Allen's small committee which served the Home Secretary's Steering Committee on Pay Negotiations was doing the job already but promised to 'ensur[e] that all the nuts and bolts were constantly tightened up'.[266] Heath was clearly dissatisfied by this and 'rather grudgingly accepted the proposal [though] making it clear that the resulting outfit will be very much on trial, and subject to ruthless revision if it falls down on the job'.[267] Trend expressed his unease and subsequent support for Heath's warning in May 1971.[268]

The first miners' strike changed the nature of the debate. On 23 February 1972, the Prime Minister received a letter from the Cabinet Secretary urging urgent changes:

> I have now discussed the lessons of the miners' strike with the permanent secretary directly involved; and I have found general agreement that the emergency organisation, as tested by that crisis, is too large and diffuse and is staffed – in terms of departmental representation (both ministerial and official) at interdepartmental discussions – at too low a level of responsibility and competence. As a result the necessary information takes too long to reach the top and sometimes arrives in too diluted a form; and decisions reached at the top take too long to travel back to the point of executive action and run some risk of being misunderstood or distorted in the process. Measured against the two essential requirements of any crisis – namely, prompt and accurate information and swift and effective executive action – there is considerable room for improvement ... there is now, for the first time, ready acceptance of the need for greater centralisation of crisis management ...[269]

The creation of a central 'command post' had got underway with Heath telling Robert Armstrong a few months later, 'I cannot over-emphasise the importance which I attach to this project.'[270]

The Civil Contingencies Unit (Heath called it his 'Winter Emergencies Committee')[271] was created in the Cabinet Office in order to coordinate the government's response to the growing problems and was immensely secret.[272] The review was carried out by a group headed by John Hunt, Trend's deputy, and processed by a ministerial committee chaired by Jellicoe.[273] It is the only one of Heath's experiment with mixed committees of officials and Ministers which survives to this day[274] (civil servants usually found it uncomfortable to disagree with their political masters and some also felt this approach to involve a dangerous blurring of constitutional divisions).[275] The responsibility for this had previously rested with the Home Office since Parliament passed the Emergency Powers Act 1920.[276] Home Office officials were understandably unhappy with a shift that cast doubt upon their stewardship. It was expressed at the time that the true picture was not that the Home Office per se had failed to perform, but that Heath had lost confidence in his (in Hurd's words, 'hopeless')[277] Home Secretary, Reginald Maudling, who 'hadn't a grip on anything, that was part of the Irish problem, too. The Home Office has these huge responsibilities, you had a man who was shrewd and idle – everybody liked him. He didn't have a grip. But he was too important to be shoved aside. After all he'd been within a hair's breath of being leader himself. He was a big beast. He had stature, political stature he no longer deserved and this was one of the personnel problems'.[278]

Empire building on the part of the Cabinet Office was another rumoured reason for the change.[279] The creation of the CCU also led to a thoroughgoing review of the government's planning for further militant industrial action. It was conducted by Brigadier R. J. 'Dick' Bishop and identified the top 16 key vulnerable industries, headed by electricity generation.[280] The CCU continued into the twenty-first century but due to non-use had lost some of its efficiency. This was to be remedied after the fuel protests of 2000 and the increased threat of fundamentalist Islamist violence after the terrorist attacks on America in September 2001 with what was now called the Civil Contingencies Secretariat becoming ever more important and powerful.[281]

Apparatus that Heath was, by contrast, very happy to establish came in the form of a coordinating body for all things European.[282] As he himself put it:

> After both the passage of the European Communities Act and the completion of the Paris Summit, we had to learn to live as members, not as applicants for membership. I sent a personal minute to all members of the Cabinet informing them of the need to familiarise themselves with the techniques which the Community had developed for doing its business. I stressed that each department had to define its objectives and work out how they could be met in the complex bargaining situations of the Community ... [and a] European Secretariat was established in the Cabinet Office ...[283]

This was another of the few Heathite changes which has endured to the present day.

The Heath Government's rhetoric combined new central government machinery with a wish to free entrepreneurial talent and so achieve less but better government alongside a dynamic economy. Allied to this was Heath's conviction that Britain's political and economic future was firmly anchored within the integrating nations of Western Europe. In 1971 Heath managed to lift the French veto of nearly a decade and, despite difficult Commons votes, Britain finally joined the European Economic Community in January 1973. Heath passionately believed that accession to the EEC would provide a tremendous fillip to the British economy through increased competition and access to a huge, high-quality market. Once the first stage of his plan had been completed, he could turn his attention to the second. This was to prove far more difficult and problematic than sweet-talking the French President Pompidou and achieving the resulting parliamentary majorities. Continuing industrial relations unrest, rising unemployment (at the beginning of 1972 it reached 900,000) and growth of 3 per cent (compared to a target of 5 per cent due to the supposed slack evidenced by the relatively high unemployment)[284] led Heath to fear that the economy would not be in a fit state to seize the opportunities he perceived in the EEC. The aim of less government was to be abandoned to get the UK fit for Europe.[285] The scene was set for a different tack.

THE U-TURN

There had been a modest reflation of the economy in the 1971 Budget after unemployment had taken an upturn, with a reduction in taxation of £500 million, but this was slight enough to occasion no accusations of a volte-face.[286] The key year was 1972 when Heath made what became known as the 'U-turn'. Though many Conservatives were very critical of this in the late 1970s and early 1980s, there was near unanimous support for it at the time.[287] In February 1972, the lame-duck Upper Clyde Shipbuilders were bailed out (Rolls-Royce, too, was saved but this decision was about cash-flow and had international contractual and strategic repercussions – it was not really a lame-duck). Then in March, the Budget brought a clear commitment to government-led expansion with large cuts in income tax and purchase tax, April saw the pursuit of the Industry Bill, all followed by the floating of the pound in June.[288]

An Industry Bill increased Whitehall's powers in terms of regional aid and created the Industrial Development Executive to facilitate the new policy by way of discriminated intervention in selected industries.[289] Heath thought it necessary to counter his growing frustration with industry's failure to invest (stability measured by years is often required to encourage entrepreneurial investment, certainly of the sustained kind).²⁹⁰ This truly was a complete turnaround as it in effect reconstituted the Wilson Government's Industrial Reorganisation Corporation which had been gratuitously abolished early in the Heath Administration, partly as 'a sop to the right'.²⁹¹ Perhaps the closest similarity was to Reggie Maudling's 1962–4 'dash for growth' which had at its heart the aborted 'breakout' strategy – the idea that a determined push for sustained growth, superseding all other pressures (especially sterling and the balance of payments), would lead Britain out of its recent constrained economic performance.²⁹² A 'passion for growth – that's the key to understanding Ted', thinks Hurd; '[h]e believed this was the secret and because we'd failed to understand that in the years since 1945 we'd lagged behind. And there'd be obstacles and there'd be dangers but you had to press on and it would come right. This was his belief – he failed – but it was his genuine belief about what should happen to this country.'²⁹³

The Bill was drawn up behind the back of the DTI's junior Ministers – free-market men²⁹⁴ and one in particular, Nicholas Ridley, 'thoroughly indiscreet' according to Heath.²⁹⁵ It was only presented to the Secretary of State for Trade and Industry, John Davies, the lead Minister who would see his powers significantly increased,²⁹⁶ after a secret Cabinet Office team led by William Armstrong and consisting of a few officials from relevant departments and the CPRS had drafted it. (This was under the code name 'Cockaigne'²⁹⁷ – perhaps coined because Heath conducted the Elgar overture with the London Symphony Orchestra at the Festival Hall in November 1971 while the planning was taking place or even because subsidies were a dangerous drug.)²⁹⁸ Why Sir William? 'Ted,' mused Hurd, 'having this semi-French view of the power of the state and its efficacy believed that William Armstrong could deliver on prices and incomes and so on, that there were possibilities there that William was the right person to push ahead with.'²⁹⁹ Moreover, according to Peter Jay (in 1972 Economics Editor of *The Times*) 'Armstrong had credibility with whoever he spoke to.' Jay went on to say

> To achieve the agreement, the consensus necessary for the country to face the fact that it was destroying itself by the conflict between labour and capital, and more particularly the inflationary consequences and the way it was boiling. To recognise this and to draw the right conclusions. He came to believe that he was the only person who could achieve this agreement. And there were some reasons for believing that in the sense that he had extraordinary skills in that field. Our system doesn't really provide for officials, however senior, to come to occupy that pivotal role, it's supposed to be a minister ... The Prime Minister certainly lacked the skills to take people with him.³⁰⁰

Heath may also have turned to Armstrong as he found Sir Douglas Allen difficult. Sir Donald MacDougall, Chief Economic Adviser, went as far as to label the ensuing reflation of the economy not the 'Barber boom' as it has subsequently become known but the 'Armstrong spending boom'.[301] (Edmund Dell has Barber following meekly behind.)[302] Patrick Jenkin, Chief Secretary to the Treasury, was to wind up the Commons debate on the bill and only found out about the change of direction during Davies' speech, so much was the Treasury distrusted.[303]

But the final change of policy was politically the most significant. There had been a clear manifesto commitment in 1970 to keep government out of wage bargaining (except for its own employees) – 'Labour's compulsory wage control was a failure and we will not repeat it.'[304] Through the ongoing industrial unrest, Heath became more and more convinced that there should be a temporary reversion to an incomes policy – something that to differing degrees both Macmillan and Wilson had felt compelled to pursue. Heath was a leader whose ends always justified his means:[305] 'Our purpose was more pragmatic than people were led to believe' was how he put it in his memoirs.[306] Unshakeable once a decision had been made, he operated as if he were an exponent of John Maynard Keynes' famous remark 'When the facts change, I change my mind. What do you do?'[307]

The incomes policy came in three stages. First, in November 1972 there was a Counter-inflation (Temporary Provisions) Act which temporarily froze wages, and a White Paper, *A Programme for Controlling Inflation, The First Stage*.[308] Next came the January 1973 Counter-inflation Act which set up the Pay Board and Prices Commission; in February 1973 a Green Paper, *The Price and Pay Code*; and then in April 1973 another White Paper, *The Counter-inflation Programme – The Operation of Stage Two*.[309] The third stage came in November 1973 with a new pay code and the dramatic step of a state of emergency. All this was at first overseen by William Armstrong, and late in 1973 – its most crucial phase – by William Whitelaw, the ace negotiator brought back from almost achieving the impossible in Northern Ireland to become Secretary of State for Employment. William Armstrong was the prime influence over both the Industry Bill and prices and incomes. He became the 'hawk of hawks' over his complete dedication to obstruct the trade unions and their drive for high wage settlements.[310]

Heath's pragmatic nature facilitated what was an even bigger shift in the 1970–4 government. From a collegiate start to the administration, perhaps a 'model of Cabinet government',[311] responsibility gradually shifted away from Ministers – especially as Heath became all-powerful on his front bench.[312] This was not a total shift, however, as Lord Hurd explained:

> I think it remained collegiate in the sense that they remained friends. I've never known a government where that was true to a greater extent. Ted had got them together, not all of them, I'm not including Margaret Thatcher,[313] he got the sort of inner core into a group in opposition and they liked each other, they joked in the same way and they were friends to an extent which I've not seen since and that was quite important. But I suppose it's true that as the pressures multiplied, as life got harder, there was less time for that

sort of socialising, enjoying being in office, and pressures on the Prime Minister became great, his impatience with government departments increased, and so, yes, that did ebb away to some extent but not totally, they still had that feel even in the desperate times in January 1974 ... I don't think he was ever an isolated figure as far as his colleagues were concerned but he probably did take more and more and more upon himself. But never to anything like the extent that we see now.[314]

But power undeniably shifted to what was in effect a powerful coterie of senior civil servants around the Prime Minister, without a doubt the most significant example of an unannounced and unintended French-style *cabinet* in the post-war period, certainly before the Blair years. This powerfully influenced policy as 'a government with an unusually large injection of Party thinking in 1970 had become a government almost divorced from any Party advice by 1973'.[315]

The tendency toward technocratic governance began earlier than is generally appreciated. For in April 1971, Heath requested that he, Trend, William Armstrong and Rothschild should meet 'as a group from time to time to review the whole structure of events and Government policy'.[316] In November 1971, the Prime Minister wanted this stepped up to once a fortnight (though there is no evidence that this lasted very long).[317] Less a 'kitchen cabinet' than a 'study sideboard', it became *the* forum for the most controversial policies the government wished to carry out. Armstrong and his officials also handled the switch to an incomes policy and the expansion of public expenditure.[318] With the attempt to recreate Macmillan's tripartite era, Heath wrote of a 'low-key initiative' he requested which saw Rothschild and William Armstrong conduct informal meetings with both sides of industry.[319] Echoing Marcia Williams' frustration with Wilson's respect for and confidence in the Civil Service and its capacity to deliver, Hurd, her successor as Political Secretary, later wrote:

> Mr Heath had a high regard for the civil service. I sometimes wondered if this regard would have been so great if he had served longer as a backbench MP, or if he had not spent so much of his Ministerial apprenticeship in the Foreign Office. To some extent all senior Ministers are vulnerable in this way. The Private Secretaries in their own office and the very senior officials whom they themselves see day by day are usually people of the highest calibre. They talk well, listen attentively, know the world, and express themselves quickly and fluently on paper. This is particularly true of the Foreign Office. It is rather too easy to suppose that the whole public service is peopled with such agreeable paragons. In fact it is not. The traditional vices of bureaucracy are delay, excessive devotion to detail and a rigidity of thought which is reflected in authoritarian attitudes towards the citizen. These vices exist – usually at the lower level where policies are executed. The citizen is in touch with these levels, so is the conscientious backbench Member of Parliament, but the Minister is not. At the top of the civil service there is order, reason and reassurance – until the roof caves in.
>
> Because of his justified respect for his senior advisers Mr Heath tended to exaggerate

what could be achieved by new official machinery ... a little more scepticism about machinery would have been wise.[320]

The unannounced *chef de cabinet* of Heath's shift towards prime ministerial government was the most powerful civil servant in the land, Sir William Armstrong.[321] Although he undoubtedly shared power with Trend in the 1960s and early 1970s, he had eclipsed Trend in the Heath years as the Secretary of the Cabinet's influence over the Prime Minister waned. This was due to Heath wanting his senior Civil Service advisers to act in a more overtly political manner, again akin to the French Civil Service.[322] This Trend could not and would not do, being the last of the old-school Cabinet Secretaries who passionately believed in the continuation of the State and the protection of the Constitution as they understood it. Part of this was never to become too closely identified with any particular government (to the extent that Trend never voted in general elections lest it swayed his judgement).[323]

Hurd has described Trend as 'a character, a traditional character. We all regarded him as a defender of the status quo, somebody you could throw things at occasionally, I mean, you could treat him as a bit of a guy'.[324] Trend was a great believer in the Socratic method of advising his Prime Minister, that if the right questions are asked in the right order at the right time, the correct answers will naturally become apparent.[325] He also believed that detached advice – rather than advocacy – was the job of the mandarin. This led to caution, and Heath found it all too academic.[326] Trend's adherence to his concept of propriety frustrated Heath. Yet Heath did respect Trend's unparalleled knowledge and experience on matters, especially secret ones such as Anglo-American intelligence pooling.[327] But he wanted unambiguously personal advice from his advisers[328] and turned to William Armstrong as Trend refused to give it.[329] Plowden noted this tension in February 1972:

> Leading Tories are known to have become incrly dissat'd with B.Trend's Cabinet Office, which simply isnt doing for them the purposive policy-oriented job they'd anticipated when working out in Opposition their elaborate plans for a central capability of wh the CPRS was to have been only one part. It's being suggested that T – who's been in the job since 1963, far too long ('Harold Wilson burnt him out', as my father [Lord Plowden] is always saying) is about to go ...[330]

It was another year before John Hunt succeeded Trend.

THE STELLAR RISE AND TRAGIC FALL OF SIR WILLIAM ARMSTRONG

William Armstrong was central to Heath's gradual shift towards a much more prime ministerial style of government. He had grown bored with his role as

Head of the Home Civil Service, only responsible for staffing and machinery-of-government issues.[331] On 23 August 1972, Samuel Brittan had an exclusive in the *Financial Times* speculating that William Armstrong was to become head of a new Prime Minister's Department.[332] Armstrong moved quickly to rebut Brittan's article, unsurprisingly labelling it 'silly season stuff'.[333] Robert Armstrong, ever hostile to the think tank, wrote to Donald Maitland with the suspicion that the story had 'A CPRS source, I presume.'[334] Maitland replied that 'The indications are that the source is in the Party. Mark Schreiber is the leading candidate.'[335] Despite Heath's 1969 interest (see Chapter 3) in more open government, very little happened on this subject during his government. Lord Franks was asked to chair an inquiry into the Official Secrets Act[336] and in 1972 urged 'a narrower, more clearly drawn secrecy law'.[337] If Heath had been re-elected in 1974, it is likely he would have legislated along these lines.[338] As it was, reform came only in 1989.

It may or may not have been 'silly season stuff' in William Armstrong's view, but Heath asked him to consider doing exactly what he had publicly dismissed.[339] Armstrong duly responded with a meaty report. A chief of staff was considered – 'one man acting as suzerain both of the Cabinet Office and the Civil Service Department'. There would be a single department approach for 'overall government strategy and the allocation and control of resources in pursuit of that strategy'. This was quickly ruled out due to concentration of work, the overall burden and questions of ministerial responsibility. Sir William then suggested a 'department of resources and management'. This would have seen either the CSD and the Treasury reunited, or the Treasury's public expenditure division merged with the CSD's staffing side and the Cabinet Office, but Armstrong was loth to split the Treasury any further. The last option mooted was a 'cabinet and public services department', which would have involved the amalgamation of the Cabinet Office and either all or most of the CSD (staffing might have been returned to the Treasury). There was a further option – to do nothing.[340] With William Armstrong offering a deep analysis but finally coming down hard on the side of the status quo, and Robert Armstrong already a known opponent of splitting the Treasury again, there was little chance of radical change at the centre. Heath accepted this, but clearly only reluctantly:

> The Prime Minister said that another major problem was what he described as the 'No. 10 problem'. Increasingly he had found the need to force issues to the fore and process them to the point of decision from the centre. The Prime Minister's Private Office as now constituted could not do this. Ad hoc arrangements had been made for dealing with European affairs and emergencies, but it might be beginning to be necessary to provide some more definite organisational arrangements.[341]

Lord Hurd was thoughtful on Heath's 'No. 10 problem':

That was quite constant. He wasn't himself a great original thinker, Ted, at all. He needed to be fed with ideas but he felt that he wasn't being fed with ideas. He was conscious of what he needed and he needed people around him such as he had in opposition on a smaller scale. He needed people around him who would have constant original ideas and he wasn't getting that out of the machine or out of his colleagues. I think that was the driver. I don't think it was him saying 'I've got these brilliant ideas, how do we apply them,' it was him saying 'We bloody-well need these brilliant ideas, who is going to give them to me, then I'll drive them through.'[342]

Heath had identified the same problem as Wilson earlier (along with Trend and William Armstrong), that of insufficient 'strength at the centre'.[343] Perhaps due to the ever-growing complexity of government, the knotty problems governments were trying to deal with, or even the gradual expansion of the role of Prime Minister beyond being merely *primus inter pares* (maybe a combination of all three), the Prime Minister was now assuming a much more active role. Yet the Prime Minister's Office remained a very small institution, certainly compared to the offices of overseas leaders. Part of the original thinking behind the CPRS was to facilitate the Prime Minister in leading from the front. The form in which the CPRS was actually created brought some support, but clearly not enough. When Wilson formed his third administration in March 1974, he took decisive action in this regard, establishing the Downing Street Policy Unit. This initially comprised nine special advisers (including its founding father Bernard Donoughue)[344] who would be 'advisers to the Prime Minister; and they are policy advisers, appointed as civil servants, not political advisers appointed and paid by a Party political organisation. They do not intend to operate over the whole field of Government policies. They are mainly interested in day-to-day advice to the Prime Minister on selected fields of domestic policy, which particular reference to the political implications of policy'.[345] The hole had been partially filled and it was the explicitly political Policy Unit which was to prosper, expand greatly and survive to the present day.

But before the Policy Unit had been established, with Heath increasingly surrounded by supposedly impartial officials, however eminent, and with troubles which demanded political solutions crowding in, something had to give. What gave was the career of Sir William Armstrong. Promoted above his superiors to become Joint-Permanent Secretary to the Treasury in 1962, he left after six momentous years to become the first Permanent Secretary to the Civil Service Department as well as Head of the Home Civil Service. But in 1972, though still based in the CSD and retaining responsibility for machinery-of-government matters (Sir Frank Cooper thought 'William got very bored with the whole thing'),[346] he was asked to plan Heath's shift towards a more interventionist strategy. Armstrong was involved throughout as a civil servant committed to making things better, 'and without the civil servant's ultimate detachment'[347] met a driven and pragmatic Prime

Minister.[348] This was already treading a fine line when it came to impartiality, but when he was photographed sitting next to the Prime Minister in a press conference to announce a statutory incomes policy in Lancaster House on 6 November 1972, rumours and reality began to converge.[349] This identified him with the politics of the incumbent. It also encouraged gossip over his role vis-à-vis the Prime Minister. One Whitehall trade union leader, Bill Kendall of the Civil and Public Services Association, coined the phrase 'the deputy prime minister'[350] to describe Armstrong, something, according to Lord Croham, Armstrong liked the sound of.[351] Press speculation, as we have seen, even suggested that Armstrong would be put in charge of a new Prime Minister's Department.[352]

Sir William's involvement at the apex of government activity did not last very long, however. For, at the moment of acutest pressure on the government, with the second miners' dispute underway from 12 November 1973 and the oil price doubled by Christmas,[353] Armstrong's mental health broke in the early weeks of 1974, just at the time when the decision was being reached to call an early general election on the basis of 'Who Governs Britain?'. There are descriptions of him being quietly led from a committee room by Douglas Allen after weeks of strange warnings from Armstrong of infiltration by communists, moving the Red Army from here and the 'blue' army from there,[354] and finally advising his fellow Permanent Secretaries to go home early that afternoon as a sign of governmental confidence in itself.[355]

Whitehall folklore suggests that Armstrong may have had two earlier breakdowns.[356] Certainly, one ex-official explained how it came within his duties in the late 1960s to administer his ongoing medication.[357] Samuel Brittan thinks that 'His illness was always likely to break out under stress.'[358] Armstrong remained Head of the Home Civil Service throughout his convalescence, but was allowed to retire a year early in April 1974 at the age of 59 to join the Board of Midland Bank on the understanding that he would become Chairman in April 1975. Permission for this, it was claimed, was granted by Heath and reviewed and approved by Wilson.[359] Joe Haines made it plain that his leaving had avoided an embarrassing demand for his departure over his identification with Heath.[360]

As Churchill had written of Lord Curzon, 'The morning had been golden; the noontide was bronze; and the evening lead': the same could be said of Sir William.[361] Armstrong himself understood his mistake: 'when honest people can use the words "deputy prime minister" of one, then clearly something got slightly askew ... I was always determined not to be seen as another Horace Wilson, but that's what happened.'[362] It was undeniably a story of failure. Even Heath came to find fault with Armstrong, criticizing him privately, after the government fell, for claiming too much influence.[363] But it was a failure shared by Heath himself.

As Prime Minister of a government better prepared than any other (according to politicians such as Iain Macleod[364] and academics like John Ramsden)[365] steered away from its original course, Heath's reputation never recovered. Recriminations reverberated for years. The right wing of the Conservative Party thought that Heath had betrayed them and his own 'Selsdon-man' planning. The rise of Thatcher and her cult was mirrored by her followers' dismissal of Heath as without principle or a spine.[366] Others felt that Heath's reliance on senior civil servants fatally wounded him. It is clear that a coterie formed at the pinnacle of government, and that it was formed by the Prime Minister, his Principal Private Secretary and the Head of the Home Civil Service. William Waldegrave, by 1973 Hurd's successor as Heath's Political Secretary, thought that he had become 'wholly reliant' on Armstrong and Armstrong. Waldegrave was reputedly said to have seen the triumvirate walking down the stairs in No 10 and then murmured 'The Treasury have got him' (though his recollection in 2006 was of 'a very clear picture of Ted going *up* the stairs to his flat [in No 10] with Robert and William going with him and thinking that he had chosen to be surrounded by the civil service when he went to relax and talk about things. I perhaps should have said the Treasury, but ... I remember the point being that it was the civil servants and not ministerial colleagues or political advisers with whom he felt most comfortable by the end'.)[367] Talk of this kind was preposterous to Sir Samuel Goldman, public expenditure supremo in the Treasury 1968–73 and a close friend of Sir William: 'Rubbish. Absolute rubbish. Don't believe it.' William Armstrong's fate was 'Very sad.' 'He was a politician really. He had the misfortune to become the friend, if you like, protégé of Edward Heath and of course there are not many civil servants who can withstand that kind of thing when the Prime Minister makes you his particular favourite. It's a very sad story. He was a great friend of mine. His life in a sense ended in tragedy ... There's no civil servant, really, who would be capable of resisting that'.[368]

It is likely that Burke Trend would have. Lord Hurd backs Goldman's thesis: 'I think that is more true. Ted had no particular regard for the Treasury and the Treasury had to restrain him in the autumn of 1973 when the danger signals were multiplying and the Treasury was quite right.'[369] There is, though, some truth to Goldman's contention. At the aforementioned press conference to announce the second phase of the incomes policy, three chairs were placed on the platform, one for Heath, one for Barber and the final one for Maurice Macmillan. When Macmillan was delayed, Heath turned to Sir William and said 'Come on, you'd better sit there.' 'What does one do when instructed by the prime minister to sit next to him?' was Armstrong's later comment.[370] Heath the bureaucratic politician and William Armstrong the highly political official were becoming far too close for propriety.[371] William Whitelaw, upon his return from Northern Ireland to become Employment Secretary, began to speak of the 'Sir William Armstrong syndrome'.[372]

CRISES AND CULMINATION

Sir William's fall came at the end of one of the most torrid periods over which a government has presided in peacetime. Strikes leading to civil disturbance, and an economy showing unprecedentedly sickly signs of what was christened 'stagflation' by Norman MaCrae of *The Economist* (stagnant growth coupled with rising unemployment – supposedly illogical), led some to describe the country as 'ungovernable'.[373] The Civil Service could not escape some of the fallout from this distressing state of affairs. Douglas Hurd, Heath's Political Secretary until 1973 when he left to nurse a parliamentary constituency in Oxfordshire, has written critically of the Civil Service when crisis enveloped the government. A diplomat to his fingertips and therefore not a man usually given to hyperbole, Hurd described the bureaucracy's capitulation in the last months. He believed that when a government faces

> rough times, when existing policies have collapsed, a Prime Minister will find that the senior civil servants fall silent. I saw this happen once over Ireland and three times over incomes policy. They busy themselves at such times with the usual agendas and meetings, the corridors are full of scurrying figures, but nothing substantial emerges. They are, quite reasonably, waiting for the new course which only politicians can set. It is then that political advice becomes all-important ... No one who was present at any of these three meetings could believe that the civil service runs this country.[374]

Heath was largely uninterested in this 'political advice' due to his attempt always to lead in the national interest and the belief that this would be, axiomatically, politically popular.

During 1972–3 Hurd encouraged ministers, with Heath's approval, to recruit more special advisers, partly in an attempt to counter the image that politics were being ignored in favour of managerialism.[375] Hurd also voiced concerns in 1971 that the CPRS, 'a body of public servants, [was] developing political strategy that was basically the prerogative of Ministers'.[376] (The idea that Heath's governance was too technocratic found strong backing from a senior Permanent Secretary in 2005 who thought that democracy demanded greater political input than was evident during 1970–4.)[377] In the last months of the administration, Hurd tried to bring the developing network of special advisers – more than ever before, though 'the total in service does not seem to have exceeded ten; and none had the public profile of, for example, Balogh'[378] – together to bring greater strategic coherence.[379]

This challenge to the authority of the State had many repercussions. It further damaged an already shaky economy. Differing beliefs on how the growing economic malaise could be mitigated was a main factor in the overshadowing of the CPRS. Relations between the Prime Minister and Rothschild had been strong from the first, with Rothschild finding Heath 'to be a careful listener with, of course, a very sharp mind'.[380] There was also for Rothschild, from the beginning, a right of audience with the Prime Minister.[381] Rothschild did admit, however, that at the end of 1972 he only saw Heath once every five to seven weeks.[382] This was partly due to Rothschild's almost shameless sycophancy – or should one call it calculated attentiveness? For example, when the Prime Minister mentioned that he wanted a Churchillian reduction in paper coming to the Cabinet[383] (a running wish of Heath's, right through to 1973),[384] Rothschild wrote to Heath's Principal Private Secretary that, 'You may care to mention to the Prime Minister that I hope he is not going to be one jump ahead of the CPRS on every occasion. The central capability has been discussing this very matter during the last 10 days'[385] (Douglas-Home had mentioned it on Rothschild's milk-round).[386] 'That all depends on the CPRS' was Heath's reply.[387]

Rothschild was to undermine this informality and closeness to Heath with an ill-judged 'brief address' to the Letcombe Laboratory of the Agricultural Research Council near Wantage on 24 September 1973. He predicted, all too accurately as it turned out, just how far the British economy would slide if the country endured an economic future similar to its recent past:

> From the vantage point of the Cabinet Office, it seems to me that unless we take a very strong pull at ourselves and give up the idea that we are one of the wealthiest, most influential and important countries in the world ... we are likely to find ourselves in increasingly serious trouble. To give just one unpalatable example, in 1985 we shall have half the economic weight of France or Germany ... It is the knowledge that our difficulties and dangers are as severe and ominous as they were in World War II, though, of course, of a different sort ... When you have 1 million unemployed, it is not easy to scrap the Concorde, even if that were a good idea, and put another 25,000 men out of work, quite apart from the financial penalties of breaking a Treaty ... [yet] if we don't grasp this nettle, we shall not solve those difficulties I mentioned earlier which, as sure as eggs are eggs, are with us now.[388]

William Plowden has explained the genesis of the speech: 'The Rothschild speech starts with Peter Carey and myself going to the Hudson Institute in New York and talking to Herman Kahn ... and bringing Kahn back to talk to Rothschild ... Kahn sowed in Rothschild's mind the seeds of what became the Wantage speech: "You guys are going down the tubes and you don't recognise it." So I felt slightly guilty about being the cause of that'.[389]

What Plowden felt 'slightly guilty' about was that Heath had decided, on the same day as Rothschild was sharing his downbeat thoughts, to give a speech of his own in Essex, lauding the economic prospects of Britain amid rising general prosperity.[390] The phone-lines of the No 10 Press Office were soon 'besieged' over this apparent divergence at the very heart of government. In the pressured world of Downing Street, where a pin-prick can appear as a sword-wound, officials moved into crisis mode. The Civil Service nightmare of a condottiere roaming around – and sometimes venturing outside accepted boundaries – was coming true.[391] For Rothschild had 'invited the BBC and local radio to be present' and 'had circulated the text of his speech to the Press because he had learnt from experience that if you did not do so you were liable to misquotation' (though in this instance the ability to claim this would have helped him).[392]

The Director of the CPRS was tracked down to his flat after his return from Cambridge and, at the 'invitation' of John Hunt, travelled to the Cabinet Office at once. An 'interview' was conducted by Hunt and Robert Armstrong, at which Rothschild protested his innocence by professing 'to be surprised by the interest which the Press were taking and claimed that he had said nothing in his speech which had not been published in some other forum'. Rothschild's warning had, almost verbatim, also formed the main part of the discussion briefing for the CPRS's November 1972 'Review of Government Strategy'.[393]

For the two paragons of propriety, Rothschild's speech was idiotic. They were

> not concerned so much with any question of the disclosure of official information [there had not been any] but with the policy implications and the embarrassment to Ministers. The Press seemed bound to draw the conclusion that our standard of living would fall dramatically in relation to our European partners unless the Government took decisions like cancelling the Concorde to free resources. Lord Rothschild said that he had never recommended cancelling the Concorde and did not do so in his speech; but he agreed that this passage might be open to misinterpretation.[394]

The mandarins were worried lest Anglo-French relations be damaged, 'particularly since it was thought that General Bloch was currently in London for discussions with senior British officials about the Concorde programme'.[395] The British Embassy in Paris was briefed immediately.[396] (This may not have been disastrous, for Rothschild was on good terms with at least one French general, with whom he had swapped information of the exact French cost of Concorde for several bottles of Château Lafite from his private cellar.)[397]

The next day, the Prime Minister summoned Hunt and William Armstrong to consider whether Rothschild 'be dismissed or asked to resign'. The factors supporting his dismissal were 'the general embarrassment', the speech being 'a calculated act', and the fact that 'other senior officials might be encouraged to think that they could similarly break the rules over the clearance of speeches and get away with it'. Against this, 'the departure of Lord Rothschild at this juncture would not only be damaging to the development of the CPRS but might appear to give substance to the suggestion that there was a fundamental disagreement over policy between Ministers and himself'.

Heath decided to keep Rothschild,[398] but the Prime Minister subjected the head of the think tank to, in Rothschild's words, a 'rather unpleasant dressing-down'.[399] In the meeting, Heath 'made clear to Lord Rothschild the embarrassment created for him'. Rothschild again defended himself, saying that 'there was nothing in his speech with which the Prime Minister would disagree'. Heath 'did not contest this' but 'regretted that Lord Rothschild's observations on the matter had been so half-baked'. The Prime Minister then warned Rothschild that his CPRS charges should 'now be instructed to be completely discreet in their relations with journalists', this in reference to a leak to *The Times* that could only have come from within the think tank over advised public expenditure cuts (senior civil servants being generally uneasy over the think tank's perceived openness).[400]

Rothschild later wrote that he and Heath immediately put all this behind them, such was the Prime Minister's nature: 'in a very Heath-like way there came a moment in the interview when he said, "Well, now let's discuss nuclear reactors". And that was the end of it. The matter was never raised again and our relationships were perfectly OK afterwards.'[401] Certainly, a fortnight later on 10 October 1973, after the Wantage speech had caused some discomfort for the Prime Minister at the Conservative Party Conference, Rothschild again wrote to Heath to 'reiterate my apologies; and express my gratitude for the way you dealt with the entire issue'.[402] The Prime Minister responded curtly: 'I said [to an ITN interviewer] that I regarded the incident as closed – and so I do'.[403] But things did not go back to the way they had been. Heath withdrew much of his earlier trust in the think tank. Even Rothschild had to admit that it was 'never glad confident morning again'.[404]

William Waldegrave believes that the CPRS's eclipse went deeper: 'The government was becoming increasingly crisis bound, which means those who are crisis bound don't want to hear people talking about strategy. In particular, they don't want to hear people saying uncomfortable things.'[405] Lord Butler thinks that the CPRS 'was becoming more of an embarrassment than a help' and that Heath was beginning to think that 'a lot of the CPRS's ideas were zany'.[406] (Trailing the CPRS's last strategy session for the Heath Government were the words, 'Many people in this country now believe politics to be a private game', promising that in the presentation the CPRS would 'take the devil's advocate role', which lend credence to Butler's analysis.)[407] The CPRS's 'brief heady moment of creative energy' was essentially coming to an end.[408] Indeed, on 19 December John Hunt wrote to Robert Armstrong reporting 'that morale in the CPRS is currently low, partly because a lot of their work has been knocked sideways by the current situation and partly because of Lord Rothschild's recent off-stage activities.'[409]

This was very unfortunate, since it coincided exactly with the time Heath needed his creation most. For, just as his options over the economy began to narrow with the OPEC-induced inflation and the miners' second bout of industrial action, the iconoclasm inherent in the CPRS may have got him through it. Indeed, Rothschild, who himself suffered a mild heart attack in December 1973,[410] and on his doctor's orders spent the first three weeks of 1974 recuperating in Barbados,[411] suggested that global pressures were changing the domestic position. He argued, unsuccessfully as it turned out, that the oil crisis had made energy a special case; in any event he felt deeply that the miners deserved a doubled wage-packet due to their unpalatable working conditions.[412]

The road was therefore open to treat the miners outside the incomes policy to which the government was trying to tie the country. This eminently reasonable and rational analysis, exactly what the CPRS had been born to do, was rejected over the power-play of who was in charge and the country slid into a three-day week and an even deeper crisis.[413] For Plowden, the whole malaise was 'compounded by Victor Rothschild's extremely unfortunate illness, wh took him away at the moment when ... more than ever before it was critical to have a sharp cutting edge in the form of someone who was willing and able to deliver slightly unpalatable and unsolicited messages to people at the top'.[414]

The last demonstration of Heath's personal *cabinet* in action was altogether ironic. In December 1973, the four most powerful mandarins in Whitehall sent the Prime Minister a blunt message that his attempt to 'breakout' of the British economy's recent straitjacket was doomed. William Armstrong, Hunt, Allen and Robert Armstrong had a meeting to discuss economic contingency planning in order to counter the damage of an estimated £3,000 million deficit on the balance of payments for 1974. The measures would include public expenditure reductions, a cut in subsidies to public energy industries, an increase in income tax, abolition of some tax relief and a tax on land and property. Robert Armstrong minuted his Prime Minister very directly about the meeting:

> At some time between now and the announcement of a change of this kind, it would be necessary to change gear, from the sort of provisional 'business as usual' line which we have followed so far, to more overt recognition that we face a very serious situation, which means (as you have said) at least reducing the growth of the standard of living and perhaps even a decline in living standards. It is arguable that confidence is no longer served by continuing as at present: if the situation is clearly serious and calls for action, confidence is damaged, not improved, by a continuing appearance of Governmental blindness (or refusal to see) and inaction.[415]

The only people capable of stopping Heath proved to be his closest official advisers. His political colleagues were simply unwilling and unable.

CONCLUSION

The Heath Government's extensive ambition was dashed so quickly and in the most dramatic fashion. It remains the biggest failure to carry out a programme in the post-war period. But that does not mean all was in vain, even worthless. For the planning in the run-up to government was exemplary, both in its theory and as an attempt to bring practicality to that theory. Some of those ideas, too, were imaginative and bold. But it was inevitable that political planning would be amended once in government. Quite how much was adapted and changed upset some of the pre-election planners, with programme analysis and review the key disappointment. The Central Policy Review Staff, while again disappointing political figures such as David Howell, was a tremendously exciting creation. Its moment in the midday sun did not last long, perhaps only two years. However, those two years impressed all who came into contact with the think tank, and its abolition in 1983 was widely lamented. Repeated calls for a reconstitution eventually led to something akin to the CPRS gradually taking shape at the heart of government throughout the Blair years.

Nevertheless, the Heath Government's fall in February 1974 was a disaster for both the temporary and permanent sides of government, and for the faith that institutional change could turn Britain's fortunes around. Perhaps it was the domestic equivalent of the Suez Crisis, whereby humiliation was suffered by Britain from every angle and 'as in a lightning flash' the landscape was revealed. Administrative reform having been extensively tried and perceived to have failed meant that the stage was set for the leftist attempts of Tony Benn and his followers and the right-wing actuality of Thatcherism, both of them aggressively political initiatives that drew their inspiration and much of their personnel from outside government altogether. Certainly the mid-1970s now seem a pivotal moment in the post-war history of Britain and the Civil Service had a central role in it.

Conclusion

The reform of British central government during the years 1960–74 was a process of comparatively vigorous activity. Departments came and went (and sometimes merged and de-merged). The twentieth century's iron demarcation between temporary yet largely elected ministers and permanent, but unelected, officials began to break down and the gradually increasing power of the office of Prime Minister began to be recognized administratively.

We have examined the reasons why the pressure for change was considerable and varied. These were long- and short-term, social, political, economic and, in some cases, personal. The feeling that no end was in sight to relative economic decline brought great impetus for change, especially in the management and purpose of the Treasury, which during the 1950s and 1960s was going through a difficult period anyway. Pent-up antagonism towards allegedly elitist recruitment to the top ranks and the real or imagined ethos of the British Civil Service added a class-based critique to the debate. A consensus between the political parties during the tenures of Macmillan, Wilson and Heath that administrative reform was necessary to turning around the country's fortunes added to the frequency of the changes. This decade and a half of constant alteration brought with it another theme which was to dominate the 1970s – whether or not the Civil Service had its own agenda; whether it was right for unelected officials to hold what were in effect political, if not party, opinions which they were powerfully placed to promote, and which usually steered policy towards the consensual middle ground. Some Labour and Conservative figures felt that the machine was a political entity in itself.

It is worth analysing just how the individual Prime Ministers who presided over the Civil Service during the 1960s and early 1970s viewed the higher reaches of the state machine. Harold Macmillan's approach, as in so many other core areas, was complex. Macmillan demonstrated an arm's-length's dependence on the bureaucracy, as witness his unchanging belief in the Cabinet system and the corresponding trust in his Ministers, somewhat in the manner that a feudal landowner would respect his servants. This meant that he felt entirely comfortable in the way the centre was traditionally organized, with a small No 10 office supplemented by a single unpaid appointee, his friend John Wyndham, essentially there as a chum to keep Macmillan's spirits up.

Yet, especially as the decade turned, Macmillan began to take a keen interest in the running of the state and its power to steer the economy. The strong and sustained growth of France and other Western European neighbours caught Macmillan's eye and, along with a wish to recreate the unified national purpose of the war years, led to the creation of the National Economic Development Council. That, and the reorganization of the Treasury (in the wake of the Plowden report) to give it a more growth-oriented momentum, with its concomitant 'out with the old, in with the new' promotion of Sir William Armstrong above his superiors, meant that Macmillan was subtly changing the nature of the Prime Minister's role as it had been previously understood in peacetime. Certainly he never trusted the Treasury enough to allow it, or its Chancellors, free rein. As the author of the mildly statist *The Middle Way*, he believed in what he later described as 'a little *dirigisme*' which he had already demonstrated during his time as an interventionist Minister for Housing in the early 1950s. It is entirely conceivable that if Macmillan's tenure had lasted longer, he would have harnessed the State's power in a greater and greater fashion.

There are many general analyses and theories of the processes and dynamics of administrative reform, perhaps the most cogent being by Richard Chapman and J. R. Greenaway in 1980. They described the multitude of elements ranging from a premium on incrementalism for an old bureaucracy to the very long historic roots of many if not all of the reform issues, along with the short- and long-term pressure of ideas from society in general, from academia, business and indeed from within the Civil Service itself. It is worth analysing which influences held the upper hand during the three main premierships of the period 1960–74. For Macmillan, the 1930s depression combined with the lessons of Keynes, the success of the wartime British State and its move towards a mixed economy with a comprehensive welfare state after 1945 all contributed to his mildly interventionist and expansionist stewardship of the State. Macmillan wanted 'a better yesterday'[1] – and more of it.

His successor, Sir Alec Douglas-Home, had too little time to demonstrate any reforms, analytically derived or not. In office for essentially a year and all the time fighting against the odds for re-election, Douglas-Home nevertheless undid nothing of Macmillan's new dirigiste approach and even suggested that, had he prevailed at the polls in 1964, a major review of central Civil Service machinery was very much in his mind.

With Labour's victory over Douglas-Home's Conservatives, Harold Wilson was in position to enact his wishes. Having been previously a young Cabinet Minister at the Board of Trade and an even younger senior civil servant in the wartime Cabinet Office meant Wilson had plenty of experience on which to base his extensive opinions. First, he was a great believer in civil servants per se. Having been one at a senior level (and one who had been offered a permanent job at the

Treasury when the war ended), Wilson felt secure in senior officials' company, not a universal feeling in political circles. Second, he was a statistician and shared the belief that experts throughout the Service were not given the credit their learning and skills deserved. Moreover, he had been Chairman of the House of Commons Public Accounts Committee before he became Labour Leader in 1963, a role which provides solid information on financial matters generally and the Treasury's performance in particular. Add to this a belief throughout the centre and left of British politics at this time of the benefits of some form of State direction and you have a politician who believed in the State but who desired to see it changed to do more with greater effect.

Unlike Macmillan, who had taken several years to decide what he wanted to do vis-à-vis the machinery of government, Wilson began his reform of Whitehall with a flurry of activity within the first weeks. Five new departments were established, high-level special advisers were ushered into senior posts both inside the Treasury and the Cabinet Office and a new Political Secretary was appointed. All were presented as needed changes to make the Civil Service work more efficiently and in a modern fashion. All created to a lesser or greater degree friction and turf wars, especially that between the DEA and the Treasury, and between Marcia Williams and Derek Mitchell in No 10. This demonstrates a key factor in the Wilsonian model of Whitehall reform, namely that for every step forward, there was often one back. It was what Sir David Omand described as, admittedly in a different context, the machinery of government's 'law of unexpected consequences'.[2] Wilson's penchant for machinery tinkering in his first two Premierships (1964–6 and 1966–70) was endless, as was his wish to build a worthy rival to the Treasury. In 1964 it was the DEA, then in 1967 the Department of Employment and Productivity, in 1968 the Civil Service Department, then in 1969 it was Mintech's turn to take the baton. None lasted very long, displacement activity in the form of constant reorganization reigned and the Treasury remained much as it always had been.

Wilson's creation of the Fulton Committee in 1966 was due as much to his belief in across-the-board modernization as it was a wish to energize the State and unleash the potentials of the specialists therein (alongside a more mundane concern over recruitment). The true significance of the myriad recommendations contained within the Fulton Report came only with the passage of time when most of its major points were enacted in some form or another. In the short term, Fulton was essentially memorable because of the arguments which ensued over its content and implementation. This was not healthy for Wilson's desired reputation as an effective Whitehall reformer.

Yet Wilson will go down in history as a reformer of great importance. For two of his innovations did endure and evolve and have ever since been considered settled parts of the Civil Service constellation, namely special advisers and the

Policy Unit. The importation of unelected outsiders to government in peacetime was not a new phenomenon, especially if one considers the time before the Great War. But for the rest of the twentieth century this was novel, as was the fact that the major appointees were specialists, economists at that, who were placed at the very top of government, as advisers to the Prime Minister and Chancellor (and another way to dent the Treasury's monopoly of advice). The 'thin end of the wedge' for special advisers into government came in 1964 and grew greatly. As did Wilson's other lasting reform, that of the Downing Street Policy Unit. Although this came in 1974 with Wilson's return, it was clearly based upon his experiences in government, notably a wish for the Prime Minister to be able to get involved much more deeply in what had hitherto been departmental business, something Macmillan had little interest in. Wilson also claimed it was developed on the recommendation of the Fulton Report, which had included the concept of a 'Planning Unit' headed by a 'Senior Policy Adviser'. That the Policy Unit was staffed by politically appointed special advisers, his other lasting innovation, provided a neat coherency uncharacteristic of Wilson's usual technocratic tinkering.

Harold Wilson's view of the State was essentially very similar to that of Macmillan. He, too, believed in a constant push for greater expansion. Where Wilson differed, however, was that his impetus had a much more consciously political heart. The left wing of British politics had been, since at least the 1930s, fascinated by the wish to plan the economy to a lesser or greater extent. After the Attlee years whereby great changes were made to the State, the 1950s saw what was in essence a dilemma for the Labour Party over whether to push for further enlargement and much more intrusive intervention in the economy or to consolidate and recognize that changing Labour aims could be better achieved by other routes. The publication of Anthony Crosland's *The Future of Socialism* in 1956 was perhaps the key text of this debate. With Wilson becoming Leader in 1963, a circle needed to be squared, and he proceeded upon a path which promised greater intervention by government but without creating new capacity, only rearranging what was already in place. Thus the DEA and Mintech were emboldened to change the economy, yet with little or no direct controls and with the Treasury retaining its veto over government spending and strategic direction, and therefore still in the ascendant. The highly ambitious plans that Wilson's 1960s governments created were consequently disappointed. That Wilson's approach had a real ideological motivation led many within his government to retain deep suspicion that the Civil Service was politically obstructionist, despite Wilson's own confidence in individual civil servants. Moreover, the seemingly never-ending addiction to rearranging the higher reaches of the State led to a real rejection of machinery reforms in the later 1970s and 1980s, something directly linked to Wilson. He immersed himself in the minutiae of technocracy, embracing all the many influences therein, only to emerge with what almost always seemed the most politically advantageous at the time, ignoring the longer-term needs. His reputation in this area has proved to be poor.

The reason the Policy Unit thrived was clear from Edward Heath's *cri de coeur* in 1972 when he spoke of the 'No 10 problem'. He felt that he was increasingly required to run policy from the centre as Macmillan did not, yet the machinery had not caught up. Furthermore, well-placed protagonists sensed that a lack of political input into the policy-making process was a definite factor in the failure of the Heath Government. A centrally placed unit comprised of those politically motivated pushed at an open door and Prime Ministers have not looked back since.

The last months of Heath's failing administration were in stark contrast to the hope it embodied in its first. The unprecedented, and unrepeated, depth and breadth of research and planning the Conservatives conducted touched on many if not most elements of government, all in the belief that while his mentor Macmillan was on exactly the right path he had not driven there with the required urgency or efficiency. Heath wanted to see central government retain its compassion and decency but simultaneously to graft onto it business efficiency and academic analysis. The influences on Heath came from many angles. For a start, he spent a short time within the Ministry for Civil Aviation after passing the Civil Service exams, but he found the bureaucracy on the periphery of Whitehall stifling and was followed by several years as a senior Minister, thus having a view on both sides of government. A salient point here is that while he most certainly found officialdom stuffy he also respected it mightily, in the traditional Tory manner. In contrast to Wilson, another with deep respect for the Service, Heath sought to avoid turf disputes whereas Wilson had in some ways encouraged them, as witness the example of Marcia Williams and Derek Mitchell compared to Douglas Hurd and Robert Armstrong.

The research groups he oversaw pulled in a wide range of skills and experience, from senior officialdom, politics and business. It was from this mélange that emerged what were in effect two strong themes. One was the need for a much strengthened centre. The other, related to the first, was a wish for government to accept that to do better it must do less. The driving forces behind these two impulses were in the main part younger Conservatives along with businessmen they were largely coordinating. Extensive work persuasively presented impressed Heath, enough so that this most adroit of leaders led his young tyros to support their growing beliefs. But, once in government, though most of the plans were embarked upon, none were implemented to the letter. The creation of the Central Policy Review Staff is perhaps the key example. In effect, Heath understood basically what he wanted to do and change, set up political inquiries to provide him with options and then gave the results of these to the mandarins to enact (which resulted in greater power for the Civil Service than all other influences).

Heath, though fascinated by the machinery of government, was understandably much more taken by events, especially as his government encountered crises of a magnitude not seen since the war. The intricacies of Civil Service reform were pushed to the side and the easiest course was charted. This was not a time to take on vested interests in the way that Wilson and more importantly those around him had taken on senior officialdom over Fulton (albeit to little effect).

It has subsequently been understood that Heath himself was not wedded to much of the push towards less government, and that his flirtation with it pre-1970 and abandonment when in government led to great disappointment in some of his closest supporters. Where Heath was content to be bureaucratically controversial was in his treatment of the Treasury. As with Macmillan and Wilson before him, Heath was suspicious of the Treasury's power and its secretive nature which often led to Treasury-dominated solutions to crises with little prime ministerial let alone Cabinet input. Heath added to this wariness a belief that the Treasury was anti-European, believing that acceding to the EEC would do little for the UK and generally gloomy about the nation's economic prospects (in other words, that entry was more of a political than an economic decision). The Treasury was at its lowest influence during Heath's tenure in the post-war period. The idea of an explicit reforging of the centre, with a Prime Minister's Department one option, was toyed with in 1972 as part of Heath's inclination that the Premier needed greater personal power, even more than had accrued to him with the establishment of the CPRS. This thesis demonstrates that the Heath Government was a largely unrecognized experiment in extensive prime ministerialism. Though Heath perfectly observed the conventions of the constitution as they were understood and policed by those such as Trend, even encouraging robust debate around the Cabinet table, the naturally private and unexpansive Prime Minister increasingly drove policy through himself. This was partly due to his character, but also because there were few trusted Ministers of stature that he could call upon, especially after Iain Macleod's early death and before William Whitelaw's rise. It was furthermore driven by the immense pressure of events which demanded swift decisions which were facilitated by Heath leaning on his officials to be more akin to those found in the French system. This is where Sir William Armstrong stepped in to the breach, with damaging results all round.

Heath had great expectations of what the machine could do for his policies but, in contrast to Wilson's actions, he believed that he had created the extra capacity required. Seeking what was essentially a retention of the status quo but run more efficiently, Heath was far more sympathetic to a technocratic, business-like approach, one opposed to overtly political steers. This was one of the reasons he became isolated from his political colleagues as he believed, rightly,

CONCLUSION

that the Civil Service always responded to a strong ministerial lead, especially if it was in a consensual, centrist direction. The bond between politician and official was never greater than during the Heath years. The Civil Service rarely had more influence.

A few major themes consequently bind the administrative history of Britain during the 1960s and early 1970s. The first is that the spirit of the age across the broad swathe of the political centre ground was resolutely anchored to the belief in vigorous interventionism. An acceptance that the economy was the government's undoubted responsibility was allied to the fact that government also had a duty to include all agents within the economy with a view to forging a coherent plan whilst maintaining fairness. A great deal of prime ministerial time, quite likely the single greatest aspect, was spent on this as was that of the Civil Service.

A related theme is that of the self-confidence of the Civil Service. It truly did still see itself as the fourth service of the Crown after the army, navy and air force, just as Sir Warren Fisher had envisaged. This strength meant that it could fend off political change it did not believe in, whether that of a philosophical nature with the Labour plans of 1964 or those borrowed from the business world, elements of which were part of the 1970 Conservative approach. Radicalism was hardly attempted in these years, but would have been seen off easily. The *art* of the senior civil servant – establishing consensus – was still dominant and trusted.

Yet a growing feeling throughout the era studied here within the higher echelons of the State was that the machinery at the centre had to be modernized. Macmillan, Wilson, Heath, even Douglas-Home, all recognized in their own ways that change was needed. The years 1960–74 witnessed many experiments with structures and people, both elected and not. With the establishment of the Cabinet Office in 1916 a system was created that would last for half a century. 1960–74 set the pattern for the next 50 years.

In a study like this which encompasses a great deal of activity over a decade or so, it is also necessary to demonstrate what value has been added. In the case of this book, it is the archival material and the subsequent interviews which have not so much changed the prevailing conceptions as fleshed some out and deepened our understanding of others.

In terms of chronology, the first new evidence to be uncovered was the late-1964 struggle over the creation of the Department of Economic Affairs, and, more specifically, the way functions were to be shared with the Treasury. It is a given that the Treasury–DEA split was a difficult one that never really worked. What is new is that drawing up the so-called 'Concordat' between the two departments was not the easy task that Wilson claimed, but one that caused conflict and subsequently took much more time to agree than has been previously thought. In fact, a second debate over the Concordat began around the time of the 1966 election. The archival evidence presented here explains much of the simmering tension between the two departments.

A new appraisal of the role played by Marcia Williams, Wilson's Personal and Political Secretary throughout his Premierships, has perhaps cast a slightly more favourable light on her than has been true of previous treatments. For sure, she had a temperament which brought about myriad discourtesies. But, as the interview with Sir Eric Roll suggested, Williams' frustrations over alleged Civil Service obstructionism (to use her extreme analysis) has a little truth to it. While there was no impropriety on the part of officials, their naturally sceptical, if not cynical, appraisal of governments which wished to change so much, was that a good deal of work could have taken place and then been undone, all within months. This was especially so regarding a government with a small majority, which led to a practically unavoidable election just 18 months after the last one, as in the 1964–6 Parliament. There was little wish to embark on wholesale change until it was clear that it would endure.

The Fulton Committee and its subsequent Report has been looked at in comprehensive detail before. Indeed, most of the documentary evidence was seen by Geoffrey Fry long before the 30-year rule released the files to the public. However, new elements have been unearthed. The most significant was the attitude of No 10 Downing Street. We always knew that Harold Wilson was a supporter of the Fulton Report. What we did not know was just how attached to as deep a reform as possible was his Principal Private Secretary, Michael Halls. This put Halls on a collision course with the Head of the Home Civil Service, Sir William Armstrong, who was far from persuaded by the Fulton Report's more stinging criticisms of the service. The low-intensity warfare between Armstrong and a Halls-inspired No 10 lasted until Halls' untimely death in the spring of 1970. In any future study of Fulton, this intra-service dispute will have to be included.

A further aspect of the Fulton story which was not fully appreciated until the archive opened was the effort which went into looking at the issue of administrative 'hiving-off' in 1969–70. Hiving-off had been mentioned as a topic for further research in the Fulton Report and was attempted on a minor scale by the Heath Government elected in 1970. But the fact that Wilson ordered work to be done on it in the last days of his second administration adds a new slant even to the 1980s. For hiving-off at this time was not clearly separated from what was to become known as privatization. The Wilson-commissioned research was not extensive, but its existence means that we need to push the governmental genesis of this proto-Thatcherite development a year further back.

The wide-ranging research undertaken by groups affiliated to the Conservative Party while in opposition during 1964–70 is another area which brings added value to this book. The existing literature demonstrated that much happened at this time, with Heath at the centre of groups such as those chaired by Dame Evelyn Sharp and Lord Normanbrook, advice from Lords Roberthall and Plowden, and the Public Sector Research Unit (PSRU) headed by Mark Schreiber and David Howell. After two lengthy interviews, several emails and a look at the virgin territory of the surviving PSRU papers, we now know a little more about the workings of this unit. None of the resulting information is ground-breaking, but contains material which is of interest. For example, there is the possible first use of the word 'privatization' which was to sweep much of the world during the 1980s and 1990s. It also adds a few illustrations and asides about the lack of interest on the part of some of Heath's Shadow Cabinet colleagues about machinery-of-government reform.

Our view of how the Conservative planning was presented to the Civil Service during the now traditional pre-election private conversations, known as the 'Douglas-Home rules', is also amended by new evidence. As far as is known, these conversations have never before been uncovered in the archives. The material is not detailed but throws some light on the Civil Service reaction, for example, to the original thinking behind the Central Policy Review Staff. For the Senior Civil Service at this time was still relatively self-confident and its top figures were formulating their own plans for machinery-of-government reform. The clash of the two plans, and the way that figures such as Howell were still smarting after more than three decades, provided a highly symbolic victory for officialdom.

Being one of the first historians able to mine the Heath archive in full after the documents released under the 30-year rule reached 1974 in January 2005 facilitated several breakthroughs. The archive is bulging with official documents from the Conservative victory in June 1970 through to the publication in October 1970 of *The Reorganisation of Central Government* White Paper which contained the blueprint for Heath's 'new style of government'. For the Conservative plans were, in effect, given by Heath to Sir William Armstrong and Sir Burke Trend to deliver. The planning which took place within Whitehall was extensive.

The creation and development of the CPRS and the appointment of Lord Rothschild was a story in itself. It had been long known that he was not the first choice, but only with the opening of the archive did we know that Rothschild was not even among the first 11 to be considered, or that he was the third to be offered the job. About the operations of the CPRS itself, much has already been written. Access to the archive has not changed our perception very much, but has inevitably brought extra detail – for example, a trail showing how Rothschild was the conduit of warnings between Royal-Dutch Shell and Heath concerning the threat to oil supplies and prices.

The first couple of years of the CPRS represent its glory period. By 1973, its energetic iconoclasm, against a background of an ever-worsening economic picture, was becoming seen by the Whitehall regulars, in Lord Butler's word, as increasingly 'zany'. This was powerfully underlined by Rothschild's Wantage speech which painted a downbeat portrait of the UK's economic future, unfortunately on the same day as Heath gave an upbeat one. The degree to which the dressing-down that Rothschild received from the process-obsessed senior civil servants is fascinating. As is the newly released document detailing how the four most senior officials in the land in effect confronted Heath and encouraged urgent measures regarding the deteriorating economic position in December 1973.

A dawning realization during research for this book was the relative lack of material regarding Programme Analysis and Review (PAR) during the period 1970–4. This was the apparatus urged by the PSRU and enshrined in *The Reorganisation of Central Government*, to shine a penetrating light on big expenditure projects in order to reduce waste in its broadest sense. The periodic letters to his colleagues that Heath sent from 1971 onwards, encouraging them to engage with the PAR process, suggests that passion for it was lacking. This lack of interest was presaged by its initial bumpy ride through Cabinet. PAR never really achieved that which was hoped for it.

A final newly uncovered element was the realization that in 1973 Heath was far from happy about the central machinery over which he was presiding. Following the incomplete implementation of, most significantly, the PSRU's grand plans which strove to strengthen the Prime Minister's position through the think tank, PAR and a smaller Cabinet created through merging departments, Heath complained in the autumn of 1972 of 'the No 10 problem'. The Prime Minister was increasingly finding that too many issues needed him to push them through 'to the point of decision'. The complexity of modern politics and government – and the media's growing concentration on the person at the top – was adding to the pressure.

The CPRS and PAR, in their original conceptions, had been attempts to solve this problem, but their eventual creation did not fill the gap. Wilson had begun to feel the same by the end of his second administration in 1970 and his immediate creation of the Downing Street Policy Unit upon returning to No 10 in 1974 at the beginning of his third certainly alleviated the problem, if not solving it. Indeed, it is intriguing to note that perhaps the two most important changes to central government in the post-war period have been the introduction of senior and more and more numerous politically-appointed special advisers and the creation of the Downing Street Policy Unit largely staffed by just such appointees. Both were Wilsonian reforms which, compared to Heath's much more researched and holistic major changes (none of which lasted very long), stood the test of time.

Let us now turn to the theme of administrative reform during 1960–74 in the round. In 2003, Sir Samuel Goldman, the Treasury mandarin who, as head of public expenditure in the late 1960s and early 1970s, had to grapple with seemingly endless economic dislocation, explained that 'machinery of government reforms are, on the whole, a waste of time'. He was referring to the historically benign economic climate of the early twenty-first century which saw the longest sustained period of UK growth for two centuries, the lowest inflation and interest rates for 40 years, and effectively full employment. According to Goldman, two events had made all the difference – the forced withdrawal from the European Exchange Rate Mechanism in 1992 (after an ill-starred return in 1990 to a not-quite-fixed foreign exchange rate which brought back all the pressures of the Bretton Woods era) and the granting of operational independence for interest rates to the Bank of England in 1997.

These events meant that the British Government no longer had day-to-day responsibility for stabilizing the pound or controlling inflation. Government could not therefore be blamed for problems in these areas, nor could politics interfere to the degree it had previously. (There were, of course, many other reasons for the UK's relative economic boom, among the most important being the labour market reforms of the 1980s and the overall global economic climate of the mid-1990s onwards.) But Goldman's point was that until the macro-economics of the nation had been placed on a logical and robust footing, all the interference in the world could not improve the economy, indeed that ceaseless reforms did harm: 'You find again and again that great new schemes are put into effect and then within a few years they come unstuck ... If government and Ministers left things alone, a bit of *laissez-faire* as far as the machinery of government is concerned, I think on the whole the nation would benefit.'[3]

Lord Butler of Brockwell, another very well-placed observer of myriad reforms over three decades at the centre of British government, provided a contrasting view to Goldman's thinking. After a career which took in the CPRS, the Treasury, No 10 as Principal Private Secretary and the Cabinet Office as Cabinet Secretary, he was adamant that political pressure for reform and the injection of outsiders into institutions such as the Treasury undeniably pushed the Treasury to raise their horizons and their game. 'I think they were beneficial,' Butler said, 'I think they were very stimulating to government'.[4] Sir Samuel Brittan, the former DEA special adviser and *Financial Times* stalwart, supported Butler's thinking when he said 'that anything that reinforces the analytical abilities of No 10 and takes it away from the hunt of the moment is a good thing ... If you believe [issues] should come out in the open, it's quite important to have in a prime minister's department or the Cabinet Office or somewhere an analytical unit which can prepare a paper on these differences and what they amount to and how you might resolve them.'[5]

On the surface, there appears a big gulf between Goldman's views on the one hand and Butler's and Brittan's on the other. That would be incorrect.

While there is clearly a difference, one must try to put oneself into the shoes of Goldman, who presided over many changes to his public expenditure brief at a time of immense pressure. Goldman was talking without caveat and expressing his frustration of what he saw as fiddling with the machinery of government when what was actually necessary was bold action on such big-picture issues as industrial relations reform and fixed exchange rates. It is difficult to disagree with him when one considers the instances of institutional reform for largely political purposes, such as the splitting of the Treasury to create the Department of Economic Affairs and its subsequent 'creative tension' – and all the eminently avoidable difficulties that entailed.

A further factor to consider as to why so many reforms were enacted in a short period was the practical one of political pressure for something to be done in the face of problems. Although Goldman was probably right to say that 'a bit of *laissez-faire* as far as the machinery of government is concerned' would have been beneficial, rather than all the changes the period 1960–74 witnessed, government cannot continue indefinitely without adapting to the changing outside world. Political controversy will inevitably follow a government which does not reform functions or institutions which clearly demand alteration. But change for change's sake was equally wrong. This recalls Petronii Arbitri Satyricon's comment from AD66, a quotation Derek Rayner used in his report on defence procurement in 1971: 'We trained hard – but it seemed that every time we were beginning to form up into teams we would be reorganized. I was to learn later in life that we tend to meet any new situation by reorganizing, and a wonderful method it can be for creating the illusion of progress while producing confusion, inefficiency and demoralization'.[6]

In terms of the economy, the irony is that it began to improve once large-scale set-piece machinery-of-government reform had largely ceased. It is difficult to believe that the earlier changes had anything other than a very marginal effect on the economy. On the other hand, a first-order question is whether changes to the central governmental apparatus have the ability to make a strong contribution to the economy at all, as suggested by the faith of politicians and officials alike during the 1960s and 1970s. Richard Wilding, nearly three decades after he had been Secretary to the Fulton Committee, mused on this issue:

> Is it really plausible to suppose that if we had been a different set of people with different skills, the decisions that turned out good would still have been taken, while those which turned out bad would have been avoided? Or, to raise the stakes à la Balogh, that the whole fate of our country between 1945 and 1979 would have been different? ... I suggest that the reform of the civil service, taken by itself, perhaps improved the record over this period by about one per cent, and that if all possible reform of the service had been successfully carried out to the maximum, that might have raised that one to about

three per cent, with an absolute maximum five per cent, half, say, for the increase in guts and determination which the consciousness of successful reform might have given the service, and half for better knowledge and experience. That five per cent would have been well worth having, and I am far from wanting to knock it ... But it is a long way from the apocalypse.[7]

Wilding's analysis suggests that the reforms were only about government itself. In this sense, a 1 per cent improvement in national performance is about right. Yet, if the innovations to the economic machinery of government, from Neddy, the DEA, the National Plan, the Industrial Reorganisation Corporation, and through to the interventionist U-turn in 1972, had succeeded then economic performance could have risen. Nurturing industrial winners, which in effect all of this boiled down to, only happened, somewhat paradoxically, once government admitted it was unable to, and left it largely to the market (agriculture and defence excepted). The sale of government shareholding in businesses like BP, the privatizations of entire enterprises such as British Telecom, British Airways and the utilities led in several cases to the 'winners' of which the interventionist Prime Ministers dreamed.

It would be folly, however, to suggest that the 1980s drive to remove government from the economy signalled the end of the era of big government. Welfare provision formed another huge swathe of government activity, and even more by way of spending. This has not been rolled back in any large way. The reform of welfare, however, falls outside the remit of this book as very little of it took place during the Macmillan, Wilson and Heath years.

But perhaps the most revealing analysis came from Sir William Armstrong in his last days as Head of the Home Civil Service in 1974. During a retirement interview with Desmond Wilcox, Armstrong was asked 'What do you go home and say at moments of economic crisis?'

'Thank God the Government's influence is so little.'

'Would you expand on that?'

'I have a very strong suspicion that governments are nothing like as important as they think they are, and that the ordinary work of making things and moving things about, of transport, manufacture, farming, mining, is so much more important than what the Government does, that the Government can make enormous mistakes and we can still survive.'

'As long as we have our Civil Service.'

'No, no. Even in spite of it.'[8]

When the foremost apostle of administrative reform talked in this way (albeit during convalescence after his breakdown), the heady days of energetic belief by many, but not all, high-ranking civil servants in the great power of the Civil Service to effect change that no other agency of the State could, was clearly drawing to a close. In a way, these words are entirely resonant with the Conservative planners' ideas pre-1970. It is also possible that they pre-echo the Thatcherite drive to 'roll back the frontiers of the state'.[9] In any event, the career of Sir William Armstrong dovetails with the whole story of this book. Promoted above his superiors in the Treasury by Macmillan, to push through the new interventionist policy, integral to the story of the Fulton Report and finally Heath's right-hand man as the Prime Minister gravitated away from his Party towards a Civil Service embrace, Armstrong's tragic fall came just a few years before the end of consciously dirigiste governance and the rise of the New Right.

While there is a State, there will always be a Civil Service. The period 1960–74 represents an ultimately doomed attempt by decent men and women to improve and enlarge the State's instruments in order first to halt and later reverse relative economic decline, and thereby improve the lot of the UK. From the vantage point of the early twenty-first century it is hard to avoid the conclusion that the political zeitgeist encouraged successive governments to attempt too much, to take too much responsibility, certainly more than it could bear. It is also easy to understand why government did overreach, as the 'big government' experiment of the twentieth century had not yet played itself out and the immense and successful example of the State's mobilization during the Second World War was still powerfully remembered. A belief in government's unique ability to remedy or solve most difficulties was a mistake – but an entirely understandable and largely unavoidable one.

Appendix

THE FULTON REPORT

SUMMARY OF MAIN FINDINGS

1. The Home Civil Service today is still fundamentally the product of the nineteenth-century philosophy of the Northcote-Trevelyan Report. The problems it faces are those of the second half of the twentieth century. In spite of its many strengths, it is inadequate in six main respects for the most efficient discharge of the present and prospective responsibilities of government:–

    a) It is still too much based on the philosophy of the amateur (or the "generalist" or "all-rounder"). This is most evident in the Administrative Class, which holds the dominant position in the Service.

    b) The present system of classes in the Service (there are over 1400, each for the most part with its own separate pay and career structure) seriously impedes its work.

    c) Scientists, engineers and members of other specialist classes are frequently given neither the full responsibilities and opportunities nor the corresponding authority they ought to have.

    d) Too few civil servants are skilled managers.

    e) There is not enough contact between the Service and the community it is there to serve.

    f) Personnel management and career planning are inadequate.

    For these and other defects the central management of the Service, the Treasury, must accept its share of responsibility.

2. We propose a simple guiding principle for the future. The Service must continuously review the tasks it is called on to perform; it should then think out what new skills and kinds of men are needed and how these men can be found, trained and deployed.

3. A new Civil Service Department should be set up with wider functions than those now performed by the "Pay and Management" group of the Treasury, which it should take over. The new department should also absorb the Civil Service Commission.

4. The new department should be under the control of the Prime Minister. We hope that he will retain direct responsibility for senior appointments, machinery of government and questions of security. Outside this area, we suggest that the Prime Minister should delegate day-to-day responsibility to a non-departmental Minister of appropriate seniority who is also a member of the Cabinet.

5. The Permanent Secretary of the Civil Service Department should be designated Head of the Home Civil Service.

6. All classes should be abolished and replaced by a single, unified grading structure covering all civil servants from top to bottom in the non-industrial part of the Service. The correct grading of each post should be determined by job evaluation.

7. The Service should develop greater professionalism both among specialists (e.g. scientists and engineers) and administrators (i.e. the new counterparts of the present Administrative and Executive Classes). For the former this means more training in management, and opportunities for greater responsibility and wider careers. For the latter it means enabling them to specialise in particular areas of government. We identify two such areas and accordingly recommend the development of a group of economic and financial administrators, and a second group of social administrators.

8. Employing departments should have a larger role in recruitment and there should be a speeding up of procedures. A majority of us consider that in the recruitment of graduates for one or other of the groups of administrators more account should be taken of the relevance of their university courses to the job they are being recruited to do.

9. A Civil Service College should be set up. It should provide major training courses in administration and management and a wide range of shorter courses. It should also have important research functions. The courses provided by the College should not be restricted to civil servants; a proportion of places should be set aside for men and women from private industrial and commercial firms, local government and public corporations.

10. More resources should be devoted to the career management of all civil servants. All must have the opportunity to progress as far and as fast as their talents and appropriate training can take them. This involves major changes in promotion procedures.

11. While the Civil Service should remain predominantly a career Service, there should be greater mobility between it and other employments. We, therefore, recommend an expanded late entry, temporary appointments for fixed periods, short-term interchanges of staff and freer movement out of the Service. These proposals involve substantial changes in the pension scheme and the replacement of "established" status by new terms of employment.
12. In the interests of efficiency, the principles of accountable management should be applied to the organisation of the work of departments. This means the clear allocation of responsibilities and authority to accountable units with defined objectives. It also means a corresponding addition to the system of government accounting.
13. Management service units with highly qualified and experienced staff should be set up in all major departments.
14. Departments should establish Planning Units.
15. In addition to the Permanent Secretary, there should also be in most departments a Senior Policy Adviser to assist the Minister. The Senior Policy Adviser would normally be head of the Planning Unit. His prime job would be to look to and prepare for the future and to ensure that present policy decisions are taken with as full a recognition as possible of likely future developments.
16. In some of the big technical departments, there may be a need for a further senior post: a chief scientist, engineer or other specialist.
17. We do not propose that the Senior Policy Adviser and chief specialist, together with the Permanent Secretary, should constitute a formal board. The working arrangements should be informal and variable from department to department and from time to time; different Ministers' individual ways of working will do much to determine the pattern.
18. There should be one man who has overall responsibility under the Minister for all the affairs of the Department and he should continue to be the Permanent Secretary.
19. A Minister at the head of a department should be able to employ on a temporary basis such small numbers of experts as he personally considers he needs to help him.
20. We have suggested a number of further inquiries. Their subjects among others, should be:
    a) The desirability of "hiving off" activities to non-departmental organisations;
    b) Ways and means of getting rid of unnecessary secrecy both in policy-making and administration;

c) The new pattern of joint consultation that will be appropriate for the Civil Service in the light of the Government's decisions on our report. This inquiry should be conducted jointly by the Civil Service Department and the staff associations;

d) Methods of making recruitment procedures as speedy and objective as possible.

21. If our proposals are accepted, we hope that the Government will take steps to see that the progress made in their implementation is reviewed. This could be by an annual report to Parliament during the next five years. A small committee might be set up at the end of that period if needed.

22. We have seen that the Service has men and women with the ability, vision and enthusiasm needed to carry our proposals through to success. A Civil Service reconstructed on the basis of these proposals will, we believe, make possible the progressive and efficient conduct of our affairs.

Chronology

1957
January — Macmillan becomes Prime Minister

1958
July — House of Commons' Select Committee on Estimates reported on Treasury Control of Expenditure

1959
July — Appointment of Plowden Committee on public expenditure
October — Conservatives win general election
'The Apotheosis of the Dilettante' published

1960
July — Derick Heathcote Amory replaced by Selwyn Lloyd as Chancellor

1961
July — Plowden Report delivered to Lloyd
July — Sterling crisis: emergency economic measures
August — First EEC application launched
October — Henry Brooke appointed as newly revived Chief Secretary to the Treasury

1962
March — First meeting of the National Economic Development Council (NEDC)
June — Reginald Maudling replaces Lloyd as Chancellor
July — Treasury reorganization begins
October — Sir William Armstrong and Sir Laurence Helsby succeed Sir Frank Lee and Sir Norman Brook as Joint Permanent Secretaries to the Treasury

1963
January — Sir Burke Trend succeeds Sir Norman Brook as Cabinet Secretary

January	First EEC application vetoed
February	NEDC approves 4 per cent growth target
May	Centre for Administrative Studies announced
October	Macmillan resigns, Sir Alec Douglas-Home becomes Prime Minister

1964

Spring	Douglas-Home rules on Civil Service–Opposition pre-election private consultation inaugurated
	The Fabians' *The Administrators* published
October	Labour wins general election with overall majority of 5, Harold Wilson becomes Prime Minister
October	James Callaghan appointed Chancellor – Department of Economic Affairs (DEA) created, George Brown becomes Minister for Economic Affairs
October	Mintech, Welsh Office, Ministry of Land and Natural Resources, Ministry of Overseas Development (ODM) created
October	Special advisers appointed to key positions
November	Sterling crisis: emergency Budget
November	Conservative Opposition begins wide-ranging policy review

1965

July	Sterling crisis: public expenditure cuts and other financial measures
August	Edward Heath replaces Douglas-Home as Conservative Leader – policy review continues
September	National Plan published

1966

January	Commonwealth Relations Office and the Colonial Office merged to form the Commonwealth Office
February	Fulton Committee convened
March	Labour wins 1966 general election with majority of 97
May	Second EEC application launched
July	Sterling crisis: emergency economic measures
August	George Brown leaves DEA to become Foreign Secretary, Michael Stewart to DEA

1967

March	Heath establishes the Marples Unit or, as it became known, the Public Sector Research Unit

CHRONOLOGY

August	Stewart leaves DEA, replaced by Peter Shore as Secretary of Economic Affairs under direct supervision from Wilson
November	Devaluation of the pound from $2.80 to $2.40 accompanied by emergency economic measures
November	Second EEC application vetoed
November	Callaghan resigns as Chancellor, replaced by Roy Jenkins

1968

January	Sir William Armstrong appointed Head of Home Civil Service, Sir Douglas Allen succeeds him on Financial and Economic side of Treasury
January	Major public expenditure cuts announced
March	Gold–dollar–sterling crisis resulted in 'Operation Brutus' contingency planning, George Brown resigns
March	Major tax-raising Budget
April	Barbara Castle appointed to enlarged Department for Employment and Productivity; Parliamentary Committee (inner Cabinet) convened
April	Wilson relinquishes overall responsibility for DEA
June	Fulton Report published
November	Civil Service Department (CSD) created (Sir William Armstrong leaves Treasury to head it), Foreign & Commonwealth Office and Department of Health & Social Security formed
November	JIC reformed

1969

June	Open Government White Paper
October	DEA abolished
October	Major enlargement of Mintech and also Local Government and Regional Planning
October	Parliamentary Committee becomes Management Committee

1970

April	Civil Service College opened
June	Conservatives win general election with majority of 31, Heath becomes Prime Minister
June	Businessmen's team created in CSD
August	Comprehensive review of government functions launched
October	*The Reform of Central Government* White Paper
October	Department of the Environment created
October	Ministry of Fuel and Power incorporated into the merged

	Department of Trade and Industry
October	ODM merged into FCO
October	Rothschild selected to be head of CPRS after several others offered job
December	Programme Analysis and Review (PAR) first presented to Cabinet unsuccessfully

1971

January	PAR again presented to Cabinet unsuccessfully
February	Central Policy Review Staff begins work
April	PAR eventually agreed by Cabinet
August	First CPRS early warning exercise
August	First CPRS forward strategy exercise
September	Sir David Barran of Shell – through Rothschild – warned Heath of possible oil crisis

1972

January	First Miners' strike
February	U-turn – Upper Clyde Shipbuilders and Rolls-Royce bailed out
February	Second CPRS early warning exercise
March	U-turn – Budget
March	Northern Ireland Office created
April	U-turn – Industry Bill, overseen by secret Cabinet Office team led by Sir William Armstrong
April	Defence Procurement Agency hived-off
May	Second CPRS forward strategy exercise
June	U-turn – floating of the pound
June	Civil Contingencies Unit created in the Cabinet Office
July	Third CPRS early warning exercise

1973

January	European Secretariat established in the Cabinet Office
January	Counter-Inflation Act which set up the Pay Board and Prices Commission
January	Three-year PAR programme agreed (slipped to January 1974)
June	Third CPRS forward strategy exercise
September	Sir John Hunt succeeds Sir Burke Trend as Cabinet Secretary
September	Rothschild's Wantage speech
November	Second Miners' strike
December	Fourth CPRS early warning exercise begun but completed in May 1974 (after Wilson returned as PM)

December	Sir William Armstrong, Sir John Hunt, Sir Douglas Allen and Robert Armstrong warn Heath of economic danger ahead
December	Rothschild suffers mild heart attack
December	OPEC cuts supply of oil

1974

January	Sir William Armstrong suffers mental breakdown
January	Department of Energy spun-off DTI
February	Heath loses election
March	Downing Street Policy Unit created
April	Sir William Armstrong leaves Whitehall
November	Fourth (and last) CPRS forward strategy exercise held (after Wilson returned as PM)

Notes

Notes to Introduction

1. Peter Hennessy, 'Britain's Governing Tribes', *The Tablet*, 4 October 2003.
2. Philip Graham used the phrase when he bought *Newsweek*, the international news magazine, in 1961, quoted from Michael Cockerell, Peter Hennessy and David Walker, *Sources Close to the Prime Minister: Inside the Hidden World of the News Manipulators* (Macmillan, 1984), p. 89. All books were published in London unless otherwise stated.
3. Peter Hennessy, *Whitehall* (Secker and Warburg, 1989).
4. Kevin Theakston, *The Civil Service Since 1945* (Blackwell, Oxford, 1995).
5. Gavin Drewry and Tony Butcher, *The Civil Service Today* (Blackwell, Oxford, 1991).
6. Christopher Pollitt, *Manipulating the Machine* (George Allen and Unwin, 1984).
7. Geoffrey Fry, *Reforming the Civil Service* (Edinburgh University Press, Edinburgh, 1993).
8. Sir Samuel Brittan, 'A backward glance: The reappraisal of the 1960s', lecture given to the Institute of Contemporary British History, April 1997.
9. Harold Macmillan, *At the End of the Day* (Macmillan, 1973), p. 37.
10. Douglas Hurd, *An End to Promises* (Collins, 1979), p. 25.
11. Iain Dale (ed.), 'A Better Tomorrow', *Conservative Party General Election Manifestos, 1900–1997* (Routledge, Oxford, 2000), p. 197.
12. See Conservative Party Conference 1970, Conservative Research Department archives, Conservative Party Archives, Bodleian Library, Oxford University.
13. *The Reorganisation of Central Government*, Cmnd. 4506 (HMSO, 1970).
14. Philip Thornton, 'Sleight of hand fails to hide gaping holes in public purse', *Independent*, 17 March 2005; See Gordon Brown's 2005 Budget statement (www.hmrc.gov.uk/budget2005).
15. See Paul Addison, *The Road to 1945* (Cape, 1975); Dennis Kavanagh and Peter Morris, *Consensus Politics from Attlee to Major* (Blackwell, Oxford, 1994); and Harriet Jones and Michael Kandiah (eds), *The Myth of Consensus* (Macmillan, 1996).
16. *Social Insurance and Allied Services*, Cmnd. 6404 (HMSO, 1942).
17. *Employment Policy*, Cmnd. 6527 (HMSO, 1944).
18. Kevin Theakston, *Leadership in Whitehall* (Macmillan, 1999), p. 50.
19. See Hennessy, *Whitehall*, pp. 88–119.
20. Henry Pelling, *The Labour Governments 1945–51* (Macmillan, 1984), p. 90.
21. David Butler and Gareth Butler, *Twentieth-Century British Political Facts, 1900–2000* (Macmillan, 2000), p. 309.

22 David Howell, *A New Style Of Government* (Conservative Political Centre, 1970), p. 8.
23 Lord Bancroft, speaking at the Gresham College seminar, 'In the Steps of Walter Bagehot: A Constitutional Health-Check', 13 March 1995.

Notes to Chapter 1: Cracks

1   Andrew Shonfield, *British Economic Policy Since The War* (Penguin, 1958).
2   Michael Shanks, *The Stagnant Society: A Warning* (Penguin, 1961).
3   Anthony Sampson, *Anatomy of Britain* (Hodder and Stoughton, 1962).
4   Shanks's work was one of the 'Penguin Specials', many of which were concerned directly with the mid-century 'decline' question. See Matthew Grant, 'Historians, the Penguin Specials and the "State-of-the-Nation" Literature, 1958–64', *Contemporary British History*, Vol. 17, No. 3 (Autumn 2003), pp. 29–54.
5   Thomas Balogh, 'The Apotheosis of the Dilettante', in Hugh Thomas (ed.), *The Establishment* (A. Blond, 1959).
6   Fabian Society, *The Administrators* (Fabian Tract 355, 1964).
7   W. J. M. Mackenzie, 'Does Our Administration Need Reform?', *The Listener*, 21 February 1963.
8   Peter Hennessy, *Whitehall* (Secker and Warburg, 1989), p. 118.
9   Ibid., p. 54.
10 Lord Penney quoted in ibid., p. 88.
11 Hennessy, *Whitehall*, pp. 94–102.
12 George Brown probably coined the phrase according to Samuel Brittan, *Steering the Economy* (Pelican, 1971), pp. 55–6.
13 Hennessy, *Whitehall*, p. 94.
14 Brittan, *Steering the Economy*, p. 56.
15 Hennessy, *Whitehall*, pp. 106–7.
16 Ibid., pp. 114, 118.
17 *Social Insurance and Allied Services*, Cmnd. 6404 (HMSO, 1942).
18 *Employment Policy*, Cmnd. 6527 (HMSO, 1944).
19 B. W. E. Alford, *British Economic Performance 1945–1975* (Cambridge University Press, Cambridge, 1995), p. 14.
20 Kevin Theakston, *The Civil Service Since 1945* (Blackwell, Oxford, 1995), p. 68.
21 Hennessy, *Whitehall*, p. 124.
22 Ibid., p. 122.
23 Kevin Theakston, *Leadership in Whitehall* (Macmillan, 1999), p. 82.
24 Leo Pliatzky, *Getting and Spending* (Basil Blackwell, Oxford, 1982), p. 34.
25 Comment by Professor Peter Burnham, Warwick University, 27 January 2005.
26 Interview with Sir Frank Cooper, 13 June 2001.
27 Brittan, *Steering the Economy*, p. 35.
28 See the Anderson Committee (which trickled into the public domain in the 1946 Oxford Romanes Lecture) in National Archives (NA) T 273/9, 'Civil Service organisation: setting up of ministerial and official committees and papers concerning draft White Paper on

Future of Civil Service'; Hennessy, *Whitehall*, pp. 129–131; the *Royal Commission on the Civil Service* (the Priestley Commission), Cmnd. 9613, HMSO, 1955 – a 'narrow inquiry into pay and conditions of service'; Theakston, *The Civil Service Since 1945*, pp. 74–5; there was also the ongoing 'application to public administration of scientific techniques of management and routine', the so-called 'O & M' (Organisation and Methods) branches located in the Treasury, Henry Roseveare, *The Treasury* (Allen Lane, 1969), pp. 246, 304.
29 Hennessy, *Whitehall*, pp. 121–2.
30 Ibid., p. 127.
31 Kevin Theakston, *The Labour Party and Whitehall* (Routledge, Oxford, 1992), pp. 141–4.
32 His most famous works include *Authority in the Modern State* (Yale University Press, Connecticut, USA, 1919), *Parliamentary Government in Britain* (Allen and Unwin, 1938) and *A Grammar of Politics* (Allen and Unwin, 1948). Laski had been the most vociferous critic of British administration but later remarked, according to A. J. P. Taylor, that the 1945–51 governments which were 'put in power by popular vote and did what the people wanted, [were] nearer the Marxist idea than any of the governments thrown up by revolution, French, Russian or other', A. J. P. Taylor's introduction to Karl Marx and Friedrich Engels, *The Communist Manifesto* (Penguin, 1967), p. 15.
33 Richard Crossman quoted in Theakston, *The Labour Party and Whitehall*, p. 74.
34 Peter Hennessy, *The Prime Minister* (Penguin, 2000), pp. 155–6.
35 John Colville, *The Churchillians* (Weidenfeld & Nicolson, 1981), p. 64.
36 Brittan, *Steering the Economy*, p. 187.
37 Ibid., p. 37.
38 Sir Edward Bridges, 'Portrait of a Profession', Rede Lecture, University of Cambridge, 1950 (Cambridge University Press, Cambridge, 1950), p. 33.
39 Correlli Barnett interviewed in Richard English and Michael Kenny (eds), *Rethinking British Decline* (Macmillan, 2000), p. 43.
40 Richard Gardner, *Sterling-Dollar Diplomacy in Current Perspective* (Columbia University Press, New York, 1980), pp. 165–253.
41 Geoffrey Owen, *From Empire to Europe* (HarperCollins, 1999), p. 30.
42 Percy Cradock, *Know Your Enemy* (John Murray, 2002), p. 92.
43 Peter Hennessy and Caroline Anstey, 'Moneybags and Brains', Strathclyde *Analysis* Paper (1990), p. 5.
44 Kevin Theakston, 'Allen, Douglas Albert Vivian' entry in John Ramsden (ed.), *The Oxford Companion to Twentieth-Century British Politics* (Oxford University Press, Oxford, 2002), p. 13.
45 Lord Croham briefing the 'Hidden Wiring' MA option course, 9 February 2005.
46 Nicholas Crafts and Gianni Toniolo, 'Postwar Growth: An Overview', in *Economic Growth in Europe Since 1945* (Cambridge University Press, Cambridge, 1996), p. 132.
47 Interview with Sir Donald MacDougall, 21 May 2001.
48 Brittan, *Steering the Economy*, p. 193.
49 Hennessy, *Whitehall*, p. 3.
50 Sir Samuel Brittan, 'A backward glance: The reappraisal of the 1960s', lecture given to the Institute of Contemporary British History, April 1997.
51 Hamish McRae, 'Lucky Britain's great escape', *Independent*, 4 August 2002.

52 Hamish McRae, 'Renaissance of China and India is the renewal of an old relationship', *Independent*, 26 January 2006.
53 See Correlli Barnett, *The Collapse of British Power* (Sutton, 1972), *The Audit of War* (Macmillan, 1986) and *The Lost Victory* (Macmillan, 1995).
54 'The Home Civil Service ... encouraged the steady, safe, orthodox man of academic approach, rather than the man of, in the words of one senior civil servant, "intense energy, great driving force and devouring zeal"', Barnett, *The Collapse of British Power*, p. 64
55 José Harris, 'Enterprise and Welfare States: A Comparative Perspective', *Transactions of the Royal Historical Society*, No. 40, 1990, p. 180.
56 Hugo Young, *This Blessed Plot* (Macmillan, 1998), p. 106.
57 Brittan, 'A backward glance: The reappraisal of the 1960s.'
58 Ibid.
59 Stephen King, 'Yes, the Sixties were groovy – but it's time for Europe to embrace the modern world', *Independent*, 31 May 2005.
60 Interview with Sir Samuel Brittan, 30 May 2001.
61 Alec Cairncross, 'The Post-war Years 1945–77', in Roderick Floud and Donald McCloskey (eds), *The Economic History of Britain Since 1870*, Volume 2 (Cambridge University Press, Cambridge, 1981), p. 375.
62 Samuel Brittan in English and Kenny (eds), *Rethinking British Decline*, p. 99.
63 Alford, *British Economic Performance 1945–1975*, p. 1.
64 Alec Cairncross, *The British Economy Since 1945* (Blackwell, Oxford, 1992), p. 19.
65 Thomas Balogh, *Planning for Progress* (Fabian Society, 1963), p. 47; Ben Pimlott, *Harold Wilson* (HarperCollins, 1993), pp. 300–1.
66 Prince Philip quoted in W. J. M. Mackenzie, 'Does Our Administration Need Reform?', *The Listener*, 21 February 1963.
67 Sampson, *Anatomy of Britain*, p. 620.
68 Hennessy, *The Prime Minister*, p. 235.
69 Ibid., p. 246.
70 National Archives (NA), Public Record Office (PRO), PREM 11/1138, 'Lessons after Suez: thoughts of Prime Minister', Sir Anthony Eden, '"Thoughts" on the general situation after Suez'.
71 Hennessy, *Whitehall*, p. 170.
72 Sampson, *Anatomy of Britain*, p. 229.
73 Balogh, 'The Apotheosis of the Dilettante', p. 126.
74 Hennessy, *Whitehall*, pp. 172–3; private information.
75 Theakston, *The Labour Party and Whitehall*, p. 116.
76 Hennessy, *Whitehall*, p. 75.
77 The exact source of this widely quoted phrase remains elusive. It is often attributed to Winston Churchill during the Second World War.
78 Sir Warren Fisher quoted in Kevin Theakston and Geoffrey K. Fry, 'Britain's Administrative Elite', *Public Administration*, Vol. 67, Summer 1989, p. 138.
79 Sampson, *Anatomy of Britain*, p. 224.
80 Ibid., p. 227.
81 Balogh, 'The Apotheosis of the Dilettante', p. 103.

82 Brittan, *Steering the Economy*, p. 33.
83 Ibid., p. 84.
84 Interview with Sir Donald MacDougall, 21 May 2001.
85 Brittan, *Steering the Economy*, p. 54.
86 Alford, *British Economic Performance 1945–1975*, p. 17.
87 Theakston and Fry, 'Britain's Administrative Elite', p. 135.
88 Ibid., pp. 137, 141.
89 Roseveare, *The Treasury*, p. 305.
90 Sampson, *Anatomy of Britain*, p. 225.
91 Martin Wiener quoted in English and Kenny (eds), *Rethinking British Decline*, p. 30.
92 Balogh, *Planning for Progress*, p. 31.
93 Sampson, *Anatomy of Britain*, p. 174.
94 Conversation with Dr Gary Magee, 17 April 2001.
95 Sidney Pollard, *The Wasting of the British Economy* (Croom Helm, 1984), p. 6.
96 Sampson, *Anatomy of Britain*, p. 223.
97 Michael Young, *The Rise of the Meritocracy* (Thames and Hudson, 1958), p. 20.
98 The phrase is Ferdinand Lassalle's and is quoted in Balogh, 'The Apotheosis of the Dilettante', p. 83.
99 Martin Wiener quoted in English and Kenny (eds), *Rethinking British Decline*, p. 30.
100 David Marquand, *The Unprincipled Society* (Cape, 1988), p. 22.
101 Hennessy, *Whitehall*, p. 722.
102 David Edgerton, *England and the Aeroplane* (Macmillan, 1991) and 'Liberal Militarism and the British State', *New Left Review*, no. 185, pp. 118–69.
103 Lord Bridges quoted in Sir Richard Clarke (edited by Sir Alec Cairncross), *Public Expenditure, Management and Control* (Macmillan, 1978), p. xix.
104 Hennessy, *Whitehall*, p.118.
105 Brittan, 'A backward glance: The reappraisal of the 1960s'.
106 Clarke, *Public Expenditure, Management and Control*, p. 3.
107 Hugh Heclo and Aaron Wildavsky, *The Private Government of Public Money* (Macmillan, 1981), p. 207.
108 Pliatzky, *Getting and Spending*, p. 44.
109 Clarke, *Public Expenditure, Management and Control*, p. xix.
110 Heclo and Wildavsky, *The Private Government of Public Money*, p. 208.
111 Roseveare, *The Treasury*, p. 297.
112 Hennessy, *Whitehall*, p. 179.
113 Roseveare, *The Treasury*, p. 297.
114 D. N. Chester quoted in Roseveare, *The Treasury*, p. 297.
115 Clarke, *Public Expenditure, Management and Control*, p. 38.
116 Samuel Goldman quoted in Clarke, *Public Expenditure, Management and Control*, p. xi.
117 Pliatzky, *Getting and Spending*, p. 43.
118 Heclo and Wildavsky, *The Private Government of Public Money*, p. 202.
119 Ibid., p. 209.
120 Pliatzky, *Getting and Spending*, p. 49.
121 Hennessy, *The Prime Minister*, pp. 450–1.

122 Heclo and Wildavsky, *The Private Government of Public Money*, p. 202.
123 Brittan, 'A backward glance: The reappraisal of the 1960s'.
124 Clarke, *Public Expenditure, Management and Control*, p. 35.
125 Roseveare, *The Treasury*, p. 300.
126 Hennessy, *Whitehall*, p. 180.
127 Sir Richard Clarke quoted in Roseveare, *The Treasury*, p. 301.
128 Clarke, *Public Expenditure, Management and Control*, p. 36.
129 Roseveare, *The Treasury*, p. 332.
130 Ibid., p. 301.
131 Sampson, *Anatomy of Britain*, p. 275.
132 Roseveare, *The Treasury*, p. 294.
133 Theakston, *The Civil Service Since 1945*, p. 86.
134 Sampson, *Anatomy of Britain*, p. 218.
135 A. H. Halsey, 'Higher Education', in A. H. Halsey (ed.), *British Social Trends Since 1900* (Macmillan, 1988), p. 270.
136 This is difficult to prove empirically due to a lack of comparative statistics. Peter Brierley, 'Religion', ibid., p. 519.
137 Henry Fairlie, 'The Establishment at work', *The Spectator*, 23 September 1955.
138 Nevil Johnson, 'Change in the Civil Service', *Public Administration*, Vol. 63, Winter 1985, p. 419.
139 John Ramsden, *The Winds of Change* (Longman, 1996), pp. 132–3.
140 Harold Macmillan, *The Middle Way* (Macmillan, 1938 edn), pp. 237–9.
141 James Margach, *The Abuse Of Power* (W. H. Allen, 1978), pp. 116–17.
142 Peter Hennessy, *Having It So Good* (Penguin, 2006), p. 572. Macmillan was also 'close' to Sir Oswald Mosley during the latter's planned economy New Party phase in 1931, Alistair Horne, *Macmillan, 1894–1956* (Macmillan, 1988), pp. 93–4.
143 Cairncross, *The British Economy Since 1945*, p. 94.
144 Alistair Horne in *Macmillan, 1957–1986* (Macmillan, 1989), pp. 138–71.
145 John Turner, '1951–1964', in Anthony Seldon (ed.), *How Tory Governments Fall* (Fontana Press, 1996), p. 321.
146 Donald MacDougall, *Don and Mandarin* (John Murray, 1987), p. 137.
147 House of Commons, *Official Report*, 25 July 1961, cols. 218–35; *Steering the Economy*, p. 255.
148 Nicholas Crafts and Gianni Toniolo, 'Post-war Growth: An Overview', in *Economic Growth in Europe Since 1945* (Cambridge University Press, Cambridge, 1996), p. 146.
149 Owen, *From Empire to Europe*, p. 450.
150 John Maynard Keynes, *The General Theory of Employment, Interest and Money* (Macmillan, 1936).
151 Harold Macmillan, *At the End of the Day* (Macmillan, 1973), p. 89.
152 Theakston, *The Civil Service Since 1945*, p. 22.
153 Hennessy, *The Prime Minister*, p. 263.
154 Peter Thorneycroft who, as Chancellor in 1958, resigned over Macmillan's expansionist philosophy and is quoted in Hennessy, *The Prime Minister*, p. 266.
155 Edmund Dell, *The Chancellors* (HarperCollins, 1997), pp. 235–41.

156 Derick Heathcoat Amory quoted in *Macmillan, 1957–1986*, p. 140.
157 Dell, *The Chancellors*, p. 256.
158 Edmund Dell, *A Strange Eventful History* (HarperCollins, 2000), p. 36.
159 Macmillan, *At the End of the Day*, p. 385.
160 Ramsden, *The Winds of Change*, pp. 31–2.
161 Macmillan, *The Middle Way* (Macmillan, 1958 edn), pp. xiii–xxix.
162 Brittan, *Steering the Economy*, p. 255.
163 Macmillan, *At the End of the Day*, p. 35.
164 Ibid., p. 231.
165 Macmillan, *At the End of the Day*, p. 231.
166 Brittan, *Steering the Economy*, p. 232.
167 Ibid., p. 237.
168 Dell, *The Chancellors*, p. 285.
169 Cairncross, *The British Economy Since 1945*, pp. 11, 19.
170 Young, *This Blessed Plot*, p. 105.
171 Ibid., p. 107.
172 Young, *This Blessed Plot*, p. 123.
173 Ibid., p. 131.
174 Macmillan Diary, d.48, entry for 28 January 1963.
175 Owen, *From Empire to Europe*, p. 459.
176 Ibid., p. 460.
177 Hennessy, *The Prime Minister*, p. 257.
178 Brittan, *Steering the Economy*, pp. 239–40.
179 Keith Middlemas, *Industry, Unions and Government* (Macmillan, 1983), p. 11.
180 Brittan, *Steering the Economy*, pp. 243–4.
181 Roseveare, *The Treasury*, p. 333.
182 Ramsden, *The Winds of Change*, p. 173.
183 Cairncross, *The British Economy Since 1945*, p. 2.
184 Dell, *A Strange Eventful History*, p. 422.
185 Brittan, *Steering the Economy*, p. 238.
186 Ibid., p. 242.
187 See NA, PRO, T 230/657.
188 MacDougall, *Don and Mandarin*, p. 137.
189 Cairncross, *The British Economy Since 1945*, p. 143.
190 Ibid., p. 105.
191 Dell, *The Chancellors*, p. 267.
192 NA, PRO, CAB 128/35, Cabinet conclusions 1(61) –75 (61), 21 September 1961.
193 Interview with Sir Donald MacDougall, 21 May 2001.
194 Sampson, *Anatomy of Britain*, p. 242.
195 Interview with Sir Donald MacDougall, 21 May 2001.
196 Macmillan, *At the End of the Day*, p. 51.
197 Brittan, *Steering the Economy*, p. 244.
198 Ibid., p. 245.
199 Macmillan, *At the End of the Day*, p. 49.

200 Ibid., p. 37.
201 Macmillan, *The Middle Way* (1938 edn), pp. 227, 290.
202 NA, PRO, CAB 128/35, Cabinet minutes for C.C. (61), 19 September 1961.
203 Brittan, *Steering the Economy*, pp. 243–4.
204 Middlemas, *Industry, Unions and Government*, p. 21.
205 Macmillan, *At the End of the Day*, p. 37.
206 Middlemas, *Industry, Unions and Government*, p. 14.
207 Ibid., p. 1; see Keir Thorpe, '"The Missing Pillar": Economic Planning and the Machinery of Government during the Labour Administrations of 1945–51', unpublished PhD thesis (Queen Mary and Westfield, University of London, 1999).
208 Brittan, *Steering the Economy*, p. 244.
209 Dell, *The Chancellors*, p. 265; Macmillan, *At the End of the Day*, p. 51.
210 Middlemas, *Industry, Unions and Government*, p. 15.
211 MacDougall, *Don and Mandarin*, p. 138.
212 Ibid., p. 144.
213 Brittan, *Steering the Economy*, p. 244.
214 Sir James Dunnett, 'The Civil Service Administrator and the Expert', *Public Administration*, Vol. 39, Autumn 1961, p. 224.
215 Sir Alec Cairncross, 'Economists in Government', *Lloyds Bank Review*, No. 95, January 1970, p. 2.
216 Interview with Sir Donald MacDougall, 21 May 2001.
217 Hennessy, *Whitehall*, p. 177.
218 MacDougall, *Don and Mandarin*, p. 138.
219 Donald MacDougall, 'The Machinery of Economic Government: Some Personal Reflections,' in David Butler and A. H. Halsey (eds), *Policy and Politics* (Macmillan, 1978), p. 176.
220 Brittan, *Steering the Economy*, p. 15.
221 Middlemas, *Industry, Unions and Government*, p. 22.
222 Interview with Sir Donald MacDougall, 21 May 2001.
223 Middlemas, *Industry, Unions and Government*, p. 26.
224 Ibid., p. 27.
225 Brittan, *Steering the Economy*, p. 264.
226 Ibid., p. 278.
227 Pliatzky, *Getting and Spending*, pp. 51–3.
228 Clarke, *Public Expenditure, Management and Control*, p. 72.
229 Dell, *The Chancellors*, p. 266.
230 Brittan, *Steering the Economy*, pp. 265–6.
231 House of Commons, *Official Report*, vol. 551, 17 April 1956, col. 867.
232 Harold Macmillan, *Pointing The Way, 1959–61* (Macmillan, 1972), p. 221.
233 Brittan, *Steering the Economy*, p. 188.
234 Brittan, *Steering the Economy*, pp. 271–2.
235 Ibid., p. 283.
236 Ibid., p. 15.
237 The Treasury was given a second Cabinet Minister in 1961, with the revival of the old office of Chief Secretary to the Treasury; the final unification of the Ministry of Defence came

in April 1964; the same month saw Sir Edward Boyle relinquish much of his Education portfolio to become Minister of State for the universities and Quintin Hogg (the former Lord Hailsham) landing the rump Education Department; the Department of Technical Co-operation was created in 1961 to coordinate technical aid previously split between the Foreign, Colonial and Commonwealth Relations Offices and the Ministry of Labour; the Central African Office was created in 1961 and was in turn quietly merged into the Commonwealth Relations Office in April 1964.

238 Lord Home, *The Way The Wind Blows* (Collins, 1976), p. 202.
239 Hennessy, *Whitehall*, p. 174.
240 Enoch Powell quoted in Geoffrey Fry, *Reforming the Civil Service* (Edinburgh University Press, Edinburgh, 1993), p. 215.
241 Helsby and Home quoted in Pollitt, *Manipulating the Machine*, pp. 42–3.
242 Hennessy, *The Prime Minister*, p. 284.
243 NA, PRO, T 273/9, 'Civil Service organisation: setting up of ministerial and official committees and papers concerning draft White Paper on Future of Civil Service'.
244 John Turner, 'Experts and Interests', in Rory Macleod (ed.), *Government and Expertise in Nineteenth Century Britain* (Cambridge University Press, Cambridge, 1988).

Notes to Chapter 2: Hardware

1 *Let's Go with Labour for the New Britain*, reprinted in F. W. S. Craig (ed.), *British General Election Manifestos, 1959–1987* (Dartmouth, Aldershot, 1990), p. 60.
2 House of Commons, *Official Report*, 3 November 1959, Col. 862.
3 Harold Wilson, *The Labour Government, 1964–1970* (Weidenfeld & Nicolson, 1971), p. xix and *Final Term: The Labour Government, 1974–1976* (Weidenfeld & Nicolson, 1979), p. ix.
4 Lord Bancroft, speaking at the Gresham College seminar, 'In the Steps of Walter Bagehot: A Constitutional Health-Check', 13 March 1995.
5 Ben Pimlott, *Harold Wilson* (HarperCollins, 1993), p. 430.
6 Martin Wolf, 'Why Globalisation Works', speaking at the 'Globalisation Lectures', Queen Mary, University of London, 12 January 2005.
7 Peter Hennessy, *The Prime Minister* (Penguin, 2000), p. 303; Keir Thorpe, '"The Missing Pillar": Economic Planning and the Machinery of Government during the Labour Administrations of 1945–51', unpublished PhD thesis (Queen Mary and Westfield, University of London, 1999).
8 Alistair Horne, *Macmillan, 1957–1986* (Macmillan, 1989), p. 350.
9 Kevin Theakston, *The Civil Service Since 1945* (Blackwell, Oxford, 1995), p. 87.
10 Pimlott, *Harold Wilson*, pp. 252–65.
11 Ibid., pp. 154–72.
12 Pimlott, *Harold Wilson*, pp. 265–81.
13 Though some who knew him believed him to be breathtakingly clever (conversation with Andrew Graham, 19 May 2003) and personally very kind (conversation with Dr Peter Rose, 2 December 2004).

14 Eric Roll, *Crowded Hours* (Faber, 1985), p. 157.
15 The first ballot was held on 7 February 1963, when Wilson received 115 votes from the Parliamentary Labour Party, Brown 88 and Callaghan 41. In the head-to-head exactly a week later, Wilson polled 144 votes to Brown's 103.
16 Kenneth O. Morgan, *Callaghan: A Life* (Oxford University Press, Oxford, 1997), pp. 173–6.
17 National Archives (NA), Public Record Office (PRO), PREM 11/4834 'HM Opposition proposals for changes in machinery of government', Bligh to Helsby, 18 July 1963.
18 George Brown, *In My Way* (Gollancz, 1971), p. 96.
19 Interview with Lord Roll of Ipsden, 17 September 2002.
20 Hennessy, *The Prime Minister*, pp. 186–95.
21 Peter Paterson, *Tired and Emotional* (Chatto and Windus, 1993), p. 172.
22 Samuel Brittan, *Steering the Economy* (Pelican, 1971), p. 311.
23 Brown, *In My Way*, p. 96.
24 Wilson, *The Labour Government 1964–1970*, pp. 63, 221.
25 Brittan, *Steering the Economy*, p. 311.
26 NA, PRO, PREM 11/4834, Bligh to Douglas-Home, 22 April 1964.
27 Interview with Lord Roll of Ipsden, 17 September 2002.
28 See Chapter 1.
29 Pimlott, *Harold Wilson*, p. 116.
30 Tony Benn, *Out of the Wilderness: Diaries 1963–67* (Hutchison, 1987), p. 25, diary entry for 25 May 1963. Regarding Balogh's blueprint, the Balogh Papers are 'still mostly unlisted, completely unsorted and therefore not open for consultation' according to the Curator at Balliol College, email 12 October 2005, whereas Tony Benn wrote that his 'archives are being moved and I cannot trace it for the moment', letter 12 November 2005.
31 Interview with Sir Donald MacDougall, 25 September 2002.
32 House of Commons, *Official Report*, 3 November 1959, Col. 862.
33 Roll, *Crowded Hours*, p. 149.
34 Peter Hennessy, *Whitehall* (Secker and Warburg, 1989), pp. 180–1.
35 Roll, *Crowded Hours*, p. 149.
36 Lord George-Brown papers, Bodleian Library, Oxford, MS.Eng.c.5000, Roll to Brown, 3 April 1964.
37 Alec Cairncross, 'Obituary: Lord Roll of Ipsden', *Guardian*, 2 April 2005.
38 Brown, *In My Way*, p. 97.
39 Benn, *Out of the Wilderness*, p. 25, diary entry for 25 May 1963.
40 Lord Bridges in Norman Hunt, *Whitehall and Beyond* (BBC, 1964), p. 71.
41 Alec Cairncross, *Managing the British Economy in the 1960s: A Treasury Perspective* (Macmillan, 1996), p. 96.
42 Peter Hennessy, *Never Again* (Jonathan Cape, 1992), p. 338.
43 Douglas Jay, *Change and Fortune* (Hutchinson, 1980), p. 295.
44 Dell, *The Chancellors*, p. 307.
45 Paterson, *Tired and Emotional*, p. 171; Patterson quotes Jay's paper from the Lord George Brown papers, Bodleian Library, Oxford University.
46 Jay, *Change and Fortune*, p. 295.
47 Ibid., p. 295.

48 Philip Ziegler, *Wilson: The Authorised Life* (Weidenfeld and Nicolson, 1993) p. 171.
49 Wilson, *The Labour Government 1964–1970*, p. xvii.
50 NA, PRO, PREM 13/1546, 'Reorganisation of government after 1966 Election', Balogh to Wilson, 'Government Machinery', 4 April 1966.
51 Harold Wilson, *Purpose in Politics: Selected Speeches* (Weidenfeld & Nicolson, 1964), pp. 14–28.
52 Marcia Williams, *Inside No. 10* (Weidenfeld & Nicolson, 1972) p. 299.
53 Brittan, *Steering the Economy*, p. 295.
54 NA, PRO, PREM 11/4834, Bligh to Douglas-Home, 22 April 1964.
55 Ibid., hand-written 'P.S.' dated 27 April 1964 on Bligh to Douglas-Home, 22 April 1964.
56 Susan Crosland, *Tony Crosland* (Cape, 1982), p. 122.
57 Interview with Lord Roll of Ipsden, 17 September 2002; See NA, PRO, T 325/98, 'Economic Plan and Concordat co-operation between Department of Economic Affairs (DEA) and the Treasury', T 330/88 'Machinery of Government: division of functions between the Treasury and the Department of Economic Affairs (Concordat)'.
58 NA, PRO, PREM 11/4834, letter from Helsby to Bligh, 19 July 1963.
59 Interview with Lord Croham, 29 October 2002.
60 Roll, *Crowded Hours*, pp. 148–89; Dell, *The Chancellors*, pp. 306–9; Hennessy, *Whitehall*, pp. 182–6.
61 It was MacDougall who persuaded Brown not to absorb all of the NEDC and NEDO. Interview with Sir Donald MacDougall, 25 September 2002.
62 Interview with Sir Donald MacDougall, 25 September 2002.
63 Roll, *Crowded Hours*, p. 152.
64 NA, PRO, PREM 13/2126, 'Division of functions between HM Treasury and Department of Economic Affairs', Tom Caulcott to W. I. McIndoe, 27 October 1964.
65 Alec Cairncross, *The Wilson Years: A Treasury Diary, 1964–1969* (The Historian's Press, 1997), p. 15, diary entry for 16 November 1964.
66 NA, PRO, PRO PREM 13/2126, Caulcott to McIndoe, 27 October 1964.
67 Wilson, *The Labour Government 1964–1970*, p. 5.
68 NA, PRO, T 325/98, Peter Jay to Ian Bancroft and Richard Clarke, 'Concordat – Note for the Record,' 29 October 1964.
69 Andrew Blick, *People Who Live in the Dark* (Politico's, 2004), p. 88.
70 Hennessy, *Whitehall*, p. 189.
71 Blick, *People Who Live in the Dark*, pp. 321–3.
72 NA, PRO, T 325/98, A. J. Collier and J. Anson, 'Her Majesty's Treasury – Treasury Organisation Committee: Department of Economic Affairs: Note by the Secretaries', 30 September 1964.
73 Interview with Lord Roll of Ipsden, 17 September 2002.
74 NA, PRO, T 325/98, Clarke to Bancroft, 'Concordat', 29 October 1964.
75 Interview with Sir Donald MacDougall, 25 September 2002.
76 NA, PRO, T 325/98, Clarke to Sir William Armstrong, 'Concordat', 30 October 1964.
77 Hennessy, *Whitehall*, p. 182.
78 NA, PRO, T 325/98, note from the meeting of Helsby, Armstrong, Clarke, Roll, MacDougall and Jay, 'Machinery of Government (Economic): Concordat', 2 November 1964.

79 Interview with Lord Croham, 29 October 2002.
80 'This phrase was invented by Sir Michael Bichard when Permanent Secretary of Education and Employment. He used it at a private conference attended by Labour figures before the 1997 General Election and it impressed them.' Comment by Peter Hennessy, 5 July 2003.
81 NA, PRO, T 325/98, Roll to Helsby, 'Concordat', 11 November 1964.
82 NA, PRO, T 325/98, Clarke to Armstrong, 'The Control of Public Expenditure and a Plan for National Economic Development', 17 November 1964.
83 NA, PRO, T 325/98, Brown to Helsby, 4 December 1964.
84 Interview with Lord Roll of Ipsden, 17 September 2002.
85 NA, PRO, CAB 161/16, 'Committee Organisation Book, December 1964'.
86 Leo Plitatzky, *Getting and Spending* (Basil Blackwell, Oxford, 1982), p. 63.
87 Dell, *The Chancellors*, p. 309.
88 Private information.
89 NA, PRO, PREM 13/2126, Balogh to Wilson, 'Control and Planning of Investment', 28 October 1964.
90 James Callaghan quoted in Peter Hennessy, *Muddling Through* (Gollancz, 1996), p. 36.
91 Hennessy, *The Prime Minister*, p. 289.
92 NA, PRO, PREM 13/2126, Derek Mitchell to Anson, 14 December 1964.
93 James Callaghan, *Time and Chance* (Collins, 1987), p. 166.
94 Cairncross, *Managing the British Economy in the 1960s*, p. 99.
95 Callaghan, *Time and Chance*, p. 166.
96 Roll, *Crowded Hours*, p. 152.
97 Clarke and Croham quoted in Christopher Pollitt, *Manipulating the Machine* (George Allen & Unwin, 1984), p. 55.
98 Croham quoted in Pollitt, *Manipulating the Machine*, p. 55.
99 NA, PRO, T 325/98, Armstrong to all senior officials, 'Department of Economic Affairs: Division of Functions with the Treasury', 16 October 1964.
100 Brown, *In My Way*, p. 100.
101 Ziegler, *Wilson: The Authorised Life*, p. 249.
102 Dell, *The Chancellors*, p. 308.
103 Pimlott, *Harold Wilson*, p. 344.
104 Roy Jenkins, *A Life at the Centre* (Macmillan, 1991), p. 157.
105 Brown, *In My Way*, p. 96.
106 Dell, *The Chancellors*, p. 308.
107 Brown, *In My Way*, p. 99.
108 Ibid., p. 99.
109 Dell, *The Chancellors*, p. 308.
110 Brown, *In My Way*, p. 113.
111 NA, PRO, PREM 13/2126, Brown to Helsby, 4 December 1964.
112 Hennessy, *Whitehall*, p. 266.
113 Patrick Hennessy, 'Blair plots to smash Brown's Treasury powerbase', *Telegraph*, 2 January 2005.
114 Callaghan, *Time And Chance*, p. 153.

115 James Callaghan talking at 'The Department of Economic Affairs', Institute of Contemporary British History witness seminar, 5 June 1996. An edited version can be found in *Contemporary British History*, Vol. 11, Summer 1997, No. 2, pp. 117–42.
116 Pliatzky, *Getting and Spending*, p. 63.
117 Though the first two meetings of MISC1 on Saturday 17 and Sunday 18 October 1964 did not mention devaluation as such, it is clear that the preliminary discussion to these meetings detailed by Susan Crosland had looked at and rejected it. NA, PRO, CAB 130/202 'Economic Affairs: Meetings: 1–18'; Crosland, *Tony Crosland*, p. 125.
118 Dell, *The Chancellors*, p. 307.
119 Wilson, *The Labour Government 1964–1970*, p. 8.
120 Wilson, *Purpose in Politics*, pp. 18–27.
121 Craig (ed.), *British General Election Manifestos, 1959–1987*, p. 48.
122 Wilson, *The Labour Government 1964–1970*, p. 8.
123 Bruce Williams, 'Ministry of Technology' (Richard Coopey ed.), *Contemporary Record*, Vol. 5, No. 1, 1991, p. 133.
124 Pollitt, *Manipulating the Machine*, pp. 56–7.
125 Marcia Williams, *Inside Number 10* (Weidenfeld & Nicolson, 1972), p. 25.
126 Sir Lawrence Helsby quoted in Pollitt, *Manipulating the Machine*, p. 57.
127 Barbara Castle, *Fighting All the Way* (Macmillan, 1993), p. 353.
128 Callaghan, *Time and Chance*, p. 164.
129 Geoffrey Goodman, *The Awkward Warrior, Frank Cousins: His Life and Times* (Davis-Poynter, 1979), p. 437.
130 Lord Zuckerman, 'Ministry of Technology' (Richard Coopey, ed.), *Contemporary Record*, Vol. 5, No. 1, 1991, p. 133.
131 Pollitt, *Manipulating the Machine*, p. 57.
132 Wilson, *The Labour Government 1964–1970*, p. 10.
133 Ibid., p. 9; also see 'Let's Go With Labour For The New Britain' reprinted in F. W. S. Craig (ed.), *British General Election Manifestos, 1959–1987* (Dartmouth, Aldershot, 1990), pp. 43–60.
134 Rachmanism was the extortion or exploitation by a landlord of tenants of dilapidated or slum property, Williams, *Inside Number 10*, p. 25.
135 Pollitt, *Manipulating the Machine*, p. 65.
136 Richard Crossman, *The Diaries of a Cabinet Minister: Vol. 1, Minister of Housing, 1964–66* (Cape, 1975), pp. 21–5, diary entry for 22 October 1964; Pollitt, *Manipulating the Machine*, p. 64.
137 NA, PRO, PREM 13/14, 'Prime Minister wrote to Sir L Helsby expressing thanks for work of Civil Service since general election', Wilson to Helsby, 21 October 1964.
138 Williams, *Inside Number 10*, p. 122.
139 Hennessy, *The Prime Minister*, p. 295.
140 Joe Haines, *Glimmers of Twilight* (Politico's, 2003), p. 135.
141 Ibid., p. 64.
142 Ibid., p. 134.
143 Pimlott, *Harold Wilson*, p. 204.
144 Williams, *Inside Number 10*, p. 20.

145 Interview with Sir Derek Mitchell, 19 September 2002.
146 Ibid.
147 Haines, *Glimmers of Twilight*, p. 138.
148 Ibid., p. 140.
149 Hennessy, *Whitehall*, p. 189.
150 Williams, *Inside Number 10*, p. 123.
151 Tom Caulcott in Crosland, *Tony Crosland*, p. 137.
152 Pimlott, *Harold Wilson*, p. 323.
153 Williams, *Inside Number 10*, p. 37.
154 Douglas Hurd, *An End to Promises* (Collins, 1979), pp. 29–30.
155 Williams, *Inside Number 10*, p. 27.
156 Interview with Lord Roll of Ipsden, 17 September 2002.
157 Interview with Sir Derek Mitchell, 19 September 2002.
158 Williams, *Inside Number 10*, p. 14.
159 Interview with Sir Derek Mitchell, 19 September 2002.
160 Dell, *The Chancellors*, p. 304.
161 Ziegler, *Wilson: The Authorised Life*, p. 315.
162 See Pimlott, *Harold Wilson*, pp. 340–1.
163 NA, PRO, CAB 130/202, MISC 1, 1st Meeting, 17 October 1964; NA T 325/96, 'Her Majesty's Treasury, General Briefing: Economic Policy and the Balance of Payments,' 12 October 1964; Dell, *The Chancellors*, p. 311.
164 Brown, *In My Way*, p. 95.
165 Crosland, *Tony Crosland*, p. 125.
166 Wilson, *The Labour Government 1964–1970*, p. xvii.
167 Brown, *In My Way*, p. 100.
168 Edmund Dell, *A Strange Eventful History* (HarperCollins, 2000), p. 347.
169 Dell, *The Chancellors*, p. 311.
170 Interview with Sir Samuel Brittan, 4 October 2002.
171 Cairncross, *Managing the British Economy in the 1960s*, p. 92.
172 Dell, *The Chancellors*, p. 316.
173 Pimlott, *Harold Wilson*, p. 352.
174 Brittan, *Steering the Economy*, p. 291.
175 Cairncross, *The Wilson Years: A Treasury Diary*, pp. 65–75, diary entries between 4 July and 11 September 1965.
176 Cairncross, *The Wilson Years: A Treasury Diary*, pp. 2–13.
177 Alec Cairncross, *The British Economy Since 1945* (Blackwell, Oxford, 1995), p.156.
178 Ibid., p.157.
179 Dell, *The Chancellors*, p. 328; Brittan, *Steering the Economy*, p. 297.
180 Jenkins, *A Life at the Centre*, p. 128.
181 Callaghan, *Time and Chance*, p. 160.
182 Paterson, *Tired and Emotional*, p. 183.
183 Craig (ed.), *British General Election Manifestos, 1959–1987*, p. 50; Jay, *Change and Fortune*, p. 298.
184 Ziegler, *Wilson: The Authorised Life*, p. 191.

185 Blick, *People Who Live in the Dark*, p. 82.
186 Alec Cairncross, *The Wilson Years*, p. 73, diary entry for 26 July 1965 and footnote, diary entry for 29 July 1965.
187 Sir Samuel Brittan at the book launch for his *Against the Flow* (Atlantic, 2005), 17 January 2005.
188 Brown, *In My Way*, p. 96.
189 Jay, *Change and Fortune*, p. 313.
190 *The National Plan*, Cmnd. 2764 (HMSO, 1965).
191 Pliatzky, *Getting and Spending*, p. 63.
192 Paterson, *Tired and Emotional*, p. 172.
193 Brown, *In My Way*, pp. 104–6.
194 For the debate to launch it see House of Commons, *Official Report*, 3 November 1965, Cols 1041–1163.
195 Interview with Sir Donald MacDougall, 25 September 2002.
196 Pimlott, *Harold Wilson*, p. 425.
197 Hennessy, *Whitehall*, p. 187.
198 NA, PRO, PREM 13/2126, Mitchell to Helsby, 5 April 1966.
199 NA, PRO, PREM 13/2126, Michael Halls, 'Note for the Record', 25 April 1966.
200 Hennessy, *Whitehall*, p. 186.
201 Brittan, *Steering the Economy*, p. 338.
202 NA, PRO, CAB 21/5889, 'UK general economic situation', 'Record of a meeting on Economic Strategy on July 1, 1966' and 'Economic Policy: Note for the Record', 11 July 1966.
203 NA, PRO, CAB 128/46/1, 'CC(67)46th conclusions, minute 1(part) confidential annex', 'CC(66) 37', 19 July 1966.
204 Interview with Lord Roll of Ipsden, 17 September 2002.
205 Interview with Lord Roll of Ipsden, 17 September 2002.
206 Brown, *In My Way*, p. 95.
207 Jenkins, *A Life at the Centre*, p. 222.
208 Dell, *A Strange Eventful History*, p. 322.
209 Ibid., p. 321.
210 Ibid., p. 376.
211 Pimlott, *Harold Wilson*, p. 364.
212 Hennessy, *Whitehall*, p. 185.
213 Pimlott, *Harold Wilson*, p. 490.
214 Lord Lever interviewed for *All the Prime Minister's Men*, 7 May 1986.
215 Ziegler, *Wilson: The Authorised Life*, p. 173.
216 Ibid., p. 259.
217 NA, PRO, PREM 13/1434, 'National plan: part 3', Trend to Wilson, 'Future Planning Work', 18 March 1967.
218 Wilson, *The Labour Government 1964–1970*, p. 623.
219 House of Commons, *Official Report*, 26 February 1969, Cols. 1727–34.
220 NA, PRO, PREM 13/2680, 'Discussions on machinery of government changes', Halls to Armstrong, 23 September 1969.
221 NA, PRO, PREM 13/2126, Michael Stewart to Wilson, 1 December 1966.

NOTES TO PAGES 45–48

222　Barbara Castle, *The Castle Diaries, 1964–70* (Weidenfeld & Nicolson, 1984), p. 290, diary entry for 31 August 1967.
223　NA, PRO, PREM 13/1538, 'Prime Minister assumed responsibility for Department Economic Affairs', note of telephone conversation between Wilson and Shore, 30 August 1967.
224　Richard Crossman, *The Diaries of a Cabinet Minister: Vol. 2, Lord President of the Council and Leader of the House of Commons, 1966–68* (Cape, 1976), pp. 462–3, diary entry for 5 September 1967.
225　Brittan, *Steering the Economy*, p. 293.
226　Interview with Lord Croham, 29 October 2002.
227　Cairncross, *Managing The British Economy In The 1960s*, pp. 177–91.
228　See NA PREM 13/1447, 'Exchange rate: measures to devalue pound sterling; "Operation Patriarch"'.
229　Dell, *The Chancellors*, p. 355.
230　Wilson, *The Labour Government 1964–1970*, p. xvii.
231　Jon Davis, 'Industrial Reorganization Corporation' entry in John Ramsden (ed.), *The Oxford Companion to Twentieth-Century British Politics* (Oxford University Press, Oxford, 2002), p. 327.
232　Pollitt, *Manipulating the Machine*, p. 56.
233　Interview with Lord Croham, 29 October 2002.
234　Castle, *Fighting All the Way*, p. 402; House of Commons, *Official Report*, 4 April 1968, Cols 595–9.
235　Ibid., p. 398.
236　Jenkins, *A Life at the Centre*, p. 248; Castle, *Fighting All the Way*, p. 398.
237　Dell, *The Chancellors*, p. 360.
238　House of Commons, *Official Report*, 11 April 1968, Col. 1586.
239　Hennessy, *Whitehall*, p. 187.
240　Ibid., p. 187.
241　Pimlott, *Harold Wilson*, p. 436.
242　NA, PRO, PREM 13/3229, 'Rationale of Government's economic policy and structure', Halls to William Nield, 23 February 1969.
243　Crosland, *Tony Crosland*, p. 138.
244　Brown, *In My Way*, p. 117.
245　Pollitt, *Manipulating the Machine*, p. 60.
246　Tony Benn, *Office Without Power: Diaries 1968–72* (Hutchinson, 1988), pp. 203–4, diary entry for 4 October 1969; Richard Crossman, *The Diaries of a Cabinet Minister: Vol. 3, Secretary of State for Health and Social Security, 1968–70* (Cape, 1977), p. 676.
247　Williams, *Inside Number 10*, p. 252.
248　Interview with Lord Croham, 29 October 2002.
249　Pimlott, *Harold Wilson*, p. 545.
250　Pollitt, *Manipulating the Machine*, p. 48.
251　Hennessy, *Whitehall*, p. 422.
252　*Eleventh Report from the Expenditure Committee, Session 1976–77*, 'The Civil Service', Vol. II, Part II, p. 786.

253 Sir Robert Armstrong quoted in Hennessy, *The Prime Minister*, p. 307; NA, PRO, CAB 130/255–58, MISC 100, The Rhodesia Steering Committee was divided into six parts, MISC 100A–G.
254 Stephen Bailey, 'The Use of Inner Cabinets "Formal" and "Informal" Since 1968', unpublished undergraduate thesis, Department of History, Queen Mary and Westfield College, University of London, 1999.
255 Hennessy, *The Prime Minister*, pp. 319–27.
256 Castle, *The Castle Diaries, 1964–70*, p. 160. Diary entry for 10 August 1966.
257 Ibid., p. 462, diary entry for 13 June 1968.
258 See Jon Davis, 'Staring over the Precipice into the Abyss: An Anatomy and an Analysis of "Operation Brutus"', unpublished MA thesis, Queen Mary, University of London, October 1999.
259 NA, PRO, PREM 13/2688, 'Reorganisation of Central Machinery for Politico-military Planning and Intelligence, 1967–1968', Trend to Wilson, 13 March 1967; Prime Minister's Meeting of 31 July 1967, Note for the Record', 2 August 1967; Hennessy, *The Prime Minister*, p. 540.

Notes to Chapter 3: Software

1 Lord Bancroft, speaking at the Gresham College seminar, 'In the Steps of Walter Bagehot: A Constitutional Health-Check', 13 March 1995.
2 See Matthew Grant, 'Historians, the Penguin Specials and the "State-of-the-Nation" Literature, 1958–64,' *Contemporary British History*, Vol. 17, No. 3 (Autumn 2003), pp. 29–54.
3 *Let's Go With Labour* reprinted in Iain Dale (ed.), *Labour Party General Election Manifestos, 1900–1997* (Politico's, 2000), p. 124.
4 House of Commons, *Official Report*, 8 February 1966, Col. 210.
5 Letter from James Callaghan to Geoffrey Fry quoted in Fry, *Reforming the Civil Service* (Edinburgh University Press, Edinburgh, 1993), p. 8.
6 National Archives (NA), Public Record Office (PRO), PREM 13/1357, 'Size of Civil Service: management; training; setting up of committee of inquiry under chairmanship of Lord Fulton Mar 1965–Apr 1966', Callaghan to Wilson, 1 November 1965.
7 Email from Professor Robert Neild, 20 October 2004.
8 *The Times*, 28 February 1966.
9 Peter Kellner and Lord Crowther-Hunt, *The Civil Servants* (Macdonald and Janes, 1980), p. 99.
10 A. H. Halsey, 'Higher Education', in A. H. Halsey, *British Social Trends Since 1900* (Macmillan, 1988), p. 270.
11 Richard Wilding, 'The Fulton Report in retrospect', *Contemporary Record*, Vol. 9, No. 2, Autumn 1995, p. 399.
12 NA, PRO, PREM 13/1357, Helsby to Wilson, 'The Shortage of Principals', 2 June 1965.
13 Interview with Richard Wilding, 15 August 2003.
14 Richard Wilding quoted in 'Fulton: 20 Years On', *Contemporary Record*, Vol. 2, No. 2, Summer 1988, p. 44.

15 NA, PRO, PREM 13/1357, Helsby to Mitchell, 13 September 1965.
16 Lord Allen of Abbeydale quoted in 'Fulton: 20 Years On', p. 44.
17 House of Commons, *Official Report*, 8 February 1966, Col. 209.
18 House of Commons, *Sixth Report from the Estimates Committee, 1964–65*, HMSO, 1965, p. xxxv; Jeremy Bray (Elizabeth Bray, ed.), *Standing On The Shoulders Of Giants* (Elizabeth Bray, 2004), p. 64.
19 House of Commons, *Official Report*, 8 February 1966, Col. 211.
20 See Chapter 1.
21 House of Commons, *Official Report*, 8 February 1966, Col. 210.
22 Kellner and Crowther-Hunt, *The Civil Servants*, p. 28.
23 Fry, *Reforming the Civil Service*, p. 18.
24 Norman Hunt, *Whitehall and Beyond* (BBC, 1964).
25 Peter Hennessy, *Whitehall* (Secker and Warburg, 1989), pp. 190–1.
26 NA, PRO, PREM 13/1971, 'Appointment of committee, under chairmanship of Lord Fulton, to examine structure, recruitment, management and training of Civil Service: comments on report; part 3', Armstrong to Halls, 'The Fulton Report', 21 June 1968.
27 Ministry of Reconstruction, *Report of the Machinery of Government Committee*, Cmnd. 9230 (HMSO, 1918).
28 Interview with Lord Allen of Abbeydale, 7 May 2003.
29 Lord Allen of Abbeydale quoted in Fry, *Reforming the Civil Service*, p. 28.
30 Carol Davis, 'Honour without accolades', *Guardian*, 23 July 2003.
31 Interview with Lord Allen of Abbeydale, 7 May 2003.
32 NA, PRO, PREM 13/1357, Ian Bancroft, 'Note for the Record', 3 November 1965.
33 Interview with Richard Wilding, 15 August 2003.
34 Fry, *Reforming the Civil Service*, p. 15.
35 Kellner and Crowther-Hunt, *The Civil Servants*, p. 27.
36 Fry, *Reforming the Civil Service*, p. 15.
37 Kellner and Crowther-Hunt, *The Civil Servants*, p. 27.
38 Lord Allen of Abbeydale quoted in 'Fulton: 20 Years On', p. 45.
39 Interview with Professor Robert Neild, 6 May 2003.
40 Interview with Richard Wilding, 15 August 2003.
41 NA, PRO, PREM 13/1970, 'Appointment of committee, under chairmanship of Lord Fulton, to examine structure, recruitment, management and training of Civil Service: consideration of conclusions; publication of and publicity for report; parts 1 and 2', Halls to Wilson, 'The Fulton Report', 9 March 1968.
42 Lord Shackleton quoted in 'Fulton: 20 Years On', p. 48.
43 Fry, *Reforming the Civil Service*, pp. 21–2.
44 Peter Hennessy quoted in 'Fulton: 20 Years On', p. 45.
45 Allen quoted in 'Fulton: 20 Years On', p. 45.
46 Henry Roseveare, *The Treasury* (Allen Lane, 1969), p. 297.
47 *Control of Public Expenditure*, Cmnd. 1432 (HMSO, 1961).
48 Fry, *Reforming the Civil Service*, p. 26.
49 NA, PRO, PREM 13/1357, Callaghan to Wilson, 1 November 1965.
50 Kellner and Crowther-Hunt, *The Civil Servants*, p. 26.

51 Fry, *Reforming the Civil Service*, p. 26.
52 Robert Neild quoted in ibid., p. 231; the Macaulay Report and the Northcote-Trevelyan Report are found in Appendix B of the Fulton Report.
53 For example, *The Civil Service: Continuity and Change*, Cmnd. 2627 (HMSO, 1994).
54 NA, PRO, PREM 13/764, 'Fulton Committee: discussions on giving of evidence by ministers and former ministers', Allen to Halls, 18 August 1966.
55 Fry, *Reforming the Civil Service*, pp. 28, 99.
56 John Rosselli quoted in ibid., p. 235.
57 Lorna Arnold, *Britain and the H-bomb* (Palgrave, Basingstoke, 2000), p. 78.
58 Interview with Richard Wilding, 15 August 2003.
59 Formerly Economic Secretary to the Treasury 1955–6, Financial Secretary to the Treasury 1959–62 and Minister of Education 1962–4.
60 Richard Wilding, *Civil Servant* (The Memoir Club, Stanhope, 2006), p. 44.
61 Wilding, 'The Fulton Report in retrospect', p. 398.
62 Allen and Wilding quoted in Fry, *Reforming the Civil Service*, p. 20.
63 Interview with Richard Wilding, 15 August 2003.
64 Fry, *Reforming the Civil Service*, p. 20.
65 Interview with Professor Robert Neild, 6 May 2003.
66 Lord Allen of Abbeydale quoted in Fry, *Reforming the Civil Service*, p. 16.
67 NA, PRO, PREM 13/1971, Hunt to Wilson, 31 July 1968.
68 Private information.
69 Fry, *Reforming the Civil Service*, pp. 42–3.
70 Ibid., p. 55.
71 Neild quoted in 'Fulton: 20 Years On', p. 45.
72 Kellner and Crowther-Hunt, *The Civil Servants*, p. 30.
73 Fry, *Reforming the Civil Service*, p. 67. BP was clearly as influential then as it has been in the recent past, with its former Chairman, Lord Simon, assuming an unofficial role as adviser to Tony Blair on public sector reform, Peter Hennessy, *The Prime Minister* (Penguin, 2000), p. 516.
74 Fry, *Reforming the Civil Service*, p. 125.
75 Richard Chapman and J. R. Greenaway, *The Dynamics of Administrative Reform* (Croom Helm, 1980), p. 139.
76 Ibid., pp. 51–5.
77 Fry, *Reforming the Civil Service*, pp. 52–3.
78 Ibid., p. 56.
79 Kellner and Crowther-Hunt, *The Civil Servants*, p. 33.
80 Fry, *Reforming the Civil Service*, pp. 67, 70.
81 Ibid., p. 234.
82 Lord Simey quoted in ibid., pp. 234–5.
83 Wilding, 'The Fulton Report in retrospect', p. 401.
84 NA, PRO, PREM 13/1970, Halls to Wilson, 'The Fulton Report', 9 March 1968.
85 Private information.
86 NA, PRO, PREM 13/1970, Armstrong to Helsby, 25 March 1968.
87 Interview with Lord Allen of Abbeydale, 7 May 2003.

88 NA, PRO, PREM 13/1970, Armstrong to Helsby, 25 March 1968.
89 Fry, *Reforming the Civil Service*, p. 238.
90 Lord Allen of Abbeydale quoted in 'Fulton: 20 Years On', p. 45.
91 NA, PRO, PREM 13/1970, Halls to Wilson, 'Fulton', 25 February 1968.
92 Robert Neild quoted in 'Fulton: 20 Years On', pp. 46–47.
93 NA, PRO, PREM 13/1971, Hunt to Halls, 31 July 1968.
94 Hennessy, *Whitehall*, p. 204.
95 Interview with Lord Jenkins of Hillhead, 5 May 1999.
96 Wilson Papers, box 76, Wilson to Helsby, 14 February 1966, quoted in Philip Ziegler, *Wilson: The Authorised Life* (Weidenfeld & Nicolson, 1993), pp. 213–14.
97 Richard Wilding quoted in 'Fulton: 20 Years On', p. 47.
98 Ibid.
99 Fry, *Reforming the Civil Service*, p. 38.
100 Simons quoted in ibid., pp. 40, 77.
101 Richard Crossman, *The Diaries of a Cabinet Minister*, Vol. 2, *Lord President of the Council and Leader of the House of Commons 1966–68* (Hamish Hamilton and Cape, 1976), p. 200, diary entry for 17 January 1967.
102 Hennessy, *Whitehall*, pp. 191–4.
103 Wilding, 'The Fulton Report in retrospect', pp. 399–400.
104 NA, PRO, PREM 13/1970, Halls to Wilson, 'Fulton', 25 February 1968.
105 Ibid.
106 Roseveare, *The Treasury*, p. 305.
107 NA, PRO, PREM 13/1357, Helsby to Mitchell, 13 September 1965.
108 Michael Young, *The Rise of the Meritocracy* (Thames and Hudson, 1958), p. 20.
109 Fry, *Reforming the Civil Service*, p. 276; *Report of the Committee of Inquiry. The Method II System of Selection for the Administrative Class of the Home Civil Service*, Cmnd. 4156 (HMSO, 1969).
110 Fry, *Reforming the Civil Service*, p. 276.
111 Thomas Balogh, 'The Apotheosis of the Dilettante', in Hugh Thomas (ed.), *The Establishment* (A. Blond, 1959), p. 91.
112 Harold Laski, 'Introduction', in J. P. W. Mallalieu, *Passed To You Please* (Gollancz, 1942), p. 11.
113 Letter from Richard Wilding, 18 December 2005.
114 NA, PRO, PREM 13/1970, Helsby to Wilson, 'The Fulton Committee', 16 May 1967.
115 See NA, PRO, CAB 87/74 (MG(42)6), 31 December 1942.
116 See NA, PRO, T162/752; T162/805; T162/806; T162/806 'Committee on training of civil servants'; Chapman and Greenaway, *The Dynamics of Administrative Reform*, pp. 146–7.
117 Samuel Brittan, *Steering the Economy* (Pelican, 1971), p. 33.
118 NA, PRO, PREM 13/1357, Helsby to Mitchell, 'Civil Service Training', 4 August 1965.
119 Chapman and Greenaway, *The Dynamics of Administrative Reform*, p. 143.
120 NA, PRO, PREM 13/1357, Balogh to Wilson, 6 July 1965.
121 Email from Professor Julian Jackson, 12 September 2004. See William Hitchcock, *France Restored: Cold War Diplomacy and the Quest for Leadership in Europe, 1944–1954* (University of North Carolina Press, Chapel Hill, North Carolina, USA, 1998).

122 NA, PRO, PREM 13/1357, Mitchell to Helsby, 'Civil Service Training', 31 August 1965.
123 See Andrew Blick, *People Who Live in the Dark* (Politico's, 2004), pp. 97–104.
124 NA, PRO, PREM 13/1970, Halls to Wilson, 'Fulton', 25 February 1968.
125 According to Richard Wilding, 'The Fulton Report in retrospect', p. 398.
126 John Garrett, *The Management of Government* (Harmondsworth, 1972), pp. 14–15.
127 Ibid., p. 43.
128 NA, PRO, BA 1/5 C.C.S. (66) 30th Meeting Appendix B: 'Oral Evidence of the Civil Service Commission' pp. B(ii–iii), 6 December 1966; Fry, *Reforming the Civil Service*, pp. 198–207.
129 Fry, *Reforming the Civil Service*, p. 21.
130 Interview with Lord Allen of Abbeydale, 7 May 2003.
131 NA, PRO, PREM 13/1970, Halls to Wilson, 'Fulton', 25 February 1968.
132 Kevin Theakston, *Leadership in Whitehall* (Macmillan, 1999), p. 183.
133 NA, PRO, PREM 13/1970, Halls to Wilson, 'Fulton', 25 February 1968.
134 Ibid.
135 Ibid., Armstrong to Halls, 'Fulton Report', 9 May 1968.
136 Priscilla Baines, 'History and Rationale of the 1979 Reforms', in Gavin Drewry (ed.), *The New Select Committees* (Clarendon Press, Oxford, 1989), p. 20.
137 Interview with Lord Allen of Abbeydale, 7 May 2003.
138 Theakston, *Leadership in Whitehall*, p. 184.
139 NA, PRO, PREM 13/1970, Armstrong to Halls, 'Fulton Report', 9 May 1968.
140 Hennessy, *The Prime Minister*, p. 45.
141 Interview with Lord Allen of Abbeydale, 7 May 2003.
142 Conversation with Sir Samuel Brittan, 17 April 2003.
143 Interview with Lord Allen of Abbeydale, 7 May 2003.
144 Lord Croham briefing the 'Hidden Wiring' MA option course, Queen Mary, University of London, 9 February 2005.
145 *Ministerial Code: A Code Of Conduct And Guidance On Procedures For Ministers* (Cabinet Office, July 2001), paragraph 50.
146 NA, PRO, PREM 13/1970, Armstrong to Halls, 'Fulton Report', 9 May 1968.
147 Interview with Professor Robert Neild, 6 May 2003.
148 Richard Wilding quoted in 'Fulton: 20 Years On', p. 45.
149 Michael Young, *The Rise of the Meritocracy* (Transaction, New Brunswick, USA, 1999), p. xiii.
150 Wilding, 'The Fulton Report in retrospect', p. 401.
151 NA, PRO, PREM 13/1970, Halls to Wilson, 'The Fulton Report', 9 March 1968.
152 Wilding, 'The Fulton Report in retrospect', p. 401.
153 Interview with Richard Wilding, 15 August 2003.
154 Wilding, 'The Fulton Report in retrospect', pp. 401–2.
155 Kellner and Crowther-Hunt, *The Civil Servants*, p. 59.
156 NA, PRO, PREM 13/1970, Armstrong to Halls, 9 May 1968.
157 Harold Wilson, *The Labour Government 1964–1970* (Weidenfeld & Nicolson, 1971), p. 539.
158 NA, PRO, PREM 13/1970, Halls to Wilson, 'The Fulton Report', 8 June 1968.

159 Donald MacDougall, *Don and Mandarin* (Murray, 1987), p. 193.
160 Ibid., p. 193.
161 Richard Crossman, *The Diaries of a Cabinet Minister, Vol. 1: Minister of Housing, 1964–66* (Cape, 1975).
162 Sir Burke Trend, Cabinet Secretary, 1963–73; Treasury Second Secretary, 1960–2.
163 Probably Sir Alexander Johnston, Permanent Secretary and Chairman of the Inland Revenue, 1958–68; Treasury Third Secretary, 1951–8.
164 Sir William Morton, Chairman of the Board of Customs and Excise, 1965–9; Treasury Third Secretary, 1958–65.
165 Sir Arnold France, Permanent Secretary, Department of Health, 1964–8; Treasury Third Secretary, 1960.
166 Sir Thomas Padmore, Permanent Secretary, Ministry of Transport, 1962–8; Treasury Second Secretary, 1952–62.
167 Sir Philip Allen, Permanent Secretary, Home Office, 1966–72; Treasury Second Secretary, 1963–6.
168 Sir David Pitblado, Permanent Secretary, Ministry of Power, 1966–9; Treasury Third Secretary, 1960.
169 Sir Richard Clarke, Permanent Secretary, Ministry of Technology, 1966–70; Treasury Second Secretary, 1962–6.
170 NA, PRO, PREM 13/1970, Halls to Wilson, 11 May 1968.
171 Interview with Richard Wilding, 15 August 2003.
172 Hennessy, *Whitehall*, p. 198.
173 Cmnd. 3638, pp. 104.
174 Interview with Richard Wilding, 15 August 2003.
175 Ibid.
176 Lord Allen of Abbeydale quoted in Fry, *Reforming the Civil Service*, p. 239.
177 Hennessy, *Whitehall*, pp. 198–9.
178 See Jon Davis, 'Staring over the Precipice into the Abyss: An Anatomy and an Analysis of "Operation Brutus"', unpublished MA thesis, Queen Mary and Westfield College, University of London, October 1999.
179 *The Civil Service: Vol. 1 – Report of the Committee 1966–68*, Cmnd. 3638, pp. 35–40.
180 *The Civil Service: Vol. 1 – Report of the Committee 1966–68*, Cmnd. 3638, pp. 81–8.
181 Ibid., pp. 69–78.
182 See Appendix.
183 NA, PRO, PREM 13/1970, Armstrong to Halls, 'Fulton Report', 12 June 1968.
184 Ibid., Halls to Armstrong, 13 June 1968.
185 NA, PRO, PREM 13/2528, 'Fulton Report: government's consideration of recommendations; inquiry into release of official information and Official Secrets Act; part 2', Halls to Gilbraith, CSD, 22 April 1969.
186 NA, PRO, PREM 13/1970, Armstrong to Halls, 13 June 1968.
187 Ibid., 14 June 1968.
188 Ibid., Armstrong to Halls, 'Fulton Report', 18 June 1968.
189 Thomas Balogh quoted in Barbara Castle, *The Castle Diaries 1964–70* (Weidenfeld & Nicolson, 1984), p. 464, diary entry for 19 June 1968.

NOTES TO PAGES 74-76

190 Roy Jenkins, *A Life At The Centre* (Macmillan, 1991), p. 41.
191 Richard Crossman, *The Diaries of a Cabinet Minister*, Vol. III, *Secretary of State for the Social Services 1968–70* (Hamilton, 1977), p. 107, diary entry for 25 June 1968.
192 Crossman was referring to his cross-party proposals for reform of the Lords – Crossman, *The Diaries of a Cabinet Minister*, Vol. III, pp. 96–103, diary entries for 17, 18 and 19 June 1968.
193 NA, PRO, CAB 128/43, Part 2, Cabinet meeting, 20 June 1968.
194 Ibid.
195 Ibid., Cabinet meeting, 25 June 1968.
196 House of Commons, *Official Report*, 26 June 1968, Col. 459.
197 Ibid.
198 Fry, *Reforming the Civil Service*, p. 267.
199 Lord Croham briefing the 'Hidden Wiring' MA option course, Queen Mary, University of London, 9 February 2005.
200 NA, PRO, PREM 13/2692, 'Creation of Civil Service Department (CSD) following Fulton Report: discussions on location of new department', Le Cheminant to Wilson, 31 May 1968. See Chapter 2.
201 Lord Croham briefing the 'Hidden Wiring' MA option course, Queen Mary, University of London, 9 February 2005.
202 Quoted in Christopher Pollitt, *Manipulating the Machine* (Allen and Unwin, 1984), p. 78.
203 The machinery set up during the First World War to calm labour difficulties across the economy by bringing employers and trade unions together, which lasted in the Civil Service until Mrs Thatcher's tenure. It took its name from J. H. Whitley, the Deputy Speaker of the House of Commons who chaired the relevant sub-committee of the Cabinet's Reconstruction Committee. See Hennessy, *Whitehall*, p. 81.
204 NA, PRO, PREM 13/1970, Halls to Wilson, 'Fulton', 25 February 1968.
205 NA, PRO, PREM 13/3099, 'Announcement about structural changes in Civil Service grades in advance of introduction of unified grading system', Hunt to Halls, 31 December 1969; PREM 13/3100, 'Structural changes in Civil Service: introduction of unified grading structure and graduate entry into new structure; joint report by official and staff sides – "Fulton, a framework for the future"; part 2', Halls to Wilson, 'Further Steps on Fulton', 13 February 1970.
206 Kellner and Crowther-Hunt, *The Civil Servants*, p. 74.
207 NA, PRO, PREM 13/3100, Halls to Shore, 17 February 1970.
208 Ibid., Hunt to Armstrong, 12 February 1970.
209 Wilding, 'The Fulton Report in retrospect', p. 406.
210 NA, PRO, PREM 13/3099, Halls to Wilson, 'Implementation of the Fulton Report', 10 January 1970.
211 Ibid.
212 NA, PRO, PREM 13/3099, Halls to Wilson, 'Further Steps on the Unified Grading Structure', 21 November 1969.
213 *The Civil Service: Report of the Committee 1966–68*, Cmnd. 3638, Appendix K, p. 179.
214 NA, PRO, PREM 13/3099, Halls to Wilson, 18 July 1969.

215 See NA, PRO, PREM 15/2024, 'Claim against Civil Service Department by Marjorie Halls for premature death of her husband, Michael Halls (Principal Private Secretary to Harold Wilson), allegedly caused by stressful working conditions in 10 Downing Street'.
216 Joe Haines, *Glimmers of Twilight* (Politico's, 2003), p. 56.
217 Interview with Richard Wilding, 15 August 2003.
218 Haines, *Glimmers of Twilight*, pp. 56–9.
219 Interview with Lord Howell of Guildford, 8 October 2003.
220 Kellner and Crowther-Hunt, *The Civil Servants*, p. 77.
221 Sir William Armstrong quoted in Theakston, *The Civil Service Since 1945* (Blackwell, Oxford, 1995), p. 97.
222 Richard Wilding, *Civil Servant* (The Memoir Club, Stanhope, 2006), pp. 53–4.
223 NA, PRO, PREM 13/3099, Halls to Roger Dawes, 15 July 1969.
224 NA, PRO, PREM 13/3100, Halls to Wilson, 'Report to Staff Association on Fulton', 17 January 1970.
225 *Eleventh Report from the Expenditure Committee, Session 1976–77*, 'The Civil Service', Vol. II, Part II, p. 788.
226 Interview with Richard Wilding, 15 August 2003.
227 Interview with Richard Wilding, 15 August 2003.
228 *The Civil Service: Vol. 1 – Report of the Committee 1966–68*, Cmnd. 3638, p. 104.
229 Ibid., pp. 40–2.
230 Ibid., p. 33.
231 Ibid., pp. 51–4.
232 Ibid., pp. 59–61.
233 Ibid., p. 45.
234 Ibid., p. 27.
235 Fry, *Reforming the Civil Service*, p. 196.
236 *The Civil Service: Vol. 1 – Report of the Committee 1966–68*, Cmnd. 3638, p. 28.
237 Ibid.
238 Fry, *Reforming the Civil Service*, p. 263.
239 Ibid., p. 220.
240 Interview with Lord Croham, 29 October 2002.
241 Hennessy, *Whitehall*, p. 204.
242 NA, PRO, PREM 13/1972, 'Progress on implementation of Fulton report recommendations', 'Developments Since Fulton', 18 December 1968.
243 *The Civil Service: Vol. 1 – Report of the Committee 1966–68*, Cmnd. 3638, p. 106.
244 NA, PRO, PREM 13/2528, Halls to Walker, Office of the Lord Privy Seal, 23 January 1969.
245 NA, PRO, PREM 13/1972, Halls to Wilson, 23 November 1968.
246 Heath quoted in Peter Hennessy, 'Open government, Whitehall and the press since 1945', in Hugh Stephenson (ed.), *Media Voices* (Politico's, 2001), p. 320.
247 NA, PRO, PREM 13/2528, Halls to Mr Walker, Office of the Lord Privy Seal, 23 January 1969.
248 Hennessy, 'Open government, Whitehall and the press since 1945', p. 318.
249 *Information and the Public Interest*, Cmnd. 4089 (HMSO, 1969), p. 12.

250 Hennessy, 'Open government, Whitehall and the press since 1945', pp. 321–3.
251 Ibid.
252 NA, PRO, PREM 13/3242, 'Follow-up to Fulton Report: candidates for "hiving-off"; reports of Steering Group', Armstrong to his fellow permanent secretaries, 'Hiving-Off', 15 August 1969.
253 Garrett, *The Management of Government*, p. 192; *The Civil Service: Vol. 5*, Cmnd. 3638 (No. 67).
254 House of Commons, *Official Report*, 21 November 1968, Col. 1555.
255 NA, PRO, PREM 13/3097, 'Developments on Fulton Report: progress report; part 4', Wilson to Halls, 15 February 1969.
256 NA, PRO, PREM 13/3242, Hiving-Off Steering Group, 'Interim Report', around 15 August 1969.
257 NA, PRO, PREM 13/3242, Hiving-Off Steering Group, 'Second Interim Report', 17 December 1969.
258 Ibid., Armstrong to all Permanent Secretaries, 'Hiving-Off', 15 August 1969.
259 Interview with Professor Robert Neild, 6 May 2003.
260 Ibid.
261 Wilding, 'The Fulton Report in retrospect', p. 394.

Notes to Chapter 4: Strategy

1 John Ramsden, *An Appetite For Power* (HarperCollins, 1998), p. 391.
2 John Ramsden, *The Winds of Change* (Longman, 1996), p. 231.
3 Lord Home in conversation with Peter Hennessy, *The Quality of Cabinet Government:* 'The Unknown Premiership', broadcast on BBC Radio 3, 25 July 1985.
4 David Butler and Anthony King, *The British General Election of 1964* (Macmillan, 1964), p. 23.
5 D. R. Thorpe, *Alec Douglas-Home* (Sinclair-Stevenson, 1997), p. 322.
6 In the poll Heath gained 150 votes, Maudling 133 and Enoch Powell 15.
7 Douglas Hurd, *Memoirs* (Little, Brown, 2003), p. 171.
8 Peter Hennessy, *Whitehall* (Secker and Warburg, 1989), p. 211.
9 Patrick Gordon Walker, the Foreign Secretary, who lost his Smethwick seat in October 1964, did not manage to return to the Commons in the hastily arranged Leyton by-election in January 1965, thereby reducing Labour's majority to only three. See Ben Pimlott, *Harold Wilson* (HarperCollins, 1993), pp. 357–8.
10 See Conservative Research Department (CRD) archives, Conservative Party Archives (CPA), Bodleian Library, Oxford University, 3/14/3.
11 CPA, CRD 3/14/2, Heath to Sir William Robson Brown, 26 February 1965; Kevin Theakston in Anthony Seldon and Stuart Ball (eds), *The Heath Government 1970–74: A Reappraisal* (Longman, 1996), p. 78.
12 Christopher Pollitt, *Manipulating The Machine* (Allen and Unwin, 1984), p. 83.
13 CPA, CRD 3/14/3, 'Policy Group on Machinery of Government: Report on the Cabinet System', March 1966; National Archives (NA), Public Record Office (PRO), PREM 15/402,

'Review of departmental responsibilities: reorganisation of central government', Douglas Hurd to Michael Wolff, 'Reorganisation of Central Government', 14 October 1970.
14 John Campbell, *Edward Heath* (Jonathan Cape, 1993), p. 212.
15 Pimlott, *Harold Wilson*, p. 503.
16 Douglas Hurd, *An End to Promises* (Collins, 1979), p. 25.
17 Iain Dale (ed.), *Conservative Party Manifestos 1900–1997* (Politico's, 2000), pp. 161–73; John Ramsden in *The Heath Government 1970–74: A Reappraisal*, p. 24.
18 Campbell, *Edward Heath*, pp. 212–13.
19 Pollitt, *Manipulating the Machine*, p. 88.
20 Hennessy, *Whitehall*, p. 281.
21 Ibid., p. 210.
22 Peter Hennessy, *Cabinet* (Basil Blackwell, Oxford, 1986), p. 74.
23 Edward Heath, *The Course of My Life* (Hodder and Stoughton, 1998), p. 120.
24 Ramsden, *An Appetite For Power*, p. 387; Hurd, *An End to Promises*, p. 86.
25 Hurd, *An End to Promises*, p. 84.
26 Heath, *The Course of My Life*, pp. 100, 188–9, 197–8, 641.
27 Campbell, *Edward Heath*, p. 203.
28 John Ramsden in *The Heath Government 1970–74: A Reappraisal*, p. 41.
29 Peter Hennessy, *The Prime Minister* (Penguin, 2000), pp. 334–5.
30 Douglas Hurd in conversation with Michael Cockerell and quoted in ibid., p. 338.
31 M. Burch, 'Approaches to Leadership in Opposition: Edward Heath and Margaret Thatcher', in Z. Layton-Henry (ed.), *Conservative Party Politics* (Macmillan, 1980), p. 172.
32 Heath, *The Course of My Life*, p. 314.
33 NA, PRO, BA 1/38, 'Numbers 194–205', 'Meeting with Mr. Edward Heath', C.C.S. (67)197, 19 June 1967; Kevin Theakston in *The Heath Government 1970–74: A Reappraisal*, p. 76.
34 Hennessy, *Whitehall*, p. 211.
35 Alistair Horne, *Macmillan, 1894–1956* (Macmillan, 1988), pp. 336–7.
36 Francis Boyd, 'Mr Marples will not play by "Etonian" rules', *Guardian*, 21 April 1966.
37 David Howell, *The Edge Of Now* (Macmillan, 2000), p. 307.
38 This person's details have not proved to be traceable.
39 MP for Bolton East, 1970–February 1974 who had studied and worked extensively in Europe.
40 Howell, *The Edge Of Now*, p. 323.
41 'Mr Marples spells out aims of new Research Unit', press release, Conservative Central Office, 22 April 1967.
42 Howell, *The Edge Of Now*, pp. 308–9.
43 Ibid., p. 308.
44 Enoch Powell's foreword to Andrew Elliot, *The Guilty Madmen of Whitehall* (Elliot Right Way Books, Kingswood, 1969), p. xii.
45 Howell, *The Edge Of Now*, p. 317.
46 Email from Lord Howell of Guildford, 22 April 2004.
47 Howell, *The Edge Of Now*, p. 308.
48 CPA, CRD 3/14/7, Mark Schreiber, 'Report on Japan', 6 May 1966.

49 CPA, CRD 3/14/8, Mark Schreiber and Laurence Reed, 'Programme for visit to I.R.I. Italy', 16 February 1968.
50 Howell, *The Edge Of Now*, p. 327.
51 Howell, *The Edge Of Now*, p. 328.
52 Ibid., p. 308.
53 Heath, *The Course of My Life*, p. 330. T. J. Hatton and K. Alec Chrystal claim that the precise figures are 39.1 per cent taken up by government spending as a percentage of GDP in 1960 compared to 47.5 per cent in 1970, N. F. R. Crafts and N. W. C. Woodward (eds), *The British Economy Since 1945* (Clarendon, Oxford, 1991), p. 56. The discrepancy clearly does not detract from Heath's overall point.
54 Howell, *The Edge Of Now*, p. 323.
55 I am grateful to Lord Howell of Guildford for allowing me to look at his PSRU papers which are incomplete and unsorted. Lord Marlesford (Mark Schreiber) had the only other copies but disposed of them several years ago.
56 Howell, *The Edge Of Now*, p. 344.
57 Lewis Baston and Anthony Seldon in *The Heath Government 1970–74: A Reappraisal*, p. 73.
58 David Henderson, 'Two Costly British Errors', *The Unimportance of Being Right*, BBC Radio 3, 24 October 1977.
59 'All do PAR', *The Economist*, 6 February 1971.
60 Kevin Theakston in *The Heath Government 1970–74: A Reappraisal*, p. 79.
61 It comprised five from its founding until May 1917 when a Cecil Harmsworth (Liberal MP and younger brother of Lord Northcliffe, proprietor of the Harmsworth newspapers) joined, went back to five in June 1917 when David Davies (Welsh coal-owner and philanthropist) left and fell to four when Waldorf Astor (Conservative MP and proprietor of the *Observer*) departed in July 1918. The other members were Philip Kerr (editor of the imperial unity journal *The Round Table*) and Joseph Davies (a Welsh commercial statistician); John Turner, *Lloyd George's Secretariat* (Cambridge University Press, Cambridge, 1980), p. 2.
62 Tessa Blackstone and William Plowden, *Inside The Think Tank* (Heinemann, 1988), pp. 2–4.
63 Howell, *The Edge Of Now*, p. 350.
64 Conversation with Mark Schreiber (now Lord Marlesford), 15 November 2003.
65 See Hennessy, *The Prime Minister*, pp. 189–95.
66 Kevin Theakston in *The Heath Government 1970–74: A Reappraisal*, p. 90.
67 Howell, *The Edge of Now*, p. 313.
68 Heath, *The Course of My Life*, p. 315.
69 NA, PRO, BA 1/38 – 'Meeting with Mr. Edward Heath', C.C.S. (67)197, 19 June 1967.
70 David Howell, *A New Style of Government* (Conservative Political Centre, 1970), p. 13.
71 Howell, *The Edge of Now*, p. 324.
72 Ibid., p. 324.
73 Heath, *The Course of My Life*, p. 62.
74 Howell, *The Edge of Now*, p. 331.
75 Hurd, *An End to Promises*, p. 142.

NOTES TO PAGES 90–92

76 Ramsden, *The Winds of Change*, p. 251.
77 Brendon Sewill to David Clarke and quoted in Ramsden, *An Appetite for Power*, p. 394.
78 Ramsden, *An Appetite for Power*, p. 389.
79 Enoch Powell quoted in Phillip Whitehead, *The Writing on the Wall* (Michael Joseph, 1985), p. 52.
80 Angus Maude, 'Winter of Tory Discontent', *The Spectator*, 14 January 1966.
81 David Howell, 'What's Wrong with Central Office', *The Spectator*, 13 January 1967.
82 Howell, *The Edge of Now*, p. 315.
83 Ibid., p. 315.
84 Ibid., p. 310.
85 Ibid., p. 315.
86 Ibid., p. 322.
87 Howell wrote: 'Peter Drucker uses the unusually ugly word "privatisation" for this process ... it is ... hideously clumsy. Something better must be invented', Howell, *A New Style of Government*, p. 8; see also Patricia Sullivan, 'Management Visionary Peter Drucker Dies', *Washington Post*, 12 November 2005.
88 Ramsden, *An Appetite for Power*, p. 395.
89 Rasmden, *The Winds of Change*, pp. 276–86.
90 NA, PRO, PREM 15/402, Hurd to Wolff, 'Reorganisation of Central Government', 14 October 1970.
91 Public Sector Research Unit papers, 'Preparation for Government: Seminar Programme', September 1969.
92 CPA, CRD 3/14/10, 'Conservative Party "Preparation for Government" Seminar', September 1969.
93 Kevin Theakston in *The Heath Government 1970–74: A Reappraisal*, p. 80.
94 Reprinted in John Ramsden, *The Making of Conservative Party Policy* (Longman, 1980), pp. 279–83.
95 NA, PRO, PREM 15/402, Hurd to Wolff, 'Reorganisation of Central Government', 14 October 1970.
96 Public Sector Research Unit papers, 'Note on Dinner with the Shadow Cabinet', 2 December 1969.
97 NA, PRO, PREM 15/402, Hurd to Wolff, 'Reorganisation of Central Government', 14 October 1970.
98 David Howell, 'Note on Dinner with the Shadow Cabinet', Public Sector Research Unit papers, 2 December 1969.
99 Ibid.
100 Interview with Lord Howell of Guildford, 8 October 2003.
101 Email from Professor Rodney Lowe, 4 April 2007.
102 NA, PRO, BA 17/232, 'Machinery of government review: organisation of the Prime Minister's Office: paper no 3'; Public Sector Research Unit papers, 'Second Draft of Submission to Mr. Heath by Action Group I', 20 May 1970.
103 Pollitt, *Manipulating the Machine*, p. 85.
104 Blackstone and Plowden, *Inside the Think Tank*, p. 8.
105 Campbell, *Edward Heath*, p. 222.

106 CPA, CRD 3/14/2, Lord Normanbrook to Heath, 8 January 1965; Kevin Theakston in *The Heath Government 1970–74: A Reappraisal*, p. 77.
107 NA, PRO, PREM 15/402, Hurd to Wolff, 'Reorganisation of Central Government', 14 October 1970.
108 CPA, CRD 3/14/4, 'Machinery of Government', Michael Fraser to James Douglas.
109 Dr William Plowden's diary, entry for 21 March 1971. I am grateful to Dr Plowden for providing me with a copy of his diary which is not available in any archive.
110 See CPA, CRD 3/14/4.
111 Blackstone and Plowden, *Inside the Think Tank*, p. 7.
112 CPA, CRD 3/14/5, William Plowden, 'Machinery of Government Group: First Report – Second Draft', 20 January 1969.
113 Kevin Theakston in *The Heath Government 1970–74: A Reappraisal*, p. 80; Blackstone and Plowden, *Inside the Think Tank*, p. 8.
114 Kevin Theakston, *Leadership In Whitehall* (Macmillan, 1999), p. 144.
115 Blackstone and Plowden, *Inside the Think Tank*, p. 7.
116 Hennessy, *Whitehall*, p. 211.
117 Hennessy, *The Prime Minister*, p. 337.
118 James Radcliffe, *The Reorganisation of British Central Government* (Dartmouth, Aldershot, 1991), p. 68.
119 Lord Trend quoted in Hennessy, *Whitehall*, p. 221.
120 Hennessy, *Whitehall*, p. 211.
121 NA, PRO, BA 17/208, 'A general study of machinery of government in 1970: interdepartmental correspondence', Ian Bancroft, 'Machinery of Government: Mr Schreiber', 1 June 1970.
122 Interview with Lord Howell of Guildford, 8 October 2003.
123 Pollitt, *Manipulating the Machine*, p. 88.
124 Interview with Lord Marlesford, 8 October 2003.
125 NA, PRO, BA 17/208, Ian Bancroft to Gilbraith, 28 May 1970.
126 Interview with Lord Howell of Guildford, 8 October 2003.
127 Interview with Lord Howell of Guildford, 8 October 2003.
128 Public Sector Research Unit papers, 'Priority Actions to Implement Recommendations', 28 May 1970.
129 Howell, *A New Style Of Government*, p. 24.
130 See NA, PRO, BA 17/208, D. O. Henley, 'Discussion with Mark Schreiber', 2 June 1970.
131 Letter from Lord Croham, 8 October 2003.
132 Joe Haines, *The Politics Of Power* (Jonathan Cape, 1977), p. 26.
133 Pimlott, *Harold Wilson*, pp. 553–4.
134 NA, PRO, PREM 15/79, 'Central analytical capability and use of businessmen', Jellicoe to Heath, 'The Analytical Capability and the Use of Businessmen', 2 December 1970.
135 Iain Dale (ed.), *Conservative Party Manifestos 1900–1997* (Politico's, 2000), pp. 175–98; Conversation with Lord Howell of Guildford, 5 November 2003; Howell, *The Edge Of Now*, p. 341; Campbell, *Edward Heath*, p. 270.
136 F. W. S. Craig, *British General Election Manifestos 1900–1974* (Macmillan, 1975), p. 330.
137 Hurd, *Memoirs*, p. 170.
138 Baston and Seldon in *The Heath Government 1970–74: A Reappraisal*, p. 51.

139 Hurd, *An End to Promises*, p. 28.
140 Ibid., p. 31.
141 Haines, *The Politics of Power*, p. 159.
142 Campbell, *Edward Heath*, p. 291.
143 Hurd, *Memoirs*, p. 192.
144 Heath, *The Course of My Life*, p. 313.
145 Hurd, *An End to Promises*, p. 34.
146 Ibid., p. 73.
147 Baston and Seldon in *The Heath Government 1970–74: A Reappraisal*, p. 56.
148 Ibid.
149 Campbell, *Edward Heath*, p. 291.
150 Baston and Seldon in *The Heath Government 1970–74: A Reappraisal*, p. 56.
151 Ibid.
152 Colin Seymour-Ure, *Prime Ministers and the Media* (Blackwell, Oxford, 2003), pp. 186–7.
153 Hurd, *An End to Promises*, pp. 73–4.
154 Baston and Seldon in *The Heath Government 1970–74: A Reappraisal*, p. 60.
155 Comment by Peter Hennessy, 5 July 2003.
156 Theakston in *The Heath Government 1970–74: A Reappraisal*, p. 86
157 Hennessy, *The Prime Minister*, p. 341.
158 Ibid., p. 341.
159 Hurd, *Memoirs*, p. 193.
160 NA, PRO, PREM 15/402, Chilcot to Caulcott, 'Reorganisation of Central Government – Additional Supplementary Notes', 15 October 1970.
161 Howell, *A New Style Of Government*, p. 5.
162 NA, PRO, PREM 15/1341, 'Fulton report: reshaping of civil service; unified grading', Robert Armstrong to B. Gilmour, 18 November 1971.
163 Ibid., Peter Gregson (Private Secretary to the Prime Minister 1968–72) to B. Gilmour, 'Unified Grading in the Civil Service', 23 November 1971.
164 Ibid., Chilcot to Gregson, 'Unified Grading in the Civil Service', 26 November 1971.
165 From the Conservative 1970 manifesto 'A Better Tomorrow' reproduced in F. W. S. Craig, 'British General Election Manifestos, 1959–1987' (Dartmouth, 1990), p. 113.
166 Hennessy, *Whitehall*, p. 221.
167 Lord Croham quoted in 'Fulton: 20 Years On', *Contemporary Record*, Vol. 2, No. 2, Summer 1988, p. 44.
168 Theakston in *The Heath Government 1970–74: A Reappraisal*, p. 81.
169 William Waldegrave, 'Three Prime Ministers', Twentieth Century British History seminar, Institute of Historical Research, 9 March 1994.
170 Hennessy, *Whitehall*, p. 220.
171 Marcia Williams, *Inside No. 10* (Weidenfeld & Nicolson, 1972), pp. 18–19.
172 Lord Trend, 'Machinery under pressure,' *Times Literary Supplement*, 26 September 1986, p. 1076.
173 Lord Trend in conversation with Peter Hennessy, 1 October 1986, and quoted in Hennessy, *Whitehall*, p. 292.

174 Pollitt, *Manipulating the Machine*, p. 79.
175 Along with Haldane, the Committee members were: Beatrice Webb; Sir Robert Morant, former Permanent Secretary at the Board of Education; the Labour MP Jimmy Thomas; Colonel Sir Alan Dykes, a Conservative MP; Edwin Montagu for the Liberals (he left quickly after being appointed Secretary of State for India); Sir George Murray, Permanent Secretary to the Post Office; Sir Claud Schuster, Permanent Secretary to the Lord Chancellor's Department; and Michael Heseltine, the Committee secretary.
176 Theakston in *The Heath Government 1970–74: A Reappraisal*, p. 76.
177 NA, PRO, PREM 15/71, 'Review of departmental responsibilities: part 2', Sir William Armstrong to Robert Armstrong, 28 August 1970.
178 Isserlis had taken over the job on 23 April 1970 after Michael Halls' death a month earlier.
179 NA, PRO, PREM 15/70, 'Review of departmental responsibilities including defence, technology, construction, trade, environment, social services (Seebohm), industry, posts, Wales and number and designation of ministers', Colin Gilbraith to Sandy Isserlis, 'Machinery of Government 1970', 19 June 1970.
180 Hurd, *Memoirs*, p. 191.
181 Heath, *The Course of My Life*, pp. 308–9; Hennessy, *The Prime Minister*, p. 340.
182 Hurd, *Memoirs*, pp. 191–2.
183 Theakston in *The Heath Government 1970–74: A Reappraisal*, p. 85.
184 David Wood, 'Fears of Civil Service purge', *The Times*, 10 July 1970.
185 George Clark, 'Civil Service purge is denied', *The Times*, 11 July 1970.
186 Ibid.
187 Heath, *The Course of My Life*, p. 311.
188 Hennessy, *The Prime Minister*, p. 340.
189 Campbell, *Edward Heath*, p. 290.
190 The actual authors were Ian Bancroft (Under Secretary in the Civil Service Department), Frank Cooper (Deputy Secretary, CSD), John Chilcot and Tom Caulcott, telephone message from Sir John Chilcot, 22 March 2004.
191 NA, PRO, PREM 15/70, Gilbraith to Isserlis, 'Machinery of Government 1970 – The Cabinet', 19 June 1970.
192 Ibid., 'Machinery of Government 1970 – Organisation of Government Functions', 19 June 1970.
193 Ibid., 'Conclusions'.
194 NA, PRO, PREM 15/70, Gilbraith to Isserlis, 'Machinery of Government 1970 – Organisation of Government Functions', 19 June 1970.
195 Ibid., 'Machinery of Government 1970 – The Cabinet', 19 June 1970.
196 Ibid.
197 NA, PRO, PREM 15/72, 'Review of departmental responsibilities: draft White Paper; part 3', Ian Bancroft to Robert Armstrong, 'Review of Departmental Responsibility – Ministers', 22 September 1970.
198 NA, PRO, PREM 15/71, Sir William Armstrong to Robert Armstrong, 'Hiving-off – Supplies Division of MPBW and HMSO', 15 September 1970.
199 NA, PRO, PREM 15/71, Jellicoe to Heath, 'Review of Departmental Responsibility', 8 September 1970.

200 The key works which underpinned this theory were: Alfred Chandler, *Strategy and Structure* (M.I.T. Press, 1962); and Alfred Sloan, *My Years With General Motors* (Sidgwick and Jackson, 1965). My thanks to Ian Beesley for this information.
201 NA, PRO, PREM 15/70, Gilbraith to Isserlis, 'Machinery of Government 1970: Large Departments and Collective Responsibilities – Committees and Staffs', 19 June 1970.
202 Ramsden, *The Winds of Change*, p. 324.
203 Radcliffe, *The Reorganisation of British Central Government*, p. 73.
204 Theakston in *The Heath Government 1970–74: A Reappraisal*, p. 91.
205 Email from Philip Connelly who is writing a biography of Sir William Armstrong, 25 September 2005.
206 Interview with Sir Samuel Goldman, 3 November 2003.
207 Ibid.
208 Marlesford had a couple more choice Bancroft-isms: 'For a problem he would say "I think we'll have to draft around that one."' Another was provoked by Schreiber having two filing cabinets, one for official work and one for party documents. In the Cabinet Office, all files must be locked away every night and if security staff discover they are not, one is hauled up before a departmental manager. Schreiber had left unlocked the party political one. He was summoned by Bancroft who, once the facts had been established, said sardonically, 'They bowled you out but it was a no-ball!' Interview with Lord Marlesford, 8 October 2003.
209 NA, PRO, PREM 15/73, 'Review of departmental responsibilities: reorganisation of central government; part 4', Gregson to Gilbraith, Review of Departmental Responsibility: Future of the Ministry of Overseas Development', 5 October 1970.
210 NA, PRO, PREM 15/402, Robert Armstrong to Heath, 21 December 1970.
211 NA, PRO, PREM 15/71, in many documents.
212 NA, PRO, PREM 15/72, Sir William Armstrong to Robert Armstrong, 'Departmental Review – Magistrates' Courts', 17 September 1970.
213 NA, PRO, PREM 15/71, Gilbraith to Robert Armstrong, 'Review of Departmental Responsibility', 9 September 1970.
214 NA, PRO, PREM 15/402, Trend to Heath, 'White Paper on the Reorganisation of Central Government', 14 October 1970.
215 Heath, *The Course of My Life*, p. 311.
216 NA, PRO, PREM 15/70, 'Notes on Ministerial Appointments: Note by First Parliamentary Counsel', 10 June 1970.
217 NA, PRO, PREM 15/402, Trend to Heath, 'White Paper on the Reorganisation of Central Government', 14 October 1970.
218 Howell, *A New Style of Government*, p. 18.
219 NA, PRO, PREM 15/71, Sir William Armstrong to Robert Armstrong, 'Review of Departmental Responsibility', 28 August 1970.
220 Howell, *A New Style of Government*, p. 22.
221 NA, PRO, PREM 15/70, Gilbraith to Isserlis, 'Machinery of Government 1970 – Organisation of Government Functions', 19 June 1970.
222 Ibid., 'Machinery of Government 1970 – Hiving-off and Accountability', 19 June 1970.
223 NA, PRO, PREM 15/70, Gilbraith to Isserlis, 'Machinery of Government 1970: Conclusions',

19 June 1970; J. S. Mill, *Considerations on Representative Government* (George Routledge, Oxford, 1905), p. 242.
224 Interview with Lord Marlesford, 8 October 2003.
225 Baston and Seldon in *The Heath Government 1970–74: A Reappraisal*, p. 47.
226 Peter Hennessy, 'The Cabinet Office: A Magnificent Piece of Powerful Bureaucratic Machinery', *The Times*, 8 March 1976.
227 David Howell quoted by Baston and Seldon in *The Heath Government 1970–74: A Reappraisal*, p. 69.
228 Quoted in Radcliffe, *The Reorganisation of British Central Government*, p. 129.
229 Iain Dale (ed.), *Conservative Party Manifestos 1900–1997* (Politico's, 2000), p. 183.
230 Heath, *The Course of My Life*, p. 321.
231 Haines, *The Politics of Power*, p. 176.
232 Heath, *The Course of My Life*, p. 321.
233 Quoted in Stephen Fay and Hugo Young, 'The Fall of Heath', *The Sunday Times*, 22 February 1976.
234 Campbell, *Edward Heath*, p. 221.
235 Howell, *The Edge of Now*, pp. 308–49.
236 Interview with Sir Frank Cooper, 13 June 2001.
237 NA, PRO, PREM 15/72, Heath to Cabinet colleagues, 'PM's Personal Minute: The Activities of Government', 28 September 1970.
238 NA, PRO, PREM 15/78, 'Review of functions and activities of government departments: rationalisation of government activity', Jellicoe to Heath, 27 August 1970.
239 Interview with Lord Howell of Guildford, 8 October 2003.
240 NA, PRO, PREM 15/777, 'Location of government: dispersal of government work from London; Lord Privy Seal invited to lead review; interim reports of Sir Henry Hardman, Review Co-ordinator', Jellicoe to Heath, 'The Location of Government', 23 September 1970.
241 Ibid., Sir William Armstrong to Robert Armstrong, 'Regional Policy and Dispersal', 31 December 1971.
242 NA, PRO, PREM 15/1317, 'Robert Armstrong's talk with Sir Michael Swann, Chairman of Board of Governors, about dispersal of part of BBC', Robert Armstrong, 'Note for the Record', 16 October 1973.
243 NA, PRO, PREM 15/2021, 'Dispersal of government work from London: Hardman report; location of Civil Aviation Authority headquarters; part 4', FERB to Robert Armstrong, 'Dispersal', 4 December 1973.
244 NA, PRO, PREM 15/79, Gilbraith to Isserlis, 'Businessmen in Government', 30 November 1970.
245 Ibid., Jellicoe to Heath, 'The Analytical Capability and the Use of Businessmen', 2 December 1970.
246 NA, PRO, PREM 15/1346, 'Prime Minister's meetings with members of Staff Side: Civil Service National Whitley Council', 'Note of a Meeting with Representatives of National Staff Side', 10 July 1970.
247 NA, PRO, PREM 15/79, Jellicoe to Heath, 'Setting Up The Business Team', 29 December 1970. Their first names have proved elusive.

248 NA, PRO, PREM 15/923, 'Activities of Business Team: discussions about its future; part 2, "Report by the Businessmen's Team on its Initial Operations"', 1 March 1971.
249 NA, PRO, CAB 134/3008.
250 NA, PRO, PREM 15/79, Jellicoe to Heath, 'The Analytical Capability and the Use of Businessmen', 2 December 1970.
251 NA, PRO, PREM 15/406, '"Central capability": setting up of Central Policy Review Staff (CPRS) in Cabinet Office; appointment of Lord Rothschild as head', Howell, 'Management Projects Committee: Project Proposals', 3 September 1970.
252 NA, PRO, PREM 15/79, Sir William Armstrong to Robert Armstrong, 'Analysis and the Decision taking process – The Role of the Business Team', 15 December 1970.
253 Interview with Lord Butler of Brockwell, 3 November 2003.
254 Interview with Lord Hurd of Westwell, 27 April 2004.
255 Howell, *The Edge of Now*, p. 336.
256 See Chapter 5.
257 Pollitt, *Manipulating the Machine*, p. 91.
258 Edward Heath, 'The First Keeling Memorial Lecture', Royal Institute of Public Administration, 7 May 1980.
259 Even this was not strictly true as, though members became temporary civil servants during their employment in the think tank, some members such as William Waldegrave were clearly Conservative. Lord Trend in conversation with Peter Hennessy, 7 November 1983, for BBC Radio 3's *Routine Punctuated by Orgies*.
260 NA, PRO, PREM 15/406, Schreiber to Jellicoe, 14 August 1970.
261 Interview with Lord Marlesford, 8 October 2003.
262 NA, PRO, PREM 15/406, Robert Armstrong, 'Note For The Record', 4 September 1970.
263 Blackstone and Plowden, *Inside The Think Tank*, p. 25.
264 NA, PRO, PREM 15/406, Jellicoe to Heath, 'The Central Capability', 3 September 1970.
265 NA, PRO, PREM 15/72, Robert Armstrong, 'Note For The Record', 18 September 1970.
266 NA, PRO, PREM 15/406, Robert Armstrong to Trend, 'Leadership of the Central Capability', 29 September 1970.
267 Ibid., Howell to Heath, 29 September 1970.
268 Ibid., Peter Gregson, 'Note Of A Meeting', 5 October 1970.
269 Ibid., Professor Hugh Ford to Edward Heath, 12 October 1970.
270 Interview with Dr William Plowden, 10 October 2003.
271 Interview with Lord Howell of Guildford, 8 October 2003.
272 Peter Hennessy, *The Secret State* (Penguin, 2002), p. 74.
273 Kenneth Rose, *Elusive Rothschild* (Weidenfeld & Nicolson, 2003), pp. 64–93.
274 Ibid., pp. 113–15, 165.
275 NA, PRO, PREM 15/406, Press notice of the Prime Minister's answer to a Parliamentary Question from Dr Reginald Bennett MP, 29 October 1970.
276 Hennessy, *The Prime Minister*, p. 337.
277 Hennessy, *Whitehall*, p. 222.
278 NA, PRO, PREM 15/72, Robert Armstrong to Donald Maitland, 'Reorganisation of Structure of the Government', 28 September 1970.
279 Kevin Theakston, *The Civil Service Since 1945* (Blackwell, Oxford, 1995), p. 109.

280 Heath, *The Course of My Life*, p. 311.
281 NA, PRO, PREM 15/402, Hurd to Wolff, 'Reorganisation of Central Government', 14 October 1970.
282 Ibid.
283 Ramsden, *The Winds of Change*, p. 262.
284 Howell, *The Edge of Now*, p. 345.
285 Ibid., p. 349.
286 Blackstone and Plowden, *Inside The Think Tank*, p. 10.
287 Interview with Lord Howell of Guildford, 8 October 2003.
288 Private information; *Modernising Government*, Cmnd. 4310 (HMSO, 1999).
289 Hennessy, *The Prime Minister*, p. 356.

Notes to Chapter 5: Pressure

1 Lord Armstrong of Ilminster briefing the 'Hidden Wiring' MA option course, Queen Mary and Westfield College, University of London, February 2001.
2 Conversation with Professor John Ramsden, 28 August 2003.
3 Edmund Dell, *The Chancellors* (HarperCollins, 1997), p. 375 and confirmed by Professor John Ramsden who said 'it is entirely consistent with what he told me when I interviewed him – he after all saw himself much as the press saw him, as an inadequate replacement for Macleod, and as a man who would be regarded as Heath's stooge (he told me that too)', email from Professor Ramsden, 7 December 2005.
4 John Ramsden in Anthony Seldon and Stuart Ball (eds), *The Heath Government 1970–74: A Reappraisal* (Longman, 1996), p. 34.
5 Kevin Theakston in Seldon and Ball (eds), *The Heath Government 1970–74: A Reappraisal*, p. 84.
6 Interview with Lord Butler of Brockwell, 3 November 2003. Though James Callaghan, a Prime Minister who spent three years at the Treasury, remained suspicious of it.
7 Interview with Sir Samuel Brittan, 22 April 2004.
8 National Archives (NA), Public Record Office (PRO), PREM 15/70, 'Review of departmental responsibilities including defence, technology, construction, trade, environment, social services (Seebohm), industry, posts, Wales and number and designation of ministers', 'Machinery of government – Central Departments', 19 June 1970.
9 NA, PRO, PREM 15/79, 'Central analytical capability and use of businessmen', Lord Jellicoe to Edward Heath, 'The Analytical Capability and The Use of Businessmen', 2 December 1970.
10 Douglas Hurd, *Memoirs* (Little, Brown, 2003), p. 170.
11 NA, PRO, PREM 15/317, 'Future role of National Economic Development Council (NEDC): successor to Sir F. Catherwood as Director-General; correspondence with Chancellor of the Exchequer and Economic Adviser', Robert Armstrong to William Ryrie, 5 January 1971.
12 NA, PRO, PREM 15/317, Brian Reading to Robert Armstrong, 29 January 1971.
13 NA, PRO, PREM 15/84, 'Papers by Brian Reading on government structure for formulation

of economic policy', Robert Armstrong to Brian Reading, 'The Formation of Economic Policy', 15 December 1970.
14 Interview with Lord Howell of Guildford, 8 October 2003.
15 NA, PRO, PREM 15/404, 'Review of functions and activities of government departments: part 2', David Howell to Edward Heath, 12 February 1971.
16 Sir Samuel Goldman said that neither Macleod, Barber nor Maurice Macmillan, Chief Secretary to the Treasury 1970–2, ever spoke to him about a potential cleavage in the Treasury, though this does not mean that others were not talking about it; interview with Sir Samuel Goldman, 3 November 2003.
17 NA, PRO, PREM 15/405, 'Review of functions and activities of government departments: part 3', Robert Armstrong to Edward Heath, 'Review of Functions', 28 April 1971.
18 Interview with Sir Samuel Goldman.
19 Interview with Lord Howell of Guildford.
20 Interview with Lord Hurd of Westwell, 27 April 2004.
21 Interview with Sir Samuel Brittan, 22 April 2004.
22 NA, PRO, PREM 15/405, Robert Armstrong to David Howell, 30 April 1971.
23 Interview with Lord Howell of Guildford.
24 Lord Howell of Guildford at the book launch for Sir Samuel Brittan's *Against the Flow* (Atlantic, 2005), 17 January 2005.
25 *Eleventh Report from the Expenditure Committee, Session 1976–77*, 'The Civil Service', Vol. II, Part II, p. 760.
26 Edward Heath, *The Course of My Life* (Hodder and Stoughton, 1998), p. 311.
27 Dell, *The Chancellors*, pp. 376–7.
28 John Campbell, *Edward Heath* (Jonathan Cape, 1993), p. 303.
29 Dell, *The Chancellors*, pp. 389–90.
30 Lord Croham briefing the 'Hidden Wiring' MA option course, Queen Mary, University of London, 9 February 2005.
31 Kenneth Rose, *Elusive Rothschild* (Weidenfeld & Nicolson, 2003), p. 175.
32 Lord Rothschild, *Random Variables* (Collins, 1984), p. 69.
33 NA, PRO, PREM 15/406, '"Central capability": setting up of Central Policy Review Staff (CPRS) in Cabinet Office; appointment of Lord Rothschild as head', Sir Burke Trend to Edward Heath, 'Central Policy Review Staff', 25 November 1970; Rothschild, *Random Variables*, pp. 73–4.
34 Rothschild, *Random Variables*, p. 69.
35 Ibid., p. 69.
36 Tessa Blackstone and William Plowden, *Inside the Think Tank* (Heinemann, 1988), pp. 25–6.
37 Lord Hunt of Tanworth, 'Cabinet strategy and management', CIPFA/RIPA Conference, Eastbourne, 9 June 1983.
38 NA, PRO, PREM 15/406, David Howell's paper 'The Central Capability' contained in Lord Jellicoe to Edward Heath, 'Central Capability', 28 July 1970.
39 Ibid., Mark Schreiber to Lord Jellicoe, 14 August 1970.
40 NA, PRO, PREM 15/406, Peter Gregson, 'Record of a Discussion', 3 December 1970.
41 Edward Heath, *My Style of Government* (Evening Standard Publications, 1972), p. 5.
42 Peter Hennessy, *Whitehall* (Secker and Warburg, 1989), p. 124.

43　NA, PRO, PREM 15/406, Sir Burke Trend to Edward Heath, 'Management Projects and the Central Capability', 8 August 1970.
44　NA, PRO, PREM 15/79, Sir Burke Trend to Edward Heath, 'Management Projects Committee', 30 December 1970.
45　NA, PRO, PREM 15/406, Sir Burke Trend to Edward Heath, 'Work of the CPRS', 2 March 1971.
46　NA, PRO, CAB 129/155, CP(71) 17, 3 February 1971.
47　NA, PRO, PREM 15/269, 'Replacement of Sir Solly Zuckerman as Chief Scientific Adviser: relationship between post of CSA and Central Policy Review Staff (CPRS); appointment of Sir Alan Cottrell', Sir Burke Trend to Edward Heath, 1 July 1970.
48　Ibid., Robert Armstrong, 'Note for the Record', 3 March 1971.
49　Rose, *Elusive Rothschild*, p. 183.
50　NA, PRO, PREM 15/269, Robert Armstrong, 'Note for the Record', 10 February 1971.
51　NA, PRO, PREM 15/269, Robert Armstrong, 'Note for the Record – Scientific Advice at the Centre', 3 March 1971.
52　Douglas Hurd, *An End to Promises* (Collins, 1979), p. 38.
53　Hennessy, *Whitehall*, p. 226.
54　NA, PRO, PREM 15/407, 'Review of government strategy: CPRS; Cabinet meeting, Chequers, 8 Oct', undated (possibly 21 June 1971) and untitled list of CPRS members, their previous jobs and education.
55　Hugh Heclo and Aaron Wildavsky, *The Private Government Of Public Money* (Macmillan, 1981), p. 307.
56　Hennessy, *Whitehall*, p. 227.
57　Rothschild, *Random Variables*, p. 81.
58　Hennessy, *Whitehall*, p. 228.
59　Interview with Lord Waldegrave of North Hill, 29 October 2003.
60　Ibid.
61　Ibid.
62　Hennessy, *Whitehall*, p. 191.
63　Interview with Lord Hurd of Westwell.
64　Heclo and Wildavsky, *The Private Government of Public Money*, p. 310.
65　Blackstone and Plowden, *Inside the Think Tank*, p. 26.
66　Interview with Lord Butler of Brockwell.
67　Rose, *Elusive Rothschild*, pp. 177–8.
68　Hennessy, *Whitehall*, p. 224.
69　Blackstone and Plowden, *Inside the Think Tank*, p. 33.
70　Hennessy, *Whitehall*, p. 226.
71　Blackstone and Plowden, *Inside the Think Tank*, p. 26.
72　Ibid., p. 27.
73　Rothschild, *Random Variables*, p. 82.
74　Hennessy, *Whitehall*, p. 226.
75　NA, PRO, PREM 15/926, 'Review of government strategy by CPRS: meetings of ministers to discuss strategy in economic and foreign affairs; part 2', Robert Armstrong to Lord Rothschild, 2 May 1972.

76 Hennessy, *Whitehall*, p. 228.
77 Rose, *Elusive Rothschild*, p. 175.
78 Interview with Lord Hurd of Westwell.
79 Interview with Lord Waldegrave of North Hill.
80 Blackstone and Plowden, *Inside the Think Tank*, p. 28.
81 Interview with Lord Waldegrave of North Hill.
82 The diary of Dr William Plowden. Entry for 19 April 1971.
83 Heath, *The Course of My Life*, p. 315.
84 Hennessy, *Whitehall*, p. 228.
85 Interview with William Plowden, 10 October 2003.
86 A senior official in the insurance division of the DTI was accused of negligence over the collapse in 1972 of Vehicle and General, a cut-price insurance firm. See Hennessy, *Whitehall*, p. 504.
87 NA, PRO, PREM 15/927, 'Review of government strategy by CPRS: meetings of ministers to discuss strategy in economic and foreign affairs; part 3', Lord Rothschild to Edward Heath, 18 July 1972.
88 NA, PRO, PREM 15/1602, 'Problem areas for government: introduction of early warning system', Lord Rothschild to Permanent Secretaries, 'Early Warning System', 27 April 1971.
89 Ibid.
90 Ibid.
91 Ruth Cousens, 'The Central Policy Review Staff Early Warning System, 1971–1972', unpublished MA thesis, Queen Mary, University of London, 2003.
92 William Plowden cited in ibid.
93 NA, PRO, CAB 184/22, 'Arrangements for an "Early Warning System" designed to keep a watch on emerging issues that may become major topical news', Sir Douglas Allen to Lord Rothschild, 14 May 1971.
94 Dr William Plowden's diary, entry for 10 May 1971.
95 NA, PRO, CAB 184/23, Robert Armstrong to Lord Rothschild, 'Arrangements for an "Early Warning System" designed to keep a watch on emerging issues that may become topical news', 26 July 1971.
96 NA, PRO, PREM 15/1602, CWR to Mr Norbury (Cabinet Office), 17 July 1971.
97 NA, PRO, PREM 15/1602, comment by Edward Heath, 3 August 1971.
98 NA, PRO, CAB 184/22, William Plowden to Robin Butler, 5 April 1971.
99 NA, PRO, CAB 129/158, *Cabinet Papers: 76–100*, Annex A to CP(71)96, 'Note by the Central Policy Review Staff', 2 August 1971.
100 Ibid., CP(71)96, 'Note by the Central Policy Review Staff', 2 August 1971.
101 NA, PRO, CAB 184/34, CPRS Weekly Meeting, 20 December 1971.
102 Cousens, 'The Central Policy Review Staff Early Warning System, 1971–1972'.
103 NA, PRO, T 342/244, 'Departmental programmes: early warning of major policy issues; Treasury contributions', Sir Douglas Allen to Treasury colleagues, 'Departmental programmes: early warning of major policy issues; Treasury contributions', 8 September 1971.
104 NA, PRO, CAB 184/24, Robin Butler, Note for the record, 24 November 1971; Cousens, 'The Central Policy Review Staff Early Warning System, 1971–1972'.
105 Cousens, 'The Central Policy Review Staff Early Warning System, 1971–1972'.

106 NA, PRO, CAB 128/50/21, CP(72)21, 13 April 1972.
107 NA, PRO, CAB 184/34, points arising from the CPRS weekly meeting, 12 June 1972.
108 Interview with Lord Hurd of Westwell.
109 Cousens, 'The Central Policy Review Staff Early Warning System, 1971–1972'.
110 NA, PRO, CAB 164/1157, 'Setting up of an early warning system for Ministers', Robert Armstrong to Sir Burke Trend, 19 July 1972.
111 Ibid., Lord Rothschild to Edward Heath, 24 July 1972.
112 NA, PRO, PREM 15/1602, Robert Armstrong to Lord Rothschild, 'Early Warning System', 29 September 1972.
113 Ibid., Armstrong to Rothschild, 7 September 1972.
114 NA, PRO, PREM 15/1602, Sir John Hunt to Mark Schreiber, 26 October 1972.
115 Ibid., B. M. Webster, 'Meeting of Departmental Secretaries', 5 November 1973.
116 NA, PRO, PREM 15/2014, 'Appointment of John Hunt to succeed Sir Burke Trend as Cabinet Secretary; review of the Cabinet Committee structure', Robert Armstrong to Edward Heath, 7 November 1973.
117 NA, PRO, PREM 16/106, 'Cabinet Secretariat "Forward Look" exercise: business coming forward to Cabinet and Cabinet Committees', Sir John Hunt, 'Forward Look Exercise', 3 April 1974.
118 NA, PRO, PREM 16/106, Sir John Hunt to Harold Wilson, 3 May 1974.
119 The diary of Dr William Plowden, entry for 19 April 1971.
120 Ibid., entry for 25 April 1971.
121 Ibid., entry for 6 November 1971.
122 NA, PRO, PREM 15/407, Robert Armstrong to Edward Heath, 'Strategy Meeting at Chequers', 22 September 1971.
123 NA, PRO, PREM 15/421, 'Prime Minister asked departments for notes on main issues of their departmental policies requiring decisions within next few months: comparison of government achievements with manifesto promises', Robert Armstrong to Peter Gregson, 28 November 1970.
124 Blackstone and Plowden, *Inside the Think Tank*, p. 39.
125 Head of Financial Policy and Aid Department, Foreign Office, 1969–70, before joining the CPRS in 1971 as an Under Secretary.
126 See NA, PRO, CAB 163/216, 'Distribution of Joint Intelligence Committee (JIC) material to Central Policy Review Staff (CPRS)', for several documents and untitled drafts.
127 Jock Bruce-Gardyne, *Whatever Happened to the Quiet Revolution?* (C. Knight, 1974), p. 116.
128 The diary of Dr William Plowden, entry for 11 October 1971.
129 Ibid.
130 John Ramsden, *The Winds of Change* (Longman, 1996), p. 329.
131 Interview with Lord Hurd of Westwell.
132 Christopher Pollitt, *Manipulating the Machine* (George Allen & Unwin, 1984), p. 101.
133 NA, PRO, PREM 15/2099, 'Central capability: Lord Rothschild's appointment as Head of Central Policy Review Staff (CPRS); Prime Minister's discussions with Lord Rothschild on projects undertaken by CPRS; part 2', Robert Armstrong to Lord Rothschild, 26 November 1973.

134 Ibid., Lord Rothschild, 14 December 1973.
135 NA, PRO, CAB 130/536, 'Government Strategy: Meetings 1–3 (1971); Meetings 1–6 (1972); Meetings 1–3 (1973)', GEN 61 (73), 'Government Strategy', 15 June 1973.
136 Campbell, *Edward Heath*, p. 408.
137 NA, PRO, CAB 130/536, GEN 61 (73), 'Government Strategy', 15 June 1973.
138 Interview with Lord Howell of Guildford.
139 Interview with Lord Hurd of Westwell.
140 Hurd, *An End to Promises*, p. 39.
141 NA, CAB 129/179/20, C(74) 110, 'Strategy and Priorities', 14 October 1974; Barbara Castle, *The Castle Diaries 1974–76* (Weidenfeld & Nicolson, 1980), pp. 219–24.
142 Lord Wilson of Rievaulx quoted in Peter Hennessy, *Cabinet* (Basil Blackwell, Oxford, 1986), p. 86.
143 A note in Bernard Donoughue's diary says 'Wilson seemed inclined to abolish it in March 1974, but B. Donoughue argued strongly for its value and retention', Bernard Donoughue, *Downing Street Diary: With Harold Wilson in No.10* (Jonathan Cape, 2005), p. 61, entry for 6 March 1974.
144 Rothschild, *Random Variables*, pp. 73–9.
145 NA, PRO, PREM 16/39, 'Public expenditure programme: programme analysis and review (PAR); parts 1, 2 and 3', Lord Rothschild to Harold Wilson, 26 June 1974.
146 Blackstone and Plowden, *Inside The Think Tank*, p. 49.
147 Ibid., p. 43.
148 Rothschild, *Random Variables*, pp. 75–6.
149 NA, PRO, PREM 15/79, Sir Burke Trend to Edward Heath, 'Management Projects Committee', 30 December 1970.
150 NA, PRO, PREM 15/2099, Lord Rothschild to Edward Heath, Annex B, 21 January 1972.
151 Ibid., Lord Rothschild to Robert Armstrong, 31 January 1972.
152 Ibid., Lord Rothschild to Robert Armstrong, 6 March 1973.
153 Blackstone and Plowden, *Inside the Think Tank*, Appendix 1, p. 221.
154 Sir Frank Cooper quoted in Hennessy, *Whitehall*, p. 232.
155 Hennessy, *Whitehall*, p. 230.
156 Lord Rothschild quoted in Hennessy, *Whitehall*, p. 232.
157 Rose, *Elusive Rothschild*, p. 187.
158 Lord Rothschild quoted in Peter Hennessy, Susan Morrison and Richard Townsend, *Routine Punctuated by Orgies: The Central Policy Review Staff, 1970–83*, Strathclyde Papers on *Government and Politics no. 31*, Politics Department, Strathclyde University, 1985, Appendix A, pp. 104–8.
159 Hennessy, *Whitehall*, p. 233.
160 David Willetts briefing the 'Cabinet & Premiership' course, Queen Mary, University of London, 11 February 2005.
161 Hurd, *Memoirs*, p. 508.
162 Geoff Mulgan talking to the Mile End Group, 'How Do Central Governments Think? Lessons from British History and Abroad', 7 June 2005.
163 Interview with Lord Butler of Brockwell.
164 Ibid.

165 David Willetts briefing the 'Cabinet & Premiership' course, Queen Mary, University of London, 11 February 2005.
166 Rothschild, *Random Variables*, p. 82.
167 Conversation with Sir Kevin Tebbit, 29 March 2005.
168 Rothschild, *Random Variables*, p. 82.
169 NA, PRO, PREM 15/762, 'Prime Minister was concerned at length of memoranda circulated to members of Cabinet and Cabinet Committees: he asked that they contain only essentials', Sir Burke Trend to Robert Armstrong, 11 February 1971.
170 Interview with Dr William Plowden.
171 NA, PRO, PREM 15/595, 'Sir David Barran of Shell gave Prime Minister exposition of study of future energy supply and demand: papers on international oil questions; CPRS paper on oil economics and supplies; DTI study on energy policy', AJCS to Robert Armstrong, 21 September 1971.
172 NA, PRO, PREM 15/595, Shell, 'The Oil Demand and Supply Position in the Context of Future Energy Requirements (Old Edition)', September 1971, p. 16.
173 Ibid., Lord Rothschild to Edward Heath, 'Sir David Barran', 21 September 1971.
174 Interview with Lord Hurd of Westwell.
175 'Running out of puff?', *The Economist*, 16 April 2005.
176 Blackstone and Plowden, *Inside the Think Tank*, p. 77; Hennessy, *Whitehall*, p. 231.
177 Douglas Wass, *Government and the Governed: BBC Reith Lectures 1983* (Routledge & Kegan Paul, 1984), p. 38.
178 NA, PRO, PREM 15/926, Lord Rothschild to Edward Heath, 16 May 1972.
179 Interview with Lord Waldegrave of North Hill.
180 Interview with Lord Marlesford, 8 October 2003.
181 Interview with Lord Butler of Brockwell.
182 Interview with Dr William Plowden.
183 Rose, *Elusive Rothschild*, p. 164.
184 Interview with Lord Howell of Guildford.
185 *All The Prime Minister's Men*, 7 May 1986.
186 Interview with Lord Howell of Guildford.
187 *All The Prime Minister's Men*.
188 Interview with Lord Howell of Guildford.
189 Interview with Dr William Plowden.
190 Interview with Lord Butler of Brockwell.
191 NA, PRO, PREM 15/419, 'Programme Analysis and Review System (PAR) for public expenditure decisions', Lord Jellicoe to Edward Heath, 'Future Arrangements for Programme Analysis and Review (PAR)', 25 June 1971.
192 Blackstone and Plowden, *Inside the Think Tank*, p. 48.
193 Interview with Dr William Plowden.
194 Kevin Theakston, *The Civil Service Since 1945* (Blackwell, Oxford, 1995), p. 110.
195 NA, PRO, PREM 15/764, 'Lord Rothschild asked to be allowed to attend GEN 92 meeting on pay and prices policy, 21 June 1972: request was not agreed', Lord Rothschild to Edward Heath, 19 June 1972.
196 Ibid., Robert Armstrong to Sir Burke Trend, 20 June 1972.

197 Lewis Baston and Anthony Seldon in Seldon and Ball (eds), *The Heath Government 1970–74: A Reappraisal* (Longman, 1996), p. 68.
198 Interview with Richard Wilding, 15 August 2003.
199 NA, PRO, CAB 128/47, CM (70), 38th Conclusions, 17 November 1970; PREM 15/419, 'Note for the Record', 8 December 1970.
200 NA, PRO, CAB 128/49, CM (71), 1st Conclusions, 5 January 1971; 19th Conclusions, 1 April 1971.
201 Ibid., CM (71), 19th Conclusions, 1 April 1971.
202 Heclo and Wildavsky, *The Private Government of Public Money*, p. 286.
203 NA, PRO, PREM 15/274, 'Review of Civil Service manpower: report of Bellinger panel of businessmen; correspondence with Sir Robert Bellinger', Sir Robert Bellinger, 'Final Observations of the Panel of Businessmen on Civil Service Manning', 14 December 1970.
204 Campbell, *Edward Heath*, p. 526.
205 Peter Kellner and Lord Crowther-Hunt, *The Civil Servants* (Book Club Associates, 1980), p. 10.
206 NA, PRO, CAB 128/49, CM (71), 1st Conclusions, 5 January 1971.
207 NA, PRO, CAB 129/156, CP (71) 43, 'Selection of Topics for Programme Analysis and Review', Annex A: Proposed List of Programmes for Review in 1971', 29 March 1971.
208 NA, PRO, PREM 15/419, C. W. Roberts (Cabinet Office), 'Record of a Meeting', 2 October 1970.
209 Heclo and Wildavsky, *The Private Government of Public Money*, p. 277.
210 Ibid., Lord Jellicoe to Edward Heath, 'Future Arrangements for Programme Analysis and Review (PAR)', 25 June 1971.
211 Ibid., Sir Burke Trend to Edward Heath, 'Selection of Topics for Programme Analysis and Review (PAR) – The Work of the Central Policy Review Staff', 31 March 1971.
212 Leo Pliatzky, *Getting and Spending* (Basil Blackwell, Oxford, 1982), pp. 135–47
213 Theakston, *The Civil Service Since 1945*, pp. 108–9.
214 Heclo and Wildavsky, *The Private Government of Public Money*, p. 278.
215 Richard Clarke, *New Trends in Government* (HMSO, 1971), p. 46.
216 See Samuel Goldman, *The developing system of public expenditure management and control* (HMSO, 1973).
217 NA, PRO, PREM 15/1587, 'Programme Analysis and Review System (PAR) for public expenditure decisions; part 2', 'Draft Minute from the Prime Minister: Secretary of State for the Environment', 25 November 1971.
218 Ibid., Mark Schreiber to Robert Armstrong, 'PAR Selection of Topics for 1972', 8 December 1971.
219 NA, PRO, PREM 15/1587, Robert Armstrong to Mark Schreiber, 13 December 1971.
220 NA, PRO, PREM 15/926, David Howell to Robert Armstrong, 4 January 1972.
221 NA, PRO, PREM 15/1587, Patrick Jenkin to Edward Heath, 'PAR Programme 1973 to 1975', 26 January 1973.
222 Ibid., Patrick Jenkin to Edward Heath, 'PAR Programme 1973 to 1975', 26 January 1973, 'Annex'.
223 Ibid., C. R. Ross to Robert Armstrong, 'Programme Analysis and Review', 9 February 1973.

224 Senior Treasury official quoted in Hennessy, *Whitehall*, p. 235.
225 Quoted in William Plowden (ed.), *Advising the Rulers* (Blackwell, Oxford, 1987), p. 67.
226 NA, PRO, PREM 15/419, Sir Burke Trend to Edward Heath, 'Progress Report on PAR', 16 November 1971.
227 Wass, *Government and the Governed: BBC Reith Lectures 1983*, p. 18.
228 A quotation from Horace, *Ars Poetica* (The Art of Poetry), line 139.
229 NA, PRO, PREM 15/419, R. J. Andrew to Robert Armstrong, 31 March 1971.
230 Theakston, *The Civil Service Since 1945*, p. 110.
231 David Howell quoted in Hennessy, *Cabinet*, p. 170.
232 Hennessy, *Whitehall*, p. 596.
233 NA, PRO, PREM 15/79, Lord Jellicoe to Edward Heath, 'The Analytical Capability and the Use of Businessmen', 2 December 1970.
234 NA, PRO, PREM 15/923, 'Activities of Business Team: discussions about its future; part 2', 'Report by the Businessmen's Team on its Initial Operations', 1 March 1971.
235 Lord Croham briefing the 'Hidden Wiring' MA course.
236 Michael Dockrill, *British Defence Since 1945* (Basil Blackwell, Oxford, 1988), p. 6.
237 NA, PRO, PREM 15/403, 'Reorganisaton of central government: defence procurement and civil aerospace; the Rayner report; part 6', Sir William Armstrong to Robert Armstrong, 'Defence Procurement: The Chief Executive', 23 March 1971.
238 Ibid., 17 March 1971.
239 Kevin Theakston, *Leadership in Whitehall* (Macmillan, 1999), p. 229.
240 NA, PRO, PREM 15/403, Sir William Armstrong to Robert Armstrong, 'Defence Procurement: The Chief Executive', 23 March 1971.
241 NA, PRO, PREM 15/410, 'Proposals for development of government organisation', Mark Schreiber to Robert Armstrong, 'Development of Government Organisation', 12 November 1971.
242 Quoted in Pollitt, *Manipulating the Machine*, p. 101.
243 See Patrick Ainley and Mark Corney, *Training for the Future* (Cassell, 1990); Pollitt, *Manipulating the Machine*, p. 104.
244 NA, PRO, PREM 15/923, 'Report by the Businessmen's Team on its Initial Operations', 1 March 1971.
245 Ibid., Robert Armstrong to John Chilcot, 14 September 1971. Cruickshank and Sainsbury appear in the file but no evidence has been found concerning their recruitment or further personal details.
246 Pollitt, *Manipulating the Machine*, p. 103.
247 NA, PRO, PREM 15/923, Douglas Hurd to Edward Heath, 'Businessmen's Team', 24 February 1972.
248 Ibid.
249 Ibid., Robert Armstrong, 'Note for the Record', 19 January 1972.
250 Ibid., Lord Jellicoe to Edward Heath, 'Businessmen in Government', 19 April 1972.
251 Ibid., Lord Rothschild to Edward Heath, 28 April 1972.
252 Ibid., Robert Armstrong to Lord Rothschild, 9 May 1972.
253 Ibid., Sir William Armstrong to Lord Jellicoe, 'Businessmen in Government', 9 May 1972.
254 Ibid., Lord Rothschild to Robert Armstrong, 17 May 1972.

255 Ibid., Lord Rothschild to Sir William Armstrong, 23 May 1972.
256 Hennessy, *Whitehall*, p. 238.
257 Heath, *The Course of My Life*, p. 505.
258 Theakston in *The Heath Government 1970–74: A Reappraisal*, p. 92.
259 See NA, PRO, PREM 15/1043, 'Exchange of messages following setting up of Northern Ireland Office'; Heath, *The Course of My Life*, pp. 420–45.
260 Keith Jeffery and Peter Hennessy, *States of Emergency* (Routledge and Kegan Paul, 1983), p. 233.
261 Hurd, *An End to Promises*, p. 99.
262 NA, PRO, PREM 15/1600, 'Arrangements for dealing with industrial and civil emergency situations: setting up of Whitehall Command post; possible use of new Cabinet Office Emergency Room', Robert Armstrong, 'Planning for Emergencies', 15 December 1970.
263 NA, PRO, PREM 15/1600, Robert Armstrong to Sir Burke Trend, 30 December 1970.
264 Ibid., Sir Philip Allen to Sir Burke Trend, 'Planning for Emergencies', 18 December 1970.
265 Ibid., Edward Heath to Sir Philip Allen, 23 February 1971.
266 Ibid., Sir Burke Trend to Robert Armstrong, 5 January 1971.
267 Ibid., Robert Armstrong, 'Planning for Emergencies', 5 January 1971.
268 NA, PRO, PREM 15/1600, Sir Burke Trend to Robert Armstrong, 12 May 1971.
269 Ibid., Sir Burke Trend to Edward Heath, 'The Emergency Organisation', 23 February 1972.
270 Ibid., Edward Heath to Robert Armstrong, 28 April 1972.
271 Peter Hennessy, 'Surprising Slants on Reforming Whitehall', *Financial Times*, 22 February 1976.
272 Hennessy, *Whitehall*, p. 236.
273 See NA, PRO, CAB 130/590, 'Civil Contingencies Unit'; CAB 134/3472; CAB 134/3653; CAB 164/1139; CAB 164/1140; and CAB 164/1226.
274 Peter Hennessy, *The Prime Minister* (Penguin, 2000), p. 347.
275 Ibid., p. 347.
276 Hennessy, *Whitehall*, p. 236.
277 Hurd, *Memoirs*, p. 194.
278 Interview with Lord Hurd of Westwell.
279 Jeffery and Hennessy, *States of Emergency*, p. 236.
280 Ibid., p. 238.
281 See Peter Hennessy, 'The British Secret State Old and New', *Royal United Services Institute*, June 2005.
282 See NA, PRO, PREM 15/884, 'Organisation of European work in central government following UK entry into EEC'.
283 Heath, *The Course of My Life*, pp. 393–4.
284 Alec Cairncross, *The British Economy Since 1945* (Blackwell, Oxford, 1995), pp. 182, 191–2.
285 Campbell, *Edward Heath*, p. 412.
286 Cairncross, *The British Economy Since 1945*, p. 189.
287 Campbell, *Edward Heath*, p. 481.
288 Cairncross, *The British Economy Since 1945*, p. 192.

289 John Ramsden, *An Appetite For Power* (HarperCollins, 1998), p. 408.
290 Hennessy, *The Prime Minister*, p. 345.
291 Conversation with Professor John Ramsden; Ramsden, *The Winds of Change*, p. 346.
292 Dell, *The Chancellors*, p. 381.
293 Interview with Lord Hurd of Westwell.
294 Theakston in *The Heath Government 1970–74: A Reappraisal*, p. 88.
295 Heath, *The Course of My Life*, p. 399.
296 Campbell, *Edward Heath*, p. 314.
297 Peter le Cheminant, *Beautiful Ambiguities* (The Radcliffe Press, 2001), p. 129; Theakston, *Leadership in Whitehall*, p. 193.
298 Comment by Professor John Ramsden, 30 August 2006.
299 Interview with Lord Hurd of Westwell.
300 Interview with Peter Jay, 2 March 2004.
301 Sir Donald MacDougall, *Don and Mandarin* (John Murray, 1987), pp. 188–9.
302 Dell, *The Chancellors*, p. 395.
303 Ramsden in *The Heath Government 1970–74: A Reappraisal*, p. 40.
304 F. W. S. Craig (ed.), *British General Election Manifestos 1959–1987* (Dartmouth, Aldershot, 1990), p. 119.
305 Conversation with Professor John Ramsden.
306 Heath, *The Course of My Life*, p. 330.
307 This comment, widely quoted, does not appear to have been written down by Keynes – see Alfred Malabre, *Lost Prophets: An Insider's History of the Modern Economists* (Harvard Business School Press, Boston, USA, 1995), p. 220.
308 *The Price and Pay Code*, Cmnd. 5152 (HMSO, 1973).
309 *The Counter-inflation Programme – The Operation of Stage Two*, Cmnd. 5267 (HMSO, 1973).
310 Theakston, *Leadership in Whitehall*, p. 195.
311 Campbell, *Edward Heath*, p. 484.
312 Ramsden in *The Heath Government 1970–74: A Reappraisal*, p. 33.
313 Though Thatcher, at the very last Cabinet of the Heath Government, spoke of 'the wonderful experience of team loyalty that she felt she had shared since 1970', Ramsden, *The Winds of Change*, p. 359.
314 Hurd cited Tony Blair's abolition of the Lord Chancellor's Department in 2003 and the decision to call a referendum on a European constitution in 2004; interview with Lord Hurd of Westwell.
315 Ramsden, *The Heath Government 1970–74: A Reappraisal*, p. 33.
316 NA, PRO, PREM 15/611, 'Prime Minister's policy review meetings with Sir Burke Trend, Sir William Armstrong and Lord Rothschild', Robert Armstrong, minutes of a meeting, 19 April 1971.
317 Ibid., Lord Rothschild to Sir Burke Trend, 6 November 1971.
318 Ramsden in *The Heath Government 1970–74: A Reappraisal*, pp. 40–1.
319 Heath, *The Course Of My Life*, p. 353.
320 Hurd, *An End to Promises*, pp. 92–3.
321 Hennessy, *Whitehall*, p. 238.
322 Ibid., p. 238.

323 Hennessy, *Whitehall*, p. 238.
324 Interview with Lord Hurd of Westwell.
325 Hennessy, *Whitehall*, pp. 237–8.
326 Baston and Seldon in *The Heath Government 1970–74: A Reappraisal*, p. 65.
327 Ibid.
328 Hennessy, *Whitehall*, pp. 237–8.
329 Campbell, *Edward Heath*, p. 490.
330 The diary of Dr William Plowden. Entry for 27 February 1972.
331 Theakston, *Leadership in Whitehall*, p. 192.
332 Samuel Brittan, 'Plan for New Department to Aid PM', *Financial Times*, 23 August 1972.
333 Roy Blackman, 'Silly Season Stuff, says Sir William', *Daily Express*, 25 August 1972.
334 NA, PRO, PREM 15/1603, 'Reorganistion of central government: organisation of three central departments of Treasury, Cabinet Office (with Central Policy Review Staff) and Civil Service Department (CSD); part 8', Robert Armstrong to Donald Maitland, 5 September 1972.
335 NA, PRO, PREM 15/1603, Donald Maitland to Robert Armstrong, 7 September 1972.
336 See NA, PRO, PREM 15/512, 'Committee of Enquiry into law of defamation, contempt of court and official secrets: review of Official Secrets Act; Franks Report'.
337 Hennessy, *Whitehall*, p. 353.
338 Peter Hennessy, 'Open government, Whitehall and the press since 1945', in Hugh Stephenson (ed.), *Media Voices* (Politico's, 2001), p. 324.
339 NA, PRO, PREM 15/1603, Sir William Armstrong to Robert Armstrong, 12 September 1972.
340 Ibid.
341 Ibid., Robert Armstrong to Sir William Armstrong, 13 September 1972.
342 Interview with Lord Hurd of Westwell.
343 See Kenneth Berrill, *Strength at the Centre: The Case for a Prime Minister's Department*, the Stamp Memorial Lecture delivered on 4 December 1980 (published by University of London, 1981).
344 NA, PRO, PREM 16/104, 'Special advisers: guidance on appointment of special advisers to ministers; political activities; role of Dr Bernard Donoughue', Bernard Thimont (CSD) to Donoughue, 'No 10: Policy Unit', 20 March 1974.
345 Ibid., Hunt to 'senior Cabinet Office staff', 23 April 1974.
346 Symposium, 'The Heath Government', *Contemporary Record*, vol. 9, no. 1 (1995), p. 212.
347 Phillip Whitehead, *The Writing on the Wall* (Joseph in association with Channel 4 Television Company, 1985), p. 89.
348 Baston and Seldon in *The Heath Government 1970–74: A Reappraisal*, p. 66.
349 Hennessy, *Whitehall*, p. 239.
350 Ibid., p. 238.
351 Lord Croham briefing the 'Hidden Wiring' MA option course, Queen Mary, University of London, 9 February 2005.
352 Theakston in *The Heath Government 1970–74: A Reappraisal*, p. 88.
353 Cairncross, *The British Economy Since 1945*, p. 199.
354 Whitehead, *The Writing on the Wall*, p. 110.

355 Hennessy, *Whitehall*, p. 240.
356 Private information.
357 Ibid.
358 Interview with Sir Samuel Brittan, 22 April 2004.
359 Michael Hatfield, 'Anger over Civil Service head's move to banking', *The Times*, 11 April 1974.
360 Joe Haines, *The Politics of Power* (Cape, 1977), p. 18.
361 Churchill quoted in Roy Jenkins, *Churchill* (Macmillan, 2001), p. 510.
362 Interview with Desmond Wilcox for BBC2's *Man Alive* reproduced in *The Listener*, 28 March 1974.
363 Lord Croham briefing the 'Hidden Wiring' MA option course, Queen Mary, University of London, 9 February 2005.
364 Hennessy, *The Prime Minister*, p. 336.
365 Comment by Professor John Ramsden, 30 August 2006.
366 Campbell, *Edward Heath*, p. xviii.
367 Private information and letter to Professor Hennessy, 20 February 2006.
368 Interview with Sir Samuel Goldman.
369 Interview with Lord Hurd of Westwell.
370 *Sunday Telegraph*, 1 May 1977.
371 Campbell, *Edward Heath*, p. 491.
372 Ibid., p. 492.
373 Sir Samuel Brittan, 'Doomsters ride again: This house believes that demographics, debt and deficit spell imminent disaster for the G7', City Debate Speech Against, 24 January 2005.
374 Hurd, *An End to Promises*, pp. 36, 118.
375 Ramsden, *The Winds of Change*, p. 326; Andrew Blick, *People Who Live in the Dark* (Politico's, 2004), p. 124.
376 NA, PRO, CAB 184/34, 'CPRS weekly meetings', 'Meeting between the CPRS and the Prime Minister', 2 July 1971.
377 Private information.
378 Blick, *People Who Live in the Dark*, p. 124.
379 Baston and Seldon in *The Heath Government 1970–74: A Reappraisal*, p. 54.
380 Rothschild, *Random Variables*, p. 76.
381 Blackstone and Plowden, *Inside the Think Tank*, p. 45.
382 Heclo and Wildavsky, *The Private Government of Public Money*, p. 325.
383 NA, PRO, PREM 15/762, Sir Burke Trend to the Cabinet, 31 January 1971.
384 NA, PRO, PREM 15/2023, 'Prime Minister's instruction to departments on reduction in paperwork', C. W. Roberts (Downing Street) to N. W. Stuart (CSD), 13 September 1973.
385 NA, PRO, PREM 15/762, Lord Rothschild to Robert Armstrong, 19 February 1971.
386 Hennessy, *Whitehall*, p. 225.
387 NA, PRO, PREM 15/762, Robert Armstrong to Lord Rothschild, 22 February 1971.
388 NA, PRO, PREM 15/1342, 'Lord Rothschild's speech to Letcombe Laboratory of Agricultural Research Council, 24 September 1973', Lord Rothschild, 'Address to the Letcombe Laboratory of the Agricultural Research Council', 24 September 1973.
389 Interview with William Plowden.

390 Lord Rothschild, *Meditations of a Broomstick* (Collins, 1977), pp. 89–96; Blackstone and Plowden, *Inside the Think Tank*, pp. 54–5.
391 Hurd, *An End to Promises*, p. 38.
392 NA, PRO, PREM 15/1342, Sir John Hunt, 'Note For The Record', 25 September 1973.
393 NA, PRO, CAB 129/166, CPRS, 'Mid-Term Strategy: Is the Balance Right?', 17 November 1972.
394 NA, PRO, PREM 15/1342, Sir John Hunt, 'Note For The Record', 25 September 1973.
395 Ibid.
396 Ibid.
397 Rose, *Elusive Rothschild*, p. 180.
398 NA, PRO, PREM 15/1342, Sir John Hunt, 'Note For The Record', 25 September 1973.
399 Lord Rothschild quoted in Hennessy, *Whitehall*, p. 235.
400 NA, PRO, PREM 15/1342, Sir John Hunt, 'Staff In Confidence', 25 September 1973.
401 Lord Rothschild quoted in Hennessy, *Whitehall*, p. 235.
402 NA, PRO, PREM 15/1342, Lord Rothschild to Edward Heath, 10 October 1973.
403 Ibid., Edward Heath to Lord Rothschild, 17 October 1973.
404 Rose, *Elusive Rothschild*, p. 192.
405 Interview with Lord Waldegrave of North Hill.
406 Interview with Lord Butler of Brockwell.
407 NA, PRO, CAB 129/170/5, CP (73) 65, 8 June 1973.
408 Campbell, *Edward Heath*, p. 319.
409 NA, PRO, PREM 15/2099, Sir John Hunt to Robert Armstrong, 19 December 1973.
410 Rose, *Elusive Rothschild*, p. 193.
411 NA, PRO, PREM 15/2099, Lord Rothschild to Edward Heath, 16 December 1973.
412 Rose, *Elusive Rothschild*, p. 189.
413 Blackstone and Plowden, *Inside the Think Tank*, pp. 55, 93–4.
414 The diary of Dr William Plowden, entry for 4 February 1974.
415 NA, PRO, PREM 15/1429, 'Economic statement 17 Dec 1973 (public expenditure reductions, taxation and consumer credit measures)', Robert Armstrong to Edward Heath, 6 December 1973.

Notes to Conclusion

1 Ralf Dahrendorf quoted in Peter Hennessy, *The Prime Minister* (Penguin, 2000), p. 335.
2 Sir David Omand, 'In the National Interest: Organising Government for National Security', The Demos Annual Security Lecture, 20 December 2006.
3 Interview with Sir Samuel Goldman, 3 November 2003.
4 Interview with Lord Butler of Brockwell, 3 November 2003.
5 Interview with Sir Samuel Brittan, 22 April 2004.
6 Petronii Arbitri Satyricon attributed to Gaius Petronius and quoted in government organisation for *Defence Procurement and Civil Aerospace*, Cmnd 4641, April 1971.
7 Richard Wilding, 'The Fulton Report in retrospect', *Contemporary Record*, Vol. 9, No. 2, Autumn 1995, p. 396.

8 Interview with Desmond Wilcox for BBC2's *Man Alive* reproduced in *The Listener*, 28 March 1974.
9 'We have not successfully rolled back the frontiers of the state in Britain, only to see them re-imposed at a European level', Margaret Thatcher to the College of Europe (the 'Bruges' speech), 20 September 1988.

Bibliography

UNPUBLISHED PRIMARY SOURCES

PUBLIC RECORD OFFICE, THE NATIONAL ARCHIVES, KEW

BA 1 Civil Service Department: Committee on the Civil Service (Fulton Committee): Minutes, Papers and Report

BA 17 Civil Service Department: Machinery of Government Group: Machinery of Government (MG Series)

CAB 21 Cabinet Office Registered Files

CAB 87 War Cabinet and Cabinet: Committees on Reconstruction, Supply and other matters: Minutes and Papers

CAB 128 Cabinet: Minutes

CAB 129 Cabinet: Memoranda

CAB 130 Cabinet: Miscellaneous Committees: Minutes and Papers

CAB 134 Cabinet: Miscellaneous Committees: Minutes and Papers

CAB 161 Cabinet Office: Committee Organisation Books

CAB 164 Cabinet Office: Subject (Theme Series) Files

CAB 184 Central Policy Review Staff: Files

DEFE 7 Ministry of Defence prior to 1964

PREM 5 Prime Ministers patronage papers for Macmillan, Home, Wilson & Heath

PREM 11 Prime Minister's Office: Correspondence and Papers, 1951–1964

PREM 13 Prime Minister's Office: Correspondence and Papers, 1964–1970

PREM 15 Prime Minister's Office: Correspondence and Papers 1970–1974

PREM 16 Records of the Prime Ministers Office: Correspondence and Papers 1973–1978

T 230 Cabinet Office, Economic Section, and Treasury, Economic Advisory Section

T 273 Treasury: Papers of Lord Bridges

T 325 Treasury and other departments: Sir R. W. B. (Otto) Clarke Papers

T 330 Treasury and Civil Service Department: Management Services Division

T 342 Treasury: Industrial and Incomes Policy Division: Registered Files

BODLEIAN LIBRARY, OXFORD UNIVERSITY
Conservative Research Department (CRD) archive
Lord George-Brown papers

PRIVATE PAPERS
Public Sector Research Unit papers
Dr William Plowden's diary

INTERVIEWS

Lord Allen of Abbeydale (7 May 2003)
Brittan, Sir Samuel (30 May 2001, 4 October 2002, 17 April 2003 and 22 April 2004)
Lord Butler of Brockwell (3 November 2003)
Cooper, Sir Frank (13 June 2001)
Lord Croham (29 October 2002)
Goldman, Sir Samuel (3 November 2003)
Lord Howell of Guildford (8 October 2003)
Lord Hurd of Westwell (27 April 2004)
Jay, Peter (2 March 2004)
Lord Jenkins of Hillhead (5 May 1999)
MacDougall, Sir Donald (21 May 2001 and 25 September 2002)
Magee, Dr Gary (17 April 2001)
Lord Marlesford (8 October 2003)
Mitchell, Sir Derek (19 September 2002)
Neild, Professor Robert (6 May 2003)
Plowden, Dr William (10 October 2003)
Lord Roll of Ipsden (17 September 2002)
Lord Waldegrave of North Hill (29 October 2003)
Wilding, Richard (15 August 2003)

PUBLISHED PRIMARY SOURCES
OFFICIAL
Control of Public Expenditure, Cmnd. 1432 (HMSO, 1961)
Employment Policy, Cmnd. 6527 (HMSO, 1944)
Information and the Public Interest, Cmnd. 4089 (HMSO, 1969)

Ministerial Code: A Code Of Conduct And Guidance On Procedures For Ministers (HMSO, 2001)
Modernising Government, Cmnd. 4310 (HMSO, 1999)
Report of the Machinery of Government Committee, Cmnd. 9230 (HMSO, 1918)
Royal Commission on the Civil Service (the Priestley Commission), Cmnd. 9613 (HMSO, 1955)
Social Insurance and Allied Services, Cmnd. 6404 (HMSO, 1942)
The Civil Service: Continuity and Change, Cmnd. 2627 (HMSO, 1994)
The Civil Service: Report of the Committee 1966–68, Cmnd. 3638 (HMSO, 1968)
The Counter-inflation Programme – The Operation of Stage Two, Cmnd. 5267 (HMSO, 1973)
The Method II System of Selection for the Administrative Class of the Home Civil Service, Cmnd. 4156 (HMSO, 1969)
The National Plan, Cmnd. 2764 (HMSO, 1965)
The Price and Pay Code, Cmnd. 5152 (HMSO, 1973)
The Reorganisation of Central Government, Cmnd. 4506 (HMSO, 1970)
House of Commons, *Sixth Report from the Estimates Committee*, 1964–65 (HMSO, 1965)
House of Commons, *Eleventh Report from the Expenditure Committee*, Session 1976–77, 'The Civil Service' (HMSO, 1977)
House of Commons, *Official Report*, various volumes
Gordon Brown's 2005 Budget statement (www.hmrc.gov.uk/budget2005)

BOOKS/PAMPHLETS

Balogh, Thomas, *Planning for Progress* (Fabian Society, 1963)
Bridges, Edward, 'Portrait of a Profession', Rede Lecture, University of Cambridge, 1950 (printed by CUP, 1950)
Goldman, Samuel, *The developing system of public expenditure management and control* (HMSO, 1973)
Heath, Edward, *My Style of Government* (Evening Standard Publications, 1972)
Howell, David, *A New Style Of Government* (Conservative Political Centre, 1970)
Hunt, Norman, *Whitehall and Beyond* (BBC, 1964)
Wass, Douglas, *Government and the Governed: BBC Reith Lectures 1983* (Routledge & Kegan Paul, 1984)
Wilson, Harold, *Purpose in Politics: Selected Speeches* (Weidenfeld & Nicolson, 1964)

MEMOIRS/DIARIES

Benn, Tony, *Out of the Wilderness: Diaries 1963–67* (Hutchinson, 1987)
Benn, Tony, *Office Without Power: Diaries 1968–72* (Hutchinson, 1988)
Brown, George, *In My Way* (Gollancz, 1971)
Cairncross, Alec, *Managing the British Economy in the 1960s: A Treasury Perspective* (Macmillan, 1996)
Cairncross, Alec, *The Wilson Years: A Treasury Diary, 1964–1969* (The Historian's Press, 1997)
Callaghan, James, *Time and Chance* (Collins, 1987)
Castle, Barbara, *Fighting All the Way* (Macmillan, 1993)
Castle, Barbara, *The Castle Diaries, 1964–70* (Weidenfeld & Nicolson, 1984)
Castle, Barbara, *The Castle Diaries 1974–76* (Weidenfeld & Nicolson, 1980)
Crossman, Richard, *The Diaries of a Cabinet Minister: Vol.1, Minister of Housing, 1964–66* (Cape, 1975)
Crossman, Richard, *The Diaries of a Cabinet Minister: Vol. 2, Lord President of the Council and Leader of the House of Commons, 1966–68* (Cape, 1976)
Crossman, Richard, *The Diaries of a Cabinet Minister: Vol. 3, Secretary of State for the Social Services 1968–70* (Hamilton, 1977)
Donoughue, Bernard, *Downing Street Diary: With Harold Wilson in No. 10* (Jonathan Cape, 2005)
Douglas-Home, Alec, *The Way The Wind Blows* (Collins, 1976)
Haines, Joe, *Glimmers of Twilight* (Politico's, 2003)
Haines, Joe, *The Politics of Power* (Jonathan Cape, 1977)
Heath, Edward, *The Course of My Life* (Hodder and Stoughton, 1998)
Hurd, Douglas, *An End to Promises* (Collins, 1979)
Hurd, Douglas, *Memoirs* (Little, Brown, 2003)
Jay, Douglas, *Change and Fortune* (Hutchinson, 1980)
Jenkins, Roy, *A Life at the Centre* (Macmillan, 1991)
Le Cheminant, Peter, *Beautiful Ambiguities* (The Radcliffe Press, 2001)
MacDougall, Donald, *Don and Mandarin* (John Murray, 1987)
Macmillan, Harold, *At the End of the Day* (Macmillan, 1973)
Macmillan, Harold, *Pointing the Way, 1959–61* (Macmillan, 1972)
Roll, Eric, *Crowded Hours* (Faber, 1985)
Rothschild, Victor, *Meditations of a Broomstick* (Collins, 1977)
Rothschild, Victor, *Random Variables* (Collins, 1984)
Wilding, Richard, *Civil Servant* (The Memoir Club, 2006)
Williams, Marcia, *Inside No. 10* (Weidenfeld & Nicolson, 1972)
Wilson, Harold, *The Labour Government 1964–1970* (Weidenfeld & Nicolson, 1971)

SECONDARY WORKS

Ainley, Patrick and Mark Corney, *Training For the Future* (Cassell, 1990)
Alford, B. W. E., *British Economic Performance 1945–1975* (Cambridge University Press, 1995)
Arnold, Lorna, *Britain and the H-bomb* (Palgrave, 2000)
Barnett, Correlli, *The Audit of War* (Macmillan, 1986)
Barnett, Correlli, *The Collapse of British Power* (Sutton, 1972)
Barnett, Correlli, *The Lost Victory* (Macmillan, 1995)
Blackstone, Tessa, and William Plowden, *Inside the Think Tank* (Heinemann, 1988)
Blick, Andrew, *People Who Live in the Dark* (Politico's, 2004)
Bray, Jeremy (Elizabeth Bray, ed.), *Standing on The Shoulders of Giants* (Elizabeth Bray, 2004)
Brittan, Samuel, *Steering the Economy* (Pelican, 1971)
Bruce–Gardyne, Jock, *Whatever Happened to the Quiet Revolution?* (C. Knight, 1974)
Butler, David and Anthony King, *The British General Election of 1964* (Macmillan, 1964)
Cairncross, Alec, *The British Economy Since 1945* (Blackwell, 1992)
Campbell, John, *Edward Heath* (Jonathan Cape, 1993)
Chandler, Alfred, *Strategy and Structure* (M.I.T. Press, 1962)
Chapman, Richard and J. R. Greenaway, *The Dynamics of Administrative Reform* (Croom Helm, 1980)
Clarke, Richard (Alec Cairncross, ed.), *Public Expenditure, Management and Control* (Macmillan, 1978)
Cockerell, Michael, Peter Hennessy and David Walker, *Sources Close to the Prime Minister* (Macmillan, 1984)
Colville, John, *The Churchillians* (Weidenfeld & Nicolson, 1981)
Craddock, Percy, *Know Your Enemy* (John Murray, 2002)
Crosland, Susan, *Tony Crosland* (Cape, 1982)
Dell, Edmund, *A Strange Eventful History* (HarperCollins, 2000)
Dell, Edmund, *The Chancellors* (HarperCollins, 1997)
Dockrill, Michael, *British Defence Since 1945* (Basil Blackwell, 1988)
Drewry, Gavin and Tony Butcher, *The Civil Service Today* (Blackwell, 1991)
Edgerton, David, *England and the Aeroplane* (Macmillan, 1991)
English, Richard and Michael Kenny (eds), *Rethinking British Decline* (Macmillan, 2000)
Fry, Geoffrey, *Reforming the Civil Service* (Edinburgh University Press, 1993)
Gardner, Richard, *Sterling–Dollar Diplomacy in Current Perspective* (Columbia University Press, 1980)
Garrett, John, *The Management of Government* (Harmondsworth, 1972)

Goodman, Geoffrey, *The Awkward Warrior, Frank Cousins: His Life and Times* (Davis-Poynter, 1979)
Halsey, A. H., *British Social Trends Since 1900* (Macmillan, 1988)
Heclo, Hugh and Aaron Wildavsky, *The Private Government of Public Money* (Macmillan, 1981)
Hennessy, Peter, *Cabinet* (Basil Blackwell, 1986)
Hennessy, Peter, *Having It So Good* (Penguin, 2006)
Hennessy, Peter, *Muddling Through* (Gollancz, 1996)
Hennessy, Peter, *Never Again* (Jonathan Cape, 1992)
Hennessy, Peter, *The Prime Minister* (Penguin, 2000)
Hennessy, Peter, *The Secret State* (Penguin, 2002)
Hennessy, Peter, *Whitehall* (Secker and Warburg, 1989)
Hitchcock, William, *France Restored* (University of North Carolina Press, 1998)
Horne, Alistair, *Macmillan, 1894–1956* (Macmillan, 1988)
Horne, Alistair, *Macmillan, 1957–1986* (Macmillan, 1989)
Howell, David, *The Edge Of Now* (Macmillan, 2000)
Jeffery, Keith, and Peter Hennessy, *States of Emergency* (Routledge and Kegan Paul, 1983)
Jenkins, Roy, *Churchill* (Macmillan, 2001)
Kellner, Peter and Lord Crowther-Hunt, *The Civil Servants* (Macdonald and Janes, 1980)
Keynes, John Maynard, *The General Theory of Employment, Interest and Money* (Macmillan, 1936)
Laski, Harold, *A Grammar of Politics* (Allen and Unwin, 1948)
Laski, Harold, *Authority in the Modern State* (Yale University Press, 1919)
Laski, Harold, *Parliamentary Government in Britain* (Allen and Unwin, 1938)
Macmillan, Harold, *The Middle Way* (Macmillan, 1938 and 1958)
Malabre, Alfred, *Lost Prophets: An Insider's History of the Modern Economists* (Harvard Business School Press, 1995)
Margach, James, *The Abuse Of Power* (W. H. Allen, 1978)
Marquand, David, *The Unprincipled Society* (Cape, 1988)
Middlemas, Keith, *Industry, Unions and Government* (Macmillan, 1983)
Morgan, Kenneth O., *Callaghan: A Life* (Oxford, 1997)
Owen, Geoffrey, *From Empire to Europe* (HarperCollins, 1999)
Paterson, Peter, *Tired and Emotional* (Chatto and Windus, 1993)
Pimlott, Ben, *Harold Wilson* (HarperCollins, 1993)
Pliatzky, Leo, *Getting and Spending* (Basil Blackwell, 1982)
Plowden, William (ed.), *Advising the Rulers* (Blackwell, 1987)
Pollard, Sidney, *The Wasting of the British Economy* (Croom Helm, 1984)
Pollitt, Christopher, *Manipulating the Machine* (George Allen and Unwin, 1984)

Radcliffe, James, *The Reorganisation of British Central Government* (Dartmouth, 1991)
Ramsden, John, *An Appetite For Power* (HarperCollins, 1998)
Ramsden, John, *The Making of Conservative Party Policy* (Longman, 1980)
Ramsden, John, (ed.), *The Oxford Companion to Twentieth-Century British Politics* (Oxford, 2002)
Ramsden, John, *The Winds of Change* (Longman, 1996)
Rose, Kenneth, *Elusive Rothschild* (Weidenfeld & Nicolson, 2003)
Roseveare, Henry, *The Treasury* (Allen Lane, 1969)
Sampson, Anthony, *Anatomy of Britain* (Hodder and Stoughton, 1962)
Seldon, Anthony and Stuart Ball (eds), *The Heath Government 1970–74: A Reappraisal* (Longman, 1996)
Shanks, Michael, *The Stagnant Society* (Penguin, 1961)
Shonfield, Andrew, *British Economic Policy Since The War* (Penguin, 1958)
Sloan, Alfred, *My Years with General Motors* (Sidgwick and Jackson, 1965)
Theakston, Kevin, *Leadership in Whitehall* (Macmillan, 1999)
Theakston, Kevin, *The Civil Service Since 1945* (Blackwell, 1995)
Theakston, Kevin, *The Labour Party and Whitehall* (Routledge, 1992)
Thorpe, D. R., *Alec Douglas-Home* (Sinclair-Stevenson, 1997)
Turner, John, *Lloyd George's Secretariat* (Cambridge University Press, 1980)
Whitehead, Phillip, *The Writing on the Wall* (Michael Joseph, 1985)
Young, Hugo, *This Blessed Plot* (Macmillan, 1998).
Young, Michael, *The Rise of the Meritocracy* (Thames and Hudson, 1958)
Ziegler, Philip, *Wilson: The Authorised Life* (Weidenfeld & Nicolson, 1993)

ARTICLES/CHAPTERS

Baines, Priscilla, 'History and Rationale of the 1979 Reforms', in Gavin Drewry (ed.), *The New Select Committees* (Clarendon Press, 1989)
Balogh, Thomas, 'The Apotheosis of the Dilettante', in Hugh Thomas (ed.), *The Establishment* (A. Blond, 1959)
Brittan, Samuel, 'A backward glance: The reappraisal of the 1960s', lecture given to the Institute of Contemporary British History, April 1997
Brittan, Samuel, 'Doomsters ride again: This house believes that demographics, debt and deficit spell imminent disaster for the G7', City Debate Speech Against, 24 January 2005
Burch, M., 'Approaches to Leadership in Opposition: Edward Heath and Margaret Thatcher', in Z. Layton-Henry (ed.), *Conservative Party Politics* (Macmillan, 1980)
Cairncross, Alec, 'Economists in Government', *Lloyds Bank Review*, No. 95, January 1970

Cairncross, Alec, 'The Post-war Years 1945–77', in Roderick Floud and Donald McCloskey (eds), *The Economic History of Britain Since 1870, Volume 2* (Cambridge University Press, 1981)

Coopey, Richard (ed.), 'Ministry of Technology', *Contemporary Record*, Vol. 5, No. 1, 1991

Crafts, N. F. R., and N. W. C. Woodward (eds), *The British Economy Since 1945* (Clarendon, 1991)

Crafts, Nicholas, and Gianni Toniolo, 'Post–war Growth: An Overview', in *Economic Growth in Europe Since 1945* (Cambridge University Press, 1996)

Dunnett, James, 'The Civil Service Administrator and the Expert', *Public Administration*, Vol. 39, Autumn 1961

Edgerton, David, 'Liberal Militarism and the British State', *New Left Review*, no. 185

Grant, Matthew, 'Historians, the Penguin Specials and the "State-of-the-Nation" Literature, 1958–64', *Contemporary British History*, Vol. 17, No. 3 (Autumn 2003)

Halsey, A. H., 'Higher Education', in A. H. Halsey (ed.), *British Social Trends Since 1900* (Macmillan, 1988)

Harris, José, 'Enterprise and Welfare States: A Comparative Perspective', *Transactions of the Royal Historical Society*, No. 40, 1990

Hennessy, Peter, and Caroline Anstey, 'Moneybags and Brains', Strathclyde Analysis Paper (1990)

Hennessy, Peter, 'Open government, Whitehall and the press since 1945', in Hugh Stephenson (ed.), *Media Voices* (Politico's, 2001)

Hennessy, Peter, Susan Morrison and Richard Townsend, *Routine Punctuated By Orgies: The Central Policy Review Staff, 1970–83*, Strathclyde Papers on Government and Politics no. 31, Politics Department, Strathclyde University, 1985

Johnson, Nevil, 'Change in the Civil Service', *Public Administration*, Vol. 63, Winter 1985

Laski, Harold, 'Introduction', in J. P. W. Mallalieu, *Passed To You Please* (Gollancz, 1942)

MacDougall, Donald, 'The Machinery of Economic Government: Some Personal Reflections', in David Butler and A. H. Halsey (eds), *Policy and Politics* (Macmillan, 1978)

Mulgan, Geoff, 'How Do Central Governments Think? Lessons from British History and Abroad', Mile End Group, Queen Mary, University of London, 7 June 2005

Powell, J. Enoch, foreword to Andrew Elliot, *The Guilty Madmen of Whitehall* (Elliot Right Way Books, 1969)

Robson, W. A., 'The reorganisation of central government', *Political Quarterly*, vol. 42, no. 1 (1971)
Symposium, 'Fulton: 20 Years On', *Contemporary Record*, Vol. 2, No. 2, Summer 1988
Symposium, 'The Department of Economic Affairs', *Contemporary British History*, Vol. 11, Summer 1997, No. 2
Wilding, Richard, 'The Fulton Report in retrospect', *Contemporary Record*, Vol. 9, No. 2, Autumn 1995
Symposium, 'The Heath Government', *Contemporary Record*, vol. 9, no. 1 (1995)
Taylor, A. J. P., introduction to Karl Marx and Friedrich Engels, *The Communist Manifesto* (Penguin, 1967)
Theakston, Kevin, and Geoffrey K. Fry, 'Britain's Administrative Elite', *Public Administration*, Vol. 67, Summer 1989
Turner, John, '1951–1964', in Anthony Seldon (ed.), *How Tory Governments Fall* (Fontana Press, 1996)
Turner, John, 'Experts and Interests', in Rory Macleod (ed.), *Government and Expertise in Nineteenth Century Britain* (Cambridge University Press, 1988)
Waldegrave, William, 'Three Prime Ministers', Twentieth Century British History seminar, Institute of Historical Research, 9 March 1994

UNPUBLISHED THESES AND PAPERS

Bailey, Stephen, 'The Use of Inner Cabinets "Formal" and "Informal" Since 1968', unpublished undergraduate thesis, Department of History, Queen Mary and Westfield College, University of London, 1999
Cousens, Ruth, 'The Central Policy Review Staff Early Warning System, 1971–1972', unpublished MA thesis, Queen Mary, University of London, 2003
Davis, Jon, 'Staring over the Precipice into the Abyss: An Anatomy and an Analysis of "Operation Brutus"', unpublished MA thesis, Queen Mary, University of London, 1999
O'Hara, Glen, 'British Economic and Social Planning 1959–1970', unpublished PhD thesis, University College London, University of London, 2002
Thorpe, Keir, '"The Missing Pillar": Economic Planning and the Machinery of Government during the Labour Administrations of 1945–51', unpublished PhD thesis, Queen Mary, University of London, 1999
Wolf, Martin, 'Why Globalisation Works', 'Globalisation Lectures', Queen Mary, University of London, 12 January 2005

NEWSPAPERS/PERIODICALS

Daily Express
Daily Telegraph
Financial Times
Guardian
Independent
Sunday Telegraph
The Economist
The Listener
The Spectator
The Sunday Times
The Times
Times Literary Supplement

Index

A Better Tomorrow (Conservative Manifesto) 95
Adams, Professor W. G. S. 88
Administrators, The (Balogh) 1
Alford, B. W. E. 8
Allen, Philip 53–5, 62, 66, 69, 78, 81, 141, 144
Allen, Douglas 32–4, 46, 69, 75, 94, 98, 116, 121–3
Andrew, Robert 136–7
'Apotheosis of the Dilettante, The' (Balogh) 1, 26, 63, 118
Armstrong, Robert
    afterword 171–2
    and the CPRS 125, 128
    and dispersal 105
    and the EWS 124
    and GEN 92 133
    and general policy 113
    and Heath 156
    and incomes policy 146
    and the Treasury 114–16, 148
Armstrong, William
    and the businessmen's team 139–40
    Civil Service Head 69
    Conservative Government 103–4, 106
    Conservative plans 93–4, 98
    and the Fulton Committee 55, 61, 63, 68–73, 75–81, 166
    grading 97
    incomes policy 145
    increased power 147
    and the Industry Bill 144
    and Isserlis 99
    rise and fall 147–52
    Treasury appointment 19
    and Wilson 34, 40, 42, 52

Ashby, Eric 56
Attlee, Clement 3–4, 12, 24, 125

Balogh, Thomas
    and the Civil Service College 66–7
    Civil Service reform 1, 7, 8, 26–7, 192n.30
    devaluation 41
    Fulton Committee 52, 63, 65
    government appointment 31, 33
    'kitchen cabinet' 40
Bancroft, Ian 101–2, 213n.190
Bank of England 169
Barber, Anthony 113, 144–5, 217n.3
'Barber Boom', the 144–5
Barnett, Correlli 5
Barran, David 130–1
Bellinger, Robert 134
Benn, Tony 47
Bevan, Aneurin 3
Beveridge Report 2
Bichard, Michael 194n.80
'Black Book' 92, 114
Blackstone, Tessa 133
Bligh, Tim 25, 29
Boyle, Edward 65, 84
BP 60, 201n.73
Bray, Jeremy 54
Bridges, Edward 3, 4, 28, 53
Brittan, Samuel 18–20, 26, 42, 69, 113, 148, 169
Brown, George 24–6, 29–30, 31–4, 41–5, 184n.12
Bruce-Gardyne, Jock 125–6
businessmen's team 137–40
Butcher, Tony ix

Butler, Robin
    comments on the Treasury 113, 217n.6
    contrast to Goldman 169
    and the CPRS 119, 121, 129, 168
    and the EWS 123
    and Lord Rothschild 132
    and the PSRU 106
Butler, Rab 84

Cabinet Office 107, 142
Cabinet, The 74
cabinets 140
Cairncross, Alec 16, 41
Callaghan, James 24–5, 33–6, 43–4, 46, 52–7, 74
Campbell, John 104
Carey, Peter 123
Carrington, Lord 91
Castle, Barbara 36, 40, 46
Caulcott, Tom 30
Central Business Advisor 140
Central Capability Unit 108
Central Policy Review Staff (CPRS)
    abolition and legacy 128–9, 131, 157, 163, 167
    in action 116–25, 216n.259
    eclipse 154–6
    and PAR 133, 135
    and policy review 127–8
    setting up of xiii 107–8
central/analytical capability 106
Centre for Administrative Studies 8, 66
Chapman, Richard 160
Chilcot, John 97
church attendance 12, 188n.136
Churchill, Winston 2, 3, 85, 88–9, 150
Civil Contingencies Unit 142–3
Civil Service
    1970 Conservative victory 97–8
    criticism 20–1
    and Douglas Hurd 39, 152
    Fulton Report *see* Fulton Report
    generalist versus expert 7–8
    and Harold Macmillan 159–60
    and Heath 98–9, 163–5
    immediate post-war 2–4, 185n.28, 186n.54
    and David Howell 93, 94, 167
    and Marcia Williams 38–40
    meritocracy 9
    own agenda 159, 165
    reform xv 1, 10–12, 24, 65–8, 167–8, 170–2
    and Thomas Balogh 1, 7, 8, 26–7, 192n.30
Civil Service College 66–7, 73–5, 81
Civil Service Commission 65, 66
Civil Service Department (CSD) 58, 74–7, 81, 98, 100–1
Civil Service Today, The (Drewry/Butcher) ix
Clarke, Otto 11, 18, 31, 101
Cooper, Geoffrey 3
Cooper, Frank 3, 104, 128
Cottrell, Alan 118
Counter-Inflation Act 1973 145
Counter-Inflation (Temporary Provisions) Act 1972 145
Cousins, Frank 36
Cripps, Stafford 28
Cromer, Lord 41
Crosland, Anthony 32–3, 41, 47, 162
Crossman, Richard 3, 40, 63, 68, 74
Crowther-Hunt, Lord 54

Dalton, Hugh 28
'dash for growth' 19
Davies, Jack 65
Davies, John 101, 116, 144
Dawes, Roger 77
de Gaulle, President Charles 15
Defence Procurement Agency 138
Dell, Edmund 44, 46
Department of Economic Affairs xii 27–34, 43, 44–8, 165
Department of Education and Science 121
Department of Employment and Productivity 46, 48
Department of Energy 140
Department of Environment 101
Department of Health and Social Security 47–8

INDEX

Department of Local Government and Regional Planning 47
Department of Trade and Industry 116
devaluation 41–2, 46
dispersal 105
Douglas-Home Rules 20, 27, 29, 93–4, 167
Douglas-Home, Alec 20, 83–4, 160
Downing Street Policy Unit 168
Drewry, Gavin ix

early warning system (EWS) 121–3
East, Richard 94
Economic Development Commmittees 17, 33
Economic Survey (1954) 5
Eden, Anthony 7
Edgerton, David 9
Employment Policy (White Paper) 2
European Economic Community (EEC) 14–15, 143
European Exchange Rate Mechanism 169

Fabian Society 7
Fairlie, Henry 12
Federation of British Industry (FBI) 15
Fisher, Warren xv 7–8, 72
Ford, Hugh 108
Foreign and Commonwealth Office 102
Framework for Government Research and Development (Rothschild) 128
France 15–16
Franks, Lord 2, 148
Fry, Geoffrey ix–x 57
FU Committee 42
Fulton, Lord John 55–6, 61–2
Fulton Report
    the Committee xii–xiii 51–6
    and the Conservative Government 97
    evidence gathering 63–4
    final report 69–73
    first draft 61
    genesis 51
    'hiving off' 89, 100, 166
    implementation 74–80
    legacy 166

    meetings 57–60
    report on recruitment 64–5
    summary 173–6
    Wilson's creation 161
Future of Socialism, The (Crosland) 162

Gaitskell, Hugh 5, 24
Galbraith, Colin 99
'Garden Suburb' (Lloyd George) 88, 209n.61
Garrett, John 60
GEN 92 133
General Theory of Employment, Interest and Money (Keynes) 13
Gilbraith, Colin 99–100, 103
'Golden Years' 18
Goldman, Peter 107
Goldman, Samuel 11, 135, 151, 168–70
Gordon Walker, Patrick 207n.9
Government Economic Service 41
Graham, Philip 183n.2
Grebenik, Eugene 75
'Green Book' (NEDC) 18
Greenaway, J. R. 160

Haines, Joe 37, 95, 104
Haldane Committee 55, 98, 100, 213n.175
Halls, Marjorie 76, 206n.215
Halls, Michael 40, 56, 61–4, 66, 68, 71–7, 166
Halsey, A. H. 60
Harris, José 6
Harrod, Roy 13
Hart, Tony 140
Haydon, Robin 96
Heath, Edward
    and the businessmen's team 138
    and the CCU 106–8
    Civil Contingencies Unit 142–3
    and the Civil Service 98–9, 163–5
    and the Civil Service College 75
    Conservative Government leader 95–7, 102–4
    Conservative party leader xi, xiii, xiv 84–6
    and the CPRS 117, 119–21, 126, 130, 156, 221n.123

Heath, Edward (*continued*)
  downfall 156–7
  and the EEC 15, 143
  and the EWS 123–4
  forward planning 83, 87–93, 209n.53
  and GEN 92 133
  and growth 144
  and incomes policy 145
  increase in power 146–9
  industrial relations 141
  legacy 167–8
  and Meyjes 139
  and the MPC 105
  Official Secrets enquiry 79–80
  and the oil crisis 130–1, 223n.171
  and PAR 136
  presentation 130, 223n.169
  and the PSRU 117
  and Rothschild 153–4
  Secretary of State 20
  and William Armstrong 147–8, 150–1
  state committment 49
  and the Treasury 113–16, 122, 164
  and White Paper 111
Heathcoat Amory, Derick 10, 14
Heclo, Hugh 119
Helsby, Lawrence 20, 32, 53, 62
Hennessy, Peter 39, 55, 57, 81, 96, 98
Home Office 141
horizontal integration 32
Hosking, Barbara 96
Howell, David
  1970 election victory 95, 97
  and the CPRS 127, 129
  discussions with the Civil Service 93, 94, 167
  Government post 103–6, 108–11
  and Lord Rothschild 132–3
  and Meyjes 139
  and the 'new style' 92
  and PAR 136–7
  Parliamentary Secretary 76
  and the PSRU 86, 89, 90
  and the Treasury 113–15

Hunt, Lord 117, 124, 142, 154–5
Hunt, Norman 54–8, 60–2, 65, 68–9, 70, 75–6, 81
Hunt, John 136
Hurd, Douglas
  and the Civil Service 39, 152
  and the CPRS 127, 128
  and the EWS 123
  growth 143
  and Heath 84–5, 95–7, 109, 118–20, 126, 145–9, 227n.314
  industrial relations 141
  the oil price 131
  William Armstrong 151
  and Trend 147

In Place of Strife (White Paper) 46
incomes policy 145
industrial relations 140–1
Industrial Reorganisation Corporation 46
Industry Bill 1972 143–4
'inner circle' 75
Isserlis, Alexander (Sandy) 76, 99, 213n.178/190

Jay, Douglas 28, 44
Jay, Peter 119, 144
Jellicoe, Lord 104, 114, 126, 133, 138–9, 142
Jenkin, Patrick 145
Jenkins, Roy 44, 46–7, 74, 95
'joined-up government' 32, 194n.80
Joint Intelligence Committee (JIC) 48
Joseph, Keith 91
Jowett, Benjamin 78
'July Measures' 14

Kellner, Peter 53, 70
Keynes, John Maynard 13
'kitchen cabinet' 40, 72
Korean War 4–5

Laski, Harold 3, 185n.32
Lee, Frank 14, 15, 16

INDEX

247

Let Us Face the Future (Attlee 1945 manifesto) 125
Lever, Harold 45
Lloyd George, David 88
Lloyd, Selwyn 13, 14, 16–17, 19
Louden, John 116
Loughnane, Mary 59

MacDougall, Donald
   and the 'Barber Boom' 144–5
   and the DEA 30, 32
   and devaluation 41
   and the Fulton Report 71–2
   and the National Plan 43
   and the Treasury 26
   and NEDC 16–18
Mackenzie, W. J. M. 1
Macleod, Ian 94, 115
McMahon, Christopher 108
Macmillan, Harold
   change of direction xi–xii
   and the Civil Service 159–60
   and Edward Heath 85–6, 124
   and Evelyn Sharpe 93
   in government 17, 19–20, 24
Maitland, Donald 96, 148
Management Consultancy Group (MCG) 60
Management Projects Comittee (MPC) 105
Manipulating The Machine (Pollitt) ix
Marples, Ernest 86–8
Marquand, David 9
Maude, Angus 90
Maudling, Reginald 17, 19, 40, 84, 92, 142, 144
Mayne, John 110, 117, 119
Meyjes, Richard 105, 108, 138–9
Minister of Programmes 94
Ministry of Land and Natural Resources (MLNR) 36–7
Ministry of Overseas Development 102
Ministry of Technology (Mintech) xii 35–6, 47, 101
MISC 205 48
MISC committees 48

Mitchell, Derek 38–40, 56, 66
Modernising Government (White Paper) 110
Mulgan, Geoff 129

National Economic Development Council (NEDC) xi 16–18, 33, 44, 114, 160
National Plan 41–3, 45
Neild, Robert 41–2, 52, 56–7, 62, 65, 69–70, 81
New Style of Government, A (1970) 91, 97
New Version of the Former National Plan, The (Green Paper) 45
Next Steps initiative 81, 139
Normanbrook, Lord 28, 92, 167
Northcote-Trevelyan Report 58, 70, 80
Northern Ireland Office (NIO) 140

oil 130–1, 167
Omand, David 161
'Operation Patriarch' 46
'Orange Book' (NEDC) 18
Owen, Geoffrey 15

Part, Anthony 101, 104
Paterson, Peter 28
planning 16, 30
Planning, Programming and Budgeting (PPB) 88
Pliatsky, Leo 11, 35, 42
Plowden Committee 54, 57
Plowden, William 92, 120, 122, 124–5, 130, 133, 147, 153
Plowden, Edwin 10, 92
Plowden Report 11
Policy Unit 149, 162–3
Pollitt, Christopher ix
'Portrait of a Profession' (Bridges) 4
post-war consensus xiv 91
Powell, Enoch 20, 87, 90, 91
'privatization' 91, 167, 210n.87
Programme Analysis and Review (PAR) xiii 132–7, 168
Programme for Controlling Inflation, A 1972 145

Public Expenditure Survey Committee (PESC) 11, 18
Public Sector Research Unit (PSRU)
   and the businessmen's team 105–6, 137–8
   focus 117
   and Isserlis 99–100
   and Lord Rothschild 132
   overview 167
   and PAR 137, 168
   pessimism 94–5
   setting up 88–91
   sidelining 103
   and the Treasury 114–15

Rachmanism 195n.134
Ramsden, John 126
Rayner, Derek 138, 170
Reading, Brian 114
Reforming The Civil Service (Fry) ix–x
Reorganisation of Central Government, The (White Paper) xiii, xiv 83, 94, 109–13, 140, 167
Ridley, Nicholas 144
Rippon, Geoffrey 98
Rise of the Meritocracy, The (Young) 9
Roberthall, Lord 92, 167
Roll, Lord 25–7, 33, 39–40, 43, 44, 166
Rolls Royce 143
Rose, Kenneth 118
Roseveare, Henry 11
Rosselli, John 58
Rothschild, Lord
   and the businessmen's team 139
   and the CCU 108–9
   and Central Business Advisor 140
   and the CPRS 116–24, 127–32
   and GEN 92 133
   and Heath 152–6, 167–8
   and Trend/Armstrong 103
Ryrie, William 63

Sampson, Anthony 7–8
Schreiber, Mark
   and Bancroft 101, 214n.208
   and businessmen's team 139
   cabinets 140
   and CCU 93
   and the CPRS 129, 131–2
   and the DPA 138
   and the EWS 124
   Government post 103, 106–8
   and Marples 86
   and PAR 135–6
   and the PSRU 89, 117, 120
Schultz, Charles 91
Scott, Maurice 18
Sewill, Brendon 90
Shackleton, Lord 57, 75, 78
Shanks, Michael 1, 184n.4
Sharp, Evelyn 92–3, 167
Sheldon, Robert 59, 60, 66
Shone, Robert 17–18
Shore, Peter 45, 46, 75
Simey, Lord 56, 61, 72
single unified grading *see* unified grading structure
sociological survey (Halsey) 60
'stagflation' 152
'Statistical Section' (Churchill) 88–9
Steering Committee on Economic Policy (SEP) 48
sterling crisis 13
Stewart, Michael 45
'stop-go' policy 13–14, 19, 40
Suez Crisis 6–7
Sundridge Park Conference 91

Tebbit, Kevin 129–30
Thatcher, Margaret 69, 128–9, 227n.313
'The Establishment' 12
'Think Tank' *see* Central Policy Review Staff/ Central Capability Unit
Thorneycroft, Peter 13–14, 188n.154
Trades Union Congress (TUC) 17
Treasury
   at the forefront 10–11
   Conservative plans 86–8, 94, 190–1n.237
   and the CPRS 121

INDEX

and the DEA 31, 33, 44–5
and the EEC 15
and Fulton 53–4, 65–6, 69, 76
  Heath's hostility 113–16, 164, 218n.16
  and Lord Butler 113, 217n.6
  and David Howell 113–15
  Macmillan's hostility 160
  and the NEDC 18–19
  and PAR 135
  and the PSRU 114–15
  reform 24–6, 102
  and Donald MacDougall 26
  and Robert Armstrong 114–16, 148
Trend, Burke
  Cabinet proposal 102–3
  Civil Service review proposal 98
  and the CPRS 106–9, 117–20, 124, 128–9, 131
  and the EWS 123
  and GEN 92 133
  and Heath 114
  industrial relations 140–1
  and PAR 136
  and power 147
  and the PSRU 93–4
  and the White Paper 110
tripartism 17, 190n.207

U-turn 143
unified grading structure 205n.205, 73–6, 97
Unprincipled Society, The (Marquand) 9
Upper Clyde Shipbuilders 143

Wade-Gery, Robert 125
Waldegrave, William 98, 119, 120, 151
Walker, Peter 116, 126, 140
Whitehall (Hennessy) 81
Whitelaw, William 121, 140, 145, 151, 220n.86

Whitley Council 75, 97, 205n.203
Wildavsky, Aaron 119
Wilding, Richard
  Appointed to Fulton 59
  Fulton Chairman discussions 56
  and the Fulton Report 53, 61–3, 70, 72, 76–8, 80–1
  and PAR 133
  and reform 170–1
Willetts, David 129
Williams, Marcia 29, 37–40, 76, 95–6, 98, 146, 166
Wilson, Harold
  and the Civil Service 37, 66–8, 160–3
  and the CPRS 127, 222n.143
  and the DEA 31, 33–4, 44–7, 165
  and devaluation 41–2, 43, 46
  and the DHSS 48
  Downing Street Policy Unit 168
  Fulton Report 52–70, 72–4, 77–8, 166
  and George Brown 44
  in government 23–9, 191n.13, 192n.15
  and the Heath Government 84–5, 96, 99, 108
  introduction xi
  and the 'kitchen cabinet' 40
  and Marcia Williams 38
  and Michael Halls 62–3
  and Mintech 36
  state committment 49
Winter Emergencies Committee *see* Civil Contingencies Unit
Wyndham, John 159

Young, Michael 9, 65, 70

Zuckerman, Solly 118